# Life Management

# Life
# Management

**Prentice Hall**
Needham, Massachusetts   Englewood Cliffs, New Jersey

**Credits:**

Program Manager: Marita A. Sullivan
Editor: Susan Judge
Contributing Writers:  Lynn Robbins
                         Helen Strahinich
Production Editor: Patricia Carda
Art Director: L. Christopher Valente
Designers:  S. Stuart Wallace
             Linda Dana Willis
             Denise D. Wallace
Design Production and Technical Art:
    PERSPECTIVES/Susan Gerould
Preparation Service Manager:
    Martha E. Ballentine
Senior Buyer: Annie Puciloski
Cover Design: Martucci Studio
Photo Research: Susan Van Etten

**FIRST EDITION:**

ISBN: 0-13-535527-3

10 9 8 7 6 5 4 3 2 1

Prentice-Hall of Australia, Pty, Ltd., Sydney
Prentice-Hall Canada Inc., Toronto
Prentice-Hall Hispanoamericana, S.A., Mexico
Prentice-Hall of India Private Ltd., New Delhi
Prentice-Hall International (UK) Limited, London
Prentice-Hall of Japan, Inc., Tokyo
Prentice-Hall of Southeast Asia Pte. Ltd., Singapore
Editora Prentice-Hall Do Brasil Ltda., Rio de Janeiro

**A Simon & Schuster Company**

**Senior Reviewers:**

Betty Lou Joanos
Coordinator of Home Economics Programs
Florida State University
Tallahassee, FL

LaNece Pope Lomonte
Homemaking Teacher
Spring Branch Independent School District
Houston, TX

*Reviewers:*

Cheryle Apple
Home Economics Instructor
Rio Vista High School
Rio Vista, CA

Regina A. Coan
Home Economics Teacher
Neptune Senior High School
Neptune, NJ

Kathleen A. Dutney
Home Economics Teacher
Simon Perkins Middle School
Akron, OH

Maudie Elizabeth Karickhoff
Assistant Professor/
Home Economics and Curriculum Project Director
Marshall University
Huntington, West Virginia

Kathleen LaRue McGrath
Home Economics Instructor
Southeastern High School
So. Charleston, OH

Margaret F. Morris
Home Economics Teacher
Washington Township High School
Sewell, NJ

Karen Thomas Reed
Vocational Home Economics Teacher
Fairfield Union High School
Lancaster, OH

Margaret A. Ryan
Home Economics Teacher
Roselle Park Middle School/High School
Roselle Park, NJ

Naomi Wetzel
Home Economics Chair
Delta High
Clarksburg, CA

# CONTENTS

## UNIT 2 Managing Work and Money Resources

**CHAPTER**

# UNIT *3*

# *Managing Time and Material Resources*

# Features

## Careers:

## Case Studies:

## Social Responsibility:

## Technology:

# Charts, Graphs, Tables

# Unit 1

# Managing Your Life

# *1*

# *The Management Process*

## *As you read, think about:*

- what life skills you need.
- what the management process is.
- how you can apply the management process to your life.
- how you make decisions.
- what influences the decisions you make.

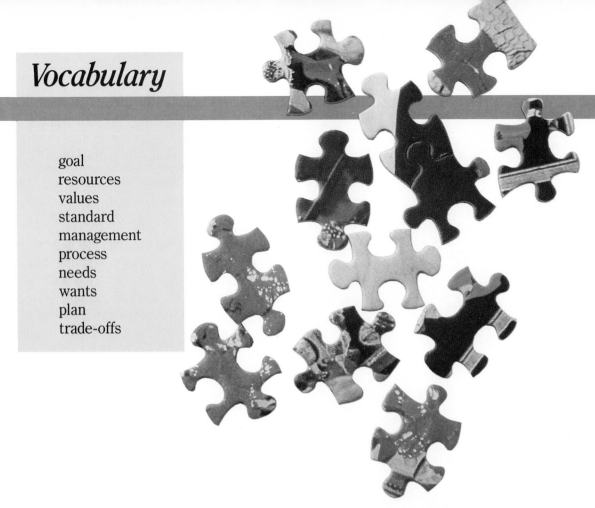

goal
resources
values
standard
management
process
needs
wants
plan
trade-offs

What are these life management skills you are about to study? Why do you need them? Can you really improve your life by applying management processes to personal decisions?

This book will try to provide answers to these questions and many others. In this first chapter, you will learn about management and the management processes. You will be reading about decision making and thinking about all of the factors that influence the decisions that you make every day.

## Why Study Life Management?

During your early years, family members and other people managed your life for you. They made decisions about the food you ate, the clothing you wore, the housing you lived in, and the health care you received. As your life roles change from child to teenager to adult, your responsibilities change. Eventually, you may be responsible for decisions about total caregiving for others.

Now, you are becoming responsible for an increasing number and variety of decisions. As you move into adulthood, you will become completely responsible for yourself. Others may offer advice, but you will make the final decisions. In reaching these decisions, you are guided by the teachings and expectations of your family, religion, and community.

Learning certain life skills can help you to make these decisions. Personal life skills, including an understanding of yourself and your relationships with others, provide an important foundation for these decisions. Skills related to work and money, material things, and leisure time also can help you to manage your life more

Reaching a goal in music requires
managing several resources.

successfully. Learning about the management
processes will enable you to apply them to your
personal decisions in all of these areas of your
everyday life.

## Personal Life Skills

You need many skills to be able to take care
of yourself physically and emotionally. You need
skills to deal with your family and the other

individuals in your life. You also need skills that
enable you to act positively in an emergency or
a crisis situation. As the events you are involved
in change and develop, you will need skills to
cope with them.

## Work and Money Skills

Throughout your life, you will need skills
related to work and money. Making career
choices, finding ways to acquire job skills, and
getting the job you want all require various
work skills. To get the most for your money, you
need consumer skills. Learning how to shop
and how to understand advertising techniques
are a part of these skills. The ability to make
a personal budget is another life skill you
will need. You need still other skills to make
wise choices when you are using credit, making
investments, or handling personal checking and
savings accounts.

## Skills to Manage Material Things and Leisure

Even choosing food, clothing, housing,
and transportation requires certain life skills.
Managing leisure time requires additional life
skills. You are already involved in making some
of these choices, and you will need to make
other choices in the future. The information in
this book will help you to make intelligent
choices and to practice life management skills.

## Learning Management Terms

Before learning about the management
process in detail, you need to know some basic
terms and their definitions. These terms often
are used when discussing the management process. Many will be explained in more detail as

they are used throughout this book. Before you begin, however, you need to understand the basic definitions of the terms *goal, resource, values, standards, management,* and *process.*

## Goals

A **goal** is what you want to accomplish. It is the end to which your effort is directed. You work toward goals every day without even thinking about them. Getting to school on time, looking your best, and completing your homework on time are among the goals you may often set for yourself.

## Resources

**Resources** are the things, knowledge, skills, abilities, services, and people that you have available to help you reach your goal or goals. The resources that you use may be either human or nonhuman.

*Human resources* include the qualities a person has within himself or herself that can be used to reach goals. Knowledge, skills, abilities, talents, attitudes, emotions and feelings, and health and energy are all a part of the strengths you may find within yourself. Friendships, family relationships, and relationships with neighbors, teachers, co-workers, and others are also human resources. Time, too, is a human resource.

*Nonhuman resources* include money, material possessions, living space, facilities provided by various levels of government, such as schools, parks, libraries, police and fire protection, and businesses and the goods they sell. Services provided by individuals and private businesses and industries, such as medical care, food preparation, interior design, and car repair, are other nonhuman resources.

Every person has many resources, both human and nonhuman, available to him or her. Nonhuman resources, such as money and mate-rial possessions, may be limited, but everyone has a wide range of unique human resources. It may not be possible always to increase certain nonhuman resources, but most human resources can be increased. Everyone can increase knowledge and learning of new skills. Everyone can work to improve relationships with others. Sometimes increasing human resources leads to an increase in nonhuman resources, perhaps a higher paying job.

The more resources that are available, the more alternatives there are for reaching a goal or solving a problem. This is why the abilities to recognize all available resources, to increase human resources, and to use resources creatively are important to effective management.

## Values

**Values** are ideas or beliefs about what is important. They are what an individual or group prizes in life. They include an individual's or group's idea of desirable behavior or desirable conditions of life. Your values demonstrate what is important to you. You act and react on

How do personal values affect the goals you choose to achieve?

the basis of your values, and you make decisions on the basis of your values. Honesty, education, good health, happiness, friendship, prestige, wealth, consideration of others, religion, and beauty are among the things and qualities people may value.

### Standards

A **standard** is a guideline for measuring your values and goals. Standards tell you how much is enough or when a task is completed to your satisfaction. They help you determine how well or how poorly you have done.

### Management

**Management** is using what you have to get what you want. "What you have" consists of all your resources, such as time, money, education, abilities, energy, community, and family. "What you want" is made up of your goals, or what you want to achieve or accomplish.

### Process

A **process** is a series of actions, thoughts, operations, or changes that lead to a particular result, condition, or end. You use processes to do many things in your life, such as prepare a meal, place an order in a restaurant, or prepare a term paper.

---

### Practical Tip: Managing Time

■ Use a calendar with large blocks for each date. Write in school, social, and work events. Be specific about times. Doing this will help you to plan ahead and manage your time more efficiently.

---

Many processes are more complex than ordering a meal. Give one example.

### For Review

1. Name three personal life skills you need.
2. What are the six basic management terms you need to understand before learning the management process?
3. Explain the difference between human and nonhuman resources.

### Understanding the Management Processes

Management processes include setting a goal or goals, analyzing resources, making a plan and assigning resources, carrying out the plan, making adjustments, and evaluating the results. These processes are the basis for the thinking you do and the actions you take. They give direction to thoughts and actions.

As you read the following descriptions of the basic management processes and learn more about management, you will begin to realize that management is a circular process.

## THE MANAGEMENT PROCESS

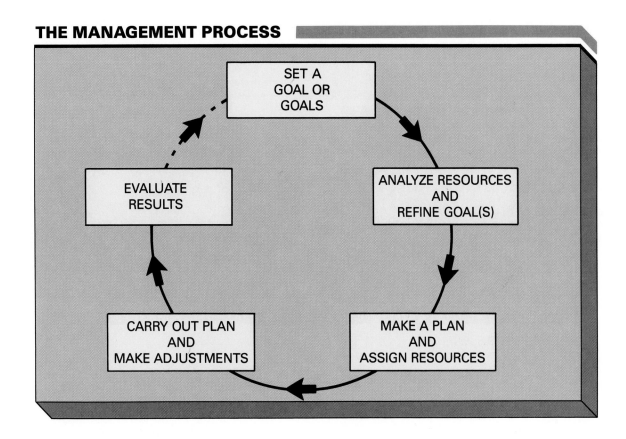

### Setting a Tentative Goal or Goals

Before you can make a plan or carry it out, you first must know what you want to accomplish, or what you want the end result, your goal, to be. Without a goal, you will not know what resources you need or what you should include in your plan.

A tentative goal is one that is not fully developed or completely worked out. You may have an idea about what you want to accomplish, but it is not specific. Once you have analyzed your resources, you can refine your goal, because you will know how the resources you have compare with the resources you need for your goal. As you refine your goal, it will become more specific and possible to achieve, using what is available to you.

**Simple and Complex Goals** Some goals are simple and easily understood. A goal of getting up at 7:00 a.m. is a good example of a simple goal. Another example is the goal of cleaning out your locker by Friday. Simple goals usually are easy to state and do not involve a lot of complicated planning.

Many goals, however, are complex goals. For example, Pete would like to keep his present grades but spend less time studying. This is a more complex goal than the earlier ones because Pete has two goals—to keep his present grades *and* to spend less time studying.

Pearl's goal is to be prepared for the tri-state music festival. She has stated it as one goal, but it is really made up of several smaller goals, including learning the music, getting homework done, getting a haircut, getting laundry done, packing a suitcase, and getting to the

What are some of the subgoals involved
in preparing to run a marathon?

bus on time. Obviously, making plans for complex goals is more involved than making plans for simple goals.

When you are considering a complex goal, it is often clearer if you break it into smaller goals. These smaller goals can be considered *subgoals,* that is, goals that are part of a larger, more general or more complex goal.

***Short-Range and Long-Range Goals***  Goals may be short-range or long-range. Short-range goals are ones to be achieved in the near future, such as making a dress for the prom or finishing a term paper or washing the dishes. Long-range goals are goals to be achieved in the more distant future. For example, Billy Joe has a long-range goal of getting a college degree. Matt has a long-range goal of losing 75 pounds.

The line between short-range goals and long-range goals is not always clear. Sometimes, reaching a long-range goal depends on reaching one or more short-range goals. Billy Joe, for example, has to take the right courses

and receive good grades to be accepted at college. Then, he has to pass his courses at college to get his degree. Each of these shorter-range goals is related to his long-range goal.

***Factors that Affect Goals***  Whether you are just beginning to formulate a goal or goals or are refining a tentative goal, there are several factors you need to consider. Some of these factors are *needs, wants, values,* and *resources.*

**Needs** are things or conditions that are necessary. **Wants** are things or conditions that are desirable. Your needs and wants can combine to affect the goals you set. They may even determine your goals. For example, your goal to get a summer job may be affected by your need to buy fall clothes for school. The new bike you may want may also affect your goal to get a summer job. The chart on page 9 shows some basic needs and wants. You will learn more about needs in Chapter 2.

Your values also affect the goals you set. If music is important to you, for example, some of your goals probably will be related to music. Perhaps your goal is to sing in the all-state chorus. Perhaps your goal is to save enough money to buy a new stereo system. If education is something you value, then your goals probably will reflect that value.

If you do not consider your own wants, needs, and values when setting your goals, you may find that you do not work to reach the goal.

Resources are still another factor that you need to consider when setting goals. You need to determine whether or not you have the resources that will allow you to reach your goal. For example, if your goal is to run at least two miles every other day all summer, and you are working two jobs, have many responsibilities at home, and have no way of obtaining running shoes, you do not have the resources you need to reach your goal.

**Stating Your Goals** Sometimes, putting your goals into words can clarify them. It may help you to realize whether they are realistic or merely vague wishes.

**Setting Goals in a Group** Sometimes, setting goals is a group activity. To establish group goals, the members of the group may have to make compromises. That is, various members of the group may have to give up something in order for the group to get what is wanted. When you set family goals or work on a committee or work with a friend, you set group goals. In these situations, you need to be accepting and understanding of the values, standards, and feelings of others in order to agree on a goal that everyone will work toward.

**Goals Set by Others** Deadlines for completing school assignments, curfews for school nights and weekends, and training requirements for a sports team are examples of goals set by someone other than yourself. Learning to meet these types of goals, even if you do not always agree with them, helps to show others that you are a responsible person. It also helps you to learn how to set goals for yourself.

Throughout your life, there will be goals that others set for you. These may be goals that you have to work toward if you are to keep your job or do other things you want to do. Being able to accept goals set by others and to make plans to work on them is a part of management. Sometimes, it is possible to discuss, change, or compromise on goals set by others. Sometimes it is not. Knowing when to spend time and

## SOME NEEDS AND WANTS

### NEEDS

- Food
- Clothing
- Housing
- Things you must have for good physical and mental health
- Resources to provide all of the needs above

### WANTS

- Extra money
- Designer clothing
- Luxury items (sports car, vacation home, fur coat)
- More leisure time

energy trying to make changes and when to accept the goals set by others can help you to manage your life effectively.

**Refining and Changing Goals** When your resources change or your needs and wants change or you and the people and situations you are involved with change, you may need to refine or change your goals. These changes may occur frequently or only occasionally.

Perhaps you have already started to carry out a plan to achieve a particular goal and have found that your resources have changed or that the situation has changed. At this point, you may need to refine or completely change your goal or goals. For example, Janelle's goal was to buy a new bicycle with the money she earned

Sometimes, unexpected events change available resources. How can this situation force a change in goals?

from baby-sitting. Unfortunately, her radio broke down and could not be repaired. After evaluating the situation, she decided her old bicycle would last a while longer, but she needed a new radio. In other words, she had to change her goal from buying a bicycle to buying a new radio.

Janelle's goal changed because her resources changed. She no longer had a radio. When she found herself without a radio, it became more important to her to have a new radio than a new bicycle.

Changing goals are a part of life. As you achieve one goal, another takes its place. Knowing when to make changes and adjustments and knowing how to make them are important parts of management.

## Analyzing Resources

After you have set a tentative goal or goals, you need to analyze your resources to decide if your goal is realistic. As you know, your resources are both human and nonhuman. They are all the things, knowledge, skills, abilities, services, and people that you have available to you to help you.

**Recognizing Resources** An important part of managing is recognizing your resources. The more resources you have, the more alternatives you have for reaching your goals.

If you are not sure you have the resources to reach your goal, you may want to think about the community resources available to you and the human resources you have, such as special talents. Think about the people you know. Sometimes, you can develop your personal resources by taking classes or by reading or talking to someone. Sometimes, you can trade an ability you have for an ability someone else has. For example, Ken decided his car needed to be washed and waxed. He could not do it himself because he had sprained his wrist and shoulder. He was going to take it to the local car wash until he discovered that he did not have enough money for a wash, wax, and gas. Just as he was about to give up his goal of a clean car, his sister Marge came home. Since Marge needed help studying for an English test the next week, she volunteered to wash and wax the car in exchange for Ken helping her study. Usually, if you think about your resources for a while, you can discover ways to expand them.

***Limitations on Resources*** Even if you have many resources available to you, you need to realize that all resources are somehow limited. For example, the money you have is always limited in that the money you spend on one thing, you cannot spend on another. Your time also is limited. There are only so many hours in each day. Although you can increase your human resources, the time you have available to do so limits how much you can increase them.

To decide how to use your resources, you need to consider how much of a given resource you have and whether or not that resource will cover all of the uses you have for it. For example, you wish to bake a cake for your father's birthday and to go to a school basketball game. There is not time to do both. These are conflicting demands on your resource of time. An important part of management is to recognize the limitations on your resources and to make your plans accordingly.

***Group Resources*** In management, group resources are sometimes called *shared resources.* These are resources that are available to more than one person. Family living space, a shared bedroom, and community resources are examples of group resources.

Shared resources can add to an individual's resources and increase alternatives for reaching goals. For example, most young people do not have enough money to have their own cars. If a family has a car, however, each person in the

Human resources include the support of friends during difficult times. What goals might an accident delay?

family can get to where he or she needs to go by sharing the resource.

Just as there are limitations on individual resources, there are limitations on group, or shared, resources. For example, a library book checked out by one person cannot be checked out by someone else until it is returned. Space occupied by one family member cannot be occupied by another.

There are also conflicting demands on group resources. For example, if one person in a family wants quiet for study in the evening and another wants loud music, there are conflicting demands on the resources of space and time.

## For Review

1. Setting a tentative goal or goals is the first of the basic management processes. What is the next process?
2. Name four factors that can affect goals.
3. Give four reasons why you may need to change your goals.

# A Day in the Life of a Manager

Imagine a career that involves daily planning and communication, transportation, purchasing, health and recreation, training and staff development, provisions, and maintenance and sanitation. The individual who enters this career is expected to perform all of these jobs and to coordinate the entire operation. M is an individual who has entered this career.

Let's look at a typical day. M is awakened by a health emergency: a junior member of the firm has a splinter. Dealing with this crisis requires delegation of provisions responsibility to a trainee—with only moderate success. The organization is falling behind schedule already! Planning and communication swings into action and switches the carpool to include the member who missed the bus. Sanitation duties are postponed.

M arrives at off-site, wage-earning facility but continues planning and communication. Telephone calls confirm an orthodontist appointment (health) and plumber's visit (maintenance). M coordinates transportation of junior member home from school with purchasing at the supermarket. Back on site, M engages in recreation supervision and training and staff development (in homework and clean-your-room skills) while catching up on sanitation left over from breakfast. Communications suffer stress when a junior member won't get off the telephone. As a result, he is demoted to walking, rather than being driven, to the orthodontist. The plumber leaves, and provision preparation gets into full swing, involving the entire staff. Salad-making and table-setting are delegated. Staff training in mashing potatoes occurs with minimum mess. Dinner is achieved. Staff must be recalled from the TV to coordinate sanitation activities. Recreation time is declared. Mother makes herself a cup of tea and mentally reviews the many operations and activities she will coordinate for herself and her family tomorrow.

## Making a Plan and Assigning Resources

Once you have set a tentative goal or goals and have analyzed your resources, you are ready to make a plan and assign resources.

A **plan** is a method outlined ahead of time for doing or making something that leads to the achieving of a goal. Planning is the process of making a plan. A plan helps you to achieve what you want, or more of what you want, with the resources you have available. A plan may be mental or written, depending on the situation and the planner.

Making plans and assigning resources involve outlining what you are going to do, how you are going to do it, when you are going to do it, and what you are going to use to carry out the plan. In other words, you're going to get organized. Many decisions are involved.

To make a plan, you need to know what needs to be done, you need to reevaluate your resources, and you need to establish a sequence of steps to achieve your goal.

Discussing details thoroughly may determine the success of a plan.

**Know What Needs to Be Done.** Before you can begin to achieve your goal, you need to identify what needs to be done. If your goal is to have a party, there are many things that need to be done. You need to decide who you want at the party and to invite them. You need to decide what to have for refreshments and to buy or make them. You need to decide what to have for music and how to provide it. You need to decide when the party will be and how long it will be. All these things need to be a part of your plan.

Sometimes you have to make plans for things you do not know much about. Before you can begin to plan, you have to find out more about what you are supposed to do. If your goal is to build a bookcase, for example, you will need to find out about building bookcases. You may check in the library, or you may talk with someone who has built bookcases. You may do both, so you can get as many ideas as possible and learn as much as you can. When you know all the steps involved, you will be able to make a more effective plan.

**Reevaluate Your Resources.** Once you know what it is that you need to do, you should reevaluate your resources. You may have all the resources you need to achieve your goal. If this is the case, you can proceed. You may find that you are short one or more resources. If this is the case, you may decide to change your goal, or you may decide to increase your resources or to make adjustments in your use of resources to accomplish what you want. You may even decide to postpone your goal until you have enough of the right resources to achieve the desired results.

Being a productive Peace Corps volunteer requires making an organized plan and putting it into action. What are some human resources you would need in this situation?

Keeping a constant check on your resources and making adjustments are important parts of management. They can make the difference between achieving a goal and not.

**Set the Sequence of Steps.** To get things done, you, as the manager, need to be able to organize activities in a way that leads to accomplishing specific objectives. There are times when the sequence of activities determines the success or failure of a plan. For example, Maria needed a new pair of shoes. She had enough money and time to go shopping, but when she arrived at the shopping center, she became interested in the attractive dresses and sports clothes. Suddenly, she discovered it was time for the stores to close, and she could not buy the shoes she needed. If Maria had changed the sequence of steps—bought shoes before looking at dresses—she might have accomplished her objective.

Sometimes, the sequence of steps doesn't determine the success or failure of the plan. It may, however, make better use of your resources and make it easier for you to achieve your goal. When you set the table, for example, it does not matter whether or not you put on the plates, glasses, or flatware first. The table will be set when you are done. If you put on the glasses first, however, the flatware next, and the plates last, you may have to move the glasses when you put on the flatware because the glasses are in the way. You may have to move both the flatware and the glasses when you put on the plates if the plates take up more space than you allowed. If you put the plates on the table first, then the flatware, and finally the glassware, you do not have to move things around as you work.

When you plan what to do in a logical order, you avoid wasting your resources, especially your resources of time and energy. Things go more smoothly. Planning the sequence of activities to carry out a plan helps to make management work for you.

## Carrying Out Plans and Making Adjustments

Carrying out a plan is the action part of management. Control is needed when you carry out a plan to be sure that you do what you planned to do.

Because plans seldom work quite as expected, adjustments may be needed. Changes, both expected and unexpected, sometimes force you to adjust your plan.

**Acting on Your Plans**  Once you have made your plan, you should carry it out. This may seem obvious, but some people find this difficult. They make elaborate plans, but they do not act on the plans. If this happens to you, perhaps you need to ask yourself some basic questions. Is your goal clear and based on your values? If you truly want to achieve your goal, is your plan suited to you? Perhaps it calls for resources you don't want to use. Perhaps it involves a great deal of new information. Maybe your plan isn't as clear as it should be.

If everything checks out, and you decide your goals, standards, and plans are appropriate, perhaps you need to stop stalling.

**Checking Your Progress**  The actions you take to carry out your plan should lead to your goal or goals. To be sure that it does, you should check your progress to be sure you are following your plan and to see how well it is working for you. When you are not familiar with the steps ahead in the plan, or when a plan requires precise, detailed steps, you may find it helpful to check more frequently.

**Making Adjustments**  Frequently, to keep a plan under control and to keep yourself on track toward your goal, you need to make adjustments in your plan. If you check your plan often, you can make adjustments as they are needed. You may even be able to prevent problems from arising later.

If you begin to carry out your plan without checking it, you may have to make larger adjustments later. It may delay you in reaching your goal, or you may not reach it at all. For example, David's goal was to go to college. He made plans to apply to several different schools. He made a list of the schools and wrote down the deadlines for mailing the applications. Unfortunately, he did not check his list until two of the deadlines had passed and the other three were coming up

Even well-organized plans may go wrong. What adjustments and additional resources may be needed here?

within a week. Although he did get the other three applications out on time, he had to spend most of his free time for a week doing so. He missed a basketball game he wanted to go to, and he was not able to spend as much time as he wanted to spend studying for an important test. If David had checked his plan sooner, he might not have had some of these problems.

Sometimes, adjustments have to be made because of changes in resources, needs, wants, or situations. These changes may be complex enough to require major changes in goals or in entire plans. For example, Sophia and her mother had planned to make all of Sophia's fall clothes, but Sophia's mother became ill and could not do any sewing. More of Sophia's time had to go into housework, and less money was available for clothes because of her mother's illness. The plan for making fall clothes could not be worked out at all, and both the goal and the plan had to be adjusted.

In this case, both Sophia and her mother faced changes in their resources of time and money. Sometimes, changes in situations force adjustments in plans. For example, suppose you plan to add clothes to your wardrobe over the next year. If you get a job that requires you to wear a uniform, or if your family moves to a different climate, your situation has changed, and your wardrobe needs will change. You will need to change your goal and plan accordingly.

The ability to make decisions about adjustments in goals, standards, and/or plans and the ability to make those adjustments as you carry out your plans are important management skills. They can mean the difference between reaching a goal or not reaching a goal. They can mean the difference between being satisfied with the results and wishing things were different.

## Evaluating the Results

When you *evaluate* something, you examine it and judge it. You decide the value of some-thing—an article, an action, a plan, or an idea. Evaluation is a natural part of management and operates throughout all of the management processes that you follow.

**The End Results**   While evaluation during the different management processes is certainly important, it is also important to evaluate your thinking, planning, and doing after you have completed your plan. You have to look at the total picture. When you do this, you learn about yourself and develop your management skills.

Think about the goal or goals and the standards you set. Were they realistic? Were they related to your values and based on the resources you had available at the time? What were the strong points of your plan? What could you have done to make your plan better or more appropriate? How well did you carry out your plan? Did you start right in carrying it out or did you hesitate? If you hesitated, did you do so because of your goal, the standards you set, your plan, or because you tend to put things off?

What could you have done differently to make things go more smoothly? Were you happy with the outcome and the way you handled things? Did you do a good job conserving your resources or were you wasteful?

**Accepting Responsibility**   One important part of the evaluation process is accepting responsibility for the decisions you make. These include your decisions about your goals, your plan, your actions, and the results of these decisions. It is easy to blame someone else or factors outside your control if things do not turn out right. Blaming other people or things does not improve your management skills.

If you evaluate yourself honestly, you may find that you have made mistakes. This is all right because this is a way to learn. It tells you that you need to try a different way next time. From the mistakes you make, you learn to manage and make the most of what you have. It is part of developing management skills.

School responsibilities include getting extra help if you need it.

If things did not turn out exactly as you planned, try to discover why. It may be something you did or did not do. If you discover why, you have learned something for another time. If the results are due to factors over which you had no control, avoid blaming yourself for what happened and get on with other things. While you can learn from the situation, you do not have to dwell on the results. Being able to evaluate and to distinguish between things you could control and things you could not are a part of accepting responsibility for yourself and your actions.

## For Review

1. What are the three steps involved in making a plan?
2. Why might you have to make adjustments in your plan?
3. How can you use mistakes constructively when you evaluate the results of your plan?

## Making Decisions

A *decision* is a conclusion reached after considering alternatives and their consequences. When you make a decision, you have to use your head. You have to think and weigh one alternative against others. You need to recognize what you are deciding. You need to have some idea of the possible outcomes and consequences of the various alternatives. When you make a choice or act on impulse without considering the alternatives or their possible consequences, or when you act out of habit, you are not making a true decision. In fact, you might call this a nondecision.

## Influences on Decision Making

To understand how you are making decisions, you need to know what factors influence your decisions. Decisions are influenced by your values and standards, your goals, your resources, various conditions and events, your peers, and trade-offs.

One decision may influence many others.

All these factors, separately and in combination, affect your decisions. Understanding how they influence you can help you to improve your decision-making skills.

**Values and Standards**  Many times, your values and standards affect or determine the decisions you make and when you make them. For example, Dolores places a high value on honesty. When she ruined the sweater she had borrowed from Amy, she decided to tell Amy the truth and offer to replace the sweater. The value she put on honesty prevented her from making up a story about what had happened.

Sometimes, the values and/or standards of other people affect your decisions. For example, Ashley's parents said she could not use the car unless she had a B average at the end of the first marking period. She worked hard to get good grades, so she could keep her driving privileges. The value she placed on using the car made her decide to meet her parents standards for grades. The value her parents placed on education set standards for Ashley to meet.

**Goals**  Goals are other factors that affect the decisions you make and the way you make your decisions. The goals may be ones that you set or that someone else sets for you. For example, if your goal is to lose 10 pounds, your decisions about food will be based on this goal. On the other hand, Marc's boss told him he would have to sell more merchandise in order to keep his job. The goal set by Marc's boss forced Marc to decide whether he would try harder or look for a different job.

**Resources**  The resources you have also affect the decisions you make. When you have many resources, and you recognize all the resources you have available, you increase the number of options you have for making decisions.

How much you have of any one resource is one way that resources affect the decisions you make. For example, if you are busy with sports and other activities after school and on most weekends, you cannot have a job after school or on weekends. You do not have enough time (a resource) available to you. The lack of this resource will affect your decision about working. If you had your afternoons and weekends free, your resource of time would not be so limited, and you could decide to take a job if you wanted to, had your parents' permission, and there were jobs available.

**Conditions and Events**  A variety of outside factors affect the decisions you make. Your health (a condition), for example, will affect the decisions you make and how you make them. Events, both planned and unplanned, also affect the decisions you make. If your school, for example, is sponsoring a pep rally (an event), you may make a decision about whether or not to go. If you break your arm, that event will affect many of the decisions you make until your arm is healed.

**Peers** Your *peers* are the people in your age group with whom you share interests. The ideas and opinions of your peers can influence your decisions greatly. Wanting to belong to a group of peers can affect the way you dress and behave. *Peer pressure* is a term used to describe this strong influence. Recognizing peer pressure and balancing it with your own goals and resources are a part of growing up.

**Trade-offs** The things or conditions you gain and/or lose when you make a specific decision are called **trade-offs.** Trade-offs definitely influence the decisions you make.

For example, you may be trying to decide between joining the track team and taking a part-time job. If you decide to join the team, you may not have money for extra clothes or entertainment. You will have less time for other activities. You will have traded these things for some other things that are more important to you.

## Processes of Decision Making

Throughout all phases of management, there are many kinds of decisions to make—large ones and small ones, ones that use many resources and ones that use few, ones that affect only a few people, and ones that affect many people. No matter what the size, complexity, or impact of a decision, however, there are certain common processes involved in it.

Advice from friends is helpful, but peers cannot make decisions for you.

## PRACTICE
## DECISION MAKING

- Increase your knowledge of what you are deciding about.
- Practice using the decision-making process, even for small decisions.
- Learn to make accurate and honest judgments about factors that affect the decision.
- Learn to gear the amount of time you spend on a decision to the importance of the decision.

Knowing the processes involved in making sound decisions can help you to make decisions with which you are pleased. These same processes can be applied when two or more people are making decisions.

Making effective decisions involves:

- Knowing the subject of the decision.
- Seeking alternative solutions.
- Thinking through the alternatives.
- Choosing and following a course of action.
- Accepting responsibility.
- Making compromises when necessary.

## Building Decision-Making Skill

You can see that the processes of decision making can be useful for all types of decisions. You can go through all the processes quickly with little thinking, or you can spend a long time investigating and thinking through alternatives. It depends on your skill in decision making, how important the decision is to you, how careful you wish to be with resources, and whether it concerns the use of a small share or a large share of certain resources.

One way to build your skill in decision making is to increase your knowledge about the subject of your decision. The more information you have, the more alternatives you can think of. For example, if you are deciding which courses to take next year, the more you know about the various courses and teachers who will be teaching them, the more informed your decisions can be.

Another way to build your skill in decision making is to take the time to go through the processes of making decisions formally when making some everyday decisions. Practice in using all the elements and processes in decision making can help you to learn the process and make them a habit. It can increase your confidence in decision making. This will make it easier when you have more complex decisions to make.

Some people consider all the factors and make decisions quickly. Other people take longer to make decisions. Sometimes, people even use paper and pencil to list all the trade-offs, or advantages and disadvantages, of the various alternatives they are considering. Taking a long time to make a decision and doing a lot of work with paper and pencil may help to improve your satisfaction with the results of some decisions, but this is not always the case. The accuracy and honesty of the judgments you make when you make a decision are more important than the amount of time you spend and the amount of writing you do.

## For Review

1. How do values and standards influence decisions? Give one example.
2. Why are the attitudes of your peers a strong influence on your decisions?
3. List the six steps involved in making effective decisions.

## Management Application: Making a Choice

Imagine yourself in the situation described below. As you read, think about how the steps of the management process might apply to this situation. Then answer the questions that follow.

### Situation

You see a new after-school job posted on the bulletin board. You read the job description and get more excited as you read. The *Valley Daily Newspaper* is looking for a student to do odd jobs at its office on Main Street. You work on your school newspaper now and have been wondering if a career in newspaper publishing would be as exciting as it seems. This experience would be great, and you could really use the extra money. Your bike needs to be fixed, and there are some new styles you just *have* to buy. Also, the money for the class trip and your yearbook is due soon. So is the big term paper you've been working on. Your parents have told you that you have to bring your grades up if you want to play basketball. Basketball! You almost forgot! Tryouts are only a week away. Let's see . . . the job is for fifteen hours a week . . . that's three hours after school every day, but so is basketball practice. If only you knew how much the coach was going to let you play. Last year you came to every practice and ended up warming the bench for every game. You stuck with it because you love the game and figured *this* would be your year. Well, it looks like it's either that perfect job or basketball.

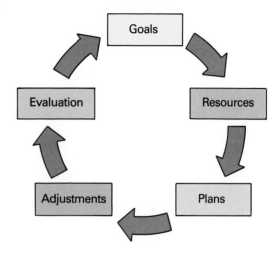

You decide to talk the problem over with a friend because you keep wondering if there is any way to fit both basketball and work into your schedule. How will you decide what you should do?

### Questions

1. How will your values help you to set a clear goal in this situation?
2. What human and nonhuman resources will you need to get and keep the newspaper job? If you decide to play basketball, what resources will you need?
3. What trade-offs will you have to make if you decide to work at the newspaper instead of playing basketball?
4. What additional information will you need to know before making a final decision?
5. Can you think of any compromises that you would try to make?
6. Which steps of the management process apply to this situation?

# *1 Chapter Review*

## *Summary*

As you move into adulthood, learning management skills related to work, money, material things, and leisure can help you to manage your life more successfully. The management processes include setting and refining goals, analyzing resources, making and carrying out plans, and evaluating results. Making decisions also means accepting responsibility for those decisions.

## *Vocabulary*

Match each of the following vocabulary words with one of the definitions below.

goal                process
resources           needs
values              wants
standard            plan
management          trade-offs

1. Using what you have to get what you want is _____ .

2. Things or conditions that are desirable are called _____ .

3. The knowledge, skills, abilities, services, people, and material things you have available to help you accomplish your aims are known as _____ .

4. A guideline for measuring one's values and goals is a _____ .

5. Something a person wants to accomplish, or the end to which one's efforts are directed, is a _____ .

6. A method, outlined ahead of time, for doing or making something that leads to achieving an end is a _____ .

7. A series of actions, thoughts, operations, or changes that lead to a particular result, condition, or end is a _____ .

8. Things or conditions you gain and/or lose when you make a specific decision are known as _____ .

9. Things or conditions that are necessary are _____ .

10. A person's ideas or beliefs about what is important are _____ .

## *Questions*

1. How do a person's responsibilities change as he or she moves into adulthood?

2. Why do limited resources affect a person's goals? What other factors sometimes affect a person's goals?

3. Give an example of a simple goal and of a complex goal. What is the difference between simple and complex goals?

4. Why must a person sometimes give up a short-range goal to accomplish his or her long-range goal?

5. Why does setting a goal in a group sometimes involve compromises?

6. How can you increase your human resources? Your nonhuman resources?

7. What must an individual do when he or she is making a plan?

8. Once you have a plan, what should you do to accomplish your goal?

9. What factors influence the decisions that an individual makes?

10. How do the goals set for you by other people influence your decisions?

## Skill Activities

**1. Resource Management.** List all the human resources that are available to you now. Then break your human resource list into two groups: Resources Within Myself and Resources Outside Myself. After you have set up your list, color code it. Put a yellow dot after each human resource that you are satisfied with and that can help you to accomplish your goals; use a green dot after each human resource that you are fairly satisfied with but want to work on; and use a blue dot after each human resource that needs work or keeps you from accomplishing your goals.

Analyze the strengths and weaknesses in your resources. What are your weakest? What steps can you take to increase your human resources? Use the results to improve the way in which you manage your resources.

**2. Critical Thinking.** Make a list of 20 simple, short-range goals. Select one of the goals, and analyze the factors (needs, wants, values, and resources) that will affect your reaching this goal.

Now, make a list of three long-term goals. Break each long-term goal into the simpler, shorter-range goals that are related to it. Which of these simpler goals seem easy to reach? Which seem more difficult? Why?

**3. Critical Thinking.** Make a list of the simple decisions you made yesterday. Your list should include the kind of decisions you make every day; for example, the food you eat for each meal, or the clothes you wear every day. Write down the first decision from the top of your list on another piece of paper. Under it, write the six steps for making a decision. Make a check next to each step that you thought about when you made the decison. Make a quick note explaining why you did or did not think about each step. Is every step valuable to you when you are making simple decisions? Why or why not?

**4. Science.** Look up in a science book the steps involved in the scientific method used to test a scientific theory. Write a short paper comparing the scientific method with the management process.

# 2 *Understanding Yourself*

## *As you read, think about:*

- how heredity, environment, needs, emotions, and attitudes affect who you are.
- how to develop a positive self-concept.
- what good communication involves.
- how to develop and maintain positive relationships.
- how to apply the management process to personal decisions about yourself.

heredity
environment
self-concept
attitude
emotions
communication
verbal communication
nonverbal communication
communication inhibitors
stereotype

Before you can manage various life situations, you need to learn how to manage yourself. Learning about your needs, emotions, and attitudes is a part of this process. You need to understand the importance of a positive self-concept. You will discover that it is easier to develop good communication skills and positive relationships with others when you understand yourself better. The knowledge and skill you gain in all of these areas will help you to live a happy, productive life.

## Learning About You

If you could be like anyone in this world, whom would you choose to be like? Why? Probably at least a part of your reason lies in your admiration of certain personal characteristics—a positive attitude, an optimistic outlook, self-confidence, an ability to deal with crises, emotional balance, patience, understanding, self-control, or an ability to make others feel good about themselves.

Most people admire these qualities in a person. They are positive qualities, and they are important to effective management. Usually, a person with positive personal characteristics has clear values and a strong sense of the direction for his or her life. When values and goals are clear, decisions are easier to make, which tends to make management easier and more effective.

Positive personal characteristics help a person to see situations realistically, to deal with difficult situations rather than to avoid them, and to look at himself or herself without being too harsh or judgmental. This greatly reduces the fear of failure and makes it easier to learn from mistakes as well as successes.

Positive personal characteristics enrich relationships with others. These relationships

Think about the positive relationships you have with family and friends. How do they enrich your life?

together. These factors are basic human needs. There are several ways to classify these needs. Some people classify them as physical needs and psychological needs. For these people, physical, or biological, needs include food, clothing, shelter, rest, activity, and protection from bodily harm. Psychological needs include the need for love, esteem, a sense of worth, recognition, status, mental stimulation, new experiences, and approval.

Other people classify these human needs as physical, emotional, mental, and social. Physical needs are those things needed to maintain life—food, clothing, shelter, and so on. Emotional needs are the need for love, esteem, a sense of worth, and approval. Mental needs include the need for knowledge and learning and for mental challenges. Social needs focus on the need for satisfying relationships with others.

Abraham Maslow, a well-known psychologist, developed still another way to classify needs. He grouped needs into five categories: physical, safety, love, esteem, and self-actualization. Physical needs include those that have been described already. Safety needs are the need for protection from physical harm and the need to feel secure and safe from harm. Love needs include the need to love and be loved and to feel a sense of belonging. Esteem needs are needs related to an individual's self-concept and self-pride as well as respect and admiration for others. Self-actualization needs include the need to develop fully one's potential. Knowledge and understanding of the self and the outside world are a part of the self-actualization needs. This knowledge and understanding will help you to meet your needs in ways that do not hurt the self or others. The ability to reach beyond oneself and to work for the betterment of others is still another part of these needs.

Although psychologists classify human needs in different ways, most agree that these

become human resources for everyone involved because supportive, positive relationships help people to reach the goals they set.

## Heredity and Environment

How do you become a totally unique person? The answer lies in the combination of heredity and environment. **Heredity** is the total of all characteristics passed on to an individual by parents and ancestors. **Environment** is the total of the conditions and life experiences an individual has in his or her surroundings. Most psychologists agree that both heredity and environment affect the development of each person. Acting together, your heredity and your environment contribute to the uniqueness of your personality.

## Human Needs

Although each individual is unique, there are several common factors that bind all people

needs are what motivate human behavior. In other words, people act in order to meet their needs. If a person is hungry, he or she will try to meet his or her food needs. If a person feels threatened, he or she will take action to reduce the threat. If a person needs approval, he or she will try to gain that approval by practicing certain behavior.

When a particular need has been met, the individual can move on to meeting other needs. If you are tired and get a good night's rest, for example, in the morning you are ready to meet other needs. If you feel the need for approval, and your parents compliment you on your report card, you can then focus your attention on meeting other needs.

If an individual does not succeed in meeting one or more needs, that person usually continues to try to meet those needs and ignores other needs. For example, if you need someone to talk to, and your best friend is not available, you may try to find someone else, or you may continue to try to get in touch with your best friend. Your actions are likely to focus on finding someone to talk to. Once you have met this need, you will be more willing to meet other important needs.

The behavior a person uses to meet needs depends on a variety of factors. One factor is the strength of the need. If the need is strong, then the behavior will be different from the behavior expressed if the need is less strong. Another factor is a person's age. A young child will seek attention and approval in ways different from an adult's ways. Intelligence, emotion, cultural background, learned responses and conditioning, and goals all affect the behavior an individual uses to meet needs.

A mature person can meet his or her needs in socially acceptable ways. The individual may postpone an activity devoted to meeting needs until a more appropriate time. For example, you might refrain from eating when you get home at 5:00 p.m. so that you will be able to eat dinner with the rest of your family at 6:00 p.m. Another example is not interrupting someone who is busy unless it is an emergency.

Sometimes, when it is appropriate, ignoring one's own needs to help another person is a sign of maturity. For example, if you are exhausted and need sleep, but your best friend needs someone to talk to, taking some time to talk to your friend may be the best thing to do. A parent who stays up with a sick child is putting the child's needs before his or her own needs. Learning how to meet needs without damaging the self or others physically or psychologically is an important part of managing your life.

## Self-Concept

One important factor affecting your personality and your ability to meet needs is your self-concept. **Self-concept** can be defined as the beliefs and feelings a person has about himself or herself. If you feel good about yourself, you feel more confident and optimistic, more positive about yourself and your situation. You

A positive self-concept helps you to relate well with others and to face the future with confidence.

feel more in control of what you do and say. You are freer to try something new or different without being overly afraid of failing or making an unfortunate mistake.

When you feel good about yourself, you are able to give more to a relationship. You may be able to listen more sympathetically to a friend or be more patient with your little sister who is overtired. You may be more willing to help with household chores because you understand that your parents are tired after working all day. When you do not feel good about yourself, it is more difficult to do these things or to be understanding of others. Your concern is more for yourself than for others.

How do you usually feel about yourself? Very positive most of the time? Fairly positive most of the time? Negative more often than you would like? While everyone has one or two "down" days occasionally, frequent negative feelings about the self can affect everything a person does or says. It is possible to increase your positive feelings about yourself, your skills, your abilities, and your worth as a person.

### How Does the Self-Concept Develop? The
self-concept begins to develop at the moment of birth. It develops out of your reactions to and perceptions of life experiences. If a baby is cared for and loved in a way to make him or her feel secure, it contributes to the child's positive self-concept. The child feels secure in the knowledge that he or she is loved and is a worthwhile human being. If only the child's physical needs are met, and love, support, and a caring attitude are not provided by parents or caregivers, the child is less likely to have strong feelings of self-worth.

As people go through life, they have many experiences. Some are positive, and some are negative. Being loved and cared about and encouraged by others are positive experiences; they help to meet human needs. Being ridiculed and criticized are negative experiences; they tend to interfere with meeting basic needs. The more positive experiences a person has, the more likely it is that a positive self-concept will develop and the easier it is to deal with the negative experiences. Too many negative experiences are likely to contribute to a negative self-concept and diminished self-confidence and feelings of self-worth. Any positive experiences at this point may be disregarded or looked at as "luck."

### The Effects of Self-Concept on Needs and Behavior Because a person with a positive self-concept has self-respect, he or she will not take actions or participate in activities that can damage his or her health or well-being. The individual with a positive self-concept behaves in a straightforward manner without putting

How can feeling good about yourself help you to get through difficult times?

himself or herself or others down or holding himself or herself above others. A positive self-concept helps a person to meet his or her needs without taking advantage of, blaming, or attacking others verbally or physically.

### Effects of Self-Concept on Relationships

An individual with a positive self-concept can think of others before himself or herself. The individual has the ability to see when this is necessary. A positive self-concept allows you to help others meet their needs. Relationships with others are based on mutual give and take. If you have a positive self-concept, you have the ability both to give to the relationship and take from the relationship. Other people's feelings and well-being are as important to you as your own feelings and well-being. There is a willingness to work on problems and to make compromises rather than ignore problems or demand one's own way.

### Effects of Self-Concept on Attitudes

A positive self-concept usually provides the basis for a positive outlook on life—a feeling that the world is a wonderful and challenging place rather than a feeling that everyone and everything is working against you. An attitude of "I can" or "I'd love to try" or "This is an interesting challenge" prevails. The words "I can't" or "I'm afraid to try because I may fail" or "This is too difficult" are seldom used.

### Developing and Maintaining a Positive Self-Concept

While a happy childhood, loving parents and family, understanding teachers, and wonderful friends can contribute to a positive self-concept, they do not guarantee a positive self-concept. Fortunately, a self-concept can be changed. Before this can happen, however, the individual must want it to change.

To improve your self-concept, you need to think positive thoughts about yourself. If you are nervous when you are taking a test, even

Friendships are based on mutual appreciation. How does the self-concept of each person affect a friendship?

when you have studied, tell yourself that you are prepared and will do well. If you receive a 90 on the test, be pleased with yourself rather than worried about the parts you missed. If you drop an egg on the floor, tell yourself that it was an accident that could have happened to anyone, not that you are clumsy. Remind yourself not of your failures, but of the things you have done well. Although changing your thoughts about yourself is not easy, once you begin to think more positively, you will begin to act in a more positive manner.

Doing things that you know you can do well will help you to build your confidence to try more challenging activities. When combined with positive thoughts, success can help you to gain self-confidence and also an improved self-concept. Once your self-confidence and self-concept have begun to grow, try more difficult and challenging tasks. If you do not, you run the risk of having negative thoughts about yourself for being afraid to try.

Sometimes, spending time with people who have a positive outlook and who are supportive of you can help. People who put you down or take advantage of you do not improve your self-concept. When you cannot avoid people who are not supportive, try not to let what they say bother you. Keep positive self-thoughts uppermost in your mind and refuse to be taken advantage of.

## For Review

1. Name and describe Abraham Maslow's five categories of human needs.
2. How does the self-concept develop?
3. Explain three things you can do to develop and maintain a positive self-concept.

## Attitudes

Some people seem to look for the best in every situation and in every person. To them, half a glass of water is half full rather than half empty. On a partly cloudy day, they enjoy the sunshine rather than complain about the clouds. These people can be said to have a positive attitude. An **attitude** is an idea or opinion a person has about himself or herself, about others, and about events and situations.

***Relationship to Self-Concept*** Usually, a positive attitude is related to a positive self-concept. When an individual feels good about himself or herself, there is a tendency to feel good about others, to feel some control over the direction of his or her life, and to accept events and situations over which there is no control.

People with negative self-concepts frequently do not feel good about themselves and their individuality. They tend to believe that others do not see them as worthwhile. They may find it difficult to trust other people, and they may feel they have no control over the direction of their lives.

***Effect on Relationships*** While almost everyone has times when they are feeling low, and their attitudes tend to be negative, people who always have negative attitudes can be annoying. Sometimes their attitudes so influence others that the others begin to think in the same ways. This can be destructive to relationships. A positive attitude makes a person much more pleasant to be around. It encourages cooperation and the free exchange of ideas.

A positive attitude can help you to accept and overcome temporary setbacks that you cannot control.

# Psychologist

Do the differences in people's personalities interest you? Do you ever wonder how learning takes place or how individuals deal with changes and crises in their lives? These are some of the areas in which psychologists do research and counseling, conduct training programs, and provide health-related services. To become a psychologist takes many years of training, but once achieved, it is a fascinating career.

Psychologists study human behavior and mental processes. They develop theories to help explain people's actions and feelings. Sometimes they help patients change those actions or feelings. Most psychologists have a specialty. The largest group, *clinical psychologists,* helps people with emotional problems. They interview patients, give diagnostic tests, and do individual, family, and group counseling. Many are in private practice; some work for health-care or social-service agencies. *Counseling psychologists* advise people on how to deal with the problems of everyday life. *Developmental psychologists* study the problems and adjustments of the different life stages, such as childhood, adolescence, and old age. *Social psychologists* are interested in how people interact in groups. *Experimental psychologists* study the basic behavior processes of human beings and lower animals. They may teach rats to run a maze to study how the animals "learn their way" and how that applies to human learning.

A doctorate is required for most professional positions. People with master's degrees can work as psychologists' assistants, counselors, or school psychologists. A master's degree in school psychology, for example, requires two years of course work and a one-year internship. A PhD degree can take three to five years of graduate work. Most states require psychologists to pass an examination before they are licensed to practice.

Learning to accept yourself and to move ahead in spite of mistakes contributes to an overall positive attitude. The way you relate to others will reflect this.

***Developing a Positive Attitude***  To develop a positive attitude, try to look at people and situations in a new way. For example, instead of becoming upset every time your friend is late, think about the qualities in your friend that you do admire. Instead of thinking of your weeknight curfew as unreasonable parental control, think of it as a sign that they care about you. If you avoid meeting people because you are afraid you will not know what to say or will say the wrong thing, try to put yourself in the other person's shoes. What would you want someone to say to you? Looking at things differently takes time and effort, but it is worthwhile.

An important part of a positive attitude is a positive self-concept. When you have a positive self-concept, it is easy to have a positive attitude and outlook. If your self-concept needs to be improved, work on it as you are working on developing a positive attitude.

## Emotions

**Emotions** are strong feelings, often combined with physiological, or bodily, responses. Love, hate, anger, guilt, loneliness, anxiety, happiness, grief, and fear are all emotions. Often these feelings are very strong. Sometimes they are difficult to express, and sometimes they are difficult to control. In fact, sometimes people refuse to recognize their emotions because they think they are "bad."

Emotions are neither bad nor good. They just exist. The way in which people deal with and express emotions, however, can have good or bad effects. Emotionally healthy people recognize and accept a wide range of emotions in themselves. They can express these emotions in ways that do not damage themselves or others either physically or mentally.

Many people judge emotions as bad or good. Often their judgments are based on past experiences. For example, if a child is punished for expressing anger, and it is not made clear to the child that the punishment is for the behavior and not for the emotion, the child may associate being angry with being "bad." If the child is not helped to find an acceptable way to express anger, he or she may try to suppress it.

Both your mental and physical health are affected when you go through life considering yourself bad because you have emotions you feel uncomfortable with. Learning to recognize, accept, and express or deal with emotions in appropriate ways is an important aspect of mental and physical health.

### Recognizing and Accepting Emotions

Recognizing emotions involves allowing yourself to feel them. If you are feeling sad, admit it. Allow yourself to feel happy when you are happy. Strange as it may seem, some people do not allow themselves to be happy because they believe they do not deserve to be happy. Some people are frightened by happiness. They believe that if they allow themselves to feel happy, the circumstances that caused their happiness will suddenly disappear.

Try not to judge yourself by the emotions you are experiencing. If you are angry or feel guilty or sad about something, accept the fact that you feel angry or guilty or sad. In other words, accept the fact that it is normal to have these emotions. Experiencing emotions that make you feel sad or uncomfortable does not mean you are a bad person.

### The Reasons Behind Emotions

Once you have recognized an emotion, particularly an emotion that you have trouble recognizing or accepting in yourself, try to understand why you are feeling that way. For example, suppose you are feeling angry. Think about why you are angry. Are you angry with yourself for having done something or for having not done something? Are you angry with someone else for a specific reason? If you realize you are feeling guilty for feeling happy, why are you feeling guilty? Once you have determined the reason for your feelings, you can begin to deal with your feelings. You may be able to express the emotion in some way or change the way you behave when you feel that emotion.

Sadness and anger are common human emotions. Why is it unhealthy to keep them inside and not express them?

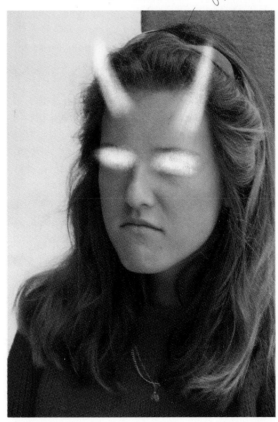

***Expressing Your Emotions and Changing Your Behavior*** Once you have discovered why you are feeling an emotion, you need to examine the strength of the emotion. Is the strength of the emotion in proportion to the reasons for it? Are you extremely angry over a minor incident, or is your anger well-founded? Are you feeling guilty for no reason, or are you justified in feeling guilty? If you can recognize that the strength of the emotion is out of proportion to the situation, the recognition may help to lessen the feeling.

If you believe the strength of the emotion is justified, you probably are justified in taking some action. This does not mean that you should tell someone off or pick a fight with someone when you are angry. It does mean giving yourself some time to cool off and then expressing your anger. Rather than accusing or attacking the other person, describe how you feel. You might say "I feel angry and hurt because you didn't keep your promise," rather than "You are the most inconsiderate person I have ever known. You must lie awake nights thinking of ways to be mean."

When you describe what you feel and why you feel that way, you make it possible to discuss the situation. When you attack the other person, you put that individual on the defensive. Conversation is likely to be nonproductive when someone is defensive.

Sometimes anger and frustration are due to several causes that, taken separately, are minor but when combined create stress and affect emotions. Often stress can be a cause of anger and frustration. Relieving the stress will relieve the impact of the emotions. Chapter 4 will give you more information about stress.

Some emotions take time to deal with. Grief over the loss of a loved one does not pass quickly. It must be recognized and dealt with in order to recover and move on with one's life. Suppressing the grief can have negative effects on behavior, attitudes, and even physical health.

Getting involved in a constructive new activity, such as helping others, may relieve negative feelings.

Sometimes, negative reactions to some emotions can be changed by a change in your thinking or behavior pattern. If you are feeling guilty or anxious about something you know is not significant, changing the way you have thought about the incident may help. Behaving in a manner that confronts the feelings may also help. If you are lonely, for example, making an effort to make friends or to participate in activities may help to overcome your loneliness. Perhaps you need to develop some interests of your own so that you do not need to depend on others for your happiness. Often the suggestions you have been given for improving your self-concept and developing a positive attitude can be used to change your behavioral response to an emotion.

## Practical Tip: Keeping A Journal

■ If you have difficulty expressing your feelings out loud, write them down in a journal. Sometimes it is easier for you to clarify your feelings when you write them down, and it may help you to express them verbally in later discussions.

Sometimes just talking with another person can help to lessen an emotion. For example, Clarissa was feeling increasingly nervous about going away to college. Among other things, she was afraid she might be homesick, that she would not do well, and that she might not make any friends. Finally, as her fears grew and her school work slipped, she told her sister Julia, who was already in college. Julia took some time to share her own experiences with Clarissa. She had had many of the same fears, and they had never come true. Just talking with Julia helped Clarissa to see that her fears probably were unfounded. Once her fears were eased, Clarissa began to look forward to going away to college.

Sometimes people experience more than one emotion at a time. This can make it difficult to recognize and deal with specific emotions. For example, if you arrive home hours after your curfew, without having notified your parents that you will be late, your parents may be relieved to know that you are safe but extremely angry because you were not home at curfew time and they were worried. If they can recognize all their emotions and let things cool down briefly, it may be possible to deal with the situation in a more satisfactory way than if they let their anger overwhelm them.

Sometimes writing down what you feel and why you feel the way you do can help you to

identify all the different emotions that are contributing to your confusion. Once you have identified specific emotions, it is easier to choose a course of action.

**When Outside Help Is Needed** Sometimes it is not possible for people to recognize, accept, and deal with their emotions on their own or by talking with friends or family. Feelings of depression, suicidal tendencies, extreme or uncontrolled anger or rage, and continuing problems with relationships are all indications that professional help is needed.

There are many sources of professional help for emotional problems. Frequently, ministers, priests, and rabbis are trained in counseling. School counselors, individual and family counselors, social workers, psychologists, and psychiatrists are trained at varying levels to help people deal with emotional difficulties. There are also many hotlines or crises centers that help people deal with emergencies. Many of these resources are explained in greater detail in Chapter 5.

How can communicating with a close friend help to put emotions in perspective and lessen stress?

1. How do attitudes effect relationships?
2. Are emotions bad or good? Explain.
3. Why is it important for you to express your emotions in some acceptable way?

## Improving Communication

Communication has many facets. It is not just skill in writing, speaking, listening, and reading. It also includes the ability to empathize and sympathize with others, to accept others for what they are and to respect differences. It requires a certain knowledge and skill in understanding and using body language and an understanding of the role played by appearance. All these skills combined can help you to develop strong relationships with others, to get along with others, and to make the most of the resources you have.

Signing is a nonverbal technique that allows deaf persons to communicate without hearing the spoken word.

## Types of Communication

**Communication** can be defined as a process by which information is exchanged among individuals through a common system of symbols, signs, or behavior. The importance of understanding is implied in this definition. If the messages that are sent or received are not clearly understood, misunderstanding occurs, and the communication has not been effective. **Verbal communication** includes written and spoken words. **Nonverbal communication** includes all the many ways people communicate without words.

***Verbal Communication*** There are many languages in the world. Each language is made up of thousands of different words. When people know the meaning of these words, they can be used as a means of communicating. Think how difficult it would be to get your messages across if there were no verbal communication.

***Nonverbal Communication*** Words are not the only way to communicate. It is possible to communicate without words by using body posture, facial expressions, and appearance. Nonverbal elements of communication can affect the verbal messages that are spoken or written. Sometimes they can contradict the verbal communication, leading to confusion.

Behavior, too, is a type of nonverbal communication. Young children who cannot yet talk rely on this form of communication. When babies or young children rub their ears and are fussy, they may be telling you that their ears hurt and that they have an ear infection. Adults also use behavior to communicate. Offering help, being there when someone needs emotional support, driving within the speed limit, talking in a soft voice, slamming doors, hitting objects or people, breaking the law, and attempting suicide are all behaviors that communicate emotions.

Your tone of voice is another aspect of non-verbal communication. Tones can give different meanings to the same words. Think about all the different meanings you can give to the words "Nice work" just by your tone of voice.

## Communication Inhibitors

Although communication should increase understanding and promote positive relationships, it does not always do so. There are many factors that can diminish the effectiveness of communication.

**Communication inhibitors** are combinations of attitudes and verbal and nonverbal communication techniques that interfere with communication. Communication inhibitors can prevent relationships from developing, or they can destroy ones that have been established. They can cause hurt feelings, misunderstandings, and diminished self-confidence. In other words, they prevent communication.

***Stereotyping*** A **stereotype** is a generalized attitude about a group of people. "All handicapped people need help in everyday living" and "All teenagers are irresponsible" are statements that reflect stereotypes.

Stereotyping perpetuates incorrect information about groups of people, not individuals. It may be true that some physically, mentally, or emotionally handicapped people need help in everyday living, and that some teenagers are irresponsible; but it is just as true that many handicapped people are self-sufficient and that many teenagers are responsible students and citizens.

Each person is an individual with individual characteristics that make him or her unique. Handicapped people are apt to be viewed as less than complete persons because others do not know how to react to them. Assuming that a person has certain characteristics because he or she is a member of a certain group or is a cer-

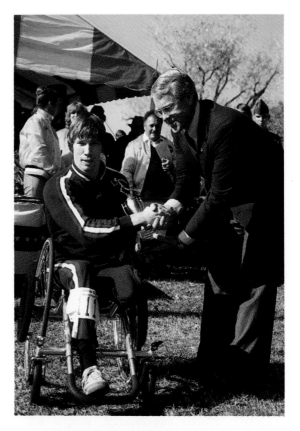

Their achievements have helped to erase stereotypes about the handicapped.

tain age does not allow you to get to know that person as he or she really is.

To avoid stereotyping, become acquainted with people as individuals. Then, you can judge for yourself what each person is like.

***Prejudice*** Prejudice is an unfair judgment or opinion about one or more individuals that is formed prior to knowing or considering the facts. Often prejudice is based on suspicion, fear, or intolerance of differences. Irrational hatred or negative opinions about all "foreigners" is one example of prejudice. There are many others.

If you have ever been a victim of prejudice, you know how unfair it can be. Whether or not you have experienced prejudice, you can take steps to prevent it by checking out facts and by waiting until you know a person before you judge him or her.

**Put-downs** Put-downs are remarks that make other people look bad or feel hurt. Destructive criticism and sarcastic, cynical, or intentionally hurtful remarks are examples of put-downs. Statements such as "How stupid can you be?" "I told you that would happen," or "Give me one good reason to trust you" all fall into this category. You probably have heard these put-downs. You may have even made some of these remarks yourself.

Sometimes, making remarks that put yourself or others down is more a matter of habit than the deliberate desire to hurt someone. You hear other people make these remarks, and you do the same. Sometimes, the remarks are not intentionally hurtful, but they have that effect anyway. Try to stop and think before you speak to be sure that what you are going to say will not attack your self-concept or another person's self-concept. If you cannot think of anything constructive to say, it may be better to say nothing.

**Blaming and/or Making Excuses** Blaming someone else for problems or unsatisfactory situations,or making excuses for the outcome of actions or the present circumstances can cause hurt feelings. Blaming and making excuses get in the way of looking at a situation realistically and doing something to change it. Saying "It's all your fault we're so far behind on this project," for example, may cause the other person to become defensive and tell you all the reasons it isn't his or her fault. Even if the other person agrees that the situation is his or her fault, blaming someone does not correct the situation. On the other hand, the statement, "We are behind on this project. What steps can we take to catch up?" opens the door to constructive communication between people.

**Using Power** Threats are one way some people use power. Other people may be physically or verbally abusive. This method of using power creates or increases fear in another person. If a person is afraid, he or she cannot be open and honest. Instead, the individual may concentrate on dealing with the fear and avoiding situations that result in someone wielding power. Other people may fight back. This blocks communication because retaliation often becomes the goal. The energy that is put into these actions is energy that is not available for developing more effective communication.

**Poor Self-Concept or a Negative Attitude** These two communication inhibitors are closely related. Either one may be the result of the other. People with poor self-concepts usually feel that they are not interesting people, do not have much to offer, and do not feel that they have much control over their lives. They may show off or try to use power or blame others as a means of getting attention or making up for real or imagined inadequacies.

A person with a negative attitude about people or situations looks at the negative aspects of a situation or a person rather than at the positive aspects. This interferes with open communication and the development of a more positive attitude.

## Communication Skills

Skills in reading, writing, speaking, and listening are all important for good communication. You use these skills every day at school or work and in family or other group situations. Improving these skills will improve communication in all areas of your life.

**Reading** Reading skills are important to every aspect of living. You have to know how to read to take the subway or bus, to get a driver's license, to do food shopping, to fill out a job

Imagine what your life would be like without reading or writing skills. Could you cope with this limitation?

application or some other type of application, and to follow written instructions for using equipment or for making or fixing things. Reading is an important component of learning. Whenever you read, you increase your knowledge and broaden your outlook on the world.

**Writing** You need writing skills to fill out forms, to take notes and to write papers in school, and to write letters. Writing is simply a visual form of communication. English classes at school are the place to learn writing skills that will help you to communicate.

If you have trouble with writing or spelling, there is probably special help available from the school. You may want to check with your teacher or guidance counselor.

**Speaking** Speaking skills include making speeches or giving presentations, but they also include carrying on conversations with other people, asking for information, registering a complaint, offering praise or encouragement, expressing emotions and opinions, and giving directions to others.

Skills in speaking are important to friendship, to business relationships, to being both a leader and follower, and to being a good citizen in the school and the community.

Practice conversational skills and try to consider any school assignments that require speaking before a group as good learning experiences. Working with a tape recorder sometimes can help you to improve your pronunciation, tone, and expression.

**Listening**  Listening is vital to communication. It is more than just hearing. Hearing involves perceiving sound, while listening involves paying attention to increase understanding.

A good listener tries to understand the message that is being sent. To do this, the listener must look for nonverbal clues, as well as listen to the words being said. A good listener also encourages the person who is speaking to express himself or herself.

## Communicating a Good Impression

When you meet someone for the first time or you apply for a job, you want to make a favorable impression. In other words, you want to communicate a positive image of yourself. The way you dress and take care of yourself, your posture, your facial expressions, and your manner, as well as the way you express yourself verbally, all contribute to this impression. Chapter 13 discusses this issue in more detail.

Body posture and facial expression communicate something about a person. Standing up straight and smiling give a message. If you slouch and frown or have a straight face, you send a different message.

The way in which a person positions himself or herself with those he or she is talking to is a means of nonverbal communication. Facing a person or leaning toward a person sends a different message from the message that is sent when you turn sideways or lean away from a person. A great deal of space between two people who are talking says something different than little space.

Personal appearance is another type of nonverbal communication. A neat, clean appearance communicates something different from that which is communicated by a dirty, disheveled appearance. Conservative clothes say something different than clothes in the latest, most modern styles.

These young people are inquiring about jobs. Do you think they are making a good impression? Why or why not?

A positive self-concept is the basis for all of these factors. If you like and respect yourself, you will want to take care of yourself and the way you look. The self-confident manner you project will create a positive impression.

### For Review

1. Explain two elements that are a part of nonverbal communication.
2. List four communication inhibitors.
3. What is the best way for you to communicate a good impression?

# Developing Positive Relationships

Throughout your life, you will experience different types of relationships with other people. There are relationships with parents, brothers and sisters, and other family members. There are relationships with friends and neighbors, teachers, co-workers, salespersons, and service persons. Each type of relationship is different, and the quality of these relationships can influence your life profoundly.

Positive relationships with others have many qualities. They help to promote positive self-concepts, and they encourage people to give of themselves. They allow for individual differences and encourage acceptance of others. They help those involved in them to meet their needs in acceptable and constructive ways. All in all, positive relationships help and encourage people to grow and to develop to their fullest capacities.

Being involved in positive relationships with others adds richness to life and provides individuals with a wealth of human resources. Love, trust, acceptance, honesty, a sense of reality, a sense of hope, and a belief in the basic goodness of people grow out of positive relationships. These qualities enable people to solve problems, cope with crises, set goals, and to work to reach those goals.

## Changing Relationships

The types of relationships you have change throughout your life. As a child, you depend on others to meet your needs. It is important that these needs are met because this frees you from feelings of insecurity and low self-esteem and allows you to develop to your fullest potential.

As you grow, you must learn to become less dependent on others to meet all your needs. You develop the abilities you need to meet your own needs in satisfactory ways. This is part of growing up and gaining maturity. Extreme dependence on others as an adult seldom provides a good foundation for healthy, positive relationships. Positive relationships with adults, particularly with parents, help you to grow and develop in positive ways. The move from dependence toward independence involves accepting responsibility for your own happiness and direction in life.

Another aspect of maturity is the development of positive interdependent relationships. These relationships involve mutual give and take and strike a balance between being dependent and independent. People who are involved in positive interdependent relationships are

Developing positive relationships with people of all ages helps you to mature.

able to meet their own needs and to help others meet their needs. Positive interdependent relationships are mutually supportive and enriching. Power is not a factor in these relationships. They are based on trust, acceptance, respect, and liking. True friendship and love can result.

Positive interdependent relationships provide strong foundations for love and marriage. The ability to function in and maintain a positive interdependent relationship develops slowly. This is why marriage at a young age seldom works. Each of the people involved may have not developed yet the ability to relate in consistently positive interdependent ways. Not all adults automatically acquire this ability. There are many who have problems with close relationships or marriage because they cannot relate to others in a consistently positive interdependent manner. However, gaining experience in relationships increases the possibility of developing the ability to relate to another person daily in a positive interdependent way.

## Improving Relationships

Think about the relationships you have with other people. Do you feel good about these relationships? It is possible to work toward more positive relationships. These suggestions may help:

- Develop positive personal qualities. These include understanding, patience, respect, and trustworthiness.
- Improve your self-concept and your skills in communication.
- Accept responsibility for yourself and the actions you take.
- Be willing to compromise.

If problems develop in a relationship, try to face them rather than avoid them. There are steps you can take toward correcting an unhappy situation. First, set up a mutually agreeable time and place to talk to the other person. Make sure you won't be distracted or interrupted. Describe the situation as you see it, and state what you think should be done. Avoid blaming and accusing, and encourage the other person to talk and to make suggestions. Decide on a plan to improve the relationship, and give it time to work. During this time, always keep the lines of communication open. These simple steps may make the difference between saving and ending some relationships.

## Developing Leader/Group Relationships

In any group, there are leaders, and there are followers. Skills in leading and in following are valuable skills. Many of the suggestions given in the preceding section apply to creating good relationships among group members.

**Group Membership Skills** Most people are leaders in some situations and followers in others. Being an intelligent follower and group member is as important as being an effective leader. Because you function within many groups, your group membership skills are needed every day. Your family group, peer group, school and club groups, and community groups are some examples. You may or may not act as a leader in these groups. However, you will always need the skills to be an intelligent, responsible group member and follower.

Having skills as both a leader and a follower can help you to increase your understanding of the other position. If you have been a group member, you have some idea about what you would like a leader to do and how you would like a leader to operate. If you have been a leader, you know how you would like members to behave.

Intelligent group members act as a check on each other and on the group leader. As a group member, you listen carefully to the leader and other members in order to understand their ideas and opinions. You participate

What are the important characteristics of a responsible group member?

group is to function effectively. A person who always wants his or her own way interferes with group progress toward reaching goals. An intelligent group member is open to new ideas and ways of doing things if the group will benefit. A willingness to help other members or give special attention to a new member are other positive characteristics of a group member.

***Leadership Skills*** Being an effective leader does not mean telling everyone else what to do. It does not mean doing all of the work yourself, without any help. It does mean knowing how to handle and deal with different types of people, being able to motivate yourself and others, and being able to work with others. It means being willing to share the work and responsibilities, being able to make use of everyone's talents and abilities, and giving recognition where recognition is due.

The people who make up a group have different personalities, different ideas and opinions, and often, different reasons for being members of the group. A leader needs to be sensitive to the different personalities and attitudes of a group. For example, some people need a lot of direction when carrying out a project. They need to be told what to do and how to do it. They may be afraid of making mistakes, or they may be unfamiliar with what they are doing. They may not be able to develop their own procedure. Other people only need to be asked to do something. They will carry out the responsibilities with little additional assistance. Recognizing these differences can help a leader to decide when to provide extra guidance and help and when to allow people to work independently on a project.

A leader needs to be able to recognize different reactions. Some people prefer to be told outright. Other people rebel when they are ordered to do something but will respond when they are asked. Still others may be most willing to do something when they have taken part in the planning.

actively by expressing your own ideas and opinions. When disagreements occur, compromises may be necessary. An intelligent follower, however, does not compromise his or her own values in order to go along with a group decision. This may occur when there is pressure within a peer group to act in a way that goes against your own values. If this happens often, you may decide that leaving the group is the wisest course of action for you—even if this is difficult. Intelligent following does not mean doing something because "everyone else is doing it." It does mean thinking things through according to your own values, making a decision, and acting on it.

When the values of the leader and group members are the same, cooperation and willingness to work together are needed if the

Different people are motivated in different ways. Some people are naturally enthusiastic about certain things or have strong opinions or feelings about something. This provides the motivation necessary for a project. Other people may have to be motivated by a leader or another member of the group or an outside force, such as a prize or extra credit or some type of personal gain. Part of a leader's job is to provide appropriate motivation for the different members of the group or to enlist the aid of others as a means of motivating as many members as possible. A leader's personal enthusiasm and strong beliefs in the importance of the group often help to motivate members.

Since all people are different, there are bound to be differences of opinion and different ideas among members. Often, individual members can work out the differences, but sometimes they cannot. A leader may need to help. One solution is to talk with each person involved and then with the people involved as a group. Sometimes, presenting the problem to the whole group for their comments, suggestions, and solutions will help settle differences. In each instance, a leader should try to respect the feelings and beliefs of every member. Compromise may be the solution.

Recognition of everyone's efforts is an important part of being a leader. Praise or public recognition can help to improve self-concepts and increase self-esteem. Often it provides the motivation to become involved again. Most people like to know that others appreciate the effort they have made.

When a group takes on a project, getting people involved in the project is part of a leader's job. Sometimes it is easy, and sometimes it is not. Learning what an individual's strong points are can help when trying to get people involved. For example, there may be a member who has a natural talent for organizing fund-raising events. This person may be willing to be in charge of, or help to plan, a fund-raiser for the group. People are often more willing to do something in which they feel they have some degree of ability.

One of the most important leadership skills is skill in communication. Knowing what you want to say and how to say it to bring out the best in other people can make all the difference in the world. Even if you do not plan to become president of the country or head of your school student council or even chairman of a committee, developing leadership skills is important. Having these skills will help you to know what to do in different situations and will give you a variety of skills to draw upon.

## Using Outside Resources to Help Relationships

For many people, the suggestions in this chapter, or the suggestions from other resources, and time and effort will help to improve and strengthen relationships with other people. Sometimes, however, there are instances when outside help is needed.

If someone has trouble making or keeping friends, a session or two with the school guidance counselor or school psychologist may be all that is needed. Perhaps the individual is being unrealistic in his or her expectations. Perhaps it is a matter of low self-esteem. For more serious problems, more sessions may be needed, or a counselor, psychologist, or other mental health personnel in the community may be needed.

## For Review

1. What are the qualities you will find in positive relationships?
2. State four suggestions you have read about for improving relationships.
3. Why are both leader and group member skills so important?

## Management Application: Making Leadership Decisions

Imagine yourself in the situation described below. As you read, think about how the steps of the management process might apply to this situation. Then answer the questions that follow.

## Situation

The student council elections were over, and Bob was the new president. The awful feeling in the pit of his stomach as he went on stage to accept the honor made him wonder why he had run for this position at all. At first, the campaign had seemed like a lot of fun—making posters, thinking of clever slogans. Bob knew he was popular, but he had never been the leader of any group or elected the president of anything before. Now, as he thought about this new responsibility, he was worried. It was his job to organize the new student council, to deal with student problems, and to plan the big dance. How could he cope with all of these things? He wondered if it was possible to be scared and excited at the same time, because at the moment, he was.

At the first student council meeting, the issue of the dance was brought up. Bob joked nervously about hiring Bruce Springsteen to play. He was beginning to feel overwhelmed. He didn't know the first thing about organizing a dance. He looked out at his fellow council members and noticed Judy. She had helped to put on the terrific Halloween dance last year. Perhaps she would help this year. Adam was a

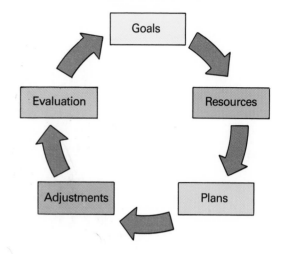

great artist. Maybe he would plan the decorations. Bob knew he had to find out what everyone else could contribute or the dance would never happen. He was a leader in need of help. He knew he could not accomplish everything by himself. What should he do?

## Questions

1. What nonhuman resources must be analyzed before Bob can begin to plan for the school dance?

2. How can Bob begin to discover the human resources of the individual members of the council?

3. How can Bob manage the students' talents and nonhuman resources to make the dance successful?

4. What leadership qualities does Bob need to develop?

5. Should Bob make decisions for the group?

6. Which of the steps of the management process apply to this situation?

# 2 Chapter Review

## Summary

Heredity and environment act together to make each person unique. A positive self-concept, however, is crucial for developing a positive attitude and meeting needs. Accepting and expressing emotions contributes to mental and physical health. People send messages through verbal and nonverbal communications. Communication inhibitors can cause hurt feelings, create misunderstandings, and diminish self-confidence. Good relationships help to promote positive self-concepts.

## Vocabulary

Complete each of the following sentences with one of the vocabulary words below.

- heredity
- environment
- self-concept
- attitudes
- emotions
- communication
- verbal communication
- nonverbal communication
- communication inhibitors
- stereotype

1. Strong feelings, often combined with bodily responses, are _____ .

2. Sending messages to other people without words is _____ .

3. The beliefs and feelings people have about themselves is the _____ .

4. The total of all characteristics passed on to an individual by parents and ancestors is _____ .

5. Attitudes and messages that can hurt feelings, create misunderstanding, and diminish self-confidence are _____ .

6. The ideas or opinions a person has about himself or herself, about others, and about events or situations are _____ .

7. A process by which information is exchanged between individuals through a common system of symbols, signs, or behavior is _____ .

8. All the conditions and life experiences an individual has in his or her surroundings are the _____ .

9. A generalized attitude or opinion about a group of people that perpetuates incorrect information is a _____ .

10. Sending messages through spoken and written words is _____ .

## Questions

1. Psychologists classify human needs in different ways, but they agree that human needs motivate human behavior. Explain how needs motivate behavior.

2. What are the factors that determine how a person meets his or her needs?

3. Why do you need a positive self-concept? How would you rate your self-concept?

4. Emotions are neither good nor bad, but the way in which people deal with them can have good or bad effects. Explain.

5. Identify each of the following as verbal or nonverbal communication: writing; body position when listening; reading; facial expressions; clapping; shaking one's head; talking; foot shuffling.

6. Give five examples of communication inhibitors. Explain how each interferes with communication.

7. What are some ways to communicate a favorable impression?

8. Why is it important for people to have positive relationships?

9. What are the qualities of a good leader?

## Skill Activities

1. **Critical Thinking.** Everyone has stereotypes and prejudices that have been learned. Stereotypes and prejudices can be unlearned, too. Part of unlearning a stereotype comes from thinking about it.

What are your stereotypes about city people/country people, young people/old people, and tall people/short people?

Write a short essay on one of your stereotypes. What has made you think or feel this way? How can you change this stereotype? Explain your answers.

2. **Communication.** Take an inventory of your communication skills. Rate yourself on the following skills as very good, good, fair, or poor.

If you think you need help, talk to your parents, teachers, or guidance counselor.

**Reading Skills**
- I can read all of the words in an assignment.
- I understand whatever I read.
- I read quickly enough to finish an assignment in the allotted time.
- I can answer questions about what I read.
- I recall what I read the next day.

**Writing Skills**
- I can express my ideas in writing.
- I use correct spelling and grammar when I am writing.
- I can easily write answers to test questions.

**Speaking Skills**
- I can carry on conversations with people.
- I can express my feelings and opinions.
- I can give directions and ask for information.

**Listening Skills**
- I can follow directions.
- I can listen to a conversation without losing my concentration.
- I look for nonverbal and verbal clues.
- I encourage people who speak to me by showing interest and asking questions.

# 3 Managing Family Life

## As you read, think about:

- [ ] what the stages of the life cycle are.
- [ ] what caregiving needs are required during each stage of the life cycle.
- [ ] how each life style needs different resources.
- [ ] how to apply the management process to decisions about family life.

life cycle
autonomy
empty nest syndrome
infatuation
nuclear family
extended family
modified extended family
blended family

*mensah*

As you grow and develop, you have needs that are met by your family. As you become more independent, you choose the life style that best suits your needs and wants. Life styles, like many other things, can change as your stage in the life cycle changes. In our country today, there are many different family structures and many different life styles. Learning about different life styles and situations can help you to make more informed decisions as you go through life.

## Understanding the Life Cycle

The course people follow as they move from birth to death is called the **life cycle.** The most recognized stages of the life cycle are: infancy, childhood, adolescence, young adulthood, middle age, and late adulthood. Each stage has its own caregiving needs, both physical and emotional. Each stage also has its own crises and roles and responsibilities.

### Infancy

Infancy lasts from birth to approximately two years of age. The first year is characterized by rapid physical growth—a baby's birth weight usually triples in the first year.

***Caregiving During Infancy*** An infant is completely dependent upon others for his or her physical and emotional needs. Infants require a great deal of physical care. They do not sleep for long periods of time. They need to be fed frequently and to have their diapers changed often. They also need a great deal of

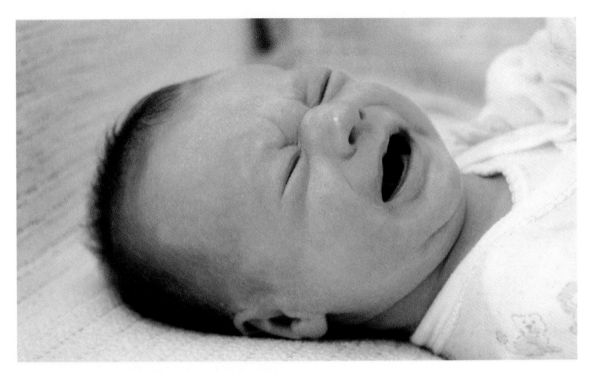

Newborn babies are totally dependent on others for their care and safety.

emotional care. They need a lot of love, which includes holding, comforting, and interacting with them in various ways. According to Erik Erikson, a noted psychologist, if an infant's needs for love, care, and reassurance are not met, the infant learns to distrust others.

**Crises During Infancy**   Crises during infancy usually involve physical illnesses, including colic, or problems with digestion. Colds and ear infections also are common during infancy. Serious birth defects can cause almost as much stress for the caregivers as for the infants, and they can place heavy demands on human and nonhuman resources.

**Roles and Responsibilities**   The infant has no responsibilities, of course. He or she is the total responsibility of others. Even so, an infant's interaction with and attachment to caregivers begins early. The infant does fill the role of giv-ing emotional feedback to the caregiver by smiling and responding positively to being fed and cared for.

## Childhood

The years of early childhood fall between the ages of three and five. Those of middle childhood include the years from the age of six to the age of twelve.

**Caregiving During Childhood**   As a child grows and develops, he or she requires physical care and an increasing amount of emotional support. In early childhood, there is still a great deal of physical care required. The child explores everything, unaware of any dangers. Young children seem to have boundless energy and an insatiable curiosity. They are into everything they can get their hands on, and they will try to put everything into their mouths. Others have to watch for their safety while allowing them to explore and learn about the world around them.

Young children are also prone to colds and ear infections because their bodies have not built up a resistance to the germs that cause these illnesses. When they do not feel well or are unhappy, they require additional attention.

Once children begin to talk, they ask questions to learn more about the world around them. It takes supervision and guidance to help them learn appropriate behavior. It takes a long time for children to develop the ability to control their actions, and they need support and help from others as they learn. During childhood, a child's discipline needs to be consistent and constructive.

***Crises During Childhood***  Physical crises include illness and accidental injuries. These are common during childhood, especially before a child learns about the harmful aspects of the surrounding environment. The healthy emotional growth of a child depends on the caregiver allowing the child to begin the move toward independence. If a child is allowed to make some choices and dress himself or herself, for example, the child gains experience and self-confidence. According to Erikson, failure to move toward independence in childhood may result in indecisiveness and a lack of self-control. In middle childhood, children need to be praised as they develop their talents and skills. If caregivers do not provide positive emotional support for the older child, the child may develop feelings of inferiority.

***Childhood Roles and Responsibilities***  The child learns many lessons about family responsibilities as he or she moves through childhood. Children who take part in helping others in the family learn that they are important and needed. The simple chores that a child may do are not as important as the fact that the

Young children require a lot of care while they are learning about the world.

caregiver relied on the child to do them and praised the child for his or her accomplishments. The child gradually learns that his or her family role is shifting from being totally cared for to helping to care for others and share a variety of responsibilities.

## Adolescence

The teenage years, from age thirteen to age nineteen, that you are now experiencing are referred to as adolescence. Adolescence is a time of dramatic change—in your body, in your emotions, and in your abilities.

***Caregiving During Adolescence***  Caregiving needs continue to change during adolescence. You need less physical care. You take care of many of your own physical needs that were supplied by others during your childhood. You become more of a caregiver as you play a role in solving family problems and working at relationships. Although physical needs for care lessen, emotional caregiving remains crucial. Loving support from family members helps you to view yourself as a worthwhile person. Positive emotional care allows you to develop self-confidence and self-esteem.

***Crises During Adolescence***   The major crisis during adolescence is the identity crisis. The establishment of your own identity is extremely important if you are to function effectively as an adult. According to Erik Erikson, a weak personality displays identity confusion while a stable personality has a strong sense of identity. If

What responsibilities can you take on during adolescence to help out at home?

a person does not establish a sense of identity during adolescence he or she may become preoccupied with how others view him or her. This dependence leads to insecurity and further blocks or weakens personality development.

Beyond any extreme illness, the physical changes in adolescence also can be termed a crisis of sorts. Growth spurts and changes in hormones can be upsetting unless they are understood as normal developments.

***Adolescent Roles and Responsibilities***   Your roles and responsibilities change and develop dramatically during adolescence. As you move toward **autonomy,** or independence, you make more of your own decisions. If decision-making roles are not defined, family problems may result. Parents often find it difficult to give up their roles as total caregivers and to allow adolescents to make their own decisions. At the same time, adolescents often want complete autonomy immediately. They may feel that they are capable of making decisions without consulting parents. Good communication is needed to clarify roles and to avoid conflict.

Your roles within the family and outside of the family expand as you move through adolescence. You may act as a caregiver for a younger sibling or as a part-time employee, as well as a student. You may add the role of boyfriend or girlfriend to your increasing number of roles. In all of these roles, you learn to handle responsibilities and to make your own decisions, but these expanding roles can be confusing. As an adolescent, you handle many changes and make many adjustments. It is important to accept all of your mistakes as well as your successes. Everyone experiences failures. With a strong sense of self-esteem, you can turn failure into learning experiences as you move toward adulthood.

***Relationships During Adolescence***   Your relationships with your parents or other care-

Friendships and romantic relationships are important parts of growing up.

givers change during adolescence. As you become older and share more family responsibilities, your relationship with your parents matures. You may help a parent with a specific problem, for example. You may be able to offer advice or emotional support during a time of family crisis.

Relationships with peers also mature as you establish new friendships that are based on similar values. Your relationships with members of the opposite sex develop further as you date and establish loving relationships.

Adolescence is a time of learning and testing relationships as boyfriends or girlfriends. You learn more about the qualities you value most in each other. You learn how to solve problems within a relationship. Since several romantic relationships may occur during adolescence, you may also learn how to end relationships. Depending upon your choice of life style, this process may be preparation for eventually choosing and making a commitment to a life partner. Whether you choose to marry or not, all of these experiences and changes in relationships help to prepare you for adulthood.

## Young Adulthood

The period of life from age twenty through approximately age forty sometimes is called young adulthood. During this period, people establish themselves in the world of work. They may marry and become parents, or they may decide to remain single.

***Caregiving During Young Adulthood*** At this stage of life, you are usually quite independent. You may be responsible for providing all of your basic living needs—food, shelter, and clothing. If you are attending college or are living at home until you can earn enough money to go out on your own, you are moving toward this point. In many cases, a young adult not only is on his or her own but already is acting as the total caregiver for a child.

***Crises During Young Adulthood*** Typical crises or stress situations during young adulthood include struggling for financial security and adjusting to parenthood. During this stage of life, problems may occur if the young adult does not have the ability to love and to commit himself or herself to others while maintaining a personal identity. If problems from adolescence are unresolved, the young adult may have difficulty establishing effective relationships with others throughout life.

## Middle Age

Middle age includes the years from age forty through approximately age sixty-five. During middle age, many people are established in their work and in chosen life style. Frequently, middle-aged adults begin to reevaluate their roles and life styles.

***Caregiving During Middle Age*** Most healthy people at this stage of life do not need to be cared for by others. In some cases, middle-aged persons may be partial or total caregivers for aging parents or relatives who once cared for them. Resources of both time and money may be necessary to meet these needs and fulfill these responsibilities. If parents and relatives are healthy and any children have left home, middle age often is a period of time that is free of caregiving responsibilities.

***Crises During Middle Age*** Often, middle age is a time of reevaluation and restlessness. Many people look at where they are in relation to their past goals. They may find these goals unsatisfactory. They may set new goals for themselves, depending on whether or not they are content with their circumstances.

Within a family, middle-age parents may experience the **empty nest syndrome.** This can occur when children leave home to become independent. Parents may experience a sense of loss, as well as a sense of freedom from responsibility. Couples who are now free to set their own schedules and pursue their own activities may find themselves bewildered by this freedom. A crisis may occur if a couple's focus has always been on the needs of their children and not on their own relationship. As the adjustment is made, couples usually become reacquainted and focus on each other as they did at the start of their marriage.

## Late Adulthood

Late adulthood, sometimes referred to as old age, follows middle age. This is the final stage of the life cycle. Depending upon health factors, late adulthood can include many happy, productive years.

***Caregiving During Late Adulthood*** As people advance into late adulthood, their health and strength diminish. If an older person is extremely ill, he or she may need total care. This last phase of life can be similar to infancy in its caregiving needs.

***Crises During Late Adulthood*** During old age, some people again become dependent on others. Poor health and the inability to do some things are difficult to accept gracefully. In this final stage, the well-adjusted older person possesses *integrity,* according to Erik Erickson. Rather than despairing over his or her situation, the older person is content and can look back on his or her life with satisfac-

Older adults have much to contribute.

tion. Older persons with integrity are at peace with themselves and secure in the knowledge that they have no strong regrets about their lives. After all, many older people live active, full lives, and a number have major success during this stage of their lives.

**Roles and Relationships** Older adults are rich sources of knowledge because of their varied life experiences. Although our society has tended to value youth, as people live longer, we have begun to realize that many people in late adulthood have much to offer us. They are capable, competent individuals who play loving, supportive roles within families.

## Understanding Different Life Styles

As you move into young adulthood, you choose a life style that is appropriate to your needs at this time. There are many different life styles that are socially acceptable in our society. Remaining single is one life style. It involves decisions about living alone or with others. Marriage is another possible life style. As you move into middle age and late adulthood, you may change your choice of life style. Understanding each of these life styles and recognizing their pressures and demands on resources are important to you as you look toward your own future.

## The Single Life

There are single people of all ages, ranging from those just out of high school to the elderly. These people are single for a variety of reasons. Their life styles and living situations vary, as do the pressures each experiences and the demands that are placed on their resources.

**Reasons for Remaining Single** Today, many people are choosing to remain single or to marry after they have established careers and had a variety of life experiences. Some people are single due to circumstances not of their choosing. They may wish to marry, but they have not found suitable partners. Other people have religious beliefs or occupations that forbid marriage, and some have extreme career demands or have sole responsibility for the care of elderly or ill parents or other relatives. Some people are single because they are divorced; still others are single because their spouses have died.

**Variations in Life Styles and Living Situations** It used to be thought that single people lived at home or shared living space with other single people only until they married. Although the costs of renting and buying living space have increased, living alone is a possibility for single persons with well-paying jobs or careers. This degree of independence is highly valued by some. Single persons with

What are some of the positive aspects of being single and living alone?

two jobs or put in overtime at work. Otherwise, they may use their free time to pursue interests or hobbies or just to socialize.

***Pressures and Demands on Resources***
Many singles today are contented with their life styles. Their time and money resources can be used for their own interests; they do not have dependents to take care of. Other singles, however, are subjected to pressure to marry. Parents may want their children to marry and have children so there will be grandchildren. Although it was more common in the past, parents and other relatives may still worry about a daughter who does not marry. They feel she should have someone to take care of her, rather than thinking of her as capable of caring for herself.

Some singles may put pressure on themselves to marry. Jobs and activities may be geared to meeting the "right" person rather than to enjoyment and self-development.

Extra demands on resources may be worthwhile to singles who value privacy and independence. Those who share living space may place less value on privacy and independence, or they may not be able to afford to live by themselves.

Singles who live at home may or may not have household responsibilities. A wide variety of arrangements exist that range from paying no room and board and having no household responsibilities to paying room and board and having shared responsibilities. Singles who are responsible for the care of elderly or invalid parents or relatives have great demands on their resources.

less well-paying jobs, however, may have no choice but to share living space with others or to live with parents or other family members.

Singles who share living space do not have to be good friends. Each one may go about his or her daily life as a separate individual with as little involvement with the group as possible. Other singles who share living space may share in the activities of each other.

Career-oriented single people may put in extra time on their jobs either at work or at home. They may take classes or pursue advanced degrees. They may belong to professional or social organizations related to their work. Sometimes their friends and activities are chosen according to their relationship to their careers.

Singles who are not career-oriented, who think of their work as only a job, may work long hours just to make ends meet. They may have

***Resources for Managing*** Whether or not an individual is single by choice or by chance, self-knowledge is vital. Knowing one's values, goals, aspirations, abilities, and limitations helps a person to get what he or she wants out of life. A positive self-concept and a positive attitude can help one to make the best of any situation.

The ability to be independent is important whether or not one is single or married. Few people are happy in a world without friends or some social contacts. Singles who live alone, who devote extra time to career development, or who are responsible for elderly or ill parents may need to make an extra effort to spend time with other people and to establish a network of friends. Other people who can be depended upon are invaluable when emotional support is needed or when one is sick or when an emergency arises and help is needed.

## Marriage

Although today's divorce rate is high, over 90 percent of all Americans will marry at some time in their lives; 60 percent of those who divorce will remarry.

What personal qualities help to make a marriage work? What is a loving relationship? Before getting married, it is important to understand these things as well as your own expectations and those of your partner.

**Loving Relationships**  There are many kinds of love. There is the love you feel for relatives, there is the love you feel for friends, and there is the love you feel for a boyfriend or girlfriend. How can you distinguish among all the loving feelings you experience? This is a question you may ask yourself more than once during your life.

When you are considering marriage, you need to know that what you feel is lasting love, not infatuation. **Infatuation** is an attraction to someone, which is often focused on only one characteristic of that person rather than the whole person. Love involves attraction to and admiration for the whole person. Infatuation usually flares explosively and then dies almost as suddenly as it flared.

You may fall in love several, perhaps many, times in your life. Realizing this may help you to recover more quickly from a broken romance. All the loving feelings you have during your life are real. In fact, as you experience loving relationships, you learn more about yourself and what characteristics you want in a marriage partner. A lasting love, you will discover, grows and changes over time.

**Personal Characteristics for Marriage**
Ideally, marriage partners should be individuals in their own right. Each one should be capable of functioning as an individual. Each should have a positive self-concept, self-confidence, and high self-esteem. When both partners have this, neither one's accomplishments will threaten the other's feelings of self-worth. When marriage partners have these characteristics, they can look at personal or marital troubles in a realistic way.

Emotional balance, patience, understanding, responsibility, and trust are also necessary for a good marriage. Being able to communicate openly and honestly will help to resolve any misunderstandings or conflicts.

Couples may sign premarital agreements dividing property in case of divorce.

# Remembering to Remember

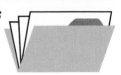

"Grandma always remembers," she used to say when she baked my favorite cookies or got me just what I wanted for my birthday. I loved visiting my grandmother when I was little. She told the greatest stories about when Dad was a kid and when she was young, and she explained *how things were*. I love my grandfather, too, of course, but he is quieter. Now he is trying to explain *how things are*—why Grandma doesn't remember things any more and gets things mixed up. I don't want to listen. I don't want to see her. I don't want to know. How could she do this to me!

\*     \*     \*     \*     \*     \*

"Now it's our turn," my Dad says. "Grandma cared for me, and even for you. Now we must help Grandpa care for her." Dad says he knows that Grandma's illness—he says it's called Alzheimer's disease—makes me angry and hurt. What makes him think he knows?!? I guess because he's angry and hurt, too. It's hard for us to explain things over and over to her when we know she'll just forget again in a minute. "Think how hard it must be for Grandpa," Dad says. "He's still a healthy, active man. He and Grandma made so many retirement plans. Imagine how he feels when she sometimes forgets who he is." So, I've gone back to calling them twice a week. Only now I mostly talk to my grandfather. If I do talk to Grandma, she doesn't remember.

\*     \*     \*     \*     \*     \*

"Always remember Grandma," my grandfather says. "Remember her the way she was . . . what she meant to you. And remember to visit her in the home. You were too young to remember her visiting you in the hospital when you had your appendix out, but she was there." So yesterday I got my mom to help me bake cookies to take to the home today. It cheers Grandma up to get cookies. Even if she doesn't know they were always our favorites, I remember.

As people mature, grow, and experience life, they usually acquire positive personal characteristics that they did not have when they were younger. Greater patience with themselves and others is one characteristic that often develops over time. These days, many people are marrying later in life, perhaps because they recognize the need to mature. This allows them to bring more positive characteristics to their marriage and increases the chances of a lasting marriage.

**Marriage Expectations** Realistic expectations of marriage, of oneself, and of one's partner contribute to a strong, mutually satisfying relationship. Unrealistic expectations often result in disappointment. In turn, disappointment can lead to accusations, blame, emotional outbursts, and a general deterioration of the relationship. Marriage, like all relationships, requires work to keep it alive and growing. One can get out of a relationship only what one puts into it. An expectation that the relationship will take care of itself once the marriage ceremony is over is unrealistic.

Sometimes, marriage is seen as an "escape" from unpleasant situations. A young person who has an unhappy home life, for example, may see marriage as the answer to all problems. A single parent may see marriage as an escape from a poor financial situation. A single person who is tired of living alone and being self-supporting or upset by remarks about his or her single life may have an idealized view of marriage. A person in one of these situations or in a similar situation may marry without giving enough thought to other important factors.

Other expectations of marriage are related to the role each partner will play. For example, the traditional role for a woman has been to take care of the house, prepare meals, raise children, and meet her husband's needs. The traditional role for a man has been to

Why is it important for couples to talk about roles before marriage?

provide for his family. Not everyone has been happy with these roles and changes in society have created the opportunity for more flexibility in the roles of women and men. For example, fathers may be at home with young children for several years while mothers work. Household responsibilities and cleaning tasks are shared more than they were in the past.

Many families today find it necessary that both partners work in order to supply family needs. It takes planning, cooperation, and skill to balance career priorities with family responsibilities, especially when both partners have careers.

Expectations about having children should be understood clearly when two people are considering marriage. If both people agree that they do not want to have children, for example, they have the same expectations. If one person definitely wants to have a child and the other person definitely does not, marriage plans may need to be discussed again and reconsidered.

Expectations about life styles and career plans should be discussed thoroughly. All money matters and priorities should be talked over so each person knows what the other person's needs and wants are.

## For Review

1. How have attitudes toward remaining single changed during recent years?

2. What are four personal qualities that are helpful in making a marriage successful?

3. What are some marriage expectations that all couples should discuss before they are married?

## Looking at Family Structure

The size and structure of the American family has changed dramatically. From the 1900s to the 1950s, two-parent households with several children were common. Today in our country, one out of every six children between the ages of six and sixteen lives in a single-parent family, and many married couples never have children. Marriage without children, two-parent families, and single-parent families are all common variations on family life styles.

The term sociologists use to describe a family unit made up of parents and their dependent children is **nuclear family.** This is still the most common type of family structure in our country today. When the children of a nuclear family have grown, they leave and establish their own families in separate homes—often far away from their original home.

The **extended family** is one that has several generations of a family living together. In extended families, there are many resources for helping each other. For example, older family members may provide care for grandchildren while parents work. This type of family is found more frequently in foreign countries than in the United States.

The **modified extended family** is one that does not have all members in the same home, but they do live nearby and interact with each other often.

The **blended family** is one that is composed of stepmothers, stepfathers, and stepchildren as a result of remarriage. Remarriage may follow the death of a spouse or divorce. Relationships within blended families may be difficult, depending on how well family members have adjusted to the divorce or death and to each other—children to children, children to stepparent, stepparent to children.

## Couples Without Children

Many married couples do not have children, and in recent years, more young people have stated their intentions to remain childless. The family unit of a childless couple consists of two people.

***Reasons for Childlessness*** Childlessness is the result of many factors. Some couples choose to remain childless. Others delay starting a family until some definite or indefinite time in the future. Still other couples are childless because of infertility or other medical problems. Financial circumstances may dictate sometimes that a couple not have any children. Finally, certain circumstances can disqualify couples from adopting children.

In an extended family, children's lives are enriched by several generations. Do you know any extended families?

**Pressures and Demands on Resources**
Couples without children sometimes face a variety of pressures. There may be subtle and not-so-subtle hints about having children from other family members or friends and acquaintances. One partner may want to have children while the other does not, or there may be a difference of opinion over when to have children. These factors can strain a relationship.

When both people work and contribute to the total household income, it would seem household tasks should be shared. However, statistics show that traditionally women continue to handle more of the household chores, whether or not they work outside the home. This places a greater demand on their time and energy, leaves less time for shared activities or activities that interest them, and can contribute to problems in the marriage. Some couples who have the money resources solve the problem of household chores by hiring someone else to do them. More often, the problem is solved by working out a plan for sharing these chores.

**Resources for Managing** A strong sense of self is an important resource for maintaining a close relationship with another person. It makes it easier to keep lines of communication open and to keep small irritations in perspective. Maturity and the ability to compromise are two other valuable personal resources needed by all married couples.

## Two-Parent Families

A two-parent family is composed of a couple and one or more children. This family may be headed by the biological parents or by a biological parent and a stepparent or by two adoptive parents.

***Reasons for Having Children*** It used to be that couples gave little thought to whether or not they would have children or how many children they would have. Many couples today still have children without giving the matter a lot of thought. There are, however, many more who give careful consideration to the matter of having children and to the timing of any births or adoptions.

Reasons for having or adopting children include, obviously, the love of children. Other reasons include love of the partner and the desire to have a child as a symbol of that love, the desire to continue the family name, and the desire to share with a child the resources and love a couple has to offer. For some couples unable to have their own children, adoption and/or foster parenthood are other ways to meet their needs to be parents and to share their lives with children.

Modern medicine has made it possible for couples who would have had to remain childless to have children. It also has developed a variety of methods of birth control that people can use. Many couples try to exercise some control over the number and spacing of the children they do have. This is because they want to be able to provide what they feel their children will need without straining the family's resources and their style of living.

What are some of the responsibilities involved in raising a child today?

**Pressures and Demands on Resources**
Today in many two-parent families, both the husband and wife work. When both parents are employed, there are greater demands on their time. If they have young children, they must make child-care arrangements. Unless the caretaker lives in or comes to the home, the children must be transported to and from the place of care. Household tasks, such as laundry, shopping, cleaning, and providing food, must be taken care of. If the children are older, they may be able to be responsible for themselves until one or both parents arrive home from work, and they may be responsible for some or all of the household tasks. However, they may be involved in activities outside of school that require transportation and perhaps participation and/or attendance by parents.

If one or both parents have highly demanding careers, demands on time and energy are even greater. If the jobs are well paying, part of the income may be earmarked for help with household tasks. Even so, career demands may conflict or compete with family demands. Trying to strike a balance that is satisfactory to all concerned can be challenging.

No matter who is working, having children costs money. Some studies estimate the cost of raising a child to the age of eighteen to be more than $150,000. Of course, it does not have to cost that much, but the fact remains that finances are an important consideration.

Particularly in their early years, children need time, energy, patience, and understanding. If one or both parents do not understand this or resent the demands that are inherent in having children, parent-child relationships can become strained, and strained husband-wife relationships can result. It takes a great deal of maturity to deal with the realities of raising a family in today's world.

Because the family ties and relationships are more complex, the pressures and strains that may exist in blended families can be great.

A stepparent, for example, may be afraid to discipline his or her spouse's children, or he or she may overdiscipline them. There can be jealousy and rivalry among stepsisters and stepbrothers. New spouses may have difficulty adjusting to an "instant family."

**Resources for Managing**  In spite of the pressures and demands on resources, many parents feel that the rewards of having children outweigh the drawbacks.

Positive personal qualities are extremely important resources for parents. Self-knowledge allows people to know their weaknesses and their strengths, what is important to them and why, and what they want from life. A positive attitude and a sense of humor can help many parents over rough spots. A positive self-concept and the ability to give of oneself make it easier to meet the needs of children. A good relationship between husband and wife is essential for good family relationships. A knowledge of management processes and the ability to use them can help parents balance their responsibilities as parents, husbands and wives, workers, citizens, and neighbors.

Knowledge of a child's stages of development, an acceptance of children for what and who they are, and the ability and willingness to meet their needs are necessary for any parent. Child-care services are important resources for working parents with small children. Some employers provide these services. There may be public or private child-care centers in the community. Sometimes, parents may find people who care for children in their homes. Sometimes, family members or relatives are willing to provide the service.

The informal support system of friends, neighbors, and relatives can be helpful in times of need. More formal support groups exist in the form of parent groups, parent-teacher groups, and groups related to specific problems that some children may have, such as learning disabilities or handicaps. When families have serious problems, there are other sources of professional help available in most communities. Chapter 5 has more information about resources for family crises.

## Single-Parent Families

The number of single-parent families used to be limited and due mainly to the death of the husband or wife. With the rise in the divorce

Divorce has left many fathers in the position of being weekend parents.

rate and other social factors in recent years, however, the number of single-parent families increased by 107 percent between 1970 and 1983. Today, one out of every four families is headed by a single parent. Ninety percent of today's single-parent families are headed by women who must support their families.

***Reasons for Single Parenthood*** While separation and divorce are important factors in the increasing incidence of single-parent families, another factor is the increase in the number of unwed mothers who keep their children. Still another contributing factor is the incidence of single persons adopting children.

***Pressures and Demands on Resources*** All of the pressures and demands on resources mentioned in the discussion of two-parent families apply to single-parent families, often to a much greater extent. A single parent usually has to fill the roles of both parents and meet the needs of the child or children alone. Sometimes, the child becomes the parent's confidante. This can place too much stress on the child. It may force him or her into an adult role too soon.

Since many women hold lower paying jobs than men, and women make up the majority of the heads of households in single-parent families, financial resources can be particularly strained in a one-parent family. If a woman has never finished high school or has never trained for a specific job or career, she may have to depend on government support. Even if she can get a job, it may be so low-paying that she cannot afford child care and a place to live, food, clothing, transportation, and medical care. These circumstances can have an extremely negative effect on self-esteem.

If a woman has been married and divorced, child support and/or alimony payments may be part of the divorce settlement, but many men do not make them or do not make

# FAMILY LIFE CYCLE

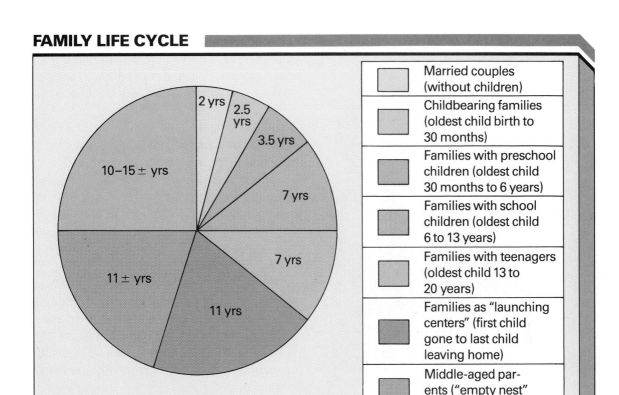

| | Married couples (without children) |
|---|---|
| | Childbearing families (oldest child birth to 30 months) |
| | Families with preschool children (oldest child 30 months to 6 years) |
| | Families with school children (oldest child 6 to 13 years) |
| | Families with teenagers (oldest child 13 to 20 years) |
| | Families as "launching centers" (first child gone to last child leaving home) |
| | Middle-aged parents ("empty nest" to retirement) |
| | Aging family members (retirement to death of both spouses) |

This graph, based on 55 to 60 years of a couple's total married life span, shows the relative amounts of time the couple can expect to spend in each stage of the family life cycle.

Source: Adapted from E.M. Duvall, *Marriage and Family Development* (N.Y.: Harper and Row, 1985).

them on time. While there are a variety of personal reasons for missing or skipping payments, some men find it difficult to support two households—one for themselves and one for their ex-wives and children. Legal means for obtaining payments vary from state to state. Frequently, it is difficult or impossible for women to get the money agreed upon at the time of divorce.

Single parents have even less time for meeting their own needs and pursuing their own interests than parents in two-parent families. There may be pressure from others to date or to get married. Some female single parents pressure themselves to find husbands as a

way out of a highly stressful and unsatisfactory financial situation. This can place unrealistic expectations on the other person and on any relationship that may develop.

The recent trend for unwed mothers to keep their babies has made single parenthood even more difficult for some. The demands of motherhood prevent most of these young women from completing high school. They are unable to get a job and, as a result, have to depend on government support. When this problem is combined with a lack of knowledge about child development, a lack of knowledge about everyday living skills, and not being able to do the same things that they did before preg-

The eldest child in a single-parent family may have to assume extra responsibility, especially if the parent works.

Management skills can be invaluable to single parents. There are major and minor decisions to be made daily. Knowing how to manage can help a person to see how all these decisions relate to each other and to the goals and values of the individuals and family. Management skills help the family to concentrate on what is important in their lives.

When a single parent has one or more young children, child-care resources are extremely important. While low-cost, high-quality care is ideal, since many working single parents are not able to pay for expensive care, it is frequently difficult to find.

For single parents with few job skills or no job skills, opportunities for job training are important resources. If child-care arrangements can be made for the duration of any job training, the end result is likely to be a self-supporting, independent family with a sense of personal pride.

Interpersonal support systems are vital to single parents. Friends, relatives, and even ex-spouses who lend a hand to help out with household tasks and child care and provide emotional support in times of need are among the informal support systems that may be available to single-parent families. More formal support systems exist in the form of locally organized or nationally affiliated single-parent groups and specific community organizations.

nancy, young single mothers face tremendous personal stress.

Statistics show that single fathers head about 10 percent of single-parent families. Unless the father has shared in caring for the child or children and in running the household, he has much to learn in addition to learning to fulfill two roles, those of mother and father. Usually, income is not as much of a problem for single fathers as it is for single mothers, but in specific instances, finances can be difficult.

**Resources for Managing** If single parents do not have an overabundance of energy, patience, understanding, and a sense of humor, they may have to develop these resources in a hurry. A very positive sense of self is necessary to cope with the demands made on time and every other personal resource.

## For Review

1. What additional pressures exist in a two-parent family if both parents work?
2. Describe three reasons for or causes of single parenthood.
3. What kinds of interpersonal support systems are especially needed by the single parent in today's society?

## Management Application: Making a Family Move

Imagine yourself in the family situation described below. As you read, think about how the steps of the management process might apply to this situation. Then answer the questions that follow.

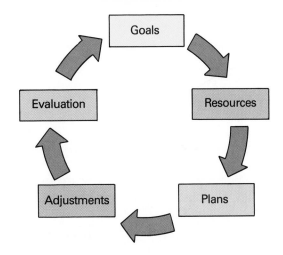

## Situation

Ann had her school year all figured out. She loved being a sophomore at Stanton High. Her courses were interesting, and so far her grades were good. She had a great group of friends. She had joined the school chorus and the Drama Club. She had even arranged for a part-time job at the supermarket. All that fall she kept thinking how well things were going. Then THE NEWS hit. Her dad's company had transferred him to Colorado. Her dad explained that this was the promotion he had been hoping to get. It also meant a raise, which would help toward college tuitions for Ann and her brother. She understood all of that, but— Colorado! That was 500 miles away—500 miles away from her friends, her school, and her *real* home! How could this be happening? Her pleas to stay in Stanton and live with her best friend's family were turned down. Although her parents were sympathetic, they said they couldn't imagine leaving her behind. The truth was Ann wanted to be with them just as much, but it was going to be so hard to start over in a new town. All the things she had planned for herself were falling apart. She realized that she was making it hard on the rest of the family. She had to stop feeling sorry for

herself and make new plans, but every time she tried, she found herself crying. Her parents had suggested that she should make a list of the pros and cons for moving. Maybe that would help to clear her mind. All she could come up with, however, were cons. How should she start this process?

## Questions

1. What new goals will Ann have to set? List some goals you would set for yourself if you were in her situation.

2. What human resources will Ann need in order to make the best of her situation?

3. Choose one goal you think Ann should have and describe a brief plan that might help her reach that goal.

4. Why are her father's goals so important in this situation?

5. Which steps of the management process apply to this situation?

# 3 *Chapter Review*

## Summary

The six stages of the life cycle are infancy, childhood, adolescence, young adulthood, middle age, and late adulthood. Each stage has its own caregiving needs, crises, roles, and responsibilities. The structure of the American family today varies from nuclear families to extended families to blended families. American society also accepts different life styles. Many adults still choose married life with or without children, but others prefer to remain single. Today, one of every four families is headed by a single parent.

## Vocabulary

Match each of the following vocabulary words with one of the definitions below.

life cycle

autonomy

empty nest syndrome

nuclear family

extended family

modified extended family

blended family

infatuation

1. A family unit made up of two parents and their dependent children is a(n) _____ .

2. An attraction to someone that is often focused on only one characteristic of that person rather than the whole person is known as _____ .

3. A family unit that does not have all its members in the same home but whose members do live nearby and interact with each other often is a(n) _____ .

4. The course people follow as they move from birth to death is the _____ .

5. A family unit that is composed of stepmothers, stepfathers, and stepchildren as a result of remarriage is a(n) _____ .

6. The sense of loss middle-aged parents may experience when their children grow up and leave home is called _____ .

7. A family unit that has several generations of a family living together is a(n) _____ .

8. Another term for independence is _____ .

## Questions

1. Compare the responsibilities of childhood with those of adolescence.

2. How is young adulthood different from the middle-age life stage?

3. Based on Erickson's ideas, explain how the concept of trust develops during infancy.

4. Define the kind of family—nuclear, extended, modified extended, or blended—each of the following children lives in.

   a. Jeanne is living with her father and mother, as well as one grandmother. Her

grandmother has taken care of her ever since she was a little girl.

b. Steve's father died in an accident. His mother remarried. He lives with his mother, stepfather, and stepsisters.

c. Ben lives with his father, mother, two brothers, and a sister.

d. Lisa lives with her father, mother, and sister. All of her grandparents live in the same town. She visits them every week.

5. What are some of the advantages of single living? What are the disadvantages?

6. What are some of the factors that can help a marriage to succeed?

7. What are some of the factors that may cause a marriage to fail?

8. How have the traditional roles of husband and wife changed over recent years?

9. What resources are helpful for married people who are raising children? What resources are helpful for single parents?

10. What pressures do you feel you face every day as an adolescent?

## Skill Activities

 1. **Reading.** Who was Erik Erikson? Go to the library and find more information about his life and his work. Write a short paper that includes basic information about his life and his ideas.

Alternative: Investigate the life and work of one of the following famous psychologists: Sigmund Freud, Jean Piaget, Carl Rogers, or Bruno Bettelheim.

 2. **Social Studies.** Anthropologists study the way people live in other societies. Investigate another culture and report on its family structure. How does its family structure differ from ours? Are there similarities?

 3. **Critical Thinking.** Develop a life-styles chart using the text and your own opinions. You may want to break your chart into such categories as: Marriage; Single People Living at Home; Single People Sharing a Living Space; Single People Living Alone.

Under each category, include the following information: advantages, disadvantages, pressures, demands on resources, and personal characteristics necessary.

 4. **Communication.** Write a short story or essay on one of the following topics:

a. "Bringing up Baby Today Is Harder Than It Looks"

b. "Why I Want to Have a Child Some Day—But Not Today"

c. "Things to Think About When Deciding Whether or Not to Have a Child"

Share your opinions in a group discussion about the human and nonhuman resources needed to raise children.

# *4* *Wellness as a Resource*

## *As you read, think about:*

- ☐ how mental and physical health affect total wellness.
- ☐ what you can do through diet and exercise to keep yourself healthy.
- ☐ how to make responsible decisions about alcohol and tobacco.
- ☐ what preventive health measures you can take.
- ☐ how to apply the management process to personal decisions about wellness.

## Vocabulary

anorexia nervosa
bulimia
aerobic exercise
stress
abstinence
STDs

Your health is the most important resource you have. Even if you are successful in other areas of your life, you cannot enjoy yourself if you are sick. Learning what you can do to promote your own physical and mental health is what this chapter is about.

## Managing Total Wellness

Good health, both physical and mental, helps you to apply all the processes of management and contributes to your success as a manager. When you are healthy, you have energy and enthusiasm. Energy and enthusiasm make it easier for you to manage your life.

You manage your health when your eating habits are based on correct nutrition information or you are involved in an exercise program or you refuse to start smoking. If you have not taken action to manage your health, perhaps it is because you don't know how to go about it. There are many things you can do to promote total wellness, which is the condition of being physically and mentally healthy.

Physical health and mental health are interrelated. One affects the other. Emotional upsets, for example, can reveal themselves as physical symptoms, such as headaches, muscle aches, or stomach problems. Physical problems can cause emotional problems when they interfere with everyday living. Your anger and frustration over limitations on activities if you fracture your leg during the first football game of the season is a good example of a physical problem that affects your mental wellness. Knowing how to manage your mental health helps you to manage your physical health; knowing how to manage your physical health helps you manage your mental health.

## Diet and Health

Your physical and mental health are affected by what you eat and drink. Most experts recommend eating a balance of different foods for good health. Chapter 11, "Making Nutrition Decisions," will provide more in-depth information about specific foods to include in your daily diet. For now, it is important to understand that a balanced intake of a variety of foods will help you to stay healthy, alert, and happy. A poor diet, on the other hand, leaves a person undernourished and more likely to become sick. A poor diet also affects your mental state. An inability to concentrate, for example, and temporary depression are caused sometimes by poor diet and any illness that may result from it.

Your weight should fall within a certain range, depending on your height.

There are at least two eating disorders that have both physical and mental causes and effects. These are anorexia nervosa (an-uh-REK-see-uh ner-VO-suh) and bulimia (byoo-LIM-ee-uh). Both of these conditions are associated with a desire to lose weight and, frequently, an impaired, or distorted, body image. People with either of these conditions lose so much weight that they sometimes endanger their own lives.

**Anorexia nervosa** is characterized by a failure to eat enough in order to become thin. Anorexics do not have a realistic image of their own bodies. They continue to feel and to view themselves as fat even when they are extremely thin. People with this disorder can starve themselves to death or die from the side effects of starvation, such as heart disorders.

**Bulimia** victims want to lose weight, but they also want to eat. They binge by consuming large amounts of food, then they make themselves vomit or take large amounts of laxatives to purge, or rid, themselves of calories.

Both of these eating disorders require long-term medical and psychological help. Teenagers are especially vulnerable to these eating disorders because they are often critical of themselves and their appearance. To make matters worse, our society has glamorized being thin. Be realistic about your own weight. If your weight is higher than average for your height, and you decide to lose weight, do it gradually, using a good nutrition plan. When you have lost the unwanted weight, do not continue to diet.

## Care of the Skin and Teeth

Skin care involves keeping it clean and protecting it from harmful substances and the sun. Unless you have special skin problems or are not overly active, you should take a bath, a shower, or a sponge bath once a day. Washing your hands frequently will help to prevent the spread of any bacteria that cause illness. If your skin is dry, you may find using a hand lotion after you have washed is helpful.

How frequently you wash your face and hair should be based on the type of skin and hair you have. Oily skin and hair should be washed more frequently than dry skin and hair. The soap and shampoo that you use should not irritate your skin and hair type.

*Acne* is caused by the clogging of oil glands beneath the skin. The hormones that are active during adolescence contribute to the problem. Skin inflammation develops, bacteria move in, and an infection occurs. The result of this process is a pimple. If you have a bad case of acne, you should see a dermatologist. External treatments and antibiotics are often prescribed and can help to reduce the severity of the acne.

Although medical professionals are not in total agreement, many feel that controlling diet is important for improving acne. Some people have reactions to certain foods that, in turn, aggravate acne. Foods to avoid include chocolate, nuts, salty foods, spicy foods, cola drinks, and high-fat dairy foods, including ice cream. The type and amount of food that will cause acne flare-ups vary with each person. It is a good idea to restrict your intake of the foods mentioned while using acne treatments. Once acne is controlled, these foods can be gradually returned to your diet. Try eating only one food at a time, such as potato chips. If your skin breaks out within a few days you will know that you should avoid that food. By gradually introducing these foods into your diet, you will find out which ones to avoid, if any.

Although having a tan is important to some people, scientists have attributed the increasing incidence of skin cancer to over exposure to the sun. Contrary to popular opinion, a tan does not eliminate the risk of skin damage or skin cancer. Overexposure to tanning rays, even in a tanning salon, may be harmful to the skin.

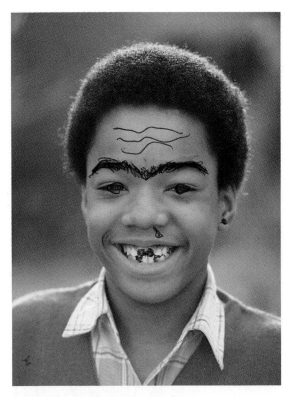

Total wellness usually is reflected in your overall appearance. How does your diet affect your health?

*Dental care* includes a proper diet to help build strong teeth, strong bones, and healthy gums. A healthy diet alone, however, does not guarantee good dental health. Regular visits to the dentist at least every six months, regular brushing at least twice a day, and the use of dental floss at least once a day will help to keep your teeth in good condition.

## Exercise and Health

Exercise plays an important role in maintaining health. Regular exercise can help a person to lose weight or to maintain the proper weight. It can help to improve the ability of the heart and lungs to supply the body with oxygen, help to improve muscular strength and endurance, and help to improve flexibility.

Athletes in training build up both muscular strength and endurance.

Recent studies have suggested that exercise can help to lower mildly elevated blood pressure and to improve the body's ability to fight off infection. Exercise that involves the long bones of the body may help them to increase or maintain their density. One recent study suggests that elderly persons who have included exercise as part of their fitness program tend to maintain hearing and speech longer.

Exercise also can help people to sleep better, to be more alert, and to have more energy. It is an effective stress reducer and sometimes helps to improve an individual's state of mind. It is frequently prescribed for people who are mildly depressed.

Aerobic (air-O-bik) endurance is the ability of the heart and lungs to supply muscles with oxygen from the bloodstream during times of sustained exertion or activity. When a person is aerobically fit, the heart and lungs work efficiently to provide the oxygen needed by the muscles to continue working. **Aerobic exercise,** exercise that can be sustained and steadily supplies sufficient oxygen to the muscles, increases the capacity of the lungs to extract oxygen from the air breathed in and to transfer the oxygen to the bloodstream. It also strengthens the heart so that it is able to pump blood throughout the body with less effort.

Although there is no definite proof, some people believe that being aerobically fit helps to protect a person from cardiovascular disease. Aerobic endurance may help to reduce heart rate and blood pressure, resulting in lower oxygen requirements for the heart. Both under exertion and at rest, the heart does not have to work so hard. It is thought that being aerobically fit may increase the size of the blood vessels, which would make them less susceptible to becoming clogged with the plaque deposits that are formed by cholesterol.

Aerobic exercise is dynamic. Dynamic exercise is exercise that involves rhythmic, repetitive motion so that blood flows continuously through the heart and large skeletal muscles. Bicycling, swimming, aerobic dance, walking, running, and jumping rope are all examples of aerobic exercise.

*Muscular fitness exercises* involve both muscle strength and muscle endurance. For example, if a person can do only one chin-up, he or she has the muscular strength to do one chin-up, but doesn't have the muscular endurance to do more. As well as increasing endurance, exercise can help to firm muscles that have become flabby from lack of use. This helps to improve appearance and strength and lessens the risk of injury while exercising or carrying out everyday activities.

Exercise for muscular fitness also must be dynamic and make use of specific muscles, such as abdominal muscles, thigh muscles, calf

# Too Much, Too Fast

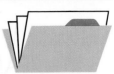

"Well, this is it," thought Sam, as he laced up his new running shoes. "I'm tired of being out of shape." He was sure that with hard work he could drop ten pounds in a week.

Alex, who ran almost every day, had been urging Sam to start exercising. He never said, "You're overweight and out of shape," but he knew that Sam was self-conscious and sometimes avoided social situations.

Now that Alex had finally convinced Sam to get out on the track, Sam was determined not to make a fool of himself. He and Alex started out at a brisk pace.

Sam was tired quickly, but he kept pushing himself. After a mile, Alex said, "Let's quit," but Sam ran on. Alex warned him not to overdo it, but Sam shook his head stubbornly.

For the next three days, it was the same. Alex stopped before he was tired, but Sam kept pushing himself to keep up with Alex. By the end of each run, Sam felt lightheaded. On the fourth day, Sam felt stabbing pains in his shins, but he ignored them, saying to himself, "No pain. No gain."

Alex asked, "Are you OK?" Sam lied, saying he was fine.

The next day, the pain was so bad that Sam couldn't run at all. A few days passed, and he still didn't feel well enough to run. By then, however, he had decided that exercise was all pain and no gain.

"Not if you do it right," said Alex. He urged Sam to try again.

The next time Sam ran, he did only a half mile. He did that for two weeks. Slowly, he worked up to two miles a day. Eventually, he did lose ten pounds. It took four months, but it didn't hurt. In fact, Sam says, "it felt pretty good!"

How could Sam have avoided some of the problems he encountered with exercise? What would you have done differently if you had been Sam? How does Alex demonstrate good sense about exercise?

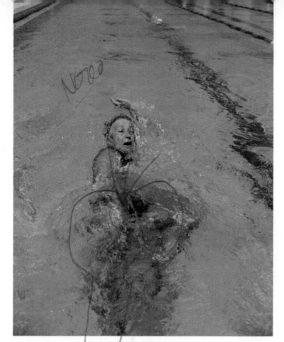

Due to the additional resistance of the water, swimming is one of the most productive and efficient forms of exercise.

muscles, and arm muscles. Sit-ups, push-ups, chin-ups, and leg lifts can improve muscular fitness. Weight-lifting also affects muscular fitness, and aerobic exercises can help to promote the muscular fitness of the muscles that are affected by the exercise.

*Flexibility exercises* increase the ability to move each joint through a wide range of motion. Motion is not restricted in any way. Flexibility makes it easier to carry out everyday tasks and decreases the risk of injury from slipping, falling, or twisting the body.

Exercises for flexibility involve exercises that stretch muscles and ligaments and promote the movement of joints, such as bending from your waist and touching your toes. These exercises should involve stretching and holding the position, not bouncing. Bouncing as a means to touch the toes can injure muscles and ligaments. Exercises involving joint movement, such as at the neck or the arm socket or elbow, should be in slow, rhythmic motions. Jerking motions increase the chance of damage.

***Exercise and Weight Control*** All three types of exercise are aids to losing weight

and maintaining weight loss because they can help to improve or maintain muscle tone. Since the body requires more calories to maintain muscle tissue than it does to maintain fat, good muscle tone aids in losing weight and maintaining weight loss.

For overweight persons, an exercise program is an important component of a weight-loss program. When the caloric intake is cut back, the body lowers its basic metabolic rate. This reduction in metabolic rate means slower weight loss and a more rapid gain when the caloric intake is increased. Exercise helps to offset the effects of a lower metabolic rate, thereby making weight loss easier.

***Developing an Exercise Program*** To be worthwhile, an exercise program should be followed on a regular basis—at least three times a week for minimum fitness, more often for maximum fitness and benefits in terms of weight loss. Each exercise session should be at least 30 minutes long, preferably 45 minutes, and should include exercises for aerobic fitness, muscular fitness, and flexibility.

If you are not used to regular exercise and/or are overweight, you should start slowly and work gradually to increase endurance and strength. Starting off too quickly or trying to do too much can cause muscle stiffness and increase your chances of injury. Each time you exercise, begin with at least five minutes of stretching exercises. This helps to increase the blood flow to the muscles and increases flexibility, thus decreasing the chance of injury. Gradually work up to a level of activity that causes you to perspire and to breathe harder than normal; maintain this level for about twenty minutes. Slow down activity toward the end of each session and repeat your stretching exercises before stopping. This gradually slows the body down and helps to stretch out muscles that were tightened during other exercises, reducing the chances of muscle pain.

It is always a good idea to get your doctor's approval before beginning any exercise program. This is especially important if you have any back problems or a chronic health problem of any kind.

## Stress and Health

One way to describe **stress** is as any factor that induces bodily or mental tension. In other words, stress is a factor or factors that place demands on physical or mental resources. Although stress is considered to be bad for you, a certain amount of stress is necessary for good health. It is the amount of stress and the way people react to it that can have negative effects, both physically and mentally.

***Types and Sources of Stress*** There are many kinds of stress. Some stress is mental stress, caused by worry over either real or imagined situations or possible consequences of actions. Boredom, monotony, and dissatisfaction with a job, with yourself, or with relationships are other sources of mental stress. Trying to balance several situations and people with different needs at the same time also can be mentally stressful.

Physical stress can be caused by a number of things. Lack of sleep, excessive noise, poor diet, lack of exercise, too much exercise, obesity, smoking, drug and alcohol abuse, untreated high blood pressure, a cold or flu, and other illnesses and conditions that affect the human body are forms of physical stress.

There are also a number of specific events that cause stress. For example, marriage, divorce, separation, having a baby, having a child leave home, the death of a friend or loved one, breaking up with a girlfriend or boyfriend, preparing for exams, and going away to college for the first time are all sources of stress. Even

## WAYS TO RELIEVE STRESS

1. Relax, take slow and measured deep breaths, slow down, take vacations.
2. Establish your priorities and make choices on how you spend your time.
3. Learn to say no. You don't need to do *everything!*
4. Avoid stressful situations that are not necessary.
5. Take advantage of personal time to do things you enjoy.
6. Alternate your routine.
7. Exercise on a regular basis (walk, jog, play sports, swim—get out and get active!).
8. Seek out friends who make you laugh.
9. Eat a well-balanced diet.
10. Get enough sleep.
11. Learn to manage your time.

Courtesy of Fallon Clinic, Worcester, MA

happy events, such as marriage or a new home, can cause stress because they are major changes in one's life. As such, they require adjustments in the way you use your physical and mental resources.

**Effects of Stress** If people do not deal with stress or with the situations that are causing stress, it can have serious effects. For example, mental and emotional problems, such as confusion, anxiety, or depression may develop. Because stress affects people both physically and mentally, physical problems can develop. For example, diseases of the digestive tract, such as ulcers, are thought to be stress-related. Skin problems may develop. Acne and other skin conditions may become more severe. Asthma may worsen. In some people, stress disturbs the normal heart rate, and if a person has angina, a type of heart disease, stress can trigger an attack.

**Dealing with Stress** Some people in stressful situations remain calm and deal with the situations in positive ways. Other people, sometimes in less stressful situations, suffer greatly from the effects of stress. What makes the difference? Usually, it has to do with the way in which the individuals perceive the situations and their degrees of control over each situation, as well as what they choose to do about the situations. For example, many people spend a lot of time and energy worrying about things that may happen. Others are able to look at specific situations and say, "I cannot control what so-and-so does, or what might happen if, so I will not worry about it. I *can* control my opinion of myself, my job performance, my diet, and how I take care of myself, so I will concentrate on doing my best in those areas." Learning how to avoid excess worry is one way to lessen stress.

A lack of clear values and goals, indecision, and procrastination, or putting off things until the last minute, all contribute to stress. Learning and applying the management processes to all aspects of life can help to reduce stress. Once your values are clear to you, it is easier to set goals, because you know what you want and do not want. Clear goals make it easier to make plans and carry them out. Skill in decision making helps you to avoid procrastination and to carry out all of the processes involved in management.

Since monotony, boredom, and too long a time spent at any one activity can contribute to stress, one way to prevent and relieve stress is to strike a balance among the types of activities you are involved in. For example, if you spend a great deal of time on school work, a leisure time activity that involves exercise may give you the balance you need. If you have a job that is repetitious or boring, other activities that provide mental stimulation can help offset the monotony and boredom. If you have a high-risk job or one that involves a lot of physical activity, activities that are relaxing and leisurely may provide the necessary balance. While a balance between work and leisure is important, each person has to decide how to achieve this balance. No matter what the source of stress is, regular exercise has been shown to reduce the feelings and physical effects associated with stress.

## Safety Tip: Filing Health Facts

■ On a sheet of paper at home, record medical information about family members including blood type, previous illnesses, and allergies. Add any family history of serious diseases. Record those facts about you on an index card to keep in your wallet in case of emergency.

We all experience sad times, but it is unhealthy to be under extreme stress. What are some ways to relieve stress?

***Improving Time Management*** One way to reduce stress in your life is to make more efficient use of your time. Some suggestions for doing this follow.

- Limit commitments on your time. Learn to say no to activities you do not want to do.
- Work to improve your decision-making skills and thus reduce stress.
- Reevaluate your work methods and habits to improve them and to save time.
- Be realistic when estimating how long each task will take.
- Learn to dovetail tasks if possible. This means fitting parts of tasks together. For example, do your homework while your clothes are in the washing machine.

## Sexual Activity and Health

If your parents have not provided sex education at home, you, as a teenager, need reliable, factual information from a trusted source. Of course, you trust your peers, but in this situation, you would probably find an older person, such as another family member, a doctor, or school or religious counselor, a more reliable source of information.

***Sexual Relationships*** Many young people between the ages of thirteen and nineteen do not have sexual relationships. Others do. You should not be pressured into doing something you are not ready for or you do not think is right. In reaching a decision, you are guided by the teachings and expectations of your family, religion, and community. Sex outside of marriage can create worry and guilt, which can hurt a relationship. The possibility of disease and an unwanted pregnancy also exists. Young people who engage in sexual activity should know about various birth control methods and their effectiveness. The most effective and universally accepted method for avoiding pregnancy is **abstinence,** that is, not having sexual relations.

***Sexually Transmitted Diseases*** Being responsible for your own health includes becoming informed about **sexually transmitted diseases (STDs),** those diseases that are passed on through sexual intercourse. If you are sexually active, you should recognize the possibility of contracting STDs. The chart on page 80 describes the causes, symptoms, and effects of STDs, as well as the treatments for them. If you have any of these symptoms, get medical treatment immediately.

AIDS (Acquired Immune Deficiency Syndrome) is a sexually transmitted fatal disease that has no known cure at this time. Medical experts believe that by 1991 an estimated 5 million Americans may be carriers of the AIDS virus. It is also predicted that in four more years AIDS will have killed more Americans than the Vietnam and Korean wars combined.

Fear and lack of education have created many misunderstandings about how AIDS is

# SEXUALLY TRANSMITTED DISEASES

(The only effective method for avoiding STD's is not having sexual relations.)

| DISEASE | CAUSE & EFFECTS | SYMPTOMS | TREATMENT |
|---------|-----------------|----------|-----------|
| **Gonorrhea** | Bacteria (Can lead to sterility, nerve disorders, blindness in newborns.) | M: Puslike discharge from penis; painful urination. F: Most affected areas have no symptoms; lower abdominal pain; discharge; burning during urination. | Penicillin or antibiotics; sexual partner needs treatment. |
| **Syphilis** | Bacteria (Can lead to brain damage, insanity, paralysis, heart disease.) | 1st stage: Pimple, blister, or sore; heals in 1–5 weeks. 2nd stage: Rash or mucus patches (highly infectious), spotty hair loss, swollen glands, and fever. | Long-acting penicillin; sexual partner needs treatment. |
| **Herpes** | Virus (Linked to cervical cancer; can infect newborns.) | Painful blisters on genitals and rectal area, around mouth; painful urination, swollen glands, and fever. | No known cure; treatment relieves symptoms. |
| **Chlamydia** (often diagnosed non-specific urethritis) | Bacteria (Can cause pelvic inflammation that leads to infertility; can infect newborns and cause eye infections. | M: Discharge from penis, painful urination. No symptoms in some cases. F: Vaginal discharge, painful urination, spotting between menstrual periods, lower abdominal pain. | Tetracycline or erythromycin. |
| **Venereal Warts** | Virus (Linked to cervical cancer.) | Local itching and wartlike growth on genitals, anus, or throat. | No known cure. May require cauterization, freezing, or surgical removal. |
| **AIDS** (Acquired Immune Deficiency Syndrome) | Virus (Can infect newborns; causes death.) | (Note: Other diseases may have similar symptoms) Enlarged lymph glands, weight loss, diarrhea, night sweats, fatigue, white spots or blemishes in the mouth. | No known cure. Treatment focuses on secondary illnesses. |

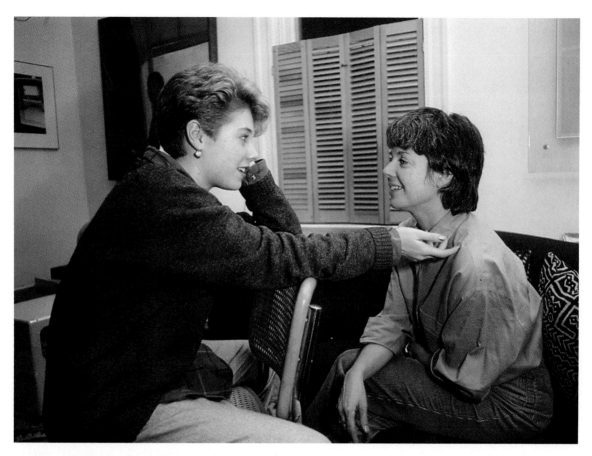

It is very important to get accurate, straightforward information about sexual matters. A discussion with a trusted adult can provide needed facts.

passed on. The AIDS virus is transmitted through the blood or sexual secretions of infected people. There have been isolated cases of AIDS contracted through blood transfusions from an infected donor, but now, donors are tested for the virus before giving blood. According to current research, the AIDS virus is not spread by kissing or sneezing.

Sexually active people must realize that they can contract AIDS if their partner is infected with the AIDS virus. A blood test can identify those people who carry the AIDS virus even before symptoms appear. These tests, however, are not always conclusive. Sci-

entists do know that it is possible to carry the virus for as long as five years without obvious symptoms of the disease.

## For Review

1. Can you separate physical health from mental health? Explain briefly.
2. Describe the physical and mental benefits of a regular exercise program.
3. What are some of the possible negative results of being sexually active?

## Learning About Substance Abuse

Substance abuse is the misuse of anything to the point of endangering your health. Any substance can be abused. The best known forms of substance abuse are those that occur with the use of tobacco, inhalants, and drugs, including alcohol and both prescription and nonprescription drugs. Most forms of substance abuse lead to some form of addiction, either psychological, physical, or both.

### Tobacco

Tobacco is dangerous to your health. This is true whether it is smokeless tobacco (chewing tobacco) or the tobacco that is used in cigarettes, pipes, or cigars. Tar and nicotine are found in all forms of tobacco. These chemicals, as well as carbon monoxide, are found in all cigarette smoke. The more a person smokes or uses smokeless tobacco, and the longer he or she has done so, the greater the risks of physical damage and premature death.

As smokers become more educated about the dangers to their health, many give up the habit. What are some dangers?

The tar in tobacco is capable of causing cancer. Smokeless tobacco users run the risk of developing cancer of the mouth and gums. Smokers who do not inhale may develop cancer of the mouth. Both may develop cancer of the throat and esophagus. Smokers who do inhale can develop cancer of the mouth, throat, esophagus, and lungs. As the smoke enters the bloodstream of a smoker who inhales, the chemicals are filtered through the bladder and excreted in the urine, which increases the chances of cancer of the bladder.

Smoking also increases the risk of heart disease and can contribute to high blood pressure because nicotine increases the heart rate. An increased heart rate makes the heart work harder and can contribute to artery damage from high blood pressure. The carbon monoxide in cigarette smoke may contribute to the deposit of plaque in the arteries, which narrows the arteries and increases the risk of heart attack. Because smoking constricts the blood vessels, which makes it more difficult for blood to flow through the body, the risk of heart attack increases even more when combined with the possibility of increased plaque deposits from smoking.

Some studies have indicated that many smokers lose more time from work than other workers because of smoking-related problems and other illnesses. This represents a loss of income to the smoking employee as well as to the employer.

Smoking not only affects smokers but may also affect others. A woman who smokes while she is pregnant is at greater risk of giving birth to a stillborn baby or a low birth-weight baby than is a nonsmoking woman. Even if of normal weight, the baby has greater chances of respiratory problems and death during infancy. Even nonsmokers who breathe the smoke from cigarettes, cigars, and pipes, as well as the smoke exhaled by smokers, may face increased risk of smoking-related health problems.

# SIGNALS OF AN ALCOHOL PROBLEM

Any of the following characteristics could mean that a person may have a problem with alcohol and should seek help.

1. Hiding the amount of drinking from family and friends
2. Experiencing loss of memory after drinking
3. Getting drunk at least once a month
4. Feeling ashamed for drinking too much
5. Arguing or fighting with family or friends when drinking too much
6. Regretting things said or done when drunk
7. Centering most social activities around drinking or partying
8. Driving while drunk
9. Experiencing a change in one's reputation due to drinking
10. Using other drugs in addition to alcohol
11. Having a parent, brother, or sister who is an alcoholic
12. Worrying about the amount of one's own drinking
13. Drinking while alone
14. Receiving complaints from friends or family about one's behavior when drinking
15. Getting into trouble with the police when drinking
16. Being injured while drinking or drunk
17. Trying repeatedly to quit or cut back on drinking
18. Drinking regularly (every day or every weekend)
19. Drinking when upset or angry with family, friends, or others
20. Drinking to gain courage or self confidence

People who exhibit 4–6 of the characteristics should talk to a professional about their drinking. Those who exhibit 7–10 characteristics have a serious problem with alcohol and very possibly are alcoholics. Having 11 or more characteristics could mean that a person should seek treatment for alcoholism.

Courtesy of Fallon Clinic, Worcester, MA

If you smoke only occasionally and do not inhale, you may feel you are in no danger of becoming a habitual smoker. However, this is how many smokers started. The sooner you stop, the easier it will be. Persons who smoke out of habit or who have become addicted to smoking or smokeless tobacco find it extremely difficult to quit.

No matter how long a person has used tobacco in any form, quitting has almost immediate benefits. The senses of taste and smell improve, and the risks from tobacco-related diseases decrease with each year a person remains a nonsmoker.

## Alcohol

Alcohol is a drug. It is a depressant that acts as a tranquilizer or relaxant. It impairs judgment and dulls the reactions of the brain and nervous system. Because even a small amount of alcohol can have this effect, the more alcohol that is consumed, the greater the effects. Speech becomes slurred, and the sense of balance may be impaired, making it difficult to stand or walk.

As it enters the human digestive system, alcohol is immediately absorbed into the blood and remains in the blood until it is broken down by the liver or passed out in the urine. Since it takes several hours to completely eliminate alcohol from the body, drinking over a period of hours has a build-up effect. The higher the alcohol content of the blood, the greater the effect of alcohol on the body and mind.

Pregnant women who have only a few drinks risk damaging their unborn children. Excessive drinking obviously increases the risk of damage. Frequent excessive drinking by anyone can permanently damage the brain, liver, and heart. Other physical problems that may occur because of excessive drinking include malnutrition, chronic stomach problems, and liver failure. Since excessive alcohol consumption leads to a lack of emotional control, relationships with family and friends frequently are affected. Because judgment, concentration, and memory are likely to be affected, school work or job performance also can suffer. Operating any motor vehicle or any kind of machinery after consuming alcohol, even in small amounts, is extremely dangerous. Over half of all automobile accidents and 90 percent of all boating accidents are related in some way to alcohol consumption.

When a person cannot perform everyday tasks without alcohol, that person is said to be an alcoholic. The dependency on alcohol is both physical and psychological. The frequency and amount of alcohol consumption that results in alcoholism varies greatly from individual to individual. Some people become dependent on alcohol quickly; others less quickly. As young people who are still growing, you run the risk of interfering with your proper development if you drink. You may also run the risk of becoming an alcoholic.

With determination and effort, those who consume alcohol out of habit may be able to stop drinking or to get it under control on their own. Those who are addicted to alcohol need medical help. Psychological help and/or emotional support is needed to help deal with the factors that led to alcoholism. Alcoholics Anonymous, Al-Anon, and Alateen are all nonprofit groups that help to provide the alcoholic and his or her family and friends with the support and understanding that is needed. Chapter 5 has more specific information about these groups. The more quickly alcohol abuse or addiction is treated, the less risk there is of serious physical and mental damage.

## Legal Drugs

Legal drugs are those purchased over the counter or prescribed by a doctor. When used properly, these substances usually are safe.

Drunk drivers cause many deaths each year. What would you do if your ride home from a party had been drinking?

However, allergic responses and the use of drugs that interact with other drugs can result in reactions ranging from mild to fatal.

If you know that you have an allergy to a particular drug, do not take it or any other drug that contains the ingredient you are allergic to. People who are allergic to aspirin, for example, not only must avoid regular aspirin but also all medications that contain aspirin, such as other remedies for headaches and the relief of cold and flu symptoms. If you are allergic to a drug, read the labels on over-the-counter drugs before purchasing anything. You may also want to remind your doctor and pharmacist about any drug allergies you have when you receive a prescription and have it filled. Many pharmacies keep records of prescriptions on computers. These can help to alert a pharmacist to potential interaction or allergy problems. For a person taking more than one type of prescribed medication, going to only one pharmacy can be a safety precaution.

Many drugs have side effects, such as drowsiness or sensitivity to the sun. Usually this information is on the label. If you have any questions, ask your pharmacist.

If you are already taking some type of medication, do not take another medication at the same time unless you have checked with your doctor or pharmacist or both. They can tell you whether one medication will interfere with the other or cause other problems. Remember that even a small amount of alcohol can be harmful or fatal when you are already

# COMMON DRUGS OF ABUSE

| DRUGS | DEPENDENCE | | HOW LONG |
| | PHYSICAL | PSYCHOLOGICAL | IT LASTS IN HOURS |
|---|---|---|---|
| **Marijuana** | Unknown | Moderate | 2–4 |
| **Alcohol** | High | High | 1–12 |
| **Barbiturates** | High–moderate | High–moderate | 1–16 |
| **Cocaine** | High | High | ½–2 |
| **Crack** | High | High | 5–10 minutes |
| **Amphetamines** | High | High | ½–2 |
| **Angel dust** | Unknown | High | Variable |
| **Heroin** | High | High | 12–24 |

| HEALTH EFFECTS | EFFECTS OF OVERDOSE |
| --- | --- |
| Can impair memory perception and judgment and raise blood pressure. Kills brain cells in rats. Contains more known carcinogens than cigarettes. May cause birth defects. | Anxiety, paranoia, loss of concentration, slower movements, time distortion. |
| Causes mental disturbance, blurred vision, staggered gait, slurred speech and muscular incoordination. Frequent use can lead to cirrhosis of liver, pancreatitis, brain disorders, vitamin deficiencies and malnutrition. Use during pregnancy can lead to mental and physical birth defects. | Shallow respiration, cold and clammy skin, dilated pupils, weak and rapid pulse, coma, possible death. |
| Can cause slurred speech, staggering gait, poor judgment and slow, uncertain reflexes, making it dangerous to drive or operate machinery. Large doses can cause unconsciousness and death. | Shallow respiration, cold and clammy skin, dilated pupils, weak and rapid pulse, coma, possible death. |
| Causes dilated pupils and increased blood pressure, heart rate, breathing rate and body temperature. Can cause anxiety, sleeplessness, paranoia, seizures, heart attacks and death. Problems increase with repeated use as well as increased doses. | Agitation, increase in body temperature, hallucinations, convulsions, tremors, possible death. |
| More and stronger cocaine is getting to the brain quicker, increasing risk of confusion, slurred speech, anxiety and serious psychological problems associated with cocaine. Like cocaine, can cause heart attacks and death. | Agitation, increase in body temperature, hallucinations, convulsions, tremors, possible death. |
| Increases heart rate, breathing rate and blood pressure. Decreases appetite and dilates pupils. Can cause sweating, headaches, blurred vision, dizziness, sleeplessness and anxiety. Higher doses can cause tremors, loss of coordination and death from stroke or heart failure. Frequent use of large amounts also can produce brain damage, ulcers and malnutrition. | Agitation, increase in body temperature, hallucinations, convulsions, tremors, possible death. |
| Can increase heart rate and blood pressure and cause flushing, sweating, dizziness and numbness. Large doses can cause drowsiness, convulsions, comas, heart and lung failure and ruptured brain vessels. | Drug effects becoming longer and more intense, psychosis. |
| Can cause restlessness, vomiting and drowsiness. Repeated use can lead to infections of heart lining and valves, skin abscesses and congested lungs. Use during pregnancy can cause spontaneous abortions, breech deliveries, premature birth and stillbirths. | Slow and shallow breathing, clammy skin, convulsions, coma, possible death. |

Source: National Institute on Drug Abuse

taking another drug. Ask your doctor or pharmacist about this if there is any chance that you may be consuming alcohol while you are taking any other drug.

A pregnant woman should not take any drug without consulting with her doctor. Many drugs are known to cause birth defects or have other harmful consequences on unborn babies. While other drugs may not cause problems, most doctors recommend taking a conservative approach to the use of any medications during pregnancy.

Abuse of over-the-counter and prescription drugs is dangerous. Abuse includes taking medication for a longer period than the directions state or taking larger amounts. Abuse also includes an individual's use of a prescription drug not prescribed for him or her.

It is also dangerous to use as inhalants products that give off toxic vapors.

**Commonly Abused Legal Drugs**  Approximately 2.5 million Americans take tranquilizers on a regular basis. Sleeping pills and diet pills are two other legal drugs that are often overused and abused.

If you use any of these legal drugs, you should be aware of signs of possible abuse. Get medical help if you cannot stop taking any drug on your own.

If an individual has abused drugs, determination to quit and a change in friends and daily living habits may be all that is needed. If an individual is addicted, professional medical and psychological help is needed. Since the line between abuse and addiction is a fine line, drug abusers who are not yet addicted often benefit from professional help.

## Illegal Drugs

Illegal drugs are those drugs that cannot be sold legally by anyone. These substances are dangerous. They upset the body chemistry and may cause serious physical or mental illness or even death. Even occasional use of illegal drugs can be harmful.

Many illegal drugs are addictive; that is, an individual becomes physically and psychologically dependent on them. The effects of addiction are devastating—physically, mentally, and emotionally. Relationships and job performance deteriorate. The need for increasing amounts of money to support the habit can lead to criminal activity. The danger of overdose is always present. As the user becomes more addicted, the amount required to feel "normal" may rise to the level that can be fatal.

Some illegal drugs that are widely used include marijuana, heroin, cocaine, and "crack," a more potent form of cocaine.

**Marijuana**  Marijuana, or "grass" or "pot," is an illegal drug that gives the user a sense of well-being when it is smoked. Studies have shown that many users of marijuana go on to using stronger drugs, such as cocaine. Marijuana alters judgment and perceptions of reality. Because of this effect, it is dangerous to drive after using it. The physical effects of marijuana include lung damage, which researchers say is more severe than the damage that is caused by smoking an equal number of regular cigarettes.

**Heroin**  Heroin is found either as a powder or as a liquid. The powder form is sniffed by the user; the liquid form is injected into the body, often into the arm. Use of heroin seems to temporarily relieve anxiety, pain, fear, or anger. However, after its effects have worn off, the user feels worse. As heroin use increases, addiction sets in, and the addict experiences physical pain, chills, and other symptoms when the drug is withdrawn. A heroin overdose can be fatal.

# HOW COCAINE AFFECTS THE BODY

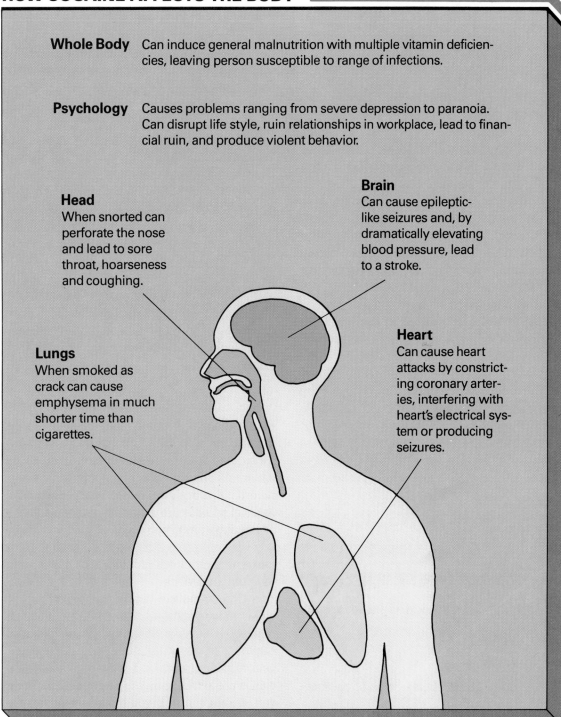

**Whole Body** Can induce general malnutrition with multiple vitamin deficiencies, leaving person susceptible to range of infections.

**Psychology** Causes problems ranging from severe depression to paranoia. Can disrupt life style, ruin relationships in workplace, lead to financial ruin, and produce violent behavior.

**Head**
When snorted can perforate the nose and lead to sore throat, hoarseness and coughing.

**Brain**
Can cause epileptic-like seizures and, by dramatically elevating blood pressure, lead to a stroke.

**Lungs**
When smoked as crack can cause emphysema in much shorter time than cigarettes.

**Heart**
Can cause heart attacks by constricting coronary arteries, interfering with heart's electrical system or producing seizures.

Source: Cocaine abuse treatment program, Columbia-Presbyterian Medical Center.

**Cocaine** Medical professionals now know that cocaine is one of the most addictive drugs in the world. It is a white powder made from the leaves of the coca plant. At least one million people in this country are addicted cocaine users. When cocaine is sniffed, the nasal passages are often damaged. Abusers may also suffer permanent hoarseness and impaired vision and breathing. These physical problems, however, are only the surface effects of cocaine use. Health specialists now realize that cocaine has far more devastating effects on the body. When cocaine is inhaled it affects all parts of the body. It has been known to cause emphysema, seizures, and heart attacks. The psychological effects of cocaine use are many and include severe depression, mood swings, and paranoid behavior.

*Crack* is a particularly potent form of cocaine. When it is smoked, it can enter the bloodstream within ten seconds. The physical and psychological effects of using crack are even more damaging than those of regular cocaine use. As a director of the cocaine abuse program at the Columbia-Presbyterian Medical Center in New York observed, people who use crack react like lab rats, becoming addicted within ten to fourteen days. Crack is the most addicting form of cocaine, which is the most addicting drug presently known.

## For Review

1. Describe the physical risks to health involved in smoking.
2. List three symptoms, or warning signs, of alcoholism.
3. Describe the physical effects of cocaine abuse on the user.

## Learning Preventive Health Measures

There are many types of preventive health measures you can take. Knowing your own body and paying attention to any noticeable changes in it are vital to your health. If you do notice any changes that seem unusual, you should see a doctor or health professional. When you do this, and you go for regular checkups, you can prevent some major health problems or at least catch them before they become more serious. For example, self-awareness and self-examination are vital in the detection of breast cancer. Keeping accurate records of your own medical history and the checkups you have had also can help you to manage your own health more effectively.

As you know, good health includes good mental health. An awareness of the signs and symptoms of serious depression can help to prevent the tragedy of suicide.

### Keeping Medical Records

Although doctors and hospitals have detailed records of their patients' medical histories, and pharmacists keep careful records of patients' prescriptions, keeping your own records at home is always a good idea. Home medical records are a summary of your health or medical problems and treatments. These records help you to know when it is time to go for certain checkups or when it is time for certain immunizations.

Home medical records also are helpful when filing medical insurance claims. Information about specific illnesses and medications can be extremely helpful if you need emergency medical care and your personal physician is not available or you do not have a doctor you see regularly. If you move, these records will be useful when you must find a new doctor, particularly if your official records have been scattered among several doctors.

Home medical records should include information about immunizations and visits to doctors and health screening clinics. If a home health-care person makes a visit, this should be recorded. For each visit to a doctor or clinic, keep track of any diagnosis that is made and any medication that is prescribed, including the dosage, the prescribed length of time for medication, directions for taking the medication, and the pharmacy where the prescription was filled. You should also note how well the medication works and any side effects it may have. You will want to keep track of any allergies and allergic reactions.

## Checkups

Infants and young children need periodic examinations by a qualified doctor to see that they are growing and developing normally and to receive immunizations against certain diseases. A family doctor or pediatrician, a doctor specializing in the care of children, can provide a schedule for these checkups.

Any woman who is pregnant should see a doctor on a regular basis. The sooner prenatal care is started, the better the chances for a healthy baby and mother.

Until recently, it was believed that adults should receive an annual physical examination. Most doctors these days, however, are changing their opinion on this matter. There is less emphasis on thorough physical exams on an annual basis unless there are special conditions or medical problems requiring regular checkups. Doctors do recommend certain medical checks and tests, such as a yearly blood pressure check, for healthy persons on a regular basis. Your own physician or local medical clinic can tell you what exams are recommended and how frequently they should be made.

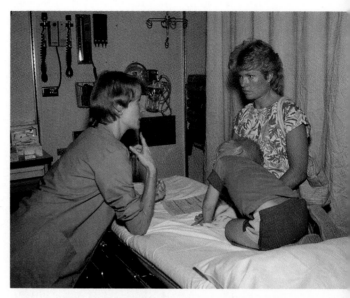

Regular checkups during childhood can detect major health problems and prevent many diseases through innoculations.

## Breast Self-Examination

In recent years, the incidence of breast cancer has increased. The reason for this has not been determined, but medical professionals agree that self-examination is the best way to identify this disease. Early detection through self-examination can save women from radical surgery and increase their chances of survival.

Many experts recommend that women examine their breasts monthly. To do this, lie flat and use your finger tips to feel all around each breast for any lump or thickening. Examine your underarm areas in the same manner. Doing this each month will provide an early warning if there are changes in the breasts.

If you discover a lump or thickening, see a doctor as soon as possible. Although most lumps are not cancerous, only medical professionals can determine this.

Similar self-examination of the testicles is a recommended health habit for men.

## Suicide Prevention

The taking of one's own life is a tragedy at any age. Over the past 30 years, the number of suicides in the under-twenty-five-year-old category has risen greatly. In this age group, suicide is the third leading cause of death.

***Causes of Suicide*** Mental health experts believe that those who suffer from continued extreme depression and feelings of hopelessness are most vulnerable to suicide. While mental or physical illness is sometimes present, more often the individual is unable to cope with a personal loss or sense of failure. Examples include the death of a friend or relative (especially by suicide), rejection by a girlfriend or boyfriend, loss of a job, or an academic or social failure. Drugs and alcohol abuse contribute to approximately 50 percent of all teenage suicide attempts.

People with low self-esteem are especially vulnerable to suicide. Perfectionists, people who demand too much of themselves, are also at risk. Of course, not all people with low self-esteem or all perfectionists attempt suicide. Many suicide victims do not fit into any particular category.

***Warning Signs*** Depression that continues for days at a time without lifting is a cause for concern. This is especially true if the person loses interest in his or her appearance, stops eating or changes eating habits drastically, cannot sleep, and/or uses drugs of any kind to try to cope.

Although talking about suicide is the most obvious sign, it is often brushed aside or not heeded as a genuine warning. Studies have revealed, however, that young people are most likely to tell a close friend that they are considering suicide. If this information is not relayed to the parents by the friend or individual, the results may be tragic. At school, an inability to learn and a drop in grades can serve as warning

How can talking over everyday problems with a relative or friend help you to put them in perspective and avoid depression?

signs if other signs of depression and hopelessness are present.

***Taking Preventive Action*** If you are feeling severely depressed, talk to someone you trust right away and see a health professional. Communication can solve problems and change feelings of desperation to hope. Do not remain lonely and isolated. The pain and hurt you are feeling now will not last forever. Many people who have attempted suicide now live happy, productive lives. Sports figures, rock stars, and people from all walks of life have overcome the depression, pain, and hurt that sometimes occur. You can too. Getting the problem out in the open and communicating are the first steps to feeling better.

If someone else, a friend or acquaintance, has confided in you that he or she is considering suicide, consider this confidence a cry for help. Be discreet, but alert his or her parents or guardians. Talk to a trusted teacher or counselor if your friend will not.

Some school systems have begun programs to help teenagers share the pressures and disappointments they feel. In Plano, Texas, after eight teenage suicides, the SWAT (Students Working All Together) program was started. SWAT pairs high-school students in a type of big brother/big sister arrangement for peer counseling and concern. Whether or not you have such a program, the key to suicide prevention is communication. Helping a suicidal person to realize that he or she is not alone is the first step. Love and unconditional support are vital, but they must be accompanied by professional help.

## Choosing Health-Care Facilities

Health-care facilities include doctors' offices, health clinics, health maintenance organizations (HMOs), and hospitals. Knowing how to use each of these facilities can help you get the medical care that you need.

### Doctors' Offices

Many doctors are in practice by themselves. Many others have practices with other doctors in a partnership or group arrangement. In a solo practice, the doctor has his or her own office space and equipment. In partnership and group practices, doctors often share space and equipment.

In a solo practice, patients will be seen by the doctor or, when there is one, by a physi-

cian's assistant. In partnership and group practices, the patient may be seen by the same doctor each time or may be seen by any one of the doctors in the practice or group. Your personal preferences should be a consideration when you choose a doctor.

Sometimes it is difficult to decide whether or not you need to be seen by a doctor. Usually a call to his or her office can help you with that decision. Describe your problem to the person who answers the telephone. He or she may be able to tell you if you should be seen by the doctor. Sometimes this person will make arrangements for the doctor to call you back, so he or she can decide what you should do.

If you know for certain that you need to see the doctor, call ahead of time to make an appointment. Be specific about your problem or what needs to be done. If it is an emergency situation, the receptionist may try to fit you in or may refer you to another source for medical help. Many walk-in clinics are open twenty-four hours a day and can provide emergency care when needed.

### Hospitals

Hospitals are institutions for the medical and surgical care that is not available from other sources. Expensive diagnostic equipment and the skilled professionals who know how to use it, the facilities and equipment necessary for surgery, and round-the-clock care for the seriously ill can be obtained at a hospital.

Most hospitals have the staff and equipment needed for dealing with emergencies at any time of the day or night. Some people tend to use the emergency room for minor ailments, instead of having a regular doctor. This can actually cost more than going to a doctor. In addition, there often is no continuity of care, and because many of the doctors on duty are specialists in emergency medicine, treatment may not be as comprehensive as treatment from a doctor who is seen regularly. Emergency rooms should be used for emergencies, that is, life-threatening health situations.

## Health Maintenance Organization (HMOs)

HMOs are programs designed to provide comprehensive health care for a fixed, prepaid premium. They combine health insurance and health services in one organization. Costs vary with the HMO used and the range of services it offers, but they are not affected by how frequently a member uses the services. There may be some out-of-pocket expenses for members, but usually these are few.

HMOs frequently employ several health-care personnel who provide services directly to members. The majority are primary care providers, that is, general practice doctors. In addition, HMOs have contracts with area hospitals so members can receive hospital care.

Membership in an HMO has several advantages. There may be fewer out-of-pocket expenses for medical care than with a traditional health insurance policy. This can result in lower overall health-care costs. Preventive checkups are usually covered by HMOs; traditional insurance policies frequently do not cover these exams unless there is a specific problem. With an HMO, there is no need to file claims with an insurance company. Sometimes, medical care may be better coordinated because of the pool of medical personnel and the desire to keep the costs of the HMO down.

There are some disadvantages to HMOs. For example, a member's choice of a doctor is limited to one who is under contract to the HMO. Services are limited to those provided by an HMO or HMO-affiliated contractor, such as a hospital or medical specialist. If a member uses services of medical personnel or facilities that are not affiliated with their HMO, they have to pay the costs. Some HMOs limit coverage when you are traveling outside the geographic area of the HMO to certain specified types of emergency care.

HMOs are not available in all areas. For example, there may be few or none in areas that are not highly populated. When they are available, many employers offer their employees a choice between traditional health insurance or membership in a local HMO. However, some HMOs open their membership to the general public. When you are deciding whether or not to join an HMO, carefully consider the specific plan offered and compare its services and your out-of-pocket expenses to having a traditional health insurance policy and related medical care.

## Public Health Services

County, state, and city health departments, as well as other publicly supported agencies, offer many services. These services usually are available at no cost or low cost.

Most schools have a school nurse to take care of minor injuries and illnesses and to provide counseling and information on various health matters. In addition, many schools have health screening clinics that screen for specific health matters, such as vision, hearing, or dental problems. These programs sometimes make arrangements and/or recommendations for follow-up care and treatment.

## For Review

1. What steps can women take for the early detection of breast cancer?
2. Describe some of the warning signs associated with suicide.
3. Name one advantage and one disadvantage of belonging to an HMO.

## Management Application: Planning Your Time

Imagine yourself in the situation described below. As you read, think about how the steps of the management process might apply to this situation. Then answer the questions that follow.

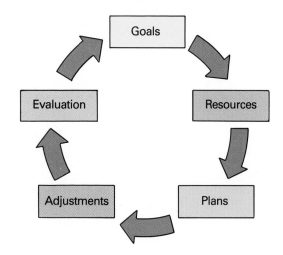

### Situation

Sandy was feeling very stressed. Usually she had her act together, but right now she felt like someone standing in the middle of a street with traffic coming at her from all directions. Next week she had two term papers due, an important math exam, and two soccer games. She had finished most of the term papers but still had to type them. She was also scheduled to work this weekend at the supermarket. Finally, she had told her neighbor weeks ago that she would babysit for her Saturday night. She hadn't realized how busy she was going to be when she had agreed to babysit, but she couldn't get out of it now. It was too late in the week to find another babysitter. Besides, she knew this night out was especially important to her neighbor. It was her anniversary.

Lately she had not been sleeping well. Sometimes she had nightmares about being stretched in three directions at once. When she did fall back to sleep, her alarm did not wake her. Because she was always late, she had been running out without breakfast. She was feeling tired all the time. Soccer practice was making her so exhausted that she had been coming home and falling asleep before

supper, which put her even further behind in her work. Panic was beginning to set in. It seemed that the more she worried, the less she actually did.

She knew she was under stress. The situation was bad and getting worse. The question was how to relieve the stress. How would she get everything done? How could she avoid being in this unhealthy situation again?

### Questions

1. What resource does Sandy need most?
2. How is poor management of time affecting Sandy's mental and physical health?
3. In this situation, will setting a goal or goals help Sandy? Why or why not?
4. If you were in this situation, how would you make a plan to resolve it?
5. How can Sandy avoid a situation like this in the future?
6. Which steps of the management process apply to this situation?

# 4 Chapter Review

## Summary

A balanced diet, good skin and dental care, and regular exercise, all play a role in maintaining good health. Learning to deal with stress in a positive way and to reduce stress by improving time management will also promote good health.

Abusing legal or illegal substances is harmful to your health. Learning about the physical and psychological effects of abusing substances, such as tobacco, alcohol, and other drugs, will help you to make informed decisions. Taking preventive measures, including having checkups and keeping medical records, can help you to manage your health more effectively. Being informed about the kinds of health facilities in your area also is important.

## Vocabulary

Complete each of the following sentences with one of the definitions below.

anorexia nervosa   abstinence
bulimia   stress
aerobic exercise

1. _____ is an eating disorder characterized by the consumption of large amounts of food, followed by vomiting or purging as a way to rid the body of calories.

2. _____ means to not have sexual relations with others.

3. _____ is an eating disorder that is characterized by the refusal to eat, to the point of endangering health, because the victim wishes to become thin.

4. _____ involves rhythmic, repetitive motion so that blood flows continuously through the heart and large skeletal muscles.

5. _____ is any factor that induces bodily or mental tension.

## Questions

1. Explain how dieting can be dangerous if it is not done with care and an understanding of the body's nutrition needs.

2. What are the health advantages of regular exercise? What types of activities might include all three types of exercise discussed on pages 74 and 76?

3. What are some sources of stress?

4. What can people do to reduce stress?

5. What are some of the disadvantages of sexual activity outside of marriage?

6. What are some of the dangers of smoking or chewing tobacco?

7. What are some legal drugs that are abused? What are some illegal drugs?

8. Describe the physical effects of heroin abuse. What are the physical effects of cocaine abuse?

9. What are some preventive health measures you can take to reduce the risk of major health problems?

10. Compare going to an HMO with going to a private physician.

11. Why is it sometimes dangerous to drink when you are taking a drug that has been prescribed for you?

## Skill Activities

**1. Resource Management.** Make a wellness chart for yourself. Keep track of your health habits during a month. Your chart should include the following areas: diet, skin care, dental care, exercise, stress control, alcohol and drug control, preventive health measures. On your chart, under each area, write out specific guidelines for good health.

At the end of a month, you should be able to review your chart for areas in which you need improvement and areas in which you are satisfied. Once you have discovered the areas that need improvement, draw up a plan to strengthen these areas.

**2. Resource Management.** Keep track of how much exercise you get each day for one week. Jot down each activity involving exercise and the length of time you spend doing it. Include time spent in gym class and

any other formal exercise classes you may take. If you are involved in a school sport, include practice and game time in your total. If you walk or bike to school, include the time it takes to get to school and home. After the week is over, look at your exercise pattern. Did you exercise every day? How much of your exercise was aerobic exercise? According to the information in this chapter, do you feel you are getting enough exercise?

**3. Communication.** Organize a class alcohol and drug abuse prevention week. Invite speakers from groups such as Al-Anon and Alateen to discuss their operations. Make posters on the danger signs of alcohol and drug problems. Do research papers on drugs, tobacco, and alcohol; find out about other programs in your area to help teens fight alcohol and drug abuse. Start a bulletin board for information, newspaper clippings, and community activities on alcohol and drug abuse.

**4. Critical Thinking.** Write a paragraph on the following topic: "Suicide Is Not an Answer." Share in a class discussion on the topic. Members of the class might want to consider the following issues for discussion: what to do for a friend in trouble; resources available for teenagers who are having problems or considering suicide; how to deal with stress in a positive way; the difficulties of growing up; and facing problems head on.

# CHAPTER 5

# Managing Crises, Emergencies, and Illnesses

## As you read, think about:

- [ ] what resources are available to help in family crises.
- [ ] how to behave effectively in emergency situations.
- [ ] how to treat common illnesses.
- [ ] how to apply the management process to personal decisions about crises, emergencies, and illnesses.

# Vocabulary

custody
violence
abuse
alcoholism
CPR
Heimlich Maneuver

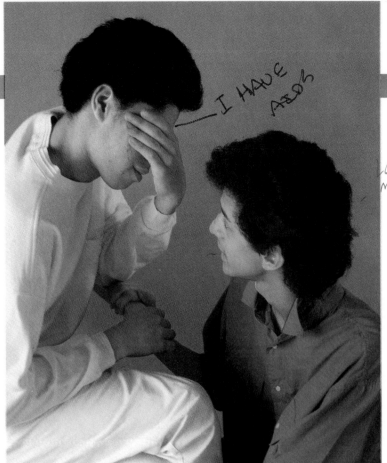

Crises, emergencies, and illnesses occur in every life. Knowing how to act in these situations sometimes can mean the difference between life and death. Learning how to treat common illnesses and learning about emergency procedures can help to prevent some dangerous situations from ever arising.

Family crises, including divorce, death, physical abuse, alcoholism and unemployment, are particularly hard to handle. If you are aware of the community resources available to you, you will know where to turn for help should you need it.

## Dealing with Family Crises

A crisis is any situation that produces severe stress. Sometimes a family can deal with a crisis without outside resources, but many times outside help is needed. Knowing what type of help is available and where to find it may make a crisis easier to handle.

## Divorce

As you learned in Chapter 3, divorce rates in this country have risen steadily. A divorce is an upsetting, stressful family crisis. Because the family unit breaks up, divorce affects both adults and children.

***Effect on Adults*** Even if both partners in a marriage have been unhappy, many are not prepared for the stresses of divorce. The problems resulting from a divorce are both practical and emotional. Practical problems include the division of common property and the question of child custody, both of which must be legally decided. **Custody** is the legal responsibility for the child or children resulting from the marriage. These issues often are the cause of bitter court battles. While it is still more common for women to receive custody of the children and for men to be required to pay child support, there are cases in which men receive custody. Depending upon the family's financial resources, one or both of the adults may suffer financial hardships. If the woman has not worked during the marriage, she may be forced to do so after the divorce. The man may suffer financial setbacks also. Since he may be paying both alimony and child support, his life style may decline considerably. Both adults commonly experience feelings of anger, depression, grief, guilt, and rejection.

**Effects on Children** The effects of divorce on children are numerous. A child usually is shocked when his or her parents separate, even if the home has not been a happy one. Anger and depression often follow the news that parents are divorcing. Behavior in school and with friends may undergo a dramatic change. Some children withdraw and suffer from feelings of low self-esteem. Others strike out and show their frustration and confusion by acting badly, even violently toward others. School grades may decline. The effects of living with one parent and visiting the other parent on a set schedule can be devastating. Depending on the details of the custody arrangement, the child may feel bounced back and forth physically and emotionally.

If the cause of the divorce is cruel or abusive behavior and the absent parent has been cruel or abusive to the child, the child's adjustment to divorce may be smoother. In an ideal situation, the children should have the chance to maintain stable, loving relationships with both parents. If this can be worked out, children will be better equipped to manage the stress of a divorce.

The crises that may occur during your life can leave you upset and confused. How can outside resources help?

Frequently, children feel guilty when their parents divorce. They may feel that they are somehow to blame for the divorce. They may remember times when they behaved badly and think that this caused the parents' unhappiness. This guilt can be destructive. It is vital for children to realize that they are not to blame for their parents' decision to divorce.

**Resources for Coping** Adults need emotional support from other relatives and friends during and after divorce. Sometimes they may need the help of a counselor or mental health professional. Community services and church organizations sometimes offer self-help groups for divorced adults. By sharing common feelings and problems in such a group, divorced individuals can overcome some of their loneliness and feelings of failure.

Children also need resources for coping. They may not always share their feelings openly with friends. Often they secretly hope and believe that their parents will get back together again, even when this hope is unrealistic. They do not want to be different from friends who still have both parents.

Because children may believe their behavior has caused their parents divorce, school counselors and child psychologists can be particularly helpful in drawing out their feelings. Another good resource is a group of peers who have also experienced divorce. Some school districts with high divorce rates have recognized the need for and have begun to create these groups. This kind of group allows children to express and share their feelings with professional supervision.

## Death

The death of a family member is a crisis for everyone. Although death is a natural part of the life process, the death of a loved one is always difficult to accept. Even when the family member has lived a long and happy life, the loss is no easier for the other family members. When there has been time to realize that the individual is dying, the death may be easier to accept. In cases of sudden death, especially the death of a young person, the shock may be greater and acceptance may be much slower.

***Talking to Children about Death*** Many psychiatrists recommend explaining death to children as simply and truthfully as possible. If a child understands that death is a normal part of life, he or she may be able to accept death more easily. Stories made up to protect children should be avoided, since they may lead to more confusion and fear. Saying that a loved one "went on a long trip" or "just went to the hospital" when they have died will not explain

death. In fact, when the person does not return, the child may feel hurt that the "trip" was taken without a goodbye or may become frightened of all hospitals because the loved one never came back.

***Resources for Coping*** There are several things you can do to ease the loss of a loved one. Although time will help, you need to allow yourself time to grieve and accept your loss. Talking it out and showing your emotions are healthy. It is normal to feel both anger and grief. Allow relatives and friends to comfort you rather than being sad alone. Think about the good memories you have of the loved one and do not dwell on any feelings of guilt about what was not said or done.

Other people may be a source for new friendships after a death. Widows, women whose husbands have died, may have a network of friends who do things together and keep each other active. The same may be true of widowers, men whose wives have died. There are often support groups for people who

Returning to school to learn new skills helps many widows and widowers to cope with the loss of their spouses.

have lost family members in similar circumstances. Parents who have lost young children, for example, may establish a support group with others in their circumstances to share their feelings.

## Violence and Abuse

Sadly, there are many cases of violence and abuse within families. Reported statistics may only scratch the surface, since many individuals do not report instances of family abuse. **Violence** involves the use of physical force or the threat of force. **Abuse** may be verbal, physical, or both verbal and physical.

**Causes of Violence and Abuse**   Violence and abuse are often part of an unbroken cycle. Often the person who abuses others was abused as a child and is passing on this destructive treatment to others. Mental illness and severe stress also cause violence and abuse. The need for power over others is frequently the motivation for abuse. Many people believe that violence is aggravated and encouraged by

Hotline phone systems are available for many situations requiring help. Volunteers usually cover the calls.

the violence that is portrayed on television and in other media.

The underlying cause of abuse seems to be closely related to low self-esteem. The abuser usually does not like himself or herself and is taking his or her hostilities out on others. The immediate tragedy of this behavior is that someone else is being injured physically and/or mentally. The long-term tragedy is that abuse creates more abusers as the cycle repeats itself.

**Types of Abuse**   Family abuse includes spouse abuse and child abuse. Many battered women stay in dangerous situations because they are afraid, have low self-esteem, or feel they cannot take care of themselves financially.

Child abuse refers to the physical, emotional, and/or sexual mistreatment of a child under the age of eighteen. Neglect, the failure to provide adequate food, clothing, shelter, or health care for a child, is another form of child abuse.

**Resources for Coping**   When violence and/or abuse surfaces, professional help is needed immediately. This is not something for individuals to try to deal with on their own. The safety of those involved is of utmost importance. Sometimes, this may mean contacting the police to remove the violent or abusive person from the situation. Sometimes, it may involve the victim seeking safety at a shelter for abuse victims. The sooner action is taken, the less physical and emotional damage done to the victim.

Despite promises to change, the abuser probably will repeat the action again and again. Counseling and/or psychiatric help is necessary to create any lasting change. Counseling for the victim is also necessary. When abuse has occurred over a prolonged period of time, permanent separation of the victim or victims and the abuser may be necessary.

# CALLS FOR HELP

- If you are thinking about running away or have **run away,**

- Call **NATIONAL RUNAWAYS HOTLINE**   800-231-6946   (in Texas, 800-392-3352)
  They provide: counseling on resolving home problems, referrals to local social service agencies and to safe shelters.  They will send help to your home in an emergency **abuse** situation or refer you to  OPERATION HOME FREE for free transportation home.
- Call **NATIONAL HOTLINE FOR MISSING CHILDREN**   800-843-5678
  They provide: counseling, referrals to local social service organizations, recommendations of local shelters.
- Call **NATIONAL RUNAWAY SWITCHBOARD**   800-621-4000
  They provide: crisis intervention (for such problems as **drug abuse, child abuse,** and **sexual abuse**), referral to local social service agencies and shelters, and transmittal of messages to parents without disclosing the runaway's location.

These hotline numbers offer confidentiality to callers.

- If you are the victim of or have observed **child abuse,**

- Call **NATIONAL CHILD ABUSE HOTLINE**   800-422-4453
  They provide: crisis intervention counseling and referrals to local services.

- If you or someone you know has a **drug problem,**

- Call **COCAINE HELPLINE**   800-662-HELP (800-662-4357) or **800-COCAINE**
  (800-262-2463)
  They provide: counseling on drug problems, referrals to local support groups (such as **NARCOTICS ANONYMOUS** and **COCAINE ANONYMOUS**), to outpatient counseling programs, and to residential treatment centers.

- If you have a **drinking problem,**

- Call **AA (ALCOHOLICS ANONYMOUS)** See your local telephone directory
  They provide: referral to their local support groups.
- If you have a parent, friend, or relative with a **drinking problem,**
- Call **ALATEEN** See your local telephone directory under **AL-ANON**
  They provide: referral to local support groups of teenagers who have relatives or friends with drinking problems.

- If you feel **depressed** or **suicidal,**

- Call a local **suicide prevention hotline.** Most telephone directories list these and other Crisis Numbers in the Community Services section at the front of the White Pages.

- If you want information about AIDS,

- Call the **NATIONAL AIDS HOTLINE**   800-443-0366.

Local religious leaders, law enforcement agencies, school guidance offices, doctors' offices, community health agencies, and the yellow pages of the telephone directory can supply information about the specific services and personnel available in your community. A crisis hotline may help both the abused individual and the abuser. Parents Anonymous, a support group for abusive parents, has a hotline number that parents can call if they feel they may be likely to abuse their children. Phone conversations try to counsel the parent and calm the situation before abuse occurs. The group also meets to work together toward changing abusive behavior.

## Alcoholism

**Alcoholism** is a disease. The alcoholic is addicted to alcohol and drinks uncontrollably once he or she has decided to drink. Health and relationships are harmed. Alcoholism in a family has devastating affects on all members of a family.

**Causes of Alcoholism** The cause of alcoholism is the misuse of alcohol. Stress and problems at work or in the family can lead to heavier drinking, which, in turn, can lead to alcoholism. Research has indicated that children of alcoholics are in more danger of becoming alcoholics than children who do not have an alcoholic parent or parents. This may be due to an inherited tendency toward alcoholism as well as to growing up in an environment where alcohol is abused.

**Effects on Families** Family members cannot rely upon an alcoholic member. Children are especially vulnerable to the effects of alcoholism. The alcoholic parent's behavior cannot be predicted. When the parent is sober, he or she acts one way; when the parent is drinking,

his or her personality may become entirely different—even abusive. Children have no sense of security in this type of environment. Teenagers experience extreme embarrassment and often become antisocial. Frequently, they try to protect and cover up for an alcoholic parent. They are afraid to get into situations where they may want to bring friends home, so they may withdraw. The alcoholic in a family becomes someone to avoid, rather than a trusted family member. Frequently, excessive drinking leads to job loss and economic hardship, which further strains family relationships. Many divorces are the result of alcoholism in the family.

Alcoholism is not limited to adult family members. As drinking has increased among teenagers, the incidence of teenage alcoholism has increased too. If you feel that you or a friend has developed a drinking problem, seek help immediately.

**Resources for Coping** The alcoholic must want to help himself or herself before anyone else can help. Once the problem is admitted, outside help can be effective. Professional help for the alcoholic can be found at local community health centers and family service agencies. The National Council on Alcoholism can provide information and refer people to sources for help. In some cases, time in a hospital or detoxification center is needed. Check the yellow pages of your telephone directory under "Alcoholism Information and Treatment Centers" for locations near you.

Three organizations that are especially valuable resources for dealing with alcoholism and its effects are Alcoholics Anonymous, Al-Anon, and Alateen.

Alcoholics Anonymous (AA) is a self-help group, composed of recovering alcoholics of any age. The support this group provides has proven successful for many people. Meetings are held regularly. Members, who are known only by their first names, offer each other encouragement and share their stories about how alcohol has affected their lives.

Al-Anon is an organization that has grown out of Alcoholics Anonymous and provides counseling and self-help for the families and friends of alcoholics. By sharing experiences, people learn how to cope with the alcoholism of a loved one. They learn effective techniques of behavior toward the alcoholic. Al-Anon members also learn how to protect themselves in their situations.

Alateen is a part of Al-Anon and Alcoholics Anonymous. It is designed for teenagers whose lives have been or are being affected by the drinking of a parent or close relative. The group allows teenagers living with an alcoholic to meet others who have the same problem. At Alateen, teens learn about alcoholism as an illness. Through sharing experiences, frustrations, and common emotions, teenagers can build their self-esteem and learn new ways to cope with their situation.

There are no membership fees or dues involved in any of these organizations. They are supported by voluntary contributions. To locate the group nearest you, look in your local telephone directory under Alcoholics Anonymous or Al-Anon.

## Premarital Pregnancy

Teenage pregnancy outside of marriage is a family crisis that requires extra physical and psychological resources. Once a pregnancy is confirmed, girls, who sometimes are barely out of childhood, are faced with the physical and emotional stress of having a child who will be totally dependent upon them. Many young girls are not mature enough to realize how dramatically their lives will change with motherhood. Formal education is usually interrupted and often ended. Boys, too, confront new stresses when faced with unexpected fatherhood. The boy may feel he should have a voice in any decision the girl makes. Guilt factors may bring about an early, unwise marriage.

An unmarried, pregnant teen faces many new stresses and difficulties.

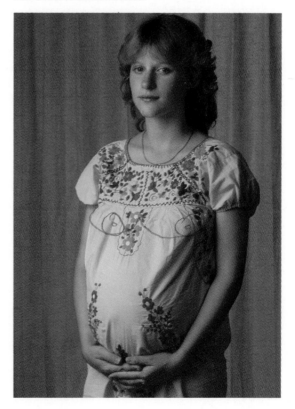

Other family members may or may not be loving and supportive during this crisis. Many are. Even in these cases, however, the extra money resources required for medical care can put a strain on family relationships. Parents who had planned on some independence as their child grew up may be involved in bringing up another baby.

**Options for Pregnant Teens** An unplanned pregnancy requires some difficult decisions. The options for an unmarried, pregnant teen include the decision to bring up her child alone, to marry or to put the child up for adoption. Each of these options and others have disadvantages. Decisions about this issue are guided by the teachings and expectations of family, religion, and community.

## Unemployment

Unemployment can result in a family crisis. The loss of job security and steady financial income can be devastating, especially if there are no savings to fall back on. The person who loses a job often feels rejected and depressed even when he or she is not responsible in any way for the job loss.

**Resources for Coping** Family support and understanding are vital in this crisis. All family members can provide emotional support. Expenses can be cut back as much as possible. If they are old enough to work, children can contribute to the family finances.

Reeducation sometimes is necessary to learn newer, more marketable skills. The family may have to talk to creditors to explain the situation and work out plans for longer payment periods on debts. Friends and relatives may become resources for learning about new job opportunities. Employment agencies are another resource. If the individual was the victim of a layoff and meets other criteria, he or

she probably is eligible to collect unemployment benefits at a state unemployment agency.

## For Review

1. List six family crises that are described in this chapter.
2. What are the suspected causes of family violence and abuse?
3. Name three organizations that are resources for help with alcoholism. Describe the purpose of each.

## Managing Emergency Situations

Knowing the steps to take if an emergency arises is your most valuable resource. Logical and calm action during an emergency is vital. The way you act in an emergency can sometimes make the difference between

Why is learning how to administer first-aid such a valuable life skill? CPR is one technique.

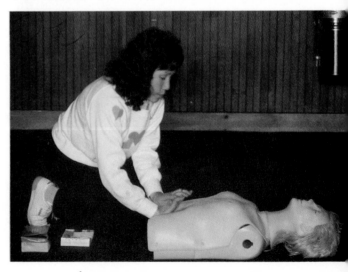

minor injuries and serious injuries or even between life and death.

Everyone should learn basic first-aid techniques. Many hospitals and local chapters of the American Red Cross offer first-aid, mouth-to-mouth resuscitation, and **CPR (cardiopulmonary resuscitation)** courses. CPR usually is applied to heart attack victims. It involves alternate breathing and heart pumping procedures. It may be applied in other cases when breathing has stopped. CPR and other techniques should be taught by health professionals. They require precise demonstrations and practice. However, you can master the CPR technique in only a few course hours. The ability to perform CPR and other life-saving procedures is an extremely valuable skill.

Volunteers work to raise funds for the American Red Cross, which provides many health services including disaster relief.

## *Poisoning*

Poisoning can occur from an overdose of legal or illegal drugs or from eating or drinking toxic chemicals. If a poisoning occurs, call a Poison Control Center, a hospital emergency room, or a physician immediately to find out what action to take. Keep these phone numbers permanently posted next to your telephone. Provide as much information as you can. The individual you speak to will want to know the victim's age, the name of the poison, how much was taken and when, whether the victim is conscious, whether the victim has vomited, and your location. The type of poison taken is extremely important to know so that proper treatment can be prescribed.

If the substance swallowed is not a strong acid, alkali, or petroleum product and the patient is conscious, you may be instructed to induce vomiting. When you call a Poison Control Center, you may be told to use ipecac or you may be told to use a particular substance readily available in the home.

If the substance swallowed is a strong acid, alkali, or petroleum product and the

patient is fully conscious, you probably will be told to give the victim water or milk to drink. Usually milk is recommended for acids and alkalis, and water is recommended for petroleum products. These fluids help to dilute and neutralize the poison. A strong acid, alkali, or petroleum product can destroy the esophagus and/or inflame the lungs if vomited.

If the victim is not fully conscious or is having convulsions, you may be told to get him or her to an emergency room or doctor as soon as possible. Take the poison container with you when you go. Do not attempt to induce vomiting; in a semiconscious or unconscious person, vomited material can go down the windpipe into the lungs.

To prevent accidental poisoning, keep medicines, cleaning products, and other dangerous substances in locked cupboards, high out of a child's reach. Mark all these substances with a "Mr. Yuk" symbol, available from the local poison center and teach children that this symbol means danger. Since many children's vitamins are flavored to taste like candy, vitamins and other dietary supplements also should be locked away.

# FIRST AID FOR CHOKING

- **ASK: Are you choking?**
- If victim cannot breathe, cough, or speak...

- **Give the Heimlich Maneuver.**
- Stand behind the victim.
- Wrap your arms around the victim's waist.
- Make a fist with one hand. PLACE your FIST (thumbside) against the victim's stomach in the midline just ABOVE THE NAVEL AND WELL BELOW THE RIB MARGIN.
- Grasp your fist with your other hand.
- PRESS INTO STOMACH WITH A QUICK UPWARD THRUST.

**1**

**2**

**3**

- **Repeat thrust if necessary.**

- **If a victim has become unconscious:**

**4** · Sweep the mouth.

**5** · Attempt rescue breathing.

**American Red Cross**

**6** · Give 6–10 abdominal thrusts.
- Repeat Steps 4, 5, and 6 as necessary

Everyone should learn how to perform the steps above for choking and how to give rescue breathing and CPR. Call your local American Red Cross chapter for information on these and other first aid techniques.
Caution: The Heimlich Maneuver (abdominal thrust) may cause injury. Do not *practice* on people.

**LOCAL EMERGENCY TELEPHONE NUMBER:** _____

## Choking

If you see someone choking, and if the person is coughing forcefully, do not interfere. Normal coughing is the most effective method for clearing a partially blocked airway. If the person seems to be choking but is not coughing forcefully, ask, "Are you choking?" If the person cannot answer, take emergency action.

Begin by calling out loud for help. Then, if the victim is conscious but cannot speak, cough, or breathe, perform the **Heimlich Maneuver**. Take the following steps for adults, and for children over the age of eight:

- Stand behind the victim, or behind the victim's chair if the person is seated.
- Wrap your arms around the victim's waist.
- Make a fist with one hand. Place your fist with the thumb side against the victim's stomach in the midline just above the navel and well below the ribs.
- Grasp your fist with the other hand.
- Press into the stomach with a quick inward and upward thrust.
- Repeat as necessary until the blocked airway is cleared or until the victim becomes unconscious.

If the victim becomes unconscious, call out again for help and, if possible, ask someone to telephone 911 for assistance. You should then perform special rescue procedures. To learn these procedures, take a course at your local hospital or American Red Cross education center.

If you are in a restaurant or with others and begin to choke, place your hands loosely across your throat. This will send a nonverbal request for help.

## Bleeding

When cuts or injuries are severe, for example, when major arteries are involved,

blood loss can be rapid. The bleeding must be stopped immediately. When an artery is damaged, blood spurts from a wound. If a wound is fairly clean, and the artery does not appear to be damaged, pressure on the wound often can stop the bleeding. If blood is spurting from a wound or pressure on the wound does not help, exerting pressure on the damaged artery between the wound and the heart can help

The Heimlich Maneuver has saved the lives of many choking victims. Even young children can perform it.

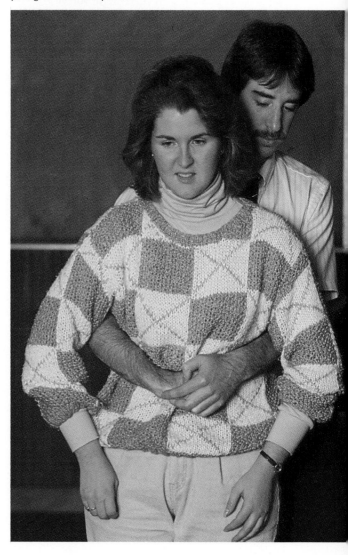

to stop the blood flow. In any of these cases when bleeding is severe, call for emergency medical help.

Most minor cuts and scrapes stop bleeding on their own because blood vessels tend to constrict when injured and blood clotting factors are released when blood vessels are injured. For minor cuts and scrapes, you should allow the wound to bleed as this tends to carry any dirt out of the wound. If there is dirt around the edges of the wound, wipe it away from the wound with clean gauze or cotton. Hydrogen peroxide (a 3 percent solution) can be used as a cleansing agent.

Cuts and scrapes heal better when they are exposed to air. If possible, they should be allowed to heal uncovered. If the cut is shallow, but the edges gape open, use small strips of surgical tape, or a "butterfly bandage," to hold the edges together. If the cut is on a finger or other place that is easily bumped and will cause the bleeding to start again, place a clean bandage over the wound. Do not apply ointment. Take the bandage off whenever possible.

A deep, gaping cut may need medical attention and stitches. A cut that does not heal well or that shows signs of infection should have medical attention.

A puncture wound is a wound that is deep and does not bleed much. If you were to step on a nail, you would receive a puncture wound. This type of wound requires medical attention because it can become infected easily. If a tetanus booster shot has not been administered within the last ten years, you should have one because there is a danger of tetanus, a serious and sometimes fatal illness.

## *Loss of Consciousness*

Loss of consciousness may be caused by many things, including epileptic seizures. *Grand mal* seizures can be recognized by loss of consciousness and involuntary movement. If this occurs, remove any objects that the individual could injure himself or herself on. The seizure will run its course. Be ready to provide reassurance if the person is disoriented upon regaining consciousness. Do *not* place any object between the teeth and do not try to restrain the individual.

If a victim is unconscious and cannot be revived, make certain that his or her airway is open. If the victim is not breathing, mouth-to-mouth resuscitation should be administered. If there is no heart beat, CPR should be administered by an individual trained in the technique. Call an ambulance and keep the victim warm to prevent shock.

If a person feels faint, having the individual sit down and lower his or her head between

There are some emergency situations that require immediate professional attention and care.

# Waste Not, Want Not

Disposal of the vast amounts of garbage and other waste materials produced every day in the United States is a matter for serious concern. Our environmental health and, in turn, our personal health is increasingly threatened by the presence of waste materials.

The Environmental Protection Agency says that over 250 million tons of hazardous waste is produced in the United States each year! Much of this is dumped into rivers, lakes, or oceans; burned in ways that pollute the air; or buried in unsealed landfills where toxic substances threaten our water sources.

The space available for waste disposal is dwindling each day. Nonbiodegradable waste, such as plastics that do not decompose for centuries, makes the situation worse. A 1989 survey of Connecticut dump sites found that of the 89 landfills in operation, 42 were near capacity, and at least 67 were unsafe. Understandably, most communities throughout the country refuse to admit new dump sites.

What can high school students do to help? A group of teenagers in the Chesapeake Bay region found a way. First, they studied the specific causes of poor waste management in their area. They then arranged to give lectures to adult groups on ways to address the problem. They explain to their audiences how phosphorous pollutes water, for example, and urge individuals to avoid buying detergents that contain phosphorous. They suggest ways to recycle nonbiodegradable waste and to safely dispose of household products such as used batteries. High school students in other parts of the country have begun to launch similar programs.

You too can help by finding safer ways to dispose of waste materials in your own household. You can also work individually or with a group to increase your community's awareness of the problem.

Paramedics make emergency rescues.

the knees usually avoids actually fainting. If someone has already fainted, place the individual flat on his or her back and elevate the legs, if possible, to increase the flow of blood to the head. Anyone who has fainted usually regains consciousness in only a few minutes. If this does not happen, get medical help as quickly as possible.

## Burns

Burns that are not deep and cover only a small area of the body are more painful than serious. Ice wrapped in a cloth applied to the area as soon as possible after the burn has occurred can ease the pain. If a blister forms, do not break it. Do not apply any ointment, cream, or grease. Leave the area uncovered unless it will be bumped or rubbed by clothing. If the area will be, cover it loosely.

Burns that are deep and cover a large area of the body need medical attention as soon as the immediate emergency is dealt with. If clothing is soaked with boiling water or hot fat, remove the clothing immediately. Cut it away if necessary. Leaving it over the skin can cause the burn to become deeper. If the clothing is stuck to the burned area, do not try to remove it. Severely burned areas generally swell, so remove jewelry, shoes, and other articles that might constrict the body.

Areas that are burned by chemicals should be held under cool running water for at least ten minutes. Other burns should have only cold water applied to them, no ointments, creams, or grease. If the burned area is large, a towel or sheet soaked in cool water can be applied. Wrap the burned area with a clean, dry dressing to help prevent contamination. Do not use cotton or any material that is fuzzy and may stick to the burned skin. Take the injured person to a doctor or hospital immediately.

Sunburn is really a type of burn. Depending on exposure to the sun or sunlamp, it can be a superficial burn or it can be deeper, causing damage to tissues beneath the outer layers of skin. Cool water or compresses can help relieve the pain from sunburn. A mild sunburn can be relieved by applying calamine lotion or cooling cream or lotion. Seek medical treatment for a severe sunburn.

### Eye Injury

If chemicals have gone into the eyes, flood the inner corner of the eye with clean water for five minutes. Cover both eyes with clean compresses and call for medical advice.

If some solid matter has gone into the eye, the eye often washes it out itself. If the object does not come out or cannot be seen, cover both eyes with clean compresses and take the person to a doctor. Do not rub the eye as this may cause the object to become embedded more deeply.

## Treating Common Illnesses

There are many common illnesses that we all experience occasionally. These include fevers, nausea, and the common cold. Simple procedures are usually enough to ease discomfort without having to see a doctor. A doctor's advice is needed, however, if the illness does not improve after a reasonable period of time, or if medications are not effective.

## Nausea and Vomiting

An upset stomach can have many causes. Usually the condition is not serious. Avoiding food and increasing liquid intake can help to ease discomfort. In young children, however, frequent vomiting can lead to dehydration, which can be serious. Give liquids freely. If the condition continues, call a physician.

There are over-the-counter products to relieve nausea and vomiting. Although these products do not cure the condition, they may make you feel more comfortable. If the nausea and vomiting continue, call a physician. Nausea and vomiting after a head injury require immediate medical attention.

### Fever

Your normal body temperature is about 98.6° F (37° C), although it may vary by one or two degrees during the day. Usually it is lowest in the morning and highest at night. Any increase above normal body temperature is considered a fever.

Often a person with a fever feels hot to the touch, even though he or she may be shivering and feeling cold. The person may look flushed and feel headachy. A child with a fever may be fussy or listless.

Most fevers are a symptom of some type of infection. Because a fever indicates the body is fighting an infection, some doctors do not recommend any action to reduce the fever if it does not go above 102° F (39° C). Check with your physician to find out what treatment he or she recommends.

Usually, aspirin or aspirin substitutes are recommended for treating a fever. While these products help to lower a fever and increase comfort, they do not cure the underlying cause. Sponging the body with lukewarm water and allowing it to evaporate can also help to lower body temperature.

A child's temperature can rise quite rapidly, and a high temperature sometimes can cause convulsions. Call a physician immediately if the child's temperature rises above 102° F (39° C).

Aspirin has been linked to Reye's syndrome, a type of encephalitis, in children and adolescents. The relationship is not clear, but most physicians recommend the use of an aspirin substitute when treating fever and pain in children and adolescents, particularly in the case of viral illnesses.

Since a fever often results in the loss of body fluids through perspiration, increased intake of liquids is recommended. Unless there is a medical reason for not eating, small amounts of easily digested foods can be eaten if the patient feels like eating.

## Headache

In children, a headache frequently is a sign of a cold or the flu or some childhood illness. In adults, a headache can be a sign of illness, but it is often a symptom of too much stress or anxiety. In fact, one type of headache is called a tension headache.

When a headache is related to an illness such as a cold or flu, aspirin or an aspirin substitute can help to relieve the pain. For headaches that are caused by tension or stress, aspirin may or may not help. Sometimes, aspirin combined with a short period of rest will relieve the pain. However, reducing the level of stress, when possible, or finding ways to deal with it can to help prevent tension headaches altogether.

## Common Cold and Flu

Unfortunately, there is no immunization for the common cold and no medicine that will cure it. Once a person catches a cold, it usually takes seven to ten days for it to run its course.

Aspirin and aspirin substitutes can help to relieve sore throat pain and headache pain as well as lower any fever. Over-the-counter cold medicines can help relieve some of the symptoms, such as sneezing and a runny nose, but they do not cure the cold. Some of these medications may cause drowsiness, and others may cause agitation, so they should be taken with care.

Flu can have some of the same symptoms as a cold, but usually there are muscle aches and pains and headache pain can be severe. A fever is usually higher with flu than with a cold. As with a cold, there is no cure for flu. Aspirin substitutes sometimes can help to relieve some of its symptoms.

Plenty of rest and an increased intake of liquids is the type of treatment usually recommended for colds and flu. Bed rest may or may not be necessary when someone has a cold. Someone with the flu usually feels miserable enough to stay in bed.

Since both colds and flu are viral infections, antibiotics will not cure either type of infections. Antibiotics such as penicillin or one of its substitutes are only effective in treating bacterial infections. Sometimes a cold or flu can lead to complications, such as strep throat, pneumonia, or other bacterial infections. In these cases, professional medical help is required, and an antibiotic probably will be prescribed for the person.

## For Review

1. Describe the steps of the Heimlich Maneuver. When would you use it?

2. How should you treat a minor burn?

3. What causes a fever? How should fevers be treated?

## Management Application: Dealing with a Crisis

Imagine yourself in the situation described below. As you read, think about how the steps of the management process might apply to this situation. Then answer the questions that follow.

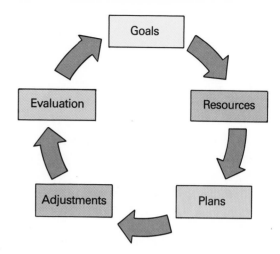

### Situation

Manuel's grandfather had had a heart condition for as long as Manuel could remember. Wanting to help his grandfather was part of the reason Manuel wanted to be a doctor. Last week his science teacher had begun a unit on the human body. His teacher took a plastic model of the human heart apart to show the class how blood flowed. She talked about what a heart attack was. Manuel asked a lot of questions about the CPR method that his teacher said could be used to revive some heart attack victims. His teacher told them that CPR had to be taught by someone trained in the method. She told the class that they could take a CPR course at the local hospital or at the Red Cross. The class was free and did not require many hours. She said that if you completed the class, you received a certificate that said you were qualified to use CPR. Manuel asked his parents if he could take the course. They thought it was a wonderful idea. His older sister agreed to provide transportation to and from the place where the course was being taught if he would do the dishes for her for one week.

Manuel registered for the class and also asked the manager of the bike shop where he worked not to schedule him on Tuesday evenings until the course was over. He attended every class and received his certificate. About three weeks later, Manuel performed CPR on his grandfather when he was stricken with a heart attack during a family party. The doctors said that Manuel had saved his grandfather's life because he had acted quickly and had known what to do.

### Questions

1. What was Manuel's short-term goal? What is his long-term goal?
2. What resources did Manuel need in order to take the CPR course?
3. What steps did Manuel have to take to make his plan complete?
4. Did he carry out his plan? Did he have to make any trade-offs?
5. Which steps of the management process apply to this situation?

# 5 *Chapter Review*

## Summary

In acute crises, like divorce or death, members of a family may need help to deal with their feelings. Other crises, such as premarital pregnancy and unemployment require family support and understanding. In cases of abuse or violence, professional help is needed immediately to ensure safety. AA, Al-Anon, and Alateen are organizations that help alcoholics and their families. To deal with emergency situations such as loss of consciousness, heart attack, poisoning, choking, burns, injury, or illness, everyone should learn some basic first-aid techniques.

## Vocabulary

Match each of the following words with one of the definitions below.

| | |
|---|---|
| custody | alcoholism |
| violence | CPR |
| abuse | Heimlich Maneuver |

1. Words or actions that are harsh or cruel are _____ .
2. Breathing and heart pumping procedures that may be applied to heart attack victims are called _____ .
3. The legal responsibility for the child or children resulting from a marriage is known as _____ .
4. An addiction to alcohol that results in uncontrollable consumption is _____ .
5. The use of physical force or the threat of force is _____ .
6. The _____ is a technique for dislodging objects that are causing a person to choke.

## Questions

1. What are some of the effects of divorce on children? What things can be done to help children handle divorce?
2. What can help people to cope with the death of a loved one?
3. What can a teenager who is living in a household with an alcoholic do to reduce the stress of the situation in addition to consulting outside organizations?
4. Explain how a situation such as teenage pregnancy outside of marriage can put stress on a family. How can unemployment cause stress within a family?
5. What steps should you take if you discover that a child has swallowed a petroleum product and is conscious? If a child has swallowed medicine?
6. What should you do if you are alone and begin to choke on a piece of food?
7. What should you do if you are babysitting and the child you are caring for burns his hand on the stove?

8. What first-aid procedures should you follow if you are painting a wall and the paint gets into your eye?

9. What is Reye's syndrome? Is there a way to avoid it?

10. What is the most effective way to treat colds and flu?

## Skill Activities

1. **Communication.** Invite the school nurse or a local medical practitioner to teach your class basic first-aid techniques. Follow up this instruction with an investigation of the local hospitals or health centers in your area that offer CPR courses. Find out the date and cost, if any, of upcoming courses. Perhaps some members of the class would like to register for the course.

2. **Communication.** Select one of the organizations listed on the chart on page 103. Look in the telephone book for the address or ask your school or local librarian to help you locate it. Write a letter asking for information about the organization. Use any information you receive to present a brief oral report to the class. Include information in your report about the specific purpose of the organization and exactly how it helps people in emergency or crisis situations.

Use all of the information that you have gathered to make a table display or bulletin board in your classroom.

3. **Science.** Write a short paper on "Hospices—A Special Kind of Treatment for Dying Patients." What things would a possible hospice patient need to consider before signing in? Do hospices fulfill a need for some people? If you do not wish to write on this topic, choose one career associated with health care. Find out how much training is needed to enter this career and exactly what its duties and responsibilities are. Nurse, doctor (including any specialty, such as pediatrician), or paramedic are some of the possible choices. Once you have your information, hold a brief class discussion about what you have learned.

4. **Critical Thinking.** Hold a group discussion about the hazards of adult drinking and driving. Look for magazine articles and books in the library that give information on ways to reduce the terrible yearly toll from drunk driving. Share your research with the group. Find out what the law in your state is concerning drinking and driving. Discuss ways to make it more effective.

Discuss also how people can avoid getting into a car with a drunk driver. For example, if they had expected to ride home with someone who has been drinking, how can they get home safely?

# Unit 2

# Managing Work and Money Resources

# 6 *Planning for Work*

## *As you read, think about:*

- ☐ how to identify reasons for working.
- ☐ how to understand the job skills required for different types of work.
- ☐ how to take steps to find a job.
- ☐ how to identify realistic expectations of both employers and employees.
- ☐ how to apply the management process to personal decisions about work.

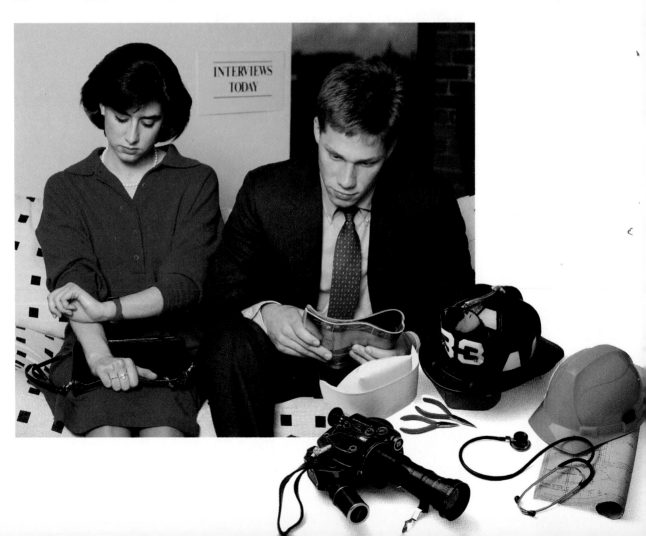

Although some people know from the time they are small children what they want to be when they "grow up," most people do not. What you thought you wanted to be when you were eleven years old may change as you grow older and have different work experiences.

Planning for a career is important because the work that you choose will affect many aspects of your life. Your choice of work will determine how much money you make, the hours you work, and the amount of leisure time you have. Where you will work will also influence your decision about where you will live.

according to individual values, goals, and resources. The most basic, practical reason for working is to earn money. Many times, however, even people who have enough money to meet their needs and wants work. Why? Working seems to satisfy a basic human need to be a useful contributor. When your work is something you enjoy and do well, you receive a sense of satisfaction from it. You feel that you are using your time constructively. All of these factors influence why you and other people work, as well as the types of work you choose to do.

## Identifying Reasons for Working

Why do people work? Everyone has personal reasons for working. These reasons vary

## Meeting Income Needs and Wants

Although money should not be your only consideration when you decide on a career, a certain amount of money is necessary to meet

A job that suits your talents and abilities
provides a sense of satisfaction.

the basic minimum needs of food, clothing, shelter, medical care, and transportation. If you have wants in addition to needs (and most people do), these, too, usually require some money, even if only a small amount. When there is a family to provide for, your income needs become greater because of your increased responsibilities. Provision for your income needs when you retire is another factor you should consider.

## Satisfying Personal Interests

Choosing a job that satisfies you is important. Statistics indicate that many men and women will be in the work force for fifty years or more. Family responsibilities, especially caring for children, will also affect your career choices.

## Becoming Self-Supporting

In past generations, most women were not encouraged to make career plans, except in terms of something to do until they were married and had a family. Their work was thought of as something they could return to if they were bored or lonely after their families had grown. If women did not marry, it was thought that they continued to work only because they had to. Women who married were expected to be supported by their husbands. If they continued to work, their income usually was considered supplementary. If they had children, they were not expected to work until their children were older or had left home. In other words, in the past, careers for women were not considered as important as careers for men.

Over the past several years, society has changed. Now, women as well as men need to have specific job skills that enable them to be self-supporting. A dramatic increase in the divorce rate has left many women partially or totally financially responsible for themselves and often their children. Changes in the job market have resulted in unemployment for many men who have been the main source of income for their families. In order for their families to survive, their wives have had to find work. Planning and training for participation in the work force might have put many of these women in a stronger position for earning income. Today, women are seeking employment in increasing numbers, not only to become self-supporting but also to find self-satisfaction from their chosen work.

## Identifying Types of Work

There are many types of work you may consider, depending on your stage of life and your changing goals, values, and resources.

### Temporary Work

As a young adult, you probably will have several different *temporary,* or *part-time,* work situations, which may or may not be related to your long-term working goal. You may need to earn spending money by working for a few hours a week as a babysitter or store clerk, for example. You may accept a temporary position to meet your financial needs simply because the hours fit into your school schedule. You know that you will not be doing this particular job for many years. It may be work that you enjoy, but it is not necessarily part of your career plan.

Occasionally, temporary work is chosen with your long-term career in mind. Many schools, for example, offer work/study pro-

grams that allow students to work at jobs they are considering as careers. In this case, you have the opportunity to work temporarily and to gain experience toward your career. As a result of this short-term work experience, you may change your mind about your intended career if you disliked the job or you may work even harder to reach your goal if you enjoyed it. Temporary work like this can be valuable because it allows you to try the job firsthand, rather than only studying or reading about it.

### Permanent Work

*Permanent work* is work that you commit to doing on a full-time, long-term basis. This may be work that you have chosen as a career or as a part of your career plan. This type of work

Resources permitting, many women choose to be at home with their children.

is goal-oriented. That is, it is work that helps you to reach your career goals. Whatever permanent work you choose, you will have to have some training or education in order to perform it.

## For Review

1. State two reasons for working other than the need to earn money for your personal needs and wants.
2. How has the attitude toward a woman's need to be self-supporting changed over the years? Why?
3. How can temporary work help you to decide on a career goal?

## Acquiring Job Skills

In today's society, job skills are a necessity. Few employers hire anyone without a high-school diploma, and jobs that do not require special skills are decreasing every year. Usually, jobs that require few or no skills are low paying, have few or no job-related benefits, may be temporary, and even when full-time, may not provide enough income to meet your basic minimum needs.

There are many ways to acquire job skills. Some cost money; others do not. The cost depends on the nature of the skills and the source of the training.

## Learning About Career Alternatives

As you are thinking about careers, you need to consider your interests and abilities, your values, and the kind of life you want to have. You may also find it helpful to think about the kinds of jobs that will be available when you enter the work force and the resources you have for obtaining specialized skills.

**Explore Career Possibilities.** A school guidance counselor is one source of information on the many possibilities for careers. The teacher of a class you particularly like is another source. The school library and the public library probably have a variety of resources that deal with interesting careers.

You may want to try to find out the types of jobs that may not be in demand in the future and the types of jobs that may develop in the future. This information will help you to avoid training for a job that will not exist in several years. It may open your eyes to possibilities you had not even considered.

Computer training is a valuable resource. How many jobs can you think of that require computer skills?

## JOB SKILLS IN SHORT SUPPLY

Job skills in demand now and at least in the near future include those in areas of:

- CUTTING EDGE TECHNOLOGIES
    (Optics, Laser, Electromagnetics)

- ELECTRICAL ENGINEERING

- MANUFACTURING ENGINEERING

- PLASTICS

- MIXED DEGREES (technical undergrad training plus an MBA, for example)

- LANGUAGES (especially Chinese, Arabic, Russian, and Japanese)

- PERSONAL COMPUTER SKILLS

- BANKING

- STATISTICS

- ACADEMIA (professors needed in business and engineering schools, especially)

Source: *Wall Street Journal*, Oct. 7, 1986

You may know people in your community who have the kind of job you think you are interested in. You may know people who work for a company that you also might like to work for. Sometimes it is helpful to talk with them about their jobs and the type of work done by their companies.

***Explore Interesting Jobs.*** As you explore different career possibilities, you may find some that sound particularly interesting. Read or ask questions to find out what the requirements are for these jobs in terms of personal qualities, special skills and education, geographical location, hours of work, special physical or mental demands, and whether or not travel is involved. The more you learn about different jobs, the more information you have on which to base your decision and the more likely you are to find the type of work that interests you.

***Evaluate Your Resources and Talents.*** You will find it helpful to take a close look at your resources and talents as you consider a satisfying career. For example, if a job requires that you have constant contact with people, will you enjoy it? Do you enjoy constantly dealing with others, or do you prefer to spend some time (or a lot of time) by yourself or with only one or two other people? If a job requires special training, is it possible for you to acquire that training? Do you have the ability, the financial resources, and the time for it?

Read about possible career choices.

Working with a hospital dietician may help you to decide on a career.

Sometimes you may not be able to get a paying job, but you may be able to *volunteer* your services. If you are interested in teaching in the elementary grades, for example, you might be able to spend some study hall time helping out in an elementary school. Volunteering some time in a hospital may help you to find out if you are truly interested in some aspect of health care.

## Learning Basic Skills

There are some skills that everyone needs for a job. These include social skills, communication skills, and mathematics skills. Computer skills are important now and eventually may be ranked among the basic job skills. Most of these skills can be acquired in your classes at school.

***Social Skills*** Social skills are those skills that focus on getting along with other people and being able to work with them. Cooperation, for example, is a social skill that is necessary for most types of jobs. Sensitivity to other people's needs and feelings is another social skill. Good manners are still another social skill that is important to any job.

***Communication Skills*** Communication skills focus on speaking, writing, and listening. Being able to express yourself clearly when you are asking questions, giving instructions, taking messages, and having discussions is important in most jobs. Listening skills allow you to hear and understand what is said to you, whether it is instruction for doing something or praise for a job well done. You need writing skills to fill out job applications, to write letters inquiring about jobs, to take notes or messages, and to leave written instructions that can be followed correctly. Many jobs require additional writing skills, such as those needed for writing business letters and reports.

If you have no idea what type of work you are interested in, there are different types of tests available for checking your interests, abilities, and aptitudes and then matching them with different types of careers. Your guidance counselor can tell you what tests are available to you and suggest other resources for helping you focus on some possible career choices.

***Work in Your Field of Choice.*** Sometimes it is impossible to get actual work experience in areas that interest you. In these cases, a part-time or temporary job as similar as possible to the one in which you are interested may help you to make up your mind one way or the other. For example, if being a veterinarian interests you, you might take a job helping to care for the animals at an animal hospital. If you are interested in construction work, a summer job as a "gofer" may help you to make up your mind.

***Math and Computer Skills*** Basic mathematics skills include being able to add, subtract, multiply, and divide, either in longhand or by using a calculator. Frequently, these skills are needed for the job you seek. Certainly, you need them to handle the money you have earned successfully.

Basic computer skills include a familiarity with computers and a basic knowledge of what they are used for and how to use them. Some beginning jobs that use computers include working with inventory, bookkeeping and accounting, word processing, and filing.

## Obtaining Specialized Knowledge and Skills

While specialized knowledge and skills are necessary for most jobs today, you do not always have to go to college to learn what you

need for a job. Often, you can get the training you need while you are in school. For example, secretarial and bookkeeping skills are taught in many schools. Computer classes are available in many school systems. Training in automobile mechanics, food service, electronics, child care, and graphic arts is offered as a part of a vocational program in many schools. These programs usually offer both classwork and actual work experience as a part of their student training.

Sometimes, specialized skills can be learned on the job at no cost to the employee. This may be in the form of training for newly hired persons or in the form of retraining for people who have been employed for some time.

Some companies prefer to educate and/or train their employees themselves. This allows the employers to give their employees the specific type of training they want them to have. When you are deciding about further

Skills in auto mechanics can lead to jobs.

education and/or looking for a job, you may want to consider a company that provides education and training.

An **apprenticeship** is a method by which a worker can learn a specific trade from one or more experienced workers. Carpenters, plumbers, and electricians often serve apprenticeships. In some states, people employed in these trades must serve apprenticeships before they can become licensed to work by themselves legally.

Special courses of study, one- and two-year vocational and technical programs, four-year college programs, and advanced study beyond college are other ways to receive the specialized knowledge and skills necessary for certain jobs. These means of gaining

Using the classified section of the newspaper is one way to find a job. What other resources are available to you?

knowledge and skills can be expensive, depending on the length of the course of study, the particular school or college, and the type of training provided.

## For Review

1. List and describe three basic skills needed for most jobs.
2. Explain how an apprenticeship can help you to learn specific job skills.
3. How can you find out more about jobs that interest you?

## Finding a Job

You may or may not have a part-time job now. Perhaps you are planning to look for a job soon. If you can manage a part-time job during the school year, your employer often will give you additional work during summer vacation if you want it and if you have performed your job well.

Many of the procedures involved in looking for and finding a job now are the same as they will be when you are older. These procedures, or steps, include locating sources to use to find a job, making out applications, and being interviewed.

### Using Job Sources

Advertisements in the classifed section of your newspaper are an important source of job listings and descriptions. Often, the salaries offered and hours needed are included in these advertisements, as well as the location of the job. You can eliminate many positions or circle those that interest you. Sometimes, part-time or temporary jobs are posted in the windows of businesses needing help. Sometimes your family members, friends, and acquaintances are the most valuable sources of job information you have. This is because they know you and the type of work or workplace you might enjoy. Often they hear about job openings that are not advertised in the newspaper and will tell you about them. Sometimes they may already work for a business that is planning to hire more employees. They may recommend you personally to the employer if you decide to try for the job. This can be especially helpful when you are trying to find your first job.

Employment agencies are another source of job information. There are public employment agencies that offer free services. These include state and government agencies. Private employment agencies are also available. You may want to check to see if a fee is required of you, the job-seeker. Usually, the fee is paid by the company that is looking for the employee.

## Filling Out an Application

Most employers ask anyone who is interested in working for them to fill out an application form. If there are immediate openings, this information is used to make a decision. If there are no immediate openings, the information is on file for the future.

If you find a job advertised in the newspaper or find out about one from someone else, you may be able to call the employer to ask for more information and to have an application sent to you. If you have questions, you may want to prepare them ahead of time, so you do not forget to ask for the information you need. If you know the name of the person to talk to about a job, ask for that specific person when you place your call. Otherwise, tell the individual answering the telephone your name and the purpose of your call. That person will help you reach the appropriate person.

Often for part-time or temporary work, you can go directly to the business to fill out an application form and find out what you want to

Why must every working person have a Social Security card and number?

know. Be sure to look neat and clean. Being well-groomed and neatly dressed will make a good impression on a potential employer.

Fill out your application form as accurately, honestly, and neatly as possible. In addition to using the information you provide, employers frequently judge you by the appearance of your application form.

**Social Security Card** If you do not have a Social Security card with your Social Security number on it, call your nearest Social Security office and ask what you will need to apply for your card. You need a Social Security number in order to be placed on the payroll where you are working. The U.S. government records all of your earnings under your Social Security number. Any Social Security benefits owed to you or your family when you retire, are disabled, or die are based on this system.

**Resumes** A **resume** is a written work history. If you are applying for your first job, you will not have anything to write about. As you have more work experiences, you will be able to list them on a formal resume. Sometimes for your first job, it is helpful to think about informal experiences you may have had that would make you more valuable as an employee. Suppose, for example, that you are applying for a job with a town or city recreation department.

Sometimes you can attend job fairs and fill out preliminary applications.

The job involves caring for young children and teaching them simple arts and crafts. Your prospective employer may be interested in knowing that you have younger brothers and sisters and have had several years of babysitting experience. Although this may not be enough information for a formal resume, it is worth telling your potential employer either on the application itself or during the course of your interview.

## Going On a Job Interview

Sometimes for part-time and temporary work, an interview may be combined with filling out an application. Sometimes, you may be asked to come for an interview after the potential employer has reviewed your application. If you are going for a formal interview, be sure you know the exact date, time, and location of the interview. It will not make a good impression if you arrive late.

***At the Interview*** Dress neatly and appropriately for the interview. Although you may want moral support, do not take anyone with you while you are being interviewed. Your manners will reveal a lot about your behavior. Be courteous and avoid interrupting the interviewer. It is a good idea not to chew gum or smoke during the interview.

You may want to have a few questions in mind to ask the interviewer. Knowing something about the business or company shows that you are interested enough in the position to do a little "homework." Your potential employer will ask you a number of questions, some of which probably will be related to any other work experience you may have had. If you haven't worked before, this is the time to provide relevant information about other experiences, such as managing a sports team or organizing a class activity or being class treasurer or teaching a class for a local youth group. You may be asked why you want the job and/or why you want to work for that particular employer. Even though your major reason for working may be "to earn money," try to focus your answer on the value of the experience you expect to gain and/or ways you feel the business can benefit from having you. Be positive in your comments about the business or company.

During the interview, speak clearly, not too loudly or too softly, so the interviewer can understand you. You will want to give your answers some thought, but avoid taking too long to answer or speaking too slowly.

If information about pay, hours, time off, and sick time, is not given, ask about it. You need this information in order to make a decision about the job.

**After the Interview** You may be offered a job before you leave the interview. Unless you are positive you want the job, ask for a short period of time to think it over. You may want to discuss certain aspects of the job with your parents or another adult. You may have other jobs you are considering. Thank the interviewer for his or her time and tell him when you will have made a decision.

If the person who interviews you says that he or she will get back to you in a few days, you both have some time to think about the situation. Once again, be sure to thank the interviewer for his or her time.

In many instances, a brief thank-you note to the person who interviewed you is appropriate. The interviewer may appreciate this gesture, which shows that you are a thoughtful person. Sometimes it may help you to get the job.

If you do not get a job, try to find out why if it is possible or practical. Perhaps the person who contacts you will tell you. Perhaps you will not hear from the business or company; many businesses use this method of letting people know they are not hired. If this happens to you, take a few minutes to evaluate the situation. Were you qualified? Do you think it was your attitude or something you said or did at the interview? Knowing why you did not get a job can help you to learn from the experience. You may be able to use the information the next time you apply for a job.

## For Review

1. What are two good sources to use when you are trying to find a job?
2. Why do you need a Social Security card?
3. What type of questions might be asked during a job interview?

Beginning a new job can be exciting and a little scary. Making sure you understand your duties is a positive way to start.

## Succeeding on the Job

Once you have a job, certain things are expected of you. If you do not perform satisfactorily, you probably will not keep your job. Some aspects of your performance will be related to your specific job. These include special skills or knowledge you are expected to have and to use. Other aspects of your performance are related to certain qualities that employers expect all employees to have.

You, too, have certain expectations about your job and your employer. As you begin to work, you will learn the exact scope of your job and all the duties related to it. These may or may not be what you had expected. You also have expectations about your paycheck, raises, and/or bonuses that may or may not be met.

# Career Resources

You've probably been asked, "What do you want to be when you grow up?" for as long as you can remember. You may recall remarks such as "Look at that sand castle! She'll make a wonderful construction engineer!" or "What long fingers! He's going to be a concert pianist!" Predictions like these don't have a great success rate. How can you find out what career would be satisfying to you for many years rather than for just a few hours in the sandbox?

One place to look for some answers is in your school guidance office. Among the resources they may have to aid you are **interest inventories,** or tests that help you evaluate your interests in an organized way. Some inventories ask you to evaluate different activities on a sliding scale from *dislike* through *indifferent* to *like*. In others, each question asks your preference among several different activities. These tests yield an *interest profile,* comparing your choices to an overall sample and to those of people who are satisfied with particular career choices or college majors.

Some guidance offices have **computer-assisted career searches,** or software programs that you can use independently. Some yield interest profiles; others search out college programs or other training for particular occupations. **Printed materials,** including books, pamphlets, catalogs, and occupational briefs and monographs, deal with interest areas and specific occupations. There are also career guides, such as the *Occupational Outlook Handbook* put out by the U.S. Department of Labor, and guides to what colleges offer particular majors. Many schools also offer **career-focus programs** in which adults who work in different fields are invited to speak to students about their careers. Your guidance counselor can offer invaluable advice and help you to find and use these and other materials.

## Employer Expectations

All employers expect you to have good work habits, including being punctual. Employers also expect you to perform the job and its duties to the best of your ability. They expect you to use the knowledge and skills you have and/or to learn new skills for the job. Employers expect you to follow the special rules or policies of the business or company. A final and important expectation is that you will display certain positive personality characteristics.

**Work Habits** There are some things that employers expect their workers to do without being told or reminded. These include being on time to work, working the number of hours agreed upon, taking only the amount of time that is allowed for coffee break and lunch, spending work time working, not goofing off or talking with friends, and working conscientiously to do a good job.

Although you may see other employees who do not seem to be working hard or who take more work breaks than they are allowed, you should realize that you are responsible for the impression you make. Be conscientious and try to develop good work habits despite what others may do. Employers usually know who is working hard and who is not. If you work hard, you will have the satisfaction of knowing that you have done your best. Your employer may reward you with a raise or bonus. If you have worked hard and you leave the job to find another one, you can be confident that you will receive a good recommendation from your former employer.

**Knowledge and Skills** You may have been hired because you possess certain specialized knowledge and skills. You may have been hired because you have indicated a willingness and the ability to acquire special knowledge and skills. Your employer expects you to use what you already know and to learn any new skills

that the job requires. At work, performance is what counts. Trying hard is important, but in the end, it is whether or not you are able to do what you are supposed to do that keeps you on a job.

When you begin a job, find out just what your employer expects you to do. You need to

### Practical Tip: Personal References

■ When you look for a job, you may need personal references. Ask teachers, neighbors, and counselors if they would be willing to give you a reference. Keep a list of the people who agree. Contact them if you do use their names. Be sure to thank them for their help.

Arriving on time for work is behavior employers expect from employees.

know what his or her standards for performance are. Standards, remember, are guidelines for measuring the level of quality or progress toward reaching a goal. If, for example, you are supposed to clean up after all the customers have gone, you need to know what specific tasks are involved in cleaning up, the procedures you are expected to follow to carry out those tasks, and what the finished appearance is supposed to be.

If you are receiving on-the-job training, find out how quickly you are expected to progress and when you will be expected to have full responsibility for using the information and skills you are learning. Knowing this can prevent misunderstandings that may be caused by your trying to take on too much responsibility too soon or by not progressing as quickly as your employer expects.

Be willing to ask questions about aspects of the job you do not understand, but think about the situation first so that you do not always ask questions that have obvious answers. Most employers would rather have their workers ask questions than to work with too little information or to make incorrect assumptions.

**Work Policies**  Work policies are rules set by a business or employer that are related to work safety, efficiency, and standards. There are policies related to missing time at work due to personal emergencies or illness. There are policies you must follow if a job-related accident occurs. There may be certain rules of dress or conduct that you are expected to follow. Some places of employment do not allow smoking or restrict smoking to certain designated areas.

All of these work policies should be fully understood for good employer-employee relations. There may be an orientation period when you first begin a job that includes an explanation of all work policies. If this does not occur, read all the company literature you have received so that you will know about any work policies. Ask your employer directly if you have any questions about rules or procedures.

**Personal Characteristics**  Certain personal characteristics are beneficial in getting and keeping a job. These include a positive self-concept, a positive attitude, a willingness to listen and learn, an ability to work with other people, reliability, responsibility, trustworthiness, self-discipline, and a neat, clean personal appearance.

As you learned in Chapter 2, a positive self-concept gives you self-confidence. You do not feel threatened when others offer suggestions. You are not uncomfortable asking questions about things you do not know. You feel sure about your ability to do the job you are supposed to do. Self-confidence will help you to present a good image of your employer and his or her business. Your self-confidence will help customers to feel confident about the business and the products.

A positive attitude makes you cheerful and pleasant to be around. It can help other

A pleasant work attitude goes a long way.

workers to develop a more positive attitude and to present a good image of the business to customers. It can make work seem easier and go faster. It also helps to promote greater cooperation among workers.

When you are willing to listen and learn from others, you are showing interest in the job. You are not afraid to try a new or different way of doing things. You are eager to learn from the experiences of others. A willingness to learn means that you are not afraid to ask questions. You take the time and make the effort to think about different situations and relate them to the work you are doing.

The ability to work with other people and to get along with them is important to almost every job. It means that you are willing to share ideas and responsibilities for successes as well as failures. When workers are cooperative, it is easier to get more work done.

Reliability means that you are dependable. You do what you say you will do. You carry out your responsibilities without being reminded. Being responsible means that you accept the tasks you are expected to do and do them as expected. Being dependable or reliable is a part of being a responsible person. It also means that you accept the consequences of any actions you take.

When you are trustworthy, you keep confidential information to yourself. You do not spread rumors or say things that are not true. You do what you are supposed to do, even when no one is watching you. You deal with your employer, your co-workers, and the customers in honest ways.

Self-discipline means that you control the things you do and say. You get yourself to work on time. You make yourself go to work when you are tempted not to. You continue working even when you are tired or when it would be easy to stop and talk with others. You avoid saying things that might make someone angry or upset, and you avoid losing your temper

A neat appearance and good communication skills are helpful on any job.

when someone makes you angry. You resist talking about your employer and/or co-workers in a negative way. Self-discipline helps you do the right thing for the situation you are in.

A neat, clean appearance includes having clean hair that is combed or brushed in a becoming style. It means having a clean body that is free from odor and clean clothes that are in good repair. It also means having clean teeth and an absence of bad breath. A neat, clean appearance says that you care about yourself and your job.

## Employee Expectations

You, as the employee, also have certain expectations when you begin a job. These include expectations about job duties and opportunities, working conditions, paychecks, and any other job benefits. Some of your

| EMERSON ENTERPRISES | | DAYTON, SADIE 0179 0000000318 | | | TAXES/DEDUCTIONS | YEAR TO DATE |
|---|---|---|---|---|---|---|
| | | | FEDERAL TAX | | 63 | 63 |
| | | | FICA | | 129 | 129 |
| | | | MASSACHUSETTS | | 86 | 86 |
| DESCRIPTION | RATE | HOURS | EARNINGS | YEAR TO DATE | | |
| REGULAR EARNING | | 475 | 1805 | 1805 | | |

| | EARNINGS | TAXES | DEDUCTIONS | NET PAY | PAY PERIOD | CHECK NUMBER | AMOUNT OF CHECK |
|---|---|---|---|---|---|---|---|
| CURRENT | 1805 | 278 | 00 | 1527 | BEGIN | 7327823 | 1527 |
| YEAR TO DATE | 1805 | 278 | | 1527 | END 12-28-86 | | |

Being aware of deduction amounts will avoid disappointment with your paycheck.

expectations may be idealistic when you begin your first job. You are less likely to be disappointed in some aspects of your work situation if you look closely at each of your expectations before you take the job. Don't forget that you can learn a lot by dealing with work-related problems or disappointments as they occur. You may come to realize that your expectations were unrealistic or that you misunderstood some information when you accepted the job. On the other hand, you may have been promised something that did not happen once you took the job. In either case, handling the situation and taking the appropriate steps to resolve issues as smoothly as possible will help you to improve your life management skills.

**Job Duties and Opportunities** You should expect some surprises when you begin a job. There may be a few additional duties that you are asked to perform. If these duties are not too unrelated to your job, and if you can learn new skills by doing them, it is usually a good idea to accept them. If they do not seem related to your job at all, you should question

them. Talk to your employer if you are asked to do many things that you did not agree to do when you accepted the job. There is a difference between being willing and cooperative and being taken advantage of. Small concerns that are not discussed sometimes grow into larger problems.

You have the right to expect the opportunities for advancement that you deserve. These opportunities may have been discussed or "promised" during your interview. If your employer told you that you would advance to a better position or receive a raise after six months, be sure to follow up on this. Perhaps you were told you would receive valuable training after three months on the job. Although these opportunities may depend on the recommendations of a supervisor, you have a right to expect them if you have worked hard and met specific employer expectations.

**Working Conditions** Your work environment includes your individual work area, any restrooms, lounges or locker areas, and any cafeteria or eating place within your workplace. You should expect these areas to be clean, safe, and healthy.

**Your Paycheck** Unless the circumstances are unusual, you will not receive all the money you earn when you receive your paycheck.

Money will be deducted from your check to pay taxes. Seeing the difference between what you earn and what you receive may be a shock if you are not aware of the deductions that will be made. If you ask your employer what deductions will be made and how much they will be, you will know what to expect. The illustration on page 136 shows a sample paycheck and some deductions that may be made. Keep in mind that paychecks for different people and from different employers are not always the same.

Deductions for social security and federal income tax are required by law. State income tax is deducted in some states to help support state governments. Local taxes also may be deducted, depending on where you live.

When you begin to work you will be asked to complete and sign a W-4 form. A **W-4 form** authorizes an employer to deduct a specific amount of federal income tax from an employee's paycheck for each pay period. You will have a chance to claim a tax exemption for yourself. If you do this, less money will be withheld from your paycheck. Ask for information about this before signing your W-4 form. If you earn less than $3,500 a year (according to existing tax laws), you will receive a refund for all federal taxes deducted after you have filed your income tax return for that year.

Other deductions are called *voluntary* deductions. This means that you, as the employee, have asked for them. You may have authorized these deductions to pay for a group insurance policy or stock or U.S. Savings Bonds. You may have decided to have some earnings put into a savings account or put toward repaying a loan.

Knowing how much money will be deducted from your paycheck can help you to plan your finances more accurately. After a few paychecks, you will know exactly what your take-home pay will be in future pay periods.

**Benefits** Common benefits for full-time employees include vacation time and the right to join group insurance, retirement, and investment plans. Life, health, and dental insurance sometimes are offered at a more reasonable rate through a company than you would pay as an individual. Disability insurance may be available. This type of insurance provides you with some income during a long illness or during recuperation from an injury that keeps you from working. Day care for children is another possible employee benefit.

As a part-time employee, you may not be entitled to many of these benefits. You may receive other benefits, however, such as a clothing discount if you are an employee of a clothing store. If you work at a restaurant, you may receive the benefit of a free meal when you work.

Although you cannot expect all of these benefits, you should ask about them when you are looking for a full-time job. A company's benefit "package" can be an important factor in your decision to take or refuse a job.

An employee discount on store products can be a valuable benefit.

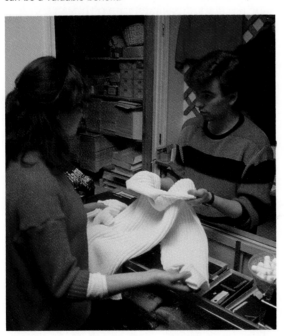

Being willing to learn and acquire new skills can lead to a better job.

## Making Job/Career Changes

Even when people are well qualified for a particular job, there may not be enough openings for everyone. Sometimes, people may be laid off from work or let go by an employer for a variety of reasons. Sometimes jobs become boring or promotions that were hoped for don't happen. Sometimes an opportunity arises that seems ideal, but it was not part of a career plan. These types of situations force people to evaluate their situations. They must either adjust to change or initiate change to keep their lives moving in the direction they want.

Like all plans, career plans need to be checked frequently in relation to your values, goals, and resources. If a plan is not leading to your goal, you need to alter it. If your marriage or family plan or situation changes, you may have to make some adjustments in your career plans to balance goals for family life with career goals.

A layoff or accident can upset the best-made career plans. When people dwell on these events and resist taking actions to find other jobs or to be retrained, they can be without work. After long periods of time, this affects their self-concept and their relationships with others, to say nothing of their hopes and dreams for the future. Taking action to adjust to the circumstances helps to keep your life headed in a positive direction.

Fear of the unknown or of doing something different stops some people from changing their careers when they are not happy with them. Some people will stay with a job, hoping for a promotion that never comes. Perhaps this is the best thing for some of them to do, but perhaps others should act to make some changes in their lives. They will never know unless they explore some alternatives. Maybe they can get a better job or a job that is more personally satisfying with another employer. Perhaps, with some thought, they can create new jobs with their present employers that are more satisfying to them and will help their employers run their businesses more efficiently or effectively.

Some career changes involve more risk than others. Changing from one employer to another does not usually involve a great deal of risk. Switching from working for someone else to running your own business involves a higher degree of risk. Although the amount of risk involved may be a factor in your decision, it should not prevent you from exploring other alternatives.

## For Review

1. What are some of the work habits that an employer expects you to have?
2. What are the paycheck deductions that are required by law? List three possible voluntary deductions.
3. What events might force an employee to change jobs?

## Management Application: Working Out a Job Problem

Imagine yourself in the situation described below. As you read, think about how the steps of the management process might apply to this situation. Then answer the questions that follow.

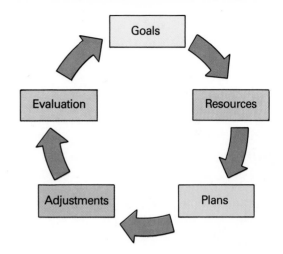

### Situation

Rose really enjoyed her part-time job at the bookstore, which she had held for a year. There was just one problem. The new evening manager, Mr. Casey, was always grouchy and seemed to be picking on her. He seemed to be expecting her to make mistakes. He was always looking over her shoulder when she rang up sales on the cash register. He made her so nervous that she found herself making silly errors. He was treating her as if she were a new employee. He assumed she needed all of the basic procedures explained to her when she didn't. Something had to be done and soon because she was so uncomfortable. Rose decided that the best way to handle the situation was to make an appointment to speak to Mr. Casey.

Although she was nervous, Rose told Mr. Casey how she felt. She explained that she liked her job and didn't want to leave, but she was upset by his lack of confidence. She told him about the added responsibilities she had taken on since she had started, including locking up on occasion. She added that she had not had problems with other employers and that she hoped they could work things out. She then asked if he had any questions about what she was doing.

Mr. Casey appeared to be surprised by everything Rose was saying. Rose found out why. He told her that he had confused her with several of the new employees. He didn't know that she had been working for a year and knew all the store procedures. He said he was glad that she had spoken up and cleared up the misunderstanding. He admitted that he was a little anxious about doing a good job himself and that he still had a lot to learn. He said he was impressed with her communication skills and told her he would recommend a raise for her within the next several weeks.

### Questions

1. What was Rose's main goal?
2. What human resources did Rose need to discuss the problem with Mr. Casey?
3. How did she carry out her plan?
4. How important are communication skills in this situation?
5. Which steps of the management process apply to this situation?

# 6 Chapter Review

## Summary

To find out about jobs that will suit your needs and wants, explore different careers, evaluate your skills and talents, and try to get job experience in areas of interest. Most jobs require social, communication, and mathematics skills. The steps for finding a job include using job sources, making out applications, and going on interviews.

Once on the job, you may be more successful if you have good work habits and a positive attitude. In order to meet your employer's expectations, you should know what all the duties related to your job are. Your job expectations also should be realistic and include knowing about paycheck deductions.

## Vocabulary

Use the vocabulary words below to complete the following paragraph.

apprenticeship

resume

work policies

W-4 form

Jack has always loved building things. For many summers he helped his father and mother make improvements on their house. This summer Jack has a(n) __(1)__ with a local carpenter, who will be teaching Jack new skills. Jack got the job by sending in his __(2)__ , which explained the different types of carpentry jobs he had done for his family and friends. Today he received a booklet with the __(3)__ , including all the rules and requirements having to do with safety and standards set by the carpenter's company. Jack will also have to fill out a __(4)__ , so that his employer can deduct taxes from his paycheck this summer.

## Questions

1. What are some of the reasons for people to work?

2. How does a person's stage in life affect his or her work decisions?

3. What is the value of taking a temporary or part-time job?

4. What are some ways of learning about different career alternatives?

5. How can you acquire specialized knowledge and skills for a job?

6. What are the three basic steps in looking for and finding a job?

7. What is a benefit package? How can it be important when you are deciding whether or not to take a job?

8. What can you do to show a prospective employer that you are interested in a job?

9. What can you do when you begin a job to help make sure your employer will be happy with your performance?

10. What are some sources to use when looking for job openings?

11. What personal characteristics will probably help you to be successful at work?

12. Why might an individual sometimes choose to change jobs?

## Skill Activities

**1. Critical Thinking.** What type of job would you enjoy? Evaluating your resources and talents is a good way to start thinking about careers. Refer to the section "Evaluate Your Resources and Talents" on page 125 in this chapter. Write a series of ten questions to help you evaluate your interests and skills.

Share your list with classmates. Develop a comprehensive evaluation sheet that will include all the different kinds of questions generated by your class. Make copies of this if possible for each member of the class.

**2. Critical Thinking.** Make a list of three careers that you have some interest in finding out about, and investigate one of the careers. Do research in the library, speak to a guidance counselor, and/or discuss the job with someone already working in your special field of interest.

Write a short paper about the career or job. Make sure that you have found out all the basic information about the job and that you can answer these questions: What responsibilities would you have on this job? What specialized skills are required? What special training or education is needed? What is the cost of the training? What are the prospects for employment in this field in the future? What are the opportunities for advancement?

**3. Communication.** Plan, as a class, a career fair. Make up several displays to illustrate the jobs chosen for Exercise 2. Prepare a list of questions and invite speakers to discuss their jobs. Then develop resumes. Create a career bulletin board using information learned from the fair.

**4. Human Relations.** Stage a mock (pretend) job interview for an after-school or summer job situation that you would be interested in getting. As a class, select four or five jobs that you would like to have. Choose an interviewer for each position. Take turns as the person seeking employment and as the interviewer. Help each other by giving constructive criticism on answers to the interviewer's questions. Also, critique the body language of both the interviewer and the prospective employee.

Record questions of the employer and answers of the prospective employee that you think are particularly good. By sharing this information, you may be better prepared when you face your next real interview situation.

# 7

# Making a Financial Plan

## As you read, think about:

- how to make a realistic budget, based on your personal financial plan.
- how to use your budget by balancing income against expenses.
- how to establish a checking account.
- how to understand the types of taxes.
- how to file income taxes.
- how to apply the management process to personal decisions about your money resources.

# Vocabulary

personal financial plan
income
budget
fixed expenses
flexible expenses
gross pay
net pay
interest
tax
income tax

Everyone has certain needs and wants that only money can provide. You can satisfy more of these needs and wants if you learn how to manage your money wisely. Making a realistic budget and using it are the first steps toward good money management. Learning about checking accounts and income taxes will also give you a clearer understanding of money issues and how they affect you.

## Deciding on Your Personal Financial Plan

Do you sometimes wonder where your money goes? Having a personal financial plan will help you to keep track of your money. A **personal financial plan** is a plan for the use of your income. **Income** is the gain, usually measured in money, that comes from a variety of sources. A personal financial plan is an individual plan that is based on your situation, your goals, and your resources, including your income. This plan will include what you spend, save, and invest. Chapter 8 includes specific information about savings accounts, credit, and investments.

What is money? Money is anything that people agree can be used in payment for goods, services, or debts. Early American settlers found the Indians using wampum, or shell beads, as money. In other times and in other places, clay tablets, stones, tobacco, and salt have been used for money. Today, coins and paper are used as money in this country. Credit cards often are referred to as "plastic money" because they, too, can be used to purchase many goods and services. Checks are still another form of money.

Today, credit cards can be used to pay for anything from medicines to vacations.

Before you create your own personal financial plan, you need to set financial goals to determine what you want your income to do for you. How you use your money will be based on these goals.

## Setting Financial Goals

Perhaps you get an allowance from your parents but do not have a paying job. Perhaps you earn money for doing chores at home or for other people. Maybe you babysit for one or more families, or maybe you have a part-time job and receive a regular paycheck. Sometimes you may receive income from gifts or other sources. No matter what your source of income is or how much or how little it is, you probably wish you had more. For most people, no matter what their income is, wants and needs expand to use it all.

Although you may or may not be able to increase your income, with some effort, you can make the income you have work harder for you. Setting some financial goals is the first step.

***Your Needs, Wants, and Values*** How many things have you bought recently that are truly needs? How many are wants? Are you satisfied with the way in which you have spent your money? Do you have other needs and wants that you are not sure you can meet? Are your spending decisions based on your values?

If you are satisfied with how you have used your money and how it is working for you, and if you know how you are going to meet future needs and wants, you probably already know what is of value to you and what is not. You may have a plan, either in your head or written down, that you follow.

If you are not satisfied with how you have spent your money, and if you have needs and wants that you cannot meet, you probably need to set some priorities. To do this, you will have to think about your needs, wants, and values. You must then decide which ones are important, which ones are less important, which ones are least important, and which ones really do not matter at all.

***Timing*** Many times, you can divide your financial goals into three categories: short-term goals, medium-term goals, and long-term goals. Perhaps you will need money for special courses or tuition in a year or two. Perhaps you need money for the prom in a month or two. Maybe you need money to make it through the week without borrowing. As you study your list of priorities, you may want to see if you can separate them into these time categories. Frequently, a time factor relates your goals to each other. As you begin to formulate your financial plan, you need to consider the relationship between your goals. Making a plan that meets only short-term goals may mean you cannot meet long-term goals.

## Changing Influences on Financial Goals

Your financial priorities may change as a result of outside forces or because your needs, wants, and values have changed. As you reach one financial goal, often it is replaced with another. Your statement of financial goals will evolve over time. It is not etched in stone.

Many factors affect your financial goals at different times. These factors include your stage in the life cycle, your marital status, and your income. As these factors change throughout your life, your financial goals also change to accommodate them.

***Stage in Life Cycle*** As you grow, you develop different needs, wants, responsibilities, and income levels, all of which influence your financial goals. For example, as a high-school student, you may not have total responsibility for meeting your everyday needs for food, clothing, and shelter. Your financial goals may focus on increasing your personal possessions and saving for further education or future independence. A young couple with small children may be working toward buying a home, having adequate life and health insurance, and building a financial plan that will allow them to save money for their children's education. A middle-aged person may be focusing on investments to insure adequate income for retirement.

***Financial Responsibilities*** Single and married people with no dependents usually have fewer financial responsibilities than single or married people who are responsible for supporting one or more persons. They have more freedom to choose what they do with their money. Their financial goals can be based on meeting their own needs and wants rather than the needs and wants of others in addition to their own.

***Income*** A limited income puts restraints on financial goals that a higher income does not.

## TOM'S FINANCIAL GOALS (AGE: 17)

| SHORT-TERM GOALS | MEDIUM-TERM GOALS | LONG-TERM GOALS |
|---|---|---|
| • To go to the movies this week | • To buy a camera next month | • To save for the class trip one year from now |
| • To buy lunch every day this week | • To buy my sister a graduation present | • To make a down payment on a car in six months |
| • To purchase a jacket at the sale this Thursday | • To get a new pair of running shoes during the next six weeks | • To buy a typewriter to use in college |

The greater the financial responsibilities of an individual or a couple, the more strain on income. In these circumstances, financial goals may have to focus on meeting everyday living needs. Long-range financial goals may not be possible.

People with job training usually increase their income as they work. An increase in income makes it possible to expand financial goals. Income that does not have to be used to meet daily needs can be put into savings, used to increase personal net worth, invested, or used in retirement plans to provide income later in life.

## For Review

1. Why is it important to have a personal financial plan?
2. Give an example of a short-term financial goal you might have.
3. Describe how stages in the life cycle can affect your financial goals.

## Making A Budget

A **budget** is an estimate of income and expenses for a fixed period of time. It is an important part of your personal financial plan, which is based on your goals.

If you want to succeed in making and using a budget, try not to think of it as a one-time project or a rigid, inflexible spending plan that controls your every move. Budgeting is a process; that is, it is something that changes over time. It is a guideline, not a law. You have control over what it includes; it is only as flexible as you make it. Since it is only an estimate based on the information you have at the time you put together the figures, it needs to change when your information changes.

Usually a budget is based on a fixed period of time, such as a week, two weeks, a month, or a year. If you have never before developed a budget, you may find it easier to start with a short period of time. If you receive a paycheck or an allowance every week, you may find it easier to develop a weekly budget. If you receive income every two weeks or every month, you may want to develop a budget for

Why is it a good idea for couples to set financial goals and a budget together?

# TYPES OF EXPENSES

| FIXED EXPENSES | FLEXIBLE EXPENSES |
|---|---|
| • housing payments | • food |
| • property taxes | • clothing |
| • estimated income taxes | • household furnishings |
| • basic telephone service | • home improvements |
| • fuel payments | • cleaning supplies |
| • trash pickup | • household items |
| • cable television service | • babysitting |
| • installment payments | • hired household help |
| • insurance payments | • gifts |
| • tuition payments | • charitable contributions |
| • room and board charges | • automobile upkeep |
| • membership dues | • health care |
| • lessons | • personal grooming |
| • subscriptions | • dry cleaning |
| • commuting fare | • entertainment |
| • parking costs | • recreation and sports |
| • automobile registration | • magazines, newspapers |
| • investments | • savings |

that period of time. If your income is irregular because you babysit or do odd jobs or substitute for your friend at work only occasionally, choose a time period you think will work.

## Identifying Expenses

Your expenses include all of the things you spend your money on. Expenses may be either fixed or flexible. **Fixed expenses** are those expenses that usually do not vary in amount and must be paid for on a regular payment schedule. Mortgage or rent payments are examples of fixed expenses. **Flexible expenses** are expenses that vary from week to week or month to month in type and amount. Examples of these include clothing

and recreation costs. The chart on this page shows other examples of fixed and flexible expenses. Later in life, you will have many expenses that you do not have now.

To start your budget, list all of your expenses over a two-week period. Record everything you spend under the type of expense it is—fixed or flexible. If you are saving any of your income toward a special purchase or in case of an unexpected expense, you should record the amount under a separate category for savings. Now, add up all of your expenses for the two-week period and write down the total amount.

When you have finished adding up your expenses, look at the chart on page 148 and compare the expenses of a high-school student with those of a twenty-three-year-old woman.

## PRESENT AND FUTURE BUDGETS: TWO EXAMPLES

### JANE'S MONTHLY BUDGET (AGE: 16)

| MONTHLY INCOME | | MONTHLY EXPENSES | |
|---|---|---|---|
| Allowance | $40.00 | **Fixed:** | |
| | | Bus fare | $60.00 |
| | | Lunch | 40.00 |
| Part-time | | **Flexible:** | |
| job | 160.00 | Clothing | 30.00 |
| | $200.00 | Entertainment | 25.00 |
| | | Savings | 40.00 |
| | | | $195.00 |
| TOTAL | | TOTAL | |
| MONTHLY | | MONTHLY | |
| INCOME: | $200.00 | EXPENSES: | $195.00 |

### ANN'S MONTHLY BUDGET (AGE: 23)

| MONTHLY INCOME | | MONTHLY EXPENSES | |
|---|---|---|---|
| Salary | $1,500 | **Fixed:** | |
| | | Rent | $700 |
| | | Car loan | 120 |
| | | Gasoline | 60 |
| | | Parking | 80 |
| | | Insurance | 100 |
| | | Telephone | 30 |
| | | SUBTOTAL: | $1,090 |
| | | **Flexible:** | |
| | | Food | 80 |
| | | Clothing | 70 |
| | | Entertainment | 75 |
| | | Health/ | |
| | | Personal care | 50 |
| | | Savings/ | |
| | | Emergency | 50 |
| | | SUBTOTAL: | $325 |
| TOTAL | | TOTAL | $1,090 |
| MONTHLY | | MONTHLY | 325 |
| INCOME: | $1,500 | EXPENSES: | $1,415 |

## Identifying Income

Just as you recorded your expenses for a two-week period, you need to record all your income. This will include any allowance you receive, any gifts, and any pay from babysitting or other part-time jobs. If you are paid by check by a business or company, be sure to record your net pay, not your **gross pay,** or total pay. **Net pay** is the amount you actually receive after any deductions have been made from your gross pay. To find out your total income for the two-week period, add all of these separate income figures together. You can record this figure on your budget sheet under the heading of income.

## Establishing Priorities

Now that you know your typical two-week expenses and income, subtract your expenses from your income. Are your expenses equal to or a little less than your income? If they are, then your budget may not need to be adjusted.

If your expenses are more than your estimated income, you may need to make some adjustments in your priorities. Unless you can work more hours or somehow increase your income, you need to figure out where you can cut back or eliminate expenses. Perhaps you should walk or take public transportation rather than drive. Maybe you should spend a little less for gifts, or maybe you should cut back on a movie or two. You are less likely to have to make more serious cutbacks in the future, such as selling your car because you cannot afford the upkeep or the insurance, if you learn to balance your budget now.

***Consider Timing.*** Some people find the different time schedules for income and expenses difficult to plan for. For example, housing, utilities, and many other payments may be due monthly, while income may be received weekly, every other week, twice a month, or monthly. To prevent financial problems, you need to know what share of monthly payments must come from each paycheck. Suppose Bernard's take-home pay is $475 every other week. Out of this take-home pay, Bernard must plan for his expenses. His share of housing expenses every month is $270; his car payment is $105 every month; his parking expenses are $20 every week; and he has insurance payments of $100 every three months. If you say that a month has approximately 4.4 weeks, Bernard has to save a minimum of $220 out of each paycheck to meet these obligations. He also has to buy food, clothing, and personal care items and be able to meet other expenses. If he does not budget carefully, he may find that he does not have enough money to meet his total expenses.

***Review Financial Goals.*** As you draw up your budget, you may find it helpful to review your estimated expenses and your financial goals. How is each expense going to help you to achieve one or more of your goals? Perhaps some of your expenses are going to get in the way of achieving your financial goals. After you

have considered any adjustments you may need to keep your budget in line with your goals, make them. If you cannot adjust your budget, you may have to postpone or revise some of your financial goals. You may even need to change your original priorities.

## Using a Budget

A budget is not useful if you do not use it. Once you have balanced your budget on paper, you can use the figures as guidelines for your spending. Once again, you will want to keep records of your income and your expenses for several pay periods. Match these records against your estimated income and expenses.

What part of your budget is used for transportation? Can you decrease it?

Did you estimate fairly closely, or are there some problems? If you are like most people, you will need to make some adjustments. You may find that you have allowed too much for some things and not enough for others. You may find that you just cannot afford certain things or cannot save as much as you planned. As you use your budget, you will see what changes should be made in it.

After you have made adjustments in your budget figures, try using the revised budget as the basis for your money management. If it works better, you are on the right track. You may or may not want to make further adjustments and refinements.

If you are realistic in your estimates of income and expenditures, your budget should be fairly accurate after two or three revisions.

If it is still not working, perhaps you are not being realistic in your estimates, or perhaps you are having problems with self-discipline. When it is time to make decisions about money, *you* are the one in charge. You have to control your actions. Your budget can be a valuable tool for wise money management, but it cannot control your actions.

## For Review

1. Explain the difference between fixed expenses and flexible expenses. Give two examples of each.
2. What are your sources of income?
3. What factors may require a change in your budget?

What are some of the advantages of having your own checking account?

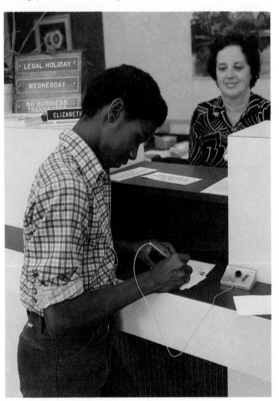

## Establishing a Checking Account

Checking accounts are among the most commonly used bank services. A checking account is a demand account; that is, the account holder has immediate access to the funds in his or her account. Funds can be withdrawn from the account at any time by writing a check, which is a written order that directs the bank to pay money as instructed.

There are many advantages to having a checking account. If you have one, you do not have to carry large amounts of money with you. You can pay for the goods and services you need by writing a personal check. Your account will provide you with a record of expenses and proof that a bill has been paid. Since some financial institutions will not cash checks unless a person has an account with them, a checking account will make it easier for you to cash checks. It also is easier to write checks and mail them to pay bills than it is to take cash to each of the persons or businesses owed money. Finally, a well-managed checking account can help you when you are applying for some forms of credit.

## Selecting a Checking Account

There are many types of checking accounts. After you have done some comparison shopping, you will want to select the one that best suits your needs. Regular checking accounts, NOW and SuperNOW accounts, Money Market Deposit Accounts, and share draft accounts are among the different types of checking accounts you will want to learn about before you make your decision.

**Regular Checking Accounts** Regular checking accounts pay no interest. **Interest** is income you earn on your own money when a bank lends it to others. Some banks require a minimum deposit to open a regular checking account and may insist that you maintain a minimum balance in the account. Usually there is no limit to the number of checks you can write and the number of withdrawals and deposits you can make, although there may be a monthly service charge, a charge for each check handled, and a charge for each deposit. Some banks waive the service charge if certain conditions are met, such as a minimum amount in a savings account. Service charges and check charges vary a great deal from financial institution to financial institution.

To use a checking account, you need checks. These are commonly available in books of fifty and are ordered through the bank that holds the account. Occasionally, checks are provided free of charge, but usually you are charged for them.

**NOW (Negotiable Order of Withdrawal) Accounts** Like checking accounts, NOW

Learn about the advantages of various checking accounts before you choose one.

accounts are demand accounts. Transactions are made in the same way that they are in regular checking accounts. Unlike checking accounts, however, NOW accounts pay interest to the account holder when certain conditions are met.

The interest rate on NOW accounts is set by the bank. Most banks require a fairly high minimum balance for this type of account to earn interest. Some banks are willing to waive the monthly service charge or charge for handling checks as long as the balance does not drop below the minimum required. The conditions for earning interest and waiving charges vary among financial institutions.

NOW accounts usually pay a lower interest rate than some types of savings accounts. If you are thinking of opening a NOW account, you may want to compare the costs of a NOW account with the costs of a regular checking account plus a savings account.

**SuperNOW Accounts** SuperNOW accounts are NOW accounts that pay a higher interest rate in return for a higher minimum balance. There are no restrictions on the number of transactions allowed in a month. The conditions for earning interest and waiving charges vary from bank to bank. SuperNOW accounts sometimes are also known as money market checking accounts.

**Money Market Deposit Accounts (MMDAs)** MMDA accounts pay the highest interest of any account on which checks are written. They are not true demand accounts, however, and are not substitutes for regular or NOW checking accounts. There are strict limitations on the number of checks that can be written (three) each month, as well as the number of preauthorized transfers (such as automatic payments) that can be made.

Some people use MMDA accounts as savings accounts. By writing one or two checks each month to deposit money in a regular or NOW checking account, they can cover the checks normally written to pay expenses.

**Share Draft Accounts** Share draft accounts are offered by credit unions. They are similar to the NOW accounts offered by banks, although there may not be a minimum balance requirement. The monthly service and check charges for share draft accounts often are lower than the charges on similar accounts at banks.

## Getting Checking Account Information

If you do not have a checking account or share draft account and would like to have one, you may want to call or visit banks near you for information on the different types of checking accounts available. If you have access to a credit union, it can supply the information you want on its share draft account.

To find out what type of account is best for you, you may want to talk with representatives of each financial institution. Explain how much money may be involved in the account, how many checks you are likely to write, and how frequently you will make deposits and withdrawals. It is a good idea to compare the costs of the different accounts at different banks. Keep in mind that some banks offer free checking if you meet certain requirements. If you are still unsure about a checking or share draft account, ask about other options.

## Opening Your Checking Account

Once you have decided on the type of account you want and where you will open it, you can begin the process of opening it. A representative at the financial institution you have chosen will help you. The first step is to fill out a signature card. The signature card is the bank's record of your signature, and the signature on it is the only signature that can be used legally to sign checks written on your account.

The card needs your name and address, your signature, and perhaps your social security number. You should sign it in the same way that you will sign your checks. When you open the account, the bank will assign you an account number and will put it on your signature card.

Obviously, opening a checking or share draft account requires money. If you have cash, the representative from the financial institution will take it and credit it to your account. If you are using a paycheck or other check, the representative will tell you how to endorse, or sign, it so that the money can be credited to your account.

After you have opened the account, you will have to order checks. Usually there is a minimum order of 200. You will find that there

What factors determine how expensive personal checks will be?

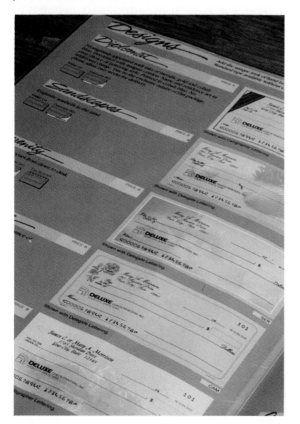

are many different styles of checks and checkbook covers from which to choose. Some banks offer checks free of charge with certain types of accounts. Otherwise, the costs range from moderate to expensive. You will be given some temporary checks to use until you receive the ones you order.

There are several things to think about when you are ordering checks. One factor is how much money you want to spend on them. Another factor is how much information you want printed on them. Some free checks and some inexpensive checks may have just the name of the account holder and the account number. The account holder then has to number each check and provide the correct address and telephone number if it is requested by the person to whom the check is written. For extra money, checks can be printed with this information. To many people, the convenience is worth the cost. Usually, the style of the check, checkbook, and check register determines the cost. Checks in color or with a special style of type or special designs are more expensive, as are special check registers and checkbook covers. The cost for the checks will be deducted from your account balance.

## Writing Checks

Checks must be made out properly for the person or business to whom the check is written to collect the money. Properly written checks also lessen the chance of tampering with the check after it is written.

If you make a mistake when writing a check, do not try to correct it because it may make it look as if the check has been tampered with. The bank has no way of knowing that you made the correction, and the person to whom it is made out may not be able to cash it. Instead, write the word VOID in large letters across the check and put it in your file of cancelled checks. Then write a new check. Use permanent ink to make out any checks. Writing in pencil or in erasable ink makes it possible for someone to change what you have written.

As you write each check, record the information in your check register and subtract the amount from your balance. This way you will avoid overdrawing your account. You will have a record of your purchases, and you will know how much you have left.

## Endorsing Checks

When you make out a check to someone else, it cannot be cashed until that person endorses it. The same is true for you. You must endorse checks made out to you that you want to cash, to deposit in an account, or to use to pay someone else. Your endorsement should be written on the back of the check and across the end that has the words "Pay to the Order of."

*To cash a check made out to you,* you may only need to sign the back, or you may have to include your account number with your signature. Do not endorse a check you want to cash

until you are at the bank or at the place where it will be cashed. If the check is endorsed and you lose it, it may be possible for someone else to cash it.

*To endorse a check to be deposited in your account,* follow the instructions given by your financial institution. Usually, if the deposit is made in person, the words "For deposit only" and your account number and signature are sufficient. If you are depositing by mail or using an automatic teller, you may be asked to write "Pay to the order of [your bank]" before writing your signature.

*If you want to use a check made out to you to pay someone else,* use the words "Pay to the order of [other person's name]" and then add your signature.

When you endorse a check, you should sign it as your name appears on the signature card. If the check is made out in a way that is different from your signature, first endorse it the way the check is made out, then endorse it using your official signature.

## Making Deposits

Depositing money in a checking or share draft account frequently can be done by mail if no cash is involved. If part or all of the money to be deposited includes cash, it would be a good idea to make the deposit in person. You can make a deposit at a window in the bank or use the automatic teller machine if your financial institution has one and if you have a card that allows you to use it.

To make a deposit, you will need a deposit slip. Fill in the date, the amount of cash and/or the bank number and amount of each check you are depositing, then fill in the total. Endorse the checks in the way that is required by your financial institution.

If you are making a deposit in person, give the deposit slip and cash and/or check(s) to be deposited to a teller. He or she will credit your

The line at the bottom left of a check allows you to record what you bought. Is this check written out correctly?

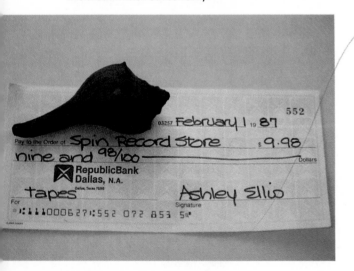

Save the dated computer statement of each automatic teller transaction.

account with the proper amount and give you a receipt of the transaction. If you are making a deposit by mail or are using an automatic teller machine, follow the instructions provided by your financial institution.

Each time you make a deposit, record the deposit in your check register and add the amount to your balance. This will make record-keeping easier and will let you track how much you have in your account.

## Making Cash Withdrawals

Taking money from a checking or share draft account can be done by writing a check. Depending on the financial institution, you may make the check out to yourself or to "Cash." It is safer to make the check out to yourself, then endorse it when you get to your bank or credit union. That way, if you lose the check before you get to the bank, someone else cannot cash it. A check made out to "Cash" can be cashed by anyone. If you want to make the check out to "Cash," wait until you get to the bank or credit union.

Another way to withdraw money from a checking account is by using the automatic teller machine. If you have a card for doing this, follow the instructions given to you by your financial institution. Remember to record the withdrawal in your check register.

## Keeping Your Account in Order

Keeping an accurate record of checks written, deposits and withdrawals made, and bank charges to you is one of the responsibilities of having a checking or share draft account. When you receive your bank statement, you should balance your account. If you don't keep accurate records, you may overdraw your account. That is, you may not have enough money in your account to cover the check or checks that you have written. Checks written when you have insufficient funds in your account are sometimes said to "bounce"; this is also referred to as an *overdraft*.

Several things happen when you overdraw your account, and not one of them is good! The person or business to whom you wrote the check will not get the money owed to them. You will be notified by your financial institution that your check was written on insufficient funds, and you will be charged a fee for a "bounced" check, which can total $20 or more.

After an individual or business receives a check that subsequently "bounces," your credibility as a responsible money manager slips. If this happens to one or more businesses too many times, they may refuse to accept checks from you. Frequently overdrawn accounts may

# *Where Has All the Money Gone?*

How much money do you have? Most people can't answer that question without some research. Today, money means more than "hard cash," or the coins and bills in your pocket. Your money includes some you may have never actually seen.

When you deposit your paycheck and then write checks to pay your bills, you are receiving and spending "unseen" money. Although you control the transactions, in truth, no *money* really changes hands. Instead, computers deduct from one account (your employer's), add to and deduct from another account (yours), and finally add to still other accounts (your landlord's or the telephone company's).

*Electronic funds transfers* (EFT) is a newer and more automated system that, in the future, may eliminate the need for most checks. EFT will automatically transfer money—or rather make additions and deductions—from one account to another. It will use *automatic clearing houses* (ACH) to receive regular deposits (such as salaries) and to pay regular expenses (such as rent). With ACH, your employer will credit your ACH account with the amount of your pay. You will direct the ACH to transfer funds to your billers' accounts each month. The computer will add and subtract the appropriate amounts, and neither cash nor checks will be necessary. Under this system, you will also use *point-of-sale terminals* and an ID card in stores to transfer the amount of your purchase immediately from your account to the store's account. Unlike using a credit card, these transactions will not involve borrowing and billing. Finally, you will use the automated teller machines found in many banks to make deposits, to transfer funds among your accounts, and to withdraw some of that strange, old-fashioned stuff—cash—if you can still think of a use for it!

cause your financial institution to look at you in a different light. If you were thinking of applying for a credit card or a loan or want to use the bank as a reference for a retail credit card, for example, a poorly managed checking account would not be a good recommendation.

Each month you will receive a statement from your financial institution. It will list all your account's activity since the last statement. Usually you will also receive your cancelled checks with your statement. These are the checks that have cleared, or have been deducted from your account.

Balancing your checkbook with your bank statement, or reconciling your account, each month simply means that you compare your records with the records of your financial institution as they are shown on your statement. Follow the directions on the back of your bank statement to do this. If your balance does not agree with the account statement from your financial institution, take your records and statement to the bank for assistance.

## Stopping Payment on a Check

If you have written a check but then have decided for some reason that you do not want it to be cashed, you can request the bank or financial institution to stop payment on it. You may want to do this if you have lost a check or if you have not received the goods or services for which you had written the check. To stop payment, contact the bank and tell them the specific check number and its amount, the date of the check, and the name of the individual or business who was to be paid. Usually, you have to pay a fee for stop payment services.

## Buying Individual Checks

For some people who do not have a lot of money or do not handle or keep money in a savings account earning interest, the expense of a checking account may not be affordable. If this is the case, what does a person do when he or she needs proof of payment or does not want to send cash through the mail?

In exchange for the cash and a fee, many banks will write a *cashier's check* or *money order* in almost any amount. The U.S. Postal Service offers a similar service in the form of postal money orders. Paying for the few checks or money orders that are needed may not be as expensive as maintaining a checking or share draft account.

Sometimes cashier's checks are used when personal checks cannot be used. Suppose, for example, you had saved enough money to buy a car and transferred what you needed from your savings account into your checking account to pay for it. The dealer may request a bank (cashier's) check as the method of payment. This is common practice when large amounts of money are involved because it lessens the risk to the seller. The seller knows a cashier's check is good; that is, there are funds to cover the check when it is cashed. The seller may not know right away whether there are enough funds to cover a personal check.

Although there is added cost involved in buying individual checks, using them may be necessary in some situations.

*Travelers' checks* are checks in fixed amounts that are insured against loss or theft by the companies that issue them. They also can be purchased with cash. Travelers' checks are sold through banks and certain travel-related organizations. Usually, there is a fee for buying them.

## For Review

1. Name five checking accounts. Which one does not pay interest?
2. Describe the correct procedure for writing out a check.
3. What happens when a check "bounces"?

## Paying Taxes

A **tax** is a charge of money imposed for public purposes on persons or property. The public purposes may include building and maintaining roads, governing on a national and local level, building and maintaining schools and paying teachers and other school personnel, providing for the national defense, and/or providing services for citizens. Federal and state income taxes, state and local sales taxes, social security taxes, excise taxes, and real estate taxes are all examples of taxes imposed by authority for public purposes.

## Income Tax

An **income tax** is a tax on the income of an individual or business. It may be a federal, state, and/or local tax. If a worker is employed by a business, income taxes are deducted from his or her paycheck by the employer and paid to the appropriate government agency. If a worker is self-employed, he or she is required to make quarterly installment payments of estimated income taxes. Federal income taxes are paid to the Internal Revenue Service (IRS). If a state or local area has mandated income taxes, these are paid to the appropriate agency (usually the tax department) in the state and/or local district.

The amount deducted from a paycheck for income taxes depends on many factors, including the size of the paycheck and the number of dependents a worker has. The W-4 form, which is filled out when you begin any job, allows an employer to determine how much to deduct from a paycheck to pay the government. The amount of estimated taxes is based on estimated income and the number of dependents. The IRS has a separate form to help self-employed persons determine how much to pay.

The federal income tax is a *graduated* or *progressive tax*. This means that lower incomes have lower rates and higher incomes have higher rates. State and local income taxes may be a percentage of the federal income tax you owe or may be figured separately. The rate of these taxes may be the same for everyone, that is, a certain percentage of the income, or it may be a graduated tax.

## Filing Your Taxes

The amount of money deducted from your paycheck for income taxes or paid to the government as estimated taxes may be more or less than what is actually owed. Between January 1 and April 15 of each year, people who have earned over a certain amount in the previous year, or who have had income taxes deducted from their pay during the previous year, are required to file an income tax return with each level of government to which they have paid income taxes. When the form is completed, you will know whether you owe additional taxes or whether the government will issue a refund for overpayment of taxes. If you have only worked during the summer and a few hours a week during the school year, you may not have earned enough in one year to require paying income tax. In that case, any income tax taken out of your paychecks will be returned to you after you have filed.

In January, people who have worked for an employer and have had income taxes and social security taxes withheld from their pay receive a W-2 form. People who have earned money from savings and investments receive a 1099 form. Both of these forms tell what information about the previous year's earnings and deductions has been given to the IRS. This information must be included on the tax return. A copy of the W-2 form must be attached to the return when it is filed with the Internal Revenue Service.

Knowing how to file an income tax return and when to file it are important parts of managing your financial resources. April 15th is the deadline for filing your tax return for the previous year. The IRS can help you to decide whether to use the 1040EZ, 1040A, or 1040 basic form. Additional forms may be needed for special circumstances.

## Social Security Tax

The social security tax is another tax that is deducted from your paycheck if you are employed by someone else. This deduction is labeled FICA, which stands for Federal Insurance Contributions Act. Social security taxes are paid by self-employed persons as part of their estimated taxes. If they underpay in a given year, they are required to make up the difference. The amount of social security any worker pays in one year is based on how much that person earns. The money that a worker pays goes into a fund that is used for retirement, old-age and survivors' insurance, and disability assistance.

## Sales Taxes

*Sales taxes* are taxes on the goods and services consumers buy. They are levied by the state or local government. These taxes are paid directly to the seller at the time of purchase. The seller is responsible for paying the state or district that mandates the tax.

Sales taxes are *direct taxes*. This means that the tax is added to the price of goods and services at the time of purchase. For example, suppose a stereo system has a price tag of $500. If there is a sales tax of 5 percent, this adds $25 to the cost of the stereo system—the total bill will be $525 not $500.

Sales taxes are considered regressive taxes because they take a higher percentage of the total income of someone earning a low income than of someone earning a high income. For example, if you earn $250 per week, a 5 percent sales tax on a $50 jacket is a higher percentage of your weekly income than it is of a weekly income of $500.

Because sales taxes are regressive taxes, some states and local districts exempt certain

Are any grocery store items taxed in your state? Are paper goods taxed?

High real estate taxes usually mean high apartment rental prices.

products from sales taxes to lessen the tax burden on people with limited incomes. There may be no sales tax on things that are considered necessities, such as food, clothing, and medicine. Sometimes, things that are considered luxuries, such as hotel rooms and restaurant food, may be taxed at a higher rate.

## Excise Taxes

*Excise taxes* are taxes on the manufacture, sale, consumption, or use of specific products. The excise tax is an *indirect tax;* that is, the tax is included in the selling price. Gasoline, tobacco products, and certain other goods have excise taxes levied on them by the federal and/ or state governments.

Sometimes an excise tax is charged on the ownership or the use of a product. For example, in some states, an excise tax is charged on all vehicles each year. If you own a car, you are billed for a percentage of the value of the car. If you own two or more cars, you receive an excise tax bill for each one.

Sometimes consumers pay both sales tax and an excise tax on a product. Cigarettes usu-

ally have an excise tax included in their price. At the time of purchase, a sales tax may be added to the price. Many people pay a sales tax on a car at the time of purchase.

## Real Estate Taxes

*Real estate taxes* are taxes paid on land by itself or on land and any buildings on it. The money is paid directly to the town or city in which the property is located. The amount of the property tax depends on the tax rate in the community. This is usually stated as a certain amount per $1000 of property value. In most communities, property taxes are used to pay for schools, community government, and community services and property.

## Inheritance Taxes

An *inheritance tax* is a tax on a person's estate after his or her death. This tax must be paid before any of the estate is passed on to the individuals, organizations, or groups named in a will or decided upon by the state if there is no will. Both federal and state governments levy inheritance taxes. At present, the federal tax is imposed only on estates valued at over $600,000. The state tax varies with the state.

## For Review

1. Name six types of taxes discussed in this chapter. Why is the sales tax considered a regressive tax and the federal income tax a progressive tax?

2. Is it possible to pay both a sales tax and an excise tax on the same product? If so, give one example.

3. When must federal income taxes be filed? What form do you need from your employer in order to do your taxes?

## Management Application: Budgeting an Allowance

Imagine yourself in the situation described below. As you read, think about how the steps of the management process might apply to this situation. Then answer the questions that follow.

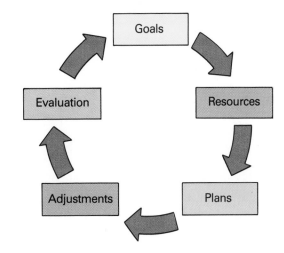

### Situation

Katie's parents had announced they were increasing her allowance. That was the good news. The bad news was that the money she received had to cover all of her expenses—lunches, school supplies, and clothing (except for major purchases such as a winter coat). Her parents explained that they were doing this to teach her how to budget her money. Katie agreed it was a good idea and received her first allowance with a smile. Two weeks later, she wasn't smiling at all. She had already spent more than half of her monthly allowance, and there was over half a month left! Where had it all gone? She tried to add up all of her expenses, but she couldn't remember them. There was that great skirt she had bought, and she had used some of her allowance to go out to eat once (well, maybe a few times) with her friends, but she couldn't have spent so much so soon. The problem was, she had.

She tried to think back to two weeks ago. She had certainly felt rich then. The first week she had even gone to two movies! Now she remembered that little shopping spree she and her friend Mimi had gone on.

Katie was determined to make ends meet without asking her parents for money. She wanted to handle this herself and prove that she could manage her own budget. She figured out that she had enough for notebooks and lunches, but nothing extra for treats. She could squeak by. Maybe she would babysit more to increase her income. From now on, though, she promised herself, she would write down all of her expenses as they occurred, and she would keep closer track of where her money was going. With some planning, she thought she could make her budget work.

### Questions

1. What is Katie's goal?
2. What happened to make Katie realize she had to reevaluate her financial plan?
3. What does Katie plan to do to make her budget work?
4. Why will she be better able to evaluate her plan after several months?
5. Which steps of the management process apply to this situation?

# Chapter Review

## 7

## Summary

To create a financial plan, you need to set goals that are based on your stage in the life cycle, your marital status, and your income. Before you start a budget, identify all your expenses, find your total income, and establish priorities. Having a checking account involves writing and endorsing checks, making deposits and withdrawals, and keeping accurate records. People who work or own property are liable for income taxes, sales taxes, social security taxes, and excise and real estate taxes.

## Vocabulary

Match each of the following vocabulary words with one of the definitions below.

| | |
|---|---|
| personal financial plan | net pay |
| income | gross pay |
| budget | interest |
| fixed expenses | tax |
| flexible expenses | income tax |

1. An estimate of income and expenses for a fixed period of time is a _____ .

2. The amount of money you receive after deductions are made from your total pay is your _____ .

3. A charge by the government imposed for public purposes on persons or property is an _____ .

4. Money that an individual pays out on a regular basis and that usually does not vary in amount is used to pay _____ .

5. A guide for the use of income is known as a _____ .

6. Total pay before deductions is _____ .

7. Money that an individual pays out that varies from week to week or month to month in the amount needed is used to pay for _____ .

8. The gain, usually measured in money, that comes from a variety of sources is _____ .

9. Income you earn on your own money when a bank lends it to others is _____ .

10. A charge by the government on the money that a business or individual makes is called a _____ .

## Questions

1. Give an example of a long-term financial goal and a medium-term financial goal.

2. Name some factors that affect your financial goals. Explain how each is important.

3. Why should a budget be flexible? Give specific examples to explain your answer.

4. Jacqueline's gross income in a two-week period is $150 dollars. Her net income is $125. She just calculated her fixed expenses for a two-week period at $100. She plans to spend an additional $50 in

flexible expenses every two weeks. Is this a workable budget for her? Explain.

5. What should Jacqueline do next?

6. Group the following expenses as fixed or flexible expenses:

tuition payments    rent payments

clothing costs      entertainment costs

gifts

dry cleaning        savings

income taxes        automobile payments

telephone service   electricity costs

7. What is the difference between a NOW account and a Money Market Deposit Account or MMDA?

8. What is an overdraft? What can you do to correct it?

9. Why might you want to put a stop payment on a check?

10. What determines the amount of income tax a person pays?

11. What is the difference between an excise tax and a sales tax?

## Skill Activities

1. **Math.** Keep track of your expenses for one week. Use a notebook or separate piece of paper to record *all* of your expenses for one week. If you are like most people, you probably do not know what your spending trends are or how you manage to spend as much as you do without realizing it. By keeping a spending diary for a week, you can begin to see if you spend small amounts of money on such things as gum, snacks, make-up, and movie tickets. Remember to record every cent that you spend. At the end of the week, bring your results to class and discuss what you learned about your spending trends.

2. **Critical Thinking.** Using the results of Skill Activity 1, think about whether or not your spending meets your needs and wants. After considering your findings, decide if you need to make changes in your spending pattern to stay within a budget or to get more of what you want.

3. **Resource Management.** Go to a local bank to find out about the requirements for opening a regular checking account. Is a minimum deposit required? Is a minimum balance required? How many checks can you write without a service charge? How many withdrawals? Is there a charge for checks? Is there a service charge? What is the cost for checks? Is any interest paid on the account? Would it be a good idea for you to open an account now or wait until you are older? If you were to open an account now, what type of identification would you need to cash a check in a store rather than a bank?

# 8

# Using Credit and Investment Resources

## As you read, think about:

- how to establish credit and manage credit purchases.
- how to arrange for a loan.
- how to establish and use a savings account.
- how to make wise short-term and long-term investments.
- how to apply the management process to personal decisions about savings, credit, and investments.

# Vocabulary

credit
equity
collateral
finance charge
annual percentage rate (APR)
inflation
credit rating
bankruptcy
investment
annual percentage yield (APY)

Learning about credit and investments is important for wise money management. As your income increases, you will begin to think about using credit cards and increasing the amount of money that you save. You may want to make other types of investments. This chapter will help you to understand more about credit, savings, and investment choices.

## Buying on Credit

There are few people who have never used credit. If you have borrowed money from a friend or from your parents or from a brother or sister, you have used credit. If you have a telephone or use electricity, you use credit because you are not billed for these utilities until after they are used. If you put an item on layaway in a store or buy a stereo from a local store and pay a certain amount each month, you use credit. When you finance the purchase of a new car or a house through a bank or some other financial institution, you use credit. Sometimes people who want to start businesses borrow money from financial institutions to do so. They are using credit.

**Credit** is the privilege of taking possession of money, goods, or services in exchange for a promise to pay for them at a future date. Sometimes, the promise is a verbal promise; other times, the promise is in writing. When you put an item on layaway in a store, you promise to pay for it within a specified time period. While you do not take possession of the item because the store holds the item until you have finished paying for it, no one else can purchase the item.

Although the privilege of taking possession of something or having it held for you may

Be careful to check all terms even when you are arranging for a short-term loan. If you sell jewelry, get a few estimates.

## Types of Consumer Credit

Consumer credit ranges from charge cards to personal loans to overdraft protection at the bank to mortgage loans. It is available from a variety of businesses and financial institutions. No matter what type of credit you use, it will fall into one of two categories: open-end or closed-end.

**Open-end Credit**  Open-end credit is credit in which the amount owed varies, depending on how much is purchased or how much of a service is used and the size of any payments made. Because the size of payments can vary, this type of credit sometimes is called non-installment credit.

The *revolving charge account* is a type of open-end credit. Under the terms of a revolving charge account, the consumer can charge purchases up to a preestablished limit. The consumer can repay all that is owed when the bill comes due or pay an installment on what is owed. The amount of the installment usually is based on a percentage of the amount owed and any applicable finance charges. Bank credit cards and many retail credit cards are revolving charge accounts. Open charge accounts and thirty-day charge accounts are two other examples of revolving charge accounts.

While a store credit card, for example, usually has a limit, other forms of open-end credit do not. Doctors and dentists, for example, usually don't stop treatment when you reach a certain limit. The telephone company does not stop service when you reach a certain limit. If you do not pay the bill, they may take action, but they do not set a limit before the service begins.

*Home-equity loans* are also a type of open-end credit. Homeowners can receive a line of credit that is worth some percentage of the equity they have in their homes. **Equity** is the owner's interest in the property over and above

be convenient and may allow you to buy some things sooner than you could otherwise, there are trade-offs involved. You give up some future purchasing power because you commit a part of your future income to paying a debt. If the payments are spread out over several months, you use a part of your income to pay the finance charges that are a part of credit purchases. The extra costs of using credit add either to the cost of what you are buying or to the amount of money you have to pay back.

Sometimes the advantages of using credit balance the trade-offs and financial costs. Sometimes the use of credit is not worth the cost and can even lead to serious financial problems. Knowing when to use credit is a part of managing your financial resources.

the claims against it. Homeowners, then, can borrow money against this amount and repay what they have borrowed according to the terms set up by the financial institution. While a home-equity loan can make a large amount of credit available at a fairly low rate to you, the rate is not as low as a mortgage. Furthermore, you must remortgage the property in order to get the line of credit, even if it is never used. With this type of credit, the property serves as collateral (kuh-LAT-uh-rul) for the loan. **Collateral** is property or goods pledged for repayment of a loan if the borrower cannot meet the payment schedule. In case of default on the loan, the property or goods can be taken over by the financial institution.

Some banks offer a *revolving credit line*. It may or may not be an extension of overdraft protection. If you qualify, you have a line of credit up to a certain limit that you can use whenever you wish. Because this type of credit does not require collateral, the interest rates may be high. Often, however, they are not as high as the rates for bank credit cards. If you do not need a large amount of money, this type of credit line may be good for you because you do not need to put up collateral.

***Closed-end Credit*** Closed-end credit involves borrowing a certain amount of money for a specified amount of time with repayment in equal installments. Because the money borrowed is repaid in installments, closed-end credit often is called *installment credit*.

Loans for purchasing housing, cars, and major appliances are examples of closed-end credit. Home improvement loans and personal loans are other examples. Some closed-end loans require collateral. These loans sometimes are called *secured loans*. For example, the property you buy using a mortgage loan serves as security, or collateral, until the mortgage is paid off. The car purchased with an auto loan serves as collateral for the loan. Major appliances usually serve as collateral when they are bought on an installment plan. If you cannot make the payments, the appliance is repossessed. Sometimes stocks and bonds or other securities can serve as collateral.

Closed-end loans that do not require collateral may be called *unsecured loans*. Personal loans are examples of unsecured loans. Personal loans may be used to pay for vacations, education, unexpected medical bills, or other unplanned expenses.

## USING CREDIT

### ADVANTAGES

- lessens the need to carry a lot of cash
- helps individuals and families meet needs and wants sooner
- allows one to take advantage of sales and discounts
- helpful for buying in quantity
- convenient
- provides records of expenses
- provides temporary solution to financial emergency

### DISADVANTAGES

- commits future income
- adds to the costs of goods and services
- can lead to overspending
- can lead to severe financial losses if payments are missed

# Financial Planner

Roxanne Fleszar counsels people about important life-management decisions. They go to her when they are planning or experiencing important transitions in their lives, such as job changes, inheriting or willing property, or retirement. She evaluates their individual needs and resources as well as factors such as age, life style, and tolerance for taking risks. Then she suggests a personalized plan to suit their particular situations. Roxanne Fleszar is a financial planner and investment counselor.

Years ago, people sought financial advice from their accountant, lawyer, stock broker, banker, or all four. "Today," says Ms. Fleszar, "the financial world is changing so rapidly it takes a specialist to keep up." A financial planner "ties the whole thing together by coordinating investments, pension plans, insurance needs, estate and tax planning, and cash flow, based on how the client wants to live his or her life."

Some clients ask, "How can I afford to keep my life style when I retire?" Others need a cash-flow analysis to find out why, with a good income, they have no money left at the end of each month. Computers are a useful tool—they provide investment and tax projections, for example—but it takes a trained human being to evaluate the data and give personalized financial advice.

"You can think of a financial planner as a financial therapist," Ms. Fleszar says. "Therefore being a good communicator—particularly a good listener—is essential." An interest in finance and economics is also important. So is knowledge of world affairs and how international politics affect the financial markets. Postgraduate study is required for the designations *Certified Financial Planner* (CFP) or *Chartered Financial Consultant.* Approval by and registration with the Securities and Exchange Commission is necessary to practice as a *Registered Investment Advisor.*

## The Costs of Credit

Sometimes, people seem to believe that credit costs nothing or very little. This is not true. Whether you borrow money, use a charge account, or buy on installment, you are using someone else's money. As you know, interest is the charge for borrowed money. It is usually a percentage of the amount borrowed. No retail store or business could keep going if it did not charge a customer for using its money.

Some stores and businesses give customers a certain number of days to pay their bills before credit costs are added to the bills. Does this mean the credit is free? Not really. Since the customers do not pay for the product or service immediately, the business may not have enough money to pay its bills. To meet this situation, the business includes all the costs of billing and collecting money and extending credit in the prices of the goods and services it offers.

***Finance Charges*** The total of all the charges for obtaining credit is the **finance charge.** When a bank or other financial institution lends money, or a business finances a purchase for a customer, there are other costs involved in addition to the amount lent to the individual. While most of these costs are interest charges, there may be charges for processing the loan, for credit checks, and for insurance.

The Consumer Credit Protection Act of 1969 and 1982, also known as the Truth-In-Lending Law, requires lenders and retail merchants to state the total dollar amount of the finance charges for closed-end credit. This amount tells the borrower how much he or she actually is paying for the use of the money.

Since interest rates on loans can be calculated in many different ways, how do you know what to compare when you try to decide on the most favorable rate? Look for a statement of the **annual percentage rate (APR).** The

Using credit cards is convenient. Why is it so important to control their use?

APR is the ratio of the dollar finance charge to the average amount of credit in use for the length of the contract. It is expressed as a yearly percentage. Because this figure reflects the true interest rate, it is usually different from other rates. Sometimes, in advertisements for loans or in the actual loan contract, there are two different interest rates given. One rate determines the way the interest charges for the credit are figured; the other is the annual percentage rate. Use the annual percentage rate when you want to compare different credit agreements. The Truth-In-Lending Law requires the disclosure of the annual percentage rate on all credit agreements.

Before paying extra costs for credit, ask yourself if you really need the item.

**Additional Factors** Many other factors, both individually and together, affect the cost of credit. Some of these factors include economic conditions, the size of the loan, the type of loan or credit agreement, the length of the loan, and the credit rating of the borrower. While credit laws do not determine the rate of interest on loans, they can place a ceiling on the rate charged for a loan.

A high demand for credit, particularly from government and business, may cause consumer interest rates to rise because less money is available to lend to consumers. **Inflation** is an increase in the general level of prices due to an increased volume of money and credit. It can cause an increase in interest rates, which will result in increased costs for people using credit.

If the credit agreement demands that the borrower put up collateral as security against the loan, the loan may have a lower interest rate than a loan without collateral. Unsecured loans may have higher interest rates than secured loans.

No matter what the size of the loan, there are certain costs involved in processing the application and conducting a credit check. When a person takes out a small loan, these costs make a higher percentage of the finance charges than they do for a large loan. For this reason, interest rates on small loans are usually higher than on large loans.

The length of time allowed for paying back a loan may or may not affect the interest rate, but it does affect the total cost of credit. The longer the payback period, the higher the total costs for interest. For revolving credit, the longer the account holder takes to pay off the bill, the higher the finance charges.

Prepaying loans, or paying them off before they are due, can save interest charges. However, if the loan agreement contains a prepayment penalty, the borrower may have to pay a penalty for paying off the loan early. Prepayment penalties are illegal in some states.

## For Review

1. State three advantages and three disadvantages of using credit when you purchase goods or services.
2. Name and describe two types of open-end credit available to consumers.
3. What is collateral? What types of loans generally do not require collateral?

## Sources of Credit/Loans

Credit is available from a variety of sources. As you already know, *retail operations and service businesses* may offer credit in the form of charge accounts or credit accounts.

Some retail stores offer installment plans for major purchases. Small retail establishments that cannot afford to offer credit plans may offer their customers an installment plan through a sales finance company. The finance company pays the retailer, and the customer pays the money back to the finance company. Interest rates can be higher or lower than the rates of banks and other financial institutions. If you decide to use a finance company, you will want to compare interest rates at several companies to get the lowest rate possible.

*Commercial banks, savings and loan associations, mutual savings banks,* and *credit unions* all offer various types of secured and unsecured loans. Many also offer credit cards and other credit services. While interest rates among these financial institutions are often competitive, the rates will vary from institution to institution for different reasons.

*Finance companies* offer loans also. These loans are usually for small amounts and often unsecured. For these reasons, interest rates at finance companies are frequently higher than bank and credit union rates. The fact that finance companies are more likely to lend money to individuals with poor credit ratings or no credit history contributes to the higher interest rates of these companies.

---

### Safety Tip: Recording Credit Card Numbers

■ Record the names and numbers of all the credit cards you own. If they are ever lost or stolen, this list will be helpful. Contacting the companies immediately and giving them your card numbers if your card is lost or stolen, limits the amount you must pay for charges made with your card.

---

*Industrial banks* originally were established to lend money to industrial workers. Now, however, they operate like commercial banks and lend money to anyone who is qualified. Interest rates may or may not be higher than the commercial bank rate.

Sometimes it is possible to obtain a loan on a life insurance policy from the company that holds the policy. Some companies make loans up to the value of the policy. The cost is often low because of the low risk.

A *pawn shop* is another place to get a cash loan. The customer gives the pawnbroker something with resale value in exchange for cash. Usually, the amount of cash received is considerably less than the item is worth. If the consumer repays the money within an agreed-upon time period, the pawnbroker returns the item. If no repayment is made, the pawnbroker sells the item, often turning a nice profit.

## Obtaining Credit

Obtaining credit depends on three factors: how a person has handled money matters in the past; what financial resources a person has, such as a car, household goods, or savings account; and the individual's ability to pay for any credit that is granted.

When you apply for credit, there is usually a form to fill out that asks such questions as how have you used credit in the past, what loans do you presently have, what is the size of your checking and savings account, what are your assets, where do you work, and what is the size of your salary or wages. It is important to be honest in filling out the application. If a creditor discovers that the applicant has not been truthful, it will hurt his or her chances of getting credit.

**Handling of Money** Creditors want to know how an individual has handled money in the past because it may be an indication of how it will be handled in the future. The responsible use of a checking account and regular deposits to a savings account are signs that the applicant is financially responsible.

Creditors also want to know an individual's credit history. If an individual has used credit before, then he or she has a credit history. Each time a person uses credit, he or she adds to that history. Prompt payment of bills and timely payments on installment loans help to make up a good credit history.

**Ability to Repay** Answers to questions about job status, income, savings and checking accounts, and other financial matters help the lender to determine how good a credit risk the individual is. If the applicant has held a job for some time, does not have many debts, and appears to have enough income to repay a loan or to make payments, it increases the chances of getting credit.

**Assets** Sometimes, an application will ask for information about the *assets* of the applicant, such as savings, investments, and ownership of property, cars, and household goods. This information helps the creditor to judge how capable a person is of handling money to increase his or her personal worth.

## Establishing a Credit Rating

A **credit rating** is a rating given to an individual to indicate how good a credit risk he or she is. Credit bureaus are agencies that are formed for the purpose of keeping records on consumer use of credit. These agencies keep files on individuals who have used credit in the past. Once you have established credit, the files contain your credit history as well as information about your personal assets, employment, and any record of legal action related to credit or other financial matters. Creditors check with credit bureaus when they evaluate

an application for credit. A good record with a credit bureau earns a person a good credit rating. A good credit rating means a person is credit-worthy, that is, that he or she probably will pay the money owed on time.

What if a person doesn't have a credit history or a credit rating because he or she has never used credit? How do you go about establishing a credit history and a good rating?

If you have a steady job and a permanent address, you have some points in your favor. People with seasonal employment or who change jobs frequently or move frequently often are considered greater credit risks than those who do not. A checking account with no history of overdrawn checks and a savings account with some money in it also help to indicate that you handle money carefully.

What personal information do you have to provide a bank or retail store in order to establish credit?

Many people just starting out will apply for a retail credit card or a bank credit card or a small loan from the bank where they have one or more accounts. They may receive a credit card with a low credit limit. This is common for people with no credit history. If you use the card wisely and pay the bills promptly, it will indicate that you are responsible. A good record of payment helps you to establish a good credit rating. After a while, you may be able to increase your credit limit.

If you apply for and receive more than one credit card or receive a bank credit card, you can charge goods and services in more places. With increased privileges, however, come increased responsibilities. There are more chances to overcharge and therefore overspend with several credit cards.

Sometimes, an individual will apply for a small loan just for the purpose of adding to his or her credit history. The money is put into a savings account and paid back out of income, according to the payment schedule. If you do this, you can earn interest on what is deposited in your savings account, which sometimes helps to offset the finance charges on the loan.

Sometimes, a creditor will grant credit to a young person or to someone with no credit history if another person with an established, favorable credit record cosigns the contract. The cosigner of a contract is responsible for the payment of the debt if the first person cannot or does not pay back the loan. Paying off the debt without depending on the cosigner helps a person to establish a good credit rating. Sometimes, young people who want to buy cars but who are not old enough to sign a contract legally will have their parents or some other responsible adult cosign the loan for them.

Once you have established a good credit history, retail businesses and banks are more willing to extend credit. If your income is adequate and not offset by a lot of debts, they are

Before signing any loan application, be sure you can meet the required payment terms.

more willing to lend larger amounts of money for such things as major appliances, furnishings, or perhaps a used or new car. A good credit rating allows you to shop around for the credit terms that best meet your needs.

## Knowing Your Credit Rights

The Equal Credit Opportunity Act of 1975 made it illegal to deny credit because of sex, marital status, race, religion, age, national origin, or receipt of public assistance. Even so, requirements related to income level, commitments for income, and other financial matters often vary from place to place. If you are turned down for credit at one place, try another. If you are unsuccessful, ask why your application was refused. The law gives you the right to know.

The Fair Credit Reporting Act of 1971 gives consumers a legal right to know what information is in their credit bureau files. If you are refused credit, you may want to ask the place where you applied for credit for the address of the credit bureau where your file is. If the information in your file is incorrect, be sure the credit bureau receives the correct information. If the information is correct and it is affecting your credit worthiness negatively, make an effort to correct the matter.

## Understanding Credit Contracts

If you are just beginning to establish a credit history, you probably will not have as many alternative sources of credit as someone who has a good credit rating and has used credit for years. To get the most value for your money and to avoid excessively high credit costs, you need to know what to look for in a credit contract and how to evaluate it.

**Types of Credit Contracts** When you apply for any type of credit, there is usually a form to fill out. If credit is granted, the creditor requires the consumer to sign a *credit contract*. For open-end credit, such as a revolving credit account or overdraft protection, the contract covers all purchases or cash advances. It is in effect for as long as the consumer has the account or until the creditor makes changes in the terms. For closed-end credit, such as installment purchases and cash loans from financial institutions, the contract usually applies only to the specific purchase or loan for which it was written. Sometimes, however, it is possible to add items to an installment contract without going through the application process again.

A credit contract for open-end credit usually is called an *agreement* or *credit agreement*. Some creditors specify the type of credit the agreement is for, such as the name of a credit card. Usually a credit agreement includes information about the interest rate and how the finance charges are computed, the payment schedule based on the amount owed, the consequences of failure to make the scheduled payments, and how long the consumer has to pay the bill before finance charges are added. If it is a retail credit card, there may be a security clause that gives the retailer the right to repossess items that have been purchased but not paid for. When you sign a credit agreement, you usually give the creditor permission to obtain information about your credit record from a credit bureau.

Officially, a credit contract for closed-end credit or installment purchase is known as a *retail installment contract and security agreement*. It is more commonly referred to as a *conditional sales contract*. This contract allows the consumer to have the merchandise at the time of purchase in exchange for the promise to fulfill the contract. The contract usually includes the interest rate and how the finance charges are computed, the payment schedule, the length of the loan, and the consequences of failure to make payments on time. Most conditional sales contracts also include the right of the seller to demand full payment or to repossess the merchandise if the consumer does not comply with the terms of the agreement.

When a consumer takes out a loan from a financial institution, he or she usually signs a *promissory note*. The interest rate, finance charges, and the terms of repayment are spelled out in the contract. If the consumer does not fulfill his or her part of the contract, the financial institution usually has the right to take the consumer to court to force repayment if necessary.

A *security agreement* may be a part of a conditional sales contract or a promissory note. This means that the consumer pledges something as security, or collateral, against

Have your entire credit contract explained
in detail before signing it.

the amount lent. In the case of a cash loan, a financial institution may require a savings account or other securities to be pledged as collateral. In case of nonpayment, the creditor has the right to take possession of the collateral, or pledged security.

**Read the Contract Carefully.** Read any credit contract thoroughly before you sign it. Make sure you understand all the terms. If you have questions, ask them. Do not sign any contract if there are blank spaces that have not been filled in. These precautions are for your protection and to prevent any misunderstanding between you and the creditor. You need to understand your responsibilities in meeting the terms of your contract. If you fail to do so, you can damage your chances for obtaining credit in the future. The chart on page 176 highlights the important things to check for on every credit contract before signing it.

## For Review

1. What are the three most important factors in determining whether or not you can obtain credit?
2. Name one way you can begin to establish a credit rating.
3. What information is usually included on a credit agreement?

## Keeping a Handle on Credit

While it can be convenient and beneficial to establish a good credit history, it is easy to overuse or misuse credit. Sometimes, people have several credit cards, use them to the limit, and then find themselves unable to make the required payments. Sometimes, they may have so many credit payments that they cannot buy anything else they need.

To avoid this situation, you may want to remind yourself that while credit can help you increase your short-term buying power, it is not additional income. Every time you use credit, you are committing some of your future income for payments. You decrease your long-term buying power. If you tie up all your future income, there is no flexibility to do other things you wish to do.

**Choose Carefully.** You should try to use credit primarily for important items, such as equipment that will be used either in running

a home or in earning a living. A refrigerator is one example. A good watch for certain kinds of employment is another example. To buy a refrigerator merely to get a later model or a different color or to buy a luxury watch can be a misuse of credit for some people. The availability of credit can tempt you to spend beyond your means.

You may want to use credit to pay for training that will increase your earning power. This is another good use for credit. When an individual borrows money to attend college or to take special classes, he or she is using money to buy knowledge and skill that will help to earn a living.

Credit is more likely to be controlled if the service or article purchased will outlast the debt. Daily food needs and personal care items add up quickly but leave you with little to show for your bills. Items of questionable quality bought on credit may need to be replaced before the debt is paid.

Each individual must decide whether or not the item justifies the use of credit. This is where management comes in. Balancing wants and needs with resources in order to reach short-term and long-term goals can help to keep the use of credit in the proper perspective for you.

**Know the Total Amount of Debt in Relation to Income.** People with serious spending problems sometimes do not know the total amount they owe and how their debt relates to their income. How is this possible? Sometimes this may happen when income varies from week to week or season to season. But, sometimes even wage- and salary-earners with fixed incomes have trouble relating total debt payments to actual income. Some people tend to think of their income in terms of gross pay rather than take-home, or net, pay. As you know, net pay is gross pay minus deductions for taxes, social security, insurance, and other

## CHECKING THE CREDIT CONTRACT

Look for this information in a credit contract:

- amount of down payment, if appropriate
- description of the merchandise, if appropriate
- the amount being financed or the cash price
- the dollar amount of finance charges and a listing of what they are
- the annual percentage rate (APR)
- the number of payments, the amount of each, and their due dates
- when finance charges begin
- late payment charges
- description of collateral or pledged security, if appropriate
- information about prepayment (paying off the debt before it is due), such as penalties or refunds on finance charges
- any special clauses or conditions

purposes. If you consider only your gross pay, you may think there is more income than there actually is. Sometimes, people are not aware of how much of their take-home pay is already committed to rent, utilities, transportation, food, and so on. They may think their take-home pay is more than enough, but if a lot of it is committed, there is little or no room for credit payments. Working out a realistic budget, as discussed in Chapter 7, will help you to know what credit payments you can afford.

### Know What the Credit Costs Will Be.

When you are thinking of buying something on credit, you should calculate how much the finance charges will add to the purchase price. As you have learned, the shorter the terms of the loan, the lower the total finance charges. Sometimes, however, short-term loans may make the monthly payments higher than desired. A long-term loan may make monthly payments smaller but also may add to the total cost of using credit and may commit future income for a longer period of time.

Before buying an item on credit, you should weigh the advantages and disadvantages of paying cash against those of using credit. Suppose, for example, you are considering a new stereo. You have priced the model you want at three stores. Store B has the lowest price. Now you are trying to decide whether to take money from your savings account to pay for it or to arrange to buy it on credit. Have you considered all the facts?

Although paying cash will cost less than what you will pay in finance charges, you know that you will lose interest on any money you take from your savings account. You have to balance your savings in finance charges if you pay cash against the fact that you will not have that money if an emergency arises.

At the same time, you cannot assume that the store with the lowest cash price will give you the best credit terms. If you do a little more investigating, you may find that another store offers more reasonable credit terms. The chart below provides an example of what you may discover. If you decide to use credit, you will get the most favorable terms at Store A. Even though the cash price is higher at Store A, you will pay less in total cost at Store A than at Store B if you buy on credit.

## BUYING A $900 STEREO

| | Selling Price | Annual Interest Rate | Monthly Payments Over One Year | Total Finance Charges | Total Cost |
|---|---|---|---|---|---|
| **STORE A** | $900.00 | 15% | $86.08 per month | $132.96 | $1,032.96 |
| **STORE B** | $875.00 (on sale) | 22% | $88.96 per month | $192.52 | $1,067.52 |

Compare the financial services offered by several banks before choosing one. Credit counseling is one of these services that you may want to use.

## Dealing with Credit Problems

Despite the best of intentions, it is possible to become overextended using credit. If this happens, you will not be able to make payments when they are due. Whether this happens through the careless use of credit or because of an unexpected financial emergency, such as extra medical expenses or a job layoff, the problem must be dealt with immediately. Ignoring it will not make it go away; it can only become worse.

### Reduce and Postpone Flexible Expenses.
Perhaps you do not have enough money to pay all your creditors this week when the bills are due, but you will have enough next week or the week after. According to your credit contracts, if you are late in paying, you will be charged a late charge, but there is no other penalty. If this is the case, now is the time to cut back on spending that is not absolutely necessary. Perhaps you can spend less on food or entertainment or use the car less and walk more or use

public transportation. Only you can decide where cuts can be made, but this may be all that you need to get back on track again.

Once you have caught up with your credit payments, you may want to take time to make a better plan for your money and to promise yourself you will stick to it. A budgeting plan for money that is based on actual income balanced against needs and wants and that is followed carefully can help to prevent many financial problems later.

### Talk with Your Creditors.
Suppose you already have cut back on expenses as much as possible, and you still do not have enough to make all the payments, and you will not be able to in a week or two. Now what? Financial experts and creditors recommend that you get in touch with all the companies, businesses, and/or banks to whom you owe money. If possible, make an appointment to talk to someone in person. Often, if creditors know the circumstances and believe that you are sincere about paying your debts, they will try to work out some way that allows you to meet your obligations and allows them to get their money.

### Seek Financial Counseling.
Sometimes creditors are unwilling to make adjustments, or there just isn't enough income to meet all the credit payments due. Some banks, businesses, and community agencies offer counseling for people who are heavily in debt and unable to meet their financial obligations. Often this counseling is free of charge. Before you go for counseling, try to get all your records in order. The counselor will need to know all about your financial situation—how much you owe and to whom, how much income you have and how regular it is, and what financial obligations you have (rent, utilities, and so on). This information makes it possible for the counselor to determine the best possible course of action for you to take.

A credit counselor can help you to set up a financial plan that allows you to pay your creditors. If there is not enough money for that to be successful, the counseling agency may be able to make arrangements with the creditors to adjust payments to a size that is manageable. This probably will result in higher interest rates and payments over a longer period, but it will allow you to pay your debts.

Under certain circumstances, a counselor may suggest that you take out a *consolidation loan* from a bank or finance company. This is a loan that is equal to all the money you owe your creditors. Usually, interest rates are high, but one payment on this single loan probably will be less than the total payments you make on all your credit bills. A consolidation loan will work only if there is enough income to make the loan payments on schedule and if no more debts are incurred for the duration of the loan. It is not additional income. It is only a way to lessen the immediate pressure of owing more money than is available.

What happens if you ignore the situation? Ignoring a credit problem does not make it go away. The longer you delay, the greater the chances that your creditor will turn your account over to an independent debt collector. The Fair Debt Collection Practices Act of 1978 protects consumers from unfair collection practices but does not eliminate the debt. You may lose anything you have bought on credit, as well as any money you have paid toward it.

If there is no other alternative, you may be forced into bankruptcy. **Bankruptcy** is a procedure that causes you to lose certain personal possessions in order to repay debts. The court takes your possessions and sells them to get money for creditors. It may be several years before it is possible for you to get credit again since bankruptcy is included in your record at credit bureaus. Bankruptcy is a drastic measure and should be avoided if there is any other way to pay back your creditors.

## For Review

1. Explain why it is important to know your total amount of debt in relation to your total income.
2. Explain how a store's annual interest rate can be more important than the price of an item you plan to purchase on credit.
3. Name three steps you can take to deal with credit problems.

Businesses that go bankrupt are forced to close down and sell all of their goods.

## Establishing a Savings Account

People use savings accounts to keep money safe for future use and to earn more money. While savings accounts have changed over the years, their purposes still are basically the same.

Savings accounts are interest-bearing accounts. They earn money because the financial institution uses your money to make money. Although it is possible to make withdrawals and deposits at any time, savings accounts are not demand accounts. Many financial institutions reserve the right to request several days notice from customers before the customer makes a withdrawal. In other words, funds do not have to be supplied on demand as they do with checking accounts. You cannot write checks on funds in savings accounts. There are other ways to withdraw your money.

The financial institutions that offer savings accounts include commercial banks, mutual savings banks, savings and loan associations, and credit unions. Because banking laws vary from state to state, you will want to check with the financial institutions within your state to find out what types of accounts are available to you.

## Investment Factors in Savings Accounts

A savings account is a type of investment. An **investment** is an outlay of money for income or profit. When you put your money into a savings account, you increase its value through the interest you earn.

When you are choosing a savings account as an investment, there are a number of factors you should consider. Although savings accounts are reasonably safe investments because they are insured by the federal government, some types of accounts require the money in them to be left there for a stated period of time. Some do not permit a balance below a specified amount. These factors mean that the money is not available to you, should you need it for emergencies. Another factor you should consider when you open a savings account is the amount of interest your account can earn. Some accounts earn more interest than others but may have more restrictions than others. They may require a specific amount of money for deposit before you can open the account.

Some people like to have several types of savings accounts. One may be for saving money for special purchases or for emergencies. One may be for earning as much interest as possible and still having the money available if needed. Still another may be for retirement. The money you save for retirement may earn a high rate of interest that cannot be taxed until it is withdrawn, but it also cannot be withdrawn before you reach a certain age.

Although they are low-risk investments, government savings bonds take years to reach full face value.

Before you open a savings account, you should consider carefully the type of account that will best meet your personal needs, wants, and goals.

## Choosing a Savings Account

When you open a savings account, you may be able to choose from regular passbook savings accounts, regular statement savings accounts, or money market savings accounts.

*Regular passbook* and *statement savings accounts* are similar. Each has a fixed rate of interest and usually no limit on deposits and withdrawals. The major difference between them lies in how transactions are handled. If you want to make a deposit or a withdrawal with a passbook account, you must present the passbook, which is given to you when the account is opened. Each time a transaction is made, the transaction and information on interest earned are recorded in the book. To make transactions on a statement savings account, you must have deposit and withdrawal slips. Every month you receive a statement of the account's transactions. There may or may not be a required minimum deposit to open a regular passbook savings account or a statement savings account. When a minimum deposit is established by a financial institution, it is usually a small amount.

*Money market savings accounts* earn interest at a rate similar to money market funds. The rate is higher than the rate for regular passbook and statement savings accounts. It may vary as money market rates vary. Although many money market savings accounts allow unlimited deposits and withdrawals, the minimum deposit needed to open the account is higher than the amount needed for passbook and statement savings accounts. At some financial institutions, if the balance falls below that minimum amount, the interest rate reverts to the rate of a regular savings

Time deposits are profitable if you do not have to make early withdrawals.

account. Sometimes, no interest is earned at all if the rate drops below a certain limit. Any interest earned is considered taxable income.

***Time Deposits*** Time deposits are deposits that must be left in an account for a fixed period of time. Interest rates may be fixed for that period of time or may be variable. At the end of that time, the deposit matures, which means that the financial institution repays the amount invested, plus interest, to you. *Certificates of deposit* (CDs) are examples of time deposits.

CDs usually have a minimum deposit requirement. The money must be left in the CD for a specified period of time, such as 30, 60, or 180 days. If the money is withdrawn before the CD matures, there is a penalty charge. Sometimes it is possible to have the CD mature on a specific date. Any interest earned on a CD is taxable as income.

***Special Savings Accounts*** A Christmas Club savings account is an example of a special savings account. When you open a Christmas Club account, you specify the amount you want to save. Most financial institutions offer Christmas Club accounts in different amounts, such as $50 or $100 or $500. You, as the depositor, are required to make a deposit of a fixed amount each week until the account reaches the desired total. Interest may be paid on the account. Any interest earned is taxable.

## Comparing Interest Rates

Interest rates vary with the savings institution and the individual savings plan. Naturally, you want your money to earn as much interest for you as it can. You may want to ask about each institution's annual percentage yield. The **annual percentage yield,** or **APY,** is the rate at which the money in a savings plan will earn interest in one year. The APY will differ from one institution to another and from one plan to another, depending on how often interest is compounded, or calculated, and added to the total account amount.

Before you open a savings account, you need to know how interest is figured under the

specific savings plan you are interested in. You will earn more interest if it is based on the average, rather than the smallest amount in your account during each time period. You also will want to know exactly how often interest is credited to the account. Some institutions credit interest every day, which allows you to earn more interest even if you make frequent withdrawals. When you are asking questions about interest, you may want to ask if minimum balances are required. Sometimes there are service charges or other penalties if the balance falls below a certain minimum. If it is not managed carefully, a savings account can cost you money rather than earn money for you.

## Opening a Savings Account

Opening a savings account is similar to opening a checking account. You will need to fill out and sign a signature card, even if you already have one for a checking account. Your financial institution keeps a signature card on file for each account you have. Once again, you will need to fill in your name, address, and other requested information and sign the card exactly as you will sign deposit slips and other transaction slips.

After you have given the money and/or checks you are going to use to open your account to the representative of the financial institution, the representative will tell you how to endorse any checks you have for deposit so your account will be credited properly.

You will be given a passbook if this is a passbook account. Your passbook will have your name, address, and account number on it. You will want to keep the passbook in a safe place, as you will need it every time you make a deposit or withdrawal. All transactions are recorded in this book at the financial institution you have decided to use. If you lose the book, notify the financial institution immediately.

How do minimum deposits vary for money market and regular savings accounts?

| THROUGH NOVEMBER 14th | Minimum | Annual Rate % | Annual Yield % |
|---|---|---|---|
| MONEY MARKET Investor Account | $2,500 | 5.65 | 5.80 |
| MONEY MARKET Investor Account | | 5.25 | 5.38 |
| | | . | . |
| 6 MONTH Certificate | $2,500 | 6.00 | . |
| 6 MONTH Certificate | $10,000 | 6.00 | . |
| 12 MONTH Certificate | $500 | 6.40 | 6.59 |
| 12 MONTH Certificate | 10,000 | 6.40 | 6.59 |

If you open a statement savings account, you will receive a register book. You do not need the register book for deposits and withdrawals. You do need it at home for keeping a record of your transactions.

## Making Deposits and Withdrawals

You can make deposits to a passbook savings account either in person or by mail. To do this in person, present your passbook to the teller along with a deposit slip and the money you are depositing. It is usually a good idea to make deposits by mail only if there is no cash involved. Be sure you have endorsed your checks properly and follow the instructions provided by the financial institution. When you send in your checks and deposit slip, you also will have to send in your passbook.

For other types of savings accounts, you need only the money you wish to deposit and a deposit slip. Fill in your name, account number, and any other information required and give the slip with your deposit to the teller. Be sure you receive a receipt for any transactions you make. If you make your deposits by mail, use the special envelope provided by the bank, fill out the deposit slip, endorse the check or checks, and drop the envelope in the mail. You should receive a receipt of the transaction.

Withdrawals are made in much the same way as deposits. If you withdraw money by mail, however, you will receive a check because banks will not send cash through the mail. You may be charged for the check.

In many places, it is possible to make savings account deposits and withdrawals by using the automatic teller machine. If you are using an automatic teller machine, follow the instructions on the machine you are using. You will want to be sure that you record the transaction in your savings account register.

Making bank deposits by mail is a convenience for many people. Why should you mail checks, not cash?

## Keeping Your Savings Account in Order

When you have a passbook savings account, your record-keeping is done for you, because each transaction is recorded in the book by the financial institution. With other types of accounts, you are responsible for keeping records of your deposits and withdrawals. You will receive a statement approximately every month. The statement will list all the deposits and withdrawals and any interest earned. You should always take time to check the statement against your records. If you find an error or you cannot get the two to balance, contact your financial institution.

## Making Investments

Do you think that investments are only for the wealthy? Many people do, but even a little money can work to make more money. This is the purpose of personal investments.

## Types of Investments

As you know, an investment is an outlay of money for income or profit. There are many ways to use money to increase its value. One way is to put money into a savings account. Other types of investments include stocks, government and corporate bonds, certain types of insurance policies, mutual funds, individual retirement plans, real estate, and collectibles (antiques and coins, for example). Investments may be either short-term or long-term, depending on the time period needed to reach the investment goal.

If you want the money that you have saved to work harder for you, or you want to start on a program of investing or have money for retirement, you need to know what your options are. Detailed information about types of investments can be obtained through the media, various classes, and the advice of any financial planners you may consult.

## Factors to Consider Before Investing

Just as there are specific factors to consider when you open a savings account, there are specific factors you should consider when you are planning to make any kind of investment. To be sure the investment is right for you, you should think carefully about each factor before deciding on it.

If you invest in collectibles, you need to learn about the factors that can raise or lower their value over time.

**Amount of Money Available** Different investments require different amounts of money. Some investment services also cost money. You should have money saved for emergencies before you use money for investments.

**Time Factors** Some investments tie money up for a specified period of time. Other investments take a while before they produce income or interest.

**Knowledge and Skill Needed** Different amounts of knowledge are needed for making informed decisions about investments. For example, the knowledge and skill needed for choosing real estate investments is different from the knowledge and skill needed for stock or bond investments or investments in various types of collectibles.

**Degree of Risk** Some investments involve more risk than others. For example, government bonds are low risk because they are insured by the government. Stocks, real estate, and some other investments involve more risk because there is no guarantee against loss.

**Rate of Return, or Yield** The rate of return, or yield, is the amount made on an investment, expressed as a percentage. The higher the rate of return, the more money that is made. Often the rate of return is related to the degree of risk. Low-risk investments usually have a lower rate of return. High-risk investments usually have the potential for earning a higher rate of return for you.

**Liquidity** Liquidity refers to how easily an investment can be converted into cash. For example, an interest-bearing bank account is easy to turn into cash. Stocks usually can be sold quickly. Time deposits and many government bonds cannot be turned into cash without a substantial penalty.

Stocks may be bought and sold daily through phone calls to brokers.

**Tax Benefits** Some investments help to reduce the amount of income that can be taxed. Some also yield interest that is not taxable. For example, money put into individual retirement plans sometimes can be deducted from taxable income. In addition, under certain circumstances, the interest earned on an individual retirement plan is not taxable. The money does become taxable, however, when withdrawals are made at retirement.

Work pension plans vary and should be supplemented by other investments for your retirement.

## Planning for Retirement

The earlier money is put away for retirement, the more income there will be after retiring. To many people, retirement seems far away. They believe there is plenty of time in the future to put away some money. There are some people who believe the deductions made from their paycheck for Social Security and their employer-sponsored retirement program will supply enough money for retirement when the time comes.

The federal government began the Social Security program in 1935 and included, as part of that plan, a provision for old-age insurance. Despite cost of living increases, Social Security alone does not provide enough income for comfortable living. Most employer-sponsored retirement programs are designed to supplement Social Security payments. Unfortunately, even with this combination of benefits, the payments often do not meet the financial needs of retired persons. While studies show that retired people can live comfortably on less income, a source of income in addition to Social Security and an employer-sponsored program is highly recommended by financial experts. Individual Retirement Accounts (IRAs) and Keogh Plans are two possible sources of retirement income. It is a sound management decision to make and carry out definite plans to have sufficient income for your retirement.

### For Review

1. Why is a certificate of deposit called a time deposit?
2. List seven important factors to consider before making any investment.
3. Does Social Security provide enough income for persons who are retired to live on comfortably?

## Management Application: Handling Credit

Imagine yourself in the situations described below. As you read, think about how the steps of the management process might apply to these situations. Then answer the questions that follow.

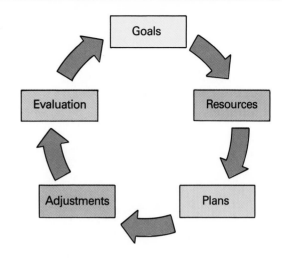

## Situations

Cheryl saw the perfect prom gown when she was shopping on Saturday. It was just the style she wanted and the color looked great on her. She tried it on, and it fit perfectly. No alterations were needed. That was the good news. The bad news was that the gown cost $150. She had planned to spend that amount on everything, including matching shoes and a beaded evening bag she had already bought. She also needed cash to have her hair done. She just didn't have enough cash on her to buy the gown. She did have one credit card. She decided to use it to buy the gown and worry about the bill when it came in. That way she would have cash on hand to have her hair done. Maybe she would also buy that cute coat she saw yesterday. She forgot that she already had charged $100 worth of clothing earlier that she hadn't paid off yet. The bill was there to remind her when she got home. The eighteen percent interest charge really made a difference! Well, she'd worry about it next month.

David had checked on the price of the tux rental, prom tickets, corsage, and dinner two months before the date of the prom. He had figured out exactly how much he would need to pay for all of this. He didn't want to take money out of his savings account, so he asked for a few more hours of work each week until the prom. He had it all figured out except that he had counted next Monday's check into his total. The prom was this Saturday night, so he needed cash right away to pay for the dinner. He decided to borrow the money from his brother, who agreed to lend it since he would be repaid in only two days.

## Questions

1. Who did a better job of analyzing resources, Cheryl or David? Explain.

2. Did David use credit for prom expenses? If so, what plan does he have for payment?

3. Explain why Cheryl's use of credit may cause problems. How can she plan to pay her debt?

4. What trade-offs does Cheryl make when she adds the gown to her credit charges?

5. Which steps of the management process apply to these two situations?

# 8 *Chapter Review*

## Summary

The convenience of buying on credit can be offset by finance charges and the commitment of future purchasing power to pay off debts. A good credit rating depends on a person's credit history, ability to pay, and assets. When credit problems arise, it is important to deal with them immediately by reducing flexible expenses and talking with creditors.

Savings accounts are a safe way to put aside money for future use. When making an investment, consider the amount of money available, time factors, degree of risk and return, tax benefits, and liquidity.

## Vocabulary

Match each of the following vocabulary words with one of the definitions below.

credit

equity

collateral

finance charge

annual percentage rate

inflation

credit rating

bankruptcy

investment

annual percentage yield

1. The standing of an individual that indicates how good a credit risk he or she is, is a _____ .

2. An outlay of money for income or profit is an _____ .

3. The ratio of the dollar finance charge to the average amount of credit in use for the length of the contract is an _____ .

4. The rate at which the money in a savings plan earns interest in one year is called the _____ .

5. An increase in the general level of prices due to an increased volume of money and credit is _____ .

6. The privilege of taking possession of money, goods, or services in exchange for a promise to pay for them at some future date is _____ .

7. Property or goods pledged for repayment of a loan if the borrower cannot meet the payment schedule is _____ .

8. A procedure that causes you to lose certain personal possessions in order to repay debts is called _____ .

9. The total of all the charges for obtaining credit is the _____ .

10. The owner's interest in a property over and above any claims against it is _____ .

## Questions

1. What are the advantages of using credit?

2. How can using credit add to the costs of goods and services?

3. How can using credit sometimes lead to overspending?

4. Compare the advantages and disadvantages of open-end credit with those of installment credit.

5. Why is it important to know the annual percentage rate before accepting credit?

6. What are the advantages and disadvantages of finance companies?

7. What was the Equal Credit Opportunity Act of 1975? *Pg 173*

8. Compare and contrast the different types of credit contracts.

9. What information should you check before you sign a credit contract?

10. If a person runs into credit problems, how should he or she deal with the situation?

11. Compare a money market savings account with a certificate of deposit.

## Skill Activities

1. **Decision Making.** Investigate the credit contracts at a retail operation, service business, or bank (for a credit card). Use the "Checking the Credit Contract" guidelines on page 176.

Compare the contract offered by the institution you investigated with those researched by other members of your class and select the best contract. You may want to compile a "Local Credit Contract Guide" by putting together and photocopying the information your class gathered.

2. **Math Skills.** What would it cost you to buy an expensive item on credit? Select some item such as a television set, a VCR, a bicycle, or a computer. Then research the cost and credit terms at three different stores in your area to determine the total cost of buying the item on credit during one year. Use the chart for "Buying A $900 Stereo on Credit" as a guideline for determining the total cost.

3. **Critical Thinking.** Ask one person you know well with a full-time job to describe his or her employer-sponsored retirement program. As a class, compile a list of the advantages and disadvantages of the different plans. Which benefits seem the most important to you? Why?

4. **Resource Management.** No matter what your income is, try to figure out if you could save a small percentage of it. You already have kept track of your expenses for one week. Are there any expenses you could have saved instead? If so, figure out what that savings would amount to after one full year. Could you use this amount toward a major purchase? Think about whether you value the savings or the weekly expenses more.

# 9

# Becoming an Informed Consumer

## As you read, think about:

- how to understand and practice your rights and responsibilities as wise consumers.
- how to evaluate advertising in order to make wise consumer decisions.
- how to find and use many sources of consumer information.
- how to understand warranties and contracts.
- how to apply the management process to personal consumer decisions.

## Vocabulary

consumer
products
services
warranty
implied warranty
express warranty
full warranty
limited warranty
contract

Being aware of your rights and responsibilities as a consumer can help you to buy more wisely and receive more value for your money. Learning to evaluate advertising, using many sources for consumer information, and understanding warranties and contracts will help you to become an informed consumer.

The way you manage consumer decisions will, of course, depend on your own individual values, goals, and resources.

## Knowing Consumer Rights and Responsibilities

What is a consumer? A **consumer** is anyone who selects and pays for goods or services. **Products** or goods are material items, such as food, clothing, and appliances. **Services** are actions or labor that have value. Services may or may not result in the production of a specific item. Health care, entertainment, cleaning, maintenance, repairs, consulting work, product installation, construction work, and insurance protection are all examples of services that you may want to purchase some day.

When you buy a new shirt or a loaf of bread or a car, you are acting as a consumer of goods. When you pay for a haircut or for someone to clean the rugs in your home, you are acting as a consumer of services. These are only a few examples of the hundreds of products and services we use every day.

In 1962, President John F. Kennedy presented to Congress four basic consumer rights: the right to choose, the right to be heard, the right to safety, and the right to be informed. In the 1970s, President Gerald R. Ford added the right to consumer education. These rights not only provide guidelines for the performance of producers and businesses but also carry certain responsibilities for the consumers of these products and services.

## The Right to Choose

Competition in the free enterprise system helps to provide you, the consumer, with a variety of products and services from which to choose and a variety of businesses from which to purchase them. There are, for example, many companies that make many different types of hairdryers and many stores and mail-order houses that sell them. There are many different telephone companies, and each offers a variety of services. The variety of goods and services you find in the marketplace allows you, as a consumer, to choose the products or services that most closely meet your needs and wants.

As a consumer, it is your responsibility to analyze the choices that are available and to make informed decisions based on these analyses. You need to let companies and businesses know when you are pleased with products and services and when you are not. You also need to express your satisfaction or dissatisfaction with stores or other places of business. When you express your satisfaction or dissatisfaction, your comments help producers and businesses to meet consumer needs.

## The Right to Be Heard

Our democratic process of government offers citizens a means of being heard. We can go to public hearings on proposed actions or legislation that will affect us as consumers. We can write to our congressional representatives or other government officials at the state or national level to comment on proposed or existing actions or legislation. Government officials frequently consider citizen opinions when proposing, discussing, or voting on some types of legislation.

Many companies have consumer departments or divisions to deal with consumer wants, needs, issues, and problems. The information these departments receive is often used when products are redesigned or services are changed. Most companies want to please consumers because consumers are the lifeline of their businesses.

As consumers, we must speak out on issues that concern us or may have an effect on us or on our community or state or nation. If we do not accept this responsibility, others will make decisions for us.

## The Right to Safety

Consumers have the right to be protected from products and services that cause health problems, illnesses, or injuries. Many government agencies, including the Consumer Product Safety Commission (CPSC), the Food

What responsibility do you have if products you buy are unsatisfactory?

and Drug Administration (FDA), the Department of Agriculture (USDA), the Environmental Protection Agency (EPA), and various local and state consumer offices, health departments, and departments of agriculture, help to establish criteria and guidelines for safe products and services. These agencies are responsible for seeing that the guidelines are met and that offenders are punished.

Producers are responsible for offering products and services that are safe and for providing directions for their safe and proper use. Consumers are responsible for using the products according to the directions provided. Companies that produce goods cannot be expected to protect consumers from their own carelessness or neglect.

## The Right to Be Informed

Consumers have the right to correct and complete information about products and services available to them. This includes truthful advertising, complete and easy-to-understand information about financing, credit costs, and any other charges, and honest answers to any questions they may have.

At the same time, consumers should use the information that is provided and ask questions when more information is desired. A well-informed consumer is more likely to make decisions that are satisfying and that use available resources wisely.

## The Right to Consumer Education

This right expands upon the right to be informed. The right to be informed focuses on information about the product or service. The right to consumer education focuses on knowledge about the *economy,* or the framework within which goods and services are bought and sold, and the relationship of consumers

Informing yourself about the quality of a product can help you to choose wisely.

and producers to each other and to their economy. An individual who has a basic understanding of the economic system is better equipped to function as an informed, responsible consumer.

Along with the right to consumer education goes the responsibility to learn about the economy and how it works and to use that information to behave in a responsible way.

## For Review

1. Name the five basic rights of consumers.
2. Explain the consumer responsibilities that correspond to each of the five basic consumer rights.
3. Why is competition among businesses so important to you as a consumer?

## CONSUMER RIGHTS AND RESPONSIBILITIES

Consumers have certain rights which carry with them certain responsibilities...

| Consumer Rights | Consumer Responsibilities |
|---|---|
| The right to choose | The responsibility to make informed decisions |
| The right to be heard | The responsibility to speak out on matters of concern to consumers |
| The right to safety | The responsibility to use products as intended |
| The right to be informed | The responsibility to make use of that information when making decisions |
| The right to consumer education | The responsibility to learn about our economic system |

## Evaluating Advertising

There are many forms of advertising all around us. Billions of dollars are spent each year by companies that want to keep their products in front of the eyes and ears of the consumer as often as possible. There are catchy tunes and jingles about goods and services on the radio and on television. There are billboard, newspaper, magazine, and television ads. Sometimes, on television, there seems to be more time devoted to advertising than to the actual programs.

Advertising informs you, the consumer who buys the goods or services; but how can you evaluate all of the advertising you see and hear? How can you sort through advertising information to make the wisest choice of goods and services? Once you understand the techniques used in advertising and how to look for factual information in advertising, you will become a wiser consumer who is more able to control spending. Learning to do these things can help you to meet your wants and needs with the resources you have.

## Truth in Advertising

While most advertisements do not actually lie about products and services, there is enough dishonest advertising around to warrant efforts to prevent deliberately misleading or untruthful ads. The advertising industry itself has guidelines and standards to follow and a board that hears complaints and makes recommendations. Radio and television companies have certain standards and guidelines for advertising. Advertisements that do not meet these standards will not be aired. Finally, the government has a role in regulating advertising. The Federal Trade Commission (FTC) receives complaints about advertising groups. It collects information about each complaint. If it finds the advertisement unfair or deceptive, it may force the company to pay a fine, stop the ad, and/or replace the advertisement with an ad that corrects the misleading information first given to the public.

## Advertising Techniques

The company whose advertisement you are reading or listening to wants you to buy its goods or services to meet its needs and wants. You, as the consumer, must decide about purchases based on *your* needs and wants. To do this, you should recognize certain advertising techniques, including product association, omission, bandwagon advertising, repetition, and bait-and-switch advertising.

**Product Association** Product association uses places, people, or things to create a happy or contented feeling that you associate with the product being advertised. For example, you may see an advertisement that shows a young, handsome, healthy-looking person riding a horse. The setting is in the mountains on a clear, sunny day. The product being advertised may be anything from soap to chewing gum. Whatever it is, the ad has been produced to leave you with the impression that you will be happier and healthier if you buy and use the product. You associate the product itself with the feeling the ad has created.

Using beautiful individuals and famous actors, actresses, and sports stars to promote products is an effective form of product association. If you admire someone's looks or accomplishments, you may want to buy the product that person is advertising. If you do this without listening for more specific facts about the product, you may end up a disappointed consumer. Try to look past the product association technique to get to the real facts before you buy goods or services.

**Omission** Omitting something means leaving it out. Advertisers naturally tell you only the best things about their products and services. An advertisement for a new sports car may tell you that it gets more miles to the gallon than a competing model, but it won't tell you that the car is so light that it did poorly in a recent crash test. It is your responsibility to investigate these omitted issues before you buy.

The misleading use of statistics falls into the omission category. For example, you may hear, "Four out of five doctors surveyed recommended product X." You may think that the product must be wonderful for 80 percent of the doctors to recommend it, but is that what the words really say? The advertisement does not say how many doctors were surveyed, so it could be that only five doctors were surveyed. Four doctors are not very many out of the total number of doctors in the country!

**Bandwagon Advertising** Bandwagon advertising makes you feel that everyone is buying goods or services and that you will be missing out if you do not join the crowd. This technique appeals to your emotional need to belong to the popular, smart group. Showing crowds of happy people enjoying a new soft drink is one example. Remember that those people are smiling because they are being paid to do the

How do these signs and billboards influence you as a consumer?

advertisement. Listen to other facts about the soft drink before deciding whether or not you want to try it.

**Repetition**   Repeating words or phrases many times in an ad or commercial may be irritating, but it is effective. Sometimes you find yourself singing part of a commercial. When that happens, the advertiser has succeeded in keeping the product in your mind.

**Bait and Switch Advertising**   This type of advertising is designed first to get you into the store, then to get you to buy more expensive goods than those shown in the original advertisements you saw or heard.

For example, you see an advertisement in the newspaper for a bicycle at a reasonable price. You go to the store, and the salesperson tells you that the only bike like that one is slightly damaged or that it isn't the best model for you. You then are shown several more expensive models. Here the advertisement is

the "bait," and the store tries to "switch" you to a different purchase.

## Making Wise Consumer Decisions

Once you can recognize certain advertising techniques, you can begin to find helpful facts in an advertisement. For example, advertisements for clothing may tell you sizes, colors, fiber content, and care needed. There may be a picture of the style. Often the advertisement tells you where you can buy the product and how much it costs. Automobile advertising may tell you about horsepower, gas mileage, special engine features, and safety features, as well as offering a picture or drawing of one or more models. Sometimes information about product or service guarantees is also given in an advertisement. Advertisers want consumers to know that certain brands, styles, and types of products and services are

What useful information should you look for in advertisements?

for sale. They also want to encourage consumers to buy. This is why advertising is both beneficial for and tempting to the shopper. Consumers need to be informed but not persuaded against their own best interests.

If a product or service sounds too good to be true, it usually is. You should expect a product or service to perform its primary function, not miracles. Learn how to use advertising and to separate the factual information from appeals to your emotions.

Resist buying things you do not need just because advertising makes them look so attractive. If you have a good hairdryer, you do not need another, although seeing repeated advertisements for ones that have more features or different shapes may make you wish you had a newer model. The newer model may not dry your hair any better or faster and may not be any easier to handle. However, if advertising can make you less happy with what you have, then producers have a better chance of convincing you to buy something new.

Read and listen to advertisements carefully to separate information from statements that are not meaningful or helpful. You may need to think carefully about statements such as "Nothing is better for your teeth than Brand A," or "No other refrigerator keeps food fresher." Perhaps nothing is better for your teeth than Brand A, but how many products are equally as good? Perhaps no other refrigerator does keep food fresher, but there may be several that are equally as good. If you closely analyze the advertisement, you will discover some of the information is valuable, and some of it is not. If you can compare the information presented about one product with the information presented about another, similar product, the information probably is useful. If a comparison is difficult, you probably are not being given enough information. Try to look for the facts in advertising. To make the best use of advertising, you should try to:

- look for specific information.
- analyze any statistical information.
- look at what the words really mean.
- enjoy the "appeals" without giving in to each one.
- avoid products or services that promise new "miracles."
- avoid products or services that promise "something for nothing."

## For Review

1. What role does the Federal Trade Commission play in maintaining truth in advertising standards?
2. Name and describe five different kinds of advertising techniques.
3. What useful information does advertising sometimes supply?

## Sources of Consumer Information

Having information about products and services can help you to decide whether or not to buy a product or service, if a product or service will meet your needs and wants, and which specific product or service will be the best for you. Making use of this information can help you to avoid wasting money and can increase your satisfaction with your use of money resources.

You can learn about products and services through the personal recommendations of others and through the mass media. You can also obtain consumer information from nonprofit, consumer organizations and from the brands, seals, and labels on the products themselves.

# The Consumer Advocacy ACT

Consumers can make a difference! Four housewives, concerned about the television programming and commercials their children were "consuming," believed in consumer power when they met to discuss "kidvid" in 1968. They pooled $3,000, invited friends and neighbors to join them in Action for Children's Television, and began by "going right to the top" to make some changes. Their first success, in 1969, was on the local scene. Pickets and petitions organized by ACT helped convince a local TV station not to interrupt a quality children's show to air another program. ACT leaders met with the station president to apply consumer pressure. That same year, they met with other influential people: U.S. senators. In testimony before the Senate, ACT protested changes in the law governing the licensing of TV and radio stations. They wanted to make sure that licenses could be challenged so that stations would have to remain responsive to consumers.

By 1971, ACT had a thousand members in 38 states and had to move from its founders' living rooms to office space. Increasing financial support and media coverage added to its "clout." Over the years, ACT has been influential in challenging deceptive toy commercials; limiting advertising of products that can be unhealthy or dangerous to young children; decreasing the minutes per hour devoted to commercials on weekend kids' shows; and encouraging quality programming. In 1973, *Time* magazine called ACT the "most effective force in children's television." Through publications, films, media spots, national conferences, awards, lawsuits, and testimony before various government bodies, four housewives—and the 15,000 others who joined them—have made consumer advocacy a great ACT to follow!

## Personal Recommendations

People who have used products and services or have special interests in certain types of products are good sources of information. For example, if a friend owns a certain brand and model of bicycle, he or she may be able to tell you what is good or what is bad about it. If someone you know has a special interest in cars or computers, then he or she may be able to tell you what to look for and what to look out for when you shop.

Some salespersons know a great deal about the products or services they sell. When they provide as much information as possible without pressuring you to buy, they can be helpful. They may be able to tell you about the special features of the products or services they sell, the care the product requires, the reliability of the product or service, and the degree to which the manufacturer or producer backs the product or service. Try to sort out the valid information from the sales "pitch." Remember that the salesperson may receive a commission, or a percent of the sale price, for each sale. Don't allow a salesperson to talk you into a purchase you really are not ready or willing to make.

Repair persons are another source of consumer information. They can tell you, for example, which products rarely need repair. If they fix all types of cars or appliances, for example, they have a good basis for the comparisons they make.

## Mass Media

Books, pamphlets and booklets, periodicals, catalogs, and newspapers are all sources of printed consumer information. Some of the information is in the form of advertisements or promotional material. Other printed information is provided by nonprofit consumer organizations that test products and publish their results for the consumer.

**Books**  Books can offer you all kinds of information on all kinds of subjects. For example, the information you learn from a book about the human body, common medical problems, and health-care procedures can help you when you are choosing health-care services or when you are dealing with health-care personnel. From books, you can learn about making living spaces more energy efficient. With this information, you will know what to ask a contractor

How can the recommendation of a mechanic help you to decide on a car?

and what to look for when evaluating work. You can learn about food and nutrition so you will be more knowledgeable when you shop and prepare food or when you eat out. Public libraries and bookstores offer books on a variety of subjects that may help you as a consumer. The federal government also publishes books that can be helpful to the consumer.

**Pamphlets and Booklets** Many free pamphlets and booklets on services and products may be obtained from the federal government. These can tell you what features to look for, what to avoid, and how to make the best use of the product or service you are interested in. Some publications tell you how to avoid being a victim of fraud. Your librarian can tell you where to write for a catalog of government publications for consumers.

Frequently, companies that produce or sell goods or services publish booklets for consumer use. Some of these may contain valuable information about specific products or services; some are more sales promotion devices than sources of information.

Look for unbiased publications to read when you need consumer product information. Avoid sales pitch pamphlets.

**Periodicals** Magazines, newspapers, and newsletters often contain information that can help you to make informed decisions. Some periodicals contain general information about products and services. Others contain detailed information about specific products and services, based on tests of the products and surveys of consumer satisfaction. Sometimes, several similar products are compared. Reports on services usually are based on information obtained from different companies that offer services, as well as consumer surveys that focus on satisfaction with services they have used.

*Consumer Reports* and *Consumers' Research Magazine* are two valuable sources of information. These magazines rate products they have researched and tested. The products are rated in terms of performance (value) in relation to price. These types of magazines are especially valuable since they are not published by the makers or sellers of goods or services. They provide unbiased, factual information. Safety and quality are their primary concern when they rate a product.

**Catalog Descriptions** Catalogs provide specific and general information for you, the consumer. They can be an efficient way to begin the shopping process because they provide a basis for price comparisons without going from store to store. You should realize, however, that the quality of the product may be hard to judge from a catalog picture.

**Newspapers** Besides general advertising, many newspapers have consumer columns that tell you about products and services. Some of these columns answer specific consumer questions and concerns.

**Radio and Television** Apart from the advertisements heard and seen on radio and television, these media also provide individual programs to inform you. Many stations have reporters who only deal with consumer issues. Public service announcements also keep you informed. Sometimes there are individual programs written and produced to deal with specific consumer problems and issues, such as the best way to shop for a used car. Radio and television talk shows often provide the opportunity to call in and ask questions as a consumer. An expert who is a guest on the show will discuss your comments and try to answer your questions. You can gain valuable consumer information just by watching and listening to some of these shows, even if you do not call in yourself.

## Nonprofit Consumer Organizations

Consumers' Union, Consumers' Research, and the Better Business Bureau (BBB) are three important nonprofit consumer organizations. As the term *nonprofit* implies, these organizations do not make any money from the sales of the goods and services they survey and report on. They exist to educate you as a consumer by researching and testing the quality of goods, services, and businesses.

Consumers' Union publishes *Consumer Reports;* Consumers' Research publishes *Consumers' Research Magazine.* The Better Business Bureau has local bureaus throughout the United States that are funded by membership dues from individual businesses. The BBB provides consumers with information about the reputation of businesses. Each local BBB keeps a file of all complaints about the goods or services of companies and businesses in that area. If you are considering buying something from a company, you may want to call the BBB to find out if any complaints have been filed against that company. This information will indicate how dissatisfied customers have been. If you are thinking of hiring a company or

How can the Better Business Bureau help you to make consumer choices?

individual to do a service for you, such as plumbing or wallpapering, you can call the BBB to find out if they have a history of complaints. Comparing businesses in terms of the number of complaints against them can help you to make a more informed and, therefore, wiser consumer choice.

## Product Brands, Seals, and Labels

Consumers who are brand-name buyers have a reason for it. Often, but not always, it is because they have learned through their own experience or the recommendations of other people that the product is reliable. Consumers frequently base their decisions on a product's or service's reliability and the company's support of its products or services.

Seals are another way that consumers can learn about a product. Various organizations give companies the right to use their seals if the products meet their requirements. For example, the seal of the American Gas Association means that a gas appliance meets the safety and design standards established by the American National Standards Institute. Approval by the American Dental Association means a dental product meets certain standards. If you are considering a product or service that has some type of seal, you may want to find out what the certification means.

Many products have labels or tags that offer specific information, such as size, brand name, care instructions, special features, ingredients, nutritional values, energy efficiency, and so on. Reading these tags and labels often can provide you with helpful information before you make a purchase.

## *For Review*

1. Explain how the personal recommendations of friends, salespersons, and repair persons can help you to make better choices as a consumer.

2. Explain how the Better Business Bureau works for the consumer.

3. Name two magazines published by non-profit consumer organizations. What types of information do they contain?

Major purchases such as cars may be made on the basis of the type of warranty.

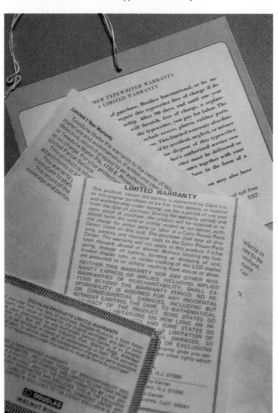

# *Understanding Warranties and Contracts*

The content of the warranty and/or contract that a business provides to insure your satisfaction with its goods or services is another important source of consumer information. Both the warranty and the contract include promises to you, the consumer. You should read and understand all warranty and contract information thoroughly before making purchases or choosing to pay for a service.

## *Warranties*

A **warranty,** or guarantee, is a written or mutually understood promise from a manufacturer or seller. The warranty tells the consumer the terms under which defective goods will be repaired or replaced. It also includes information about refunding your money if you are not satisfied with goods.

***Implied Warranties*** Warranties are not always in writing. An **implied warranty** sometimes exists simply because a sale has taken place. It is based on certain assumptions the consumer can make about the product.

All products carry with them an implied warranty of *merchantability*. This means that the product, when used properly, will do what it is supposed to do for a reasonable length of time; for example, a hairdryer will dry hair more than a few times, a pen will write for several weeks or months, depending on its use; an automatic dryer will dry clothes for more than a few months. Just by selling the product, the merchant implies that it will work properly.

When a consumer asks advice from a salesperson for a specific product for a specific situation, then buys the recommended product and uses it as directed, the product carries an implied warranty of *fitness*. This means that the product should meet the need the consumer expressed to the salesperson. Suppose, for example, you tell the salesperson in the lumber yard that you have a wall space over your desk four feet wide and five feet high for shelves. You want to know what kind of shelf supports and what type and size of lumber to use for holding heavy books. The warranty of fitness covers your purchase if you buy what the salesperson recommends.

## CHECKING A WARRANTY

Look for this information in a warranty:

- the type of warranty (full or limited or a combination of the two)
- what is covered and what is not covered
- time limitations
- if the warranty is limited to only the first buyer
- who pays for what in case repairs are needed
- limitations on who can make repairs
- who pays for damages or losses caused by a faulty product or service
- if the warranty card must be returned by the buyer
- actions that will negate the warranty
- actions that are necessary to keep the warranty in effect

## *Practical Tip: Saving Warranties*

■ Save warranties and dated sales receipts that come with merchandise in case you want to return it. Some warranty cards should be mailed in. Putting sales receipts and warranties in one place will help you to find them if needed. An old shoebox makes an inexpensive file.

Implied warranty rights vary from state to state. In some states, the consumer has three years to discover a problem and to seek some kind of resolution to the problem from the store or manufacturer. In other states, the consumer may have four or even five years.

The limitations placed on implied warranties also vary from state to state. In many states, express warranties limit implied warranties. This means that if a written warranty limits the manufacturer's responsibility for product performance to three months, the implied warranty is void after that time. In a few states, implied warranties cannot be limited by express warranties.

Although individual businesses have different policies about returning faulty products, many are willing to replace them.

***Express Warranties*** An **express warranty** is created by the seller or manufacturer of a product and includes specific statements about the product. Express warranties usually are stated in writing. However, an advertisement or even an explanation by a salesperson can be considered an express warranty. Usually consumers want to know exactly what is covered in an express warranty and are reluctant to accept anything less than a written warranty.

While there are no laws requiring sellers or manufacturers to offer written warranties with certain products or to give consumers copies of written warranties, the Magnuson-Moss Warranty Act, passed by Congress in 1975, does force any written warranties to meet certain requirements.

If a product has a written warranty and the product costs $15 or more, a copy of the warranty must be made available to the consumer before the product is purchased. You should ask about a written warranty for any product you are thinking of buying. The seller should have a copy for you to read, although he or she does not have to give you a copy to keep.

One type of express warranty is known as a full warranty. A **full warranty** is a promise to fix or replace an item, or a particular part of an item, free of charge. This type of warranty must be labeled as a full warranty and must state how long the warranty is in effect. A full warranty may cover an entire product, such as a hairdryer, or it may cover only parts of a product, such as the motor in a dishwasher or the mechanical parts of a bicycle but not the tires. Whatever is covered by the full warranty is fully covered—including repair or replacement of the product or part, parts and labor included. A full refund may be part of a full warranty if the repairs do not prove satisfactory. If the product is sold to someone else, the full warranty is still valid if the time limit has not passed. A full warranty cannot limit or disclaim any implied warranties.

Another type of express warranty is a limited warranty. A **limited warranty** limits the promises made about a product and may require certain actions on the part of the consumer. In other words, the seller or manufacturer has less responsibility than if it were a full warranty, and the consumer has more responsibility. For example, a limited warranty may be void unless the consumer sends in the warranty card. The consumer may be required to bring a product back to the store for servicing. The seller may be responsible for certain parts but not for any labor costs. There are some limited warranties that place time limits on implied warranties.

Some product warranties are a combination of full warranties and limited warranties. A product may be covered by a full warranty for 90 days (all parts and labor), and be covered by a limited warranty from the 91st day until one year from the date of purchase (parts but no labor). On the same product, there also may be a limited warranty on liability, or responsibility, for any additional expenses incurred by the consumer if the product does not work as it should.

Many people think that express warranties are more valuable than implied warranties because things are in writing. However, written warranties can contain so many restrictions in terms of time limits and manufacturer's (or seller's) responsibilities that they not be valuable to the consumer. They may, in fact, negate consumer rights as they are set forth in implied warranties.

**Warranties for Services** While there are no laws covering warranties for services, most reputable businesses or individuals do try to satisfy customers, and many guarantee the work they do. It is important to check the reputation of any service person or business you are considering hiring, however, because there are some who seem to be interested only in earning money rather than pleasing their customers. As you have learned, you can do this by contacting the Better Business Bureau. Businesses with highly satisfied customers usually have high standards of quality for all customers and stand behind their work. Some will redo the work or refund the money if the customer is not satisfied. You should try to find out about service guarantees when you are comparison shopping.

## Contracts

Like warranties, contracts do not have to be in writing, although many are. A **contract** is a legally binding agreement between two or more persons or parties. To be legally binding, both parties must be capable of bargaining, both parties must agree to the terms, both

parties must contribute something of value (such as money or a product or a service), and the agreement must be for a legal purpose. Usually, all parties involved in the contract must be at least eighteen years old. In some instances, they must be at least twenty-one years old.

An unwritten contract can be as simple as an agreement between you and a friend that you will sell him or her your bicycle, and he or she will pay you so much money for it. If either one of you does not fulfill your part of the bargain, it is possible to take legal action to carry out the contract. In this instance, however, you might just agree to cancel the contract for the moment and remain friends.

In most states, there are some situations in which contracts must be written. These instances are usually defined by the state's

## CHECKING A CONTRACT

Look for this information in a contract:

• names and addresses of all parties involved

• date of the contract

• intent or purpose of the contract

• complete description of the product or service to be provided

• date the product is to be delivered or service is to be completed (including intermediate dates, if appropriate)

• date for payment in full (including intermediate dates, if appropriate)

• the total price for the product or service

Understanding contracts before signing them is vital. Why might it be a good idea to have a written contract even when dealing with a friend?

laws. The sale or purchase of real estate, for example, usually requires a written contract. Usually the sale of goods costing more than $500 requires a written contract.

Rather than depending on verbal agreement, many people prefer to write up contracts, particularly when large amounts of money are involved or a variety of types of work are to be done.

A written contract can be short and simple or long and complex. Simple transactions usually can be covered by a simple contract. Complex transactions, such as remodeling a house or buying a car, usually require more complex contracts. In some cases when you are buying a house or contracting for building a shopping mall, for example, contracts are written or approved or negotiated by lawyers. For most general consumer transactions, however, you do not need a lawyer.

## For Review

1. Explain the major difference between implied and express warranties.

2. List ten types of information that you should check for on a warranty.

3. Give one example of an unwritten contract that might be in effect when you buy or sell a product or service.

# Management Application: Getting the Goods

Imagine yourself in the situation described below. As you read, think about how the steps of the management process might apply to this situation. Then answer the questions that follow.

## Situation

You have decided to buy a portable radio for your room. You can afford this purchase because you have received birthday money from relatives. You have seen a few radios you like, but you need more information in order to decide which one to purchase.

Saturday morning you go to the shopping mall and ask questions about the different radios. The salespeople show you several models with the features you want. You try them out and decide that they all sound pretty much alike. You have seen ads for Blabbo radios that claim that "Blabbos sound the best." You decide they don't. You also know several friends who bought Blabbos, and they needed repairs within three months.

You check in the latest *Consumer Reports* to learn how the different radios are rated. The two brands you are considering are near the top of the list, so you feel satisfied about buying either one of them. Now you feel you are ready to make your purchase.

The next day, you read an ad in the newspaper about a huge truckload sale of radios and televisions at 50 percent off the retail price. Sure enough, they have just the brand and model you want, so you buy it. What a deal! You

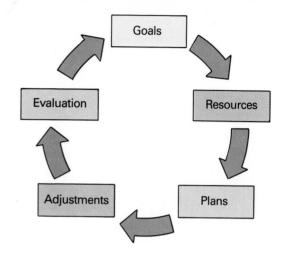

are really excited about your bargain; you hurry home and set up the radio in your room. You turn it on and start singing happily.

The radio works well for two days, then dies out. When you go to return it you realize that the truck is no longer there. Worse, your radio did not come in a box or with the usual warranty. When you reread the sale ad, you see the words "Some slightly damaged. No returns" on it.

## Questions

1. What was your goal? Did you have the resources you needed?

2. What were the steps in your consumer plan for getting information?

3. How would you evaluate the results of your plan? What went wrong?

4. Explain why paying full price is sometimes the better deal.

5. Which steps of the management process apply to this situation?

# *Chapter Review*

## *Summary*

Consumers have certain rights that carry with them responsibilities. Learning to evaluate advertising by recognizing advertising techniques can help the consumer to make the wisest choice of goods and services. Some of these advertising techniques are product association, omission, bandwagon advertising, and repetition. Once in the store, you may be the victim of bait-and-switch advertising if you are not familiar with this technique.

The consumer can learn about goods and services through personal recommendations, mass media, periodicals, product seals, and nonprofit consumer organizations. Warranties and contracts, both written and unwritten, provide further information for consumers and help to protect their interests.

## *Vocabulary*

Use each of the vocabulary words below to complete the following sentences.

consumer

products

services

warranty

implied warranty

express warranty

full warranty

limited warranty

contract

1. An _____ is a guarantee created by the seller or manufacturer of a product. It is usually in writing.

2. A _____ is a legally binding agreement between two or more persons or parties.

3. _____ , or goods, are material items, such as food, clothing, and appliances.

4. A _____ is a promise to fix or replace an item, or a part of an item, free of charge.

5. A _____ , or guarantee, is a written or mutually understood promise from a manufacturer or seller.

6. _____ are actions or labor that have value, such as health care, cleaning, maintenance, repairs, and consulting work.

7. A _____ is a guarantee that may require certain actions on the part of the consumer before the seller or manufacturer is required to take action.

8. An _____ is a guarantee concerning a product, based on assumptions the consumer can make about the product, but which is not necessarily in writing.

9. A _____ is anyone who selects and pays for goods or services.

## *Questions*

1. As a manufacturer, what are your responsibilities if a customer returns a radio after six months, claiming that it does not work? Do you have any rights?

2. As a consumer, what are your rights if you purchase an iron that gives you a shock? What are your responsibilities?

3. How does the bandwagon technique in advertising work?

4. How do advertisers use product association to sell their products?

5. Explain how a consumer can make wiser choices about products if he or she understands advertising techniques.

6. Explain how *Consumer Reports* and *Consumers' Research Magazine* can help you to exercise your rights and responsibilities as a consumer.

7. How can friends help each other to exercise their rights and responsibilities?

8. What is merchantability? How is merchantability related to warranties?

9. What is the difference between a warranty and a contract?

10. How do product seals and labels help consumers? How can they be misleading?

## Skill Activities

1. ***Communication.*** Get tuned in to advertising techniques. Look over some magazines or newspaper ads. Find two ads that show one of the advertising techniques discussed in this chapter on pages 195–196. Cut out the ads or copy them down. Explain which technique was used.

Now write your own ad, using one of the techniques studied in this chapter. For example: Football player, Sam Strong, loves Wheat-Sport cereal. It keeps him healthy and happy. You'll love it too. (Product association)

2. ***Decision Making.*** Learn to use a consumer guide. Research a product, for example, a television set, a VCR, a curling iron, or a walkman. Go to the reference area in the library and consult *Consumer Reports*. Make copies of those pages that indicate which manufacturers produce the product you are interested in buying. Decide which one is the best purchase, and then write a short paragraph defending your selection.

3. ***Critical Thinking.*** Follow up on Exercise 2. Find out what kind of warranties are offered on the item you selected. What kind of warranties are offered by the competitors? Which is the best warranty? Why?

4. ***Science.*** Test the claim of any TV commercial or magazine ad that its product performs better than a competing brand. Perform the experiment as demonstrated in the ad. For example, test the claim of a detergent ad that its product removes stains better than another detergent. Using identical pieces of cloth containing several common stains such as ink, mustard, and grease, use each detergent in identical water temperature. Report the results of your experiment to the class.

# *10 Developing Consumer Skills*

## *As you read, think about:*

- [ ] how to use your resources wisely as a consumer.
- [ ] how to decide where and when to shop to get the most for your resources.
- [ ] how to take effective steps to solve consumer complaints or problems.
- [ ] how to apply the management process to personal shopping decisions within the limits of your resources.

impulse buying
comparison shop
sales
small claims court

Knowing how to shop can help you to make the best possible use of your resources. Having a shopping plan and learning where and when to shop will help you to satisfy your own needs and wants. To be a wise consumer, you need to be able to evaluate bargains and to learn how to recognize quality in goods and services. Finally, as a wise consumer, you will want to know what steps you should take to resolve any complaints you may have about an item you have purchased.

## Deciding on a Shopping Plan

No matter what you are shopping for, you have a better chance of being satisfied with what you buy and how you have used your resources if it is part of a plan. **Impulse buying,** buying without thinking about your budget and needs, can leave you without money for the goods and services you do need. It can make you feel as if you are always trying to catch up on money matters, rather than being in control of them.

The first steps in your shopping plan should be to evaluate your resources and to decide what you need and want.

## Identifying Shopping Resources, Needs, and Wants

While some needs and wants can be met without money, many cannot. Before you can decide how to budget your money to meet your needs and wants, you must know how much money you have available. In Chapter 7, you learned about budgeting. This information can help you to determine how much you have to spend and how you should divide it. You also learned how to make and how to follow a spending and saving plan that will help you to reach your goals. Try to use what you have learned about budgeting when you set your shopping priorities.

When income is limited, planning is especially important to help guarantee that the basic needs for food, clothing, and shelter are met. After basic needs are met, each individual and family has its own personal list of needs. Individuals and families also must decide how they feel their needs should be met. For example, one person may be perfectly content with a one-room apartment; his or her need for shelter has been met adequately. Another person, however, may feel too closed-in in a one-room apartment; it does not meet his or her needs.

A clear understanding of needs and wants helps you to make a plan that will meet them as closely as possible with the resources you have. When your values and goals are clear to you, it is easier to determine your needs and wants and to make a plan to meet them.

## *Being Flexible When You Shop*

Any plan, including a shopping plan, should be flexible. New situations can change your needs or wants. Resources may change, leaving you with less or more than you had planned on. Being flexible allows you to adjust to these changes and still remain on the path toward your goals.

Sometimes when you are shopping, you will run across a bargain "too good to pass up." Should you pass it by just because it is not in your plan? Each individual and family must make that decision for themselves. If the individual or family takes advantage of the bargain without considering alternatives and consequences, the results may not be satisfactory.

Besides cost, why is it a good idea to comparison shop for tires?

Money may not be available for other needs and wants, or drastic adjustments may need to be made in plans, making it more difficult to reach desired goals. Sometimes, plans can be adjusted to accommodate the bargain. Your decision to buy or pass up a bargain should be based on a careful consideration of other alternatives and the consequences of any decision.

## *Making Shopping Decisions*

Whether you buy in stores, shop by mail or telephone, or buy from a salesperson in your home, there are certain facts you should know to make the best use of your time, effort, and money. Knowing when comparison shopping may be helpful and when it may not be is valuable. Learning how to comparison shop and deciding where and when to buy are also important consumer procedures. Bargain-hunting, sales, deciding how to pay, and ways to look for quality are all important shopping issues to learn about.

## Deciding When to Comparison Shop

When you **comparison shop,** you carefully compare and research the goods (products) or services of several different sellers before you purchase them. In other words, you find out what is being offered. You may find that everything you compared is out of your price range. You may find that nothing really meets your needs or serves the purpose you have in mind. If you had not comparison shopped, you might not have come to this conclusion. Helping you to decide whether or not to buy is one way that comparison shopping helps you to make the most of your resources.

As you comparison shop, you may want to compare the sources of the products and services, as well as the store and company policies. Comparison shopping can take a lot of time and effort, but most consumer experts agree that it is worth the time and effort when a lot of money is involved in the purchase. Comparison shopping is also worthwhile if you are shopping for a product or service that involves safety or health or that must last for a long time. In these situations, comparison shopping can help you to get the best quality and the highest degree of safety that is possible for what you have to spend. When a small amount of money is involved, or the product will be consumed or worn out shortly, comparison shopping is not as important. In fact, spending a lot of time collecting and comparing information may not be an effective use of your time in these situations.

For example, you might want to spend considerable time and effort comparison shopping for the following things: a stereo, a radio, a major appliance (such as a range, refrigerator, or washing machine), a computer, a major house repair, a bank or financial institution, or medical and dental care. You might spend less time and effort comparison shopping when you are looking for everyday clothes, an alarm clock, food, or a watch. Notebooks, notebook paper, pencils, pens, and snacks may not require any comparison shopping at all. You may simply buy what is most convenient.

Sometimes when you are just learning about a product or service, you will spend a lot of time comparison shopping. You will not need to spend that much time and effort the next time you make a similar decision. For example, Alison spent a great deal of time learning about cars, reading reports on different models, and talking with repair persons and salespersons before she decided to buy a used car. Even when she made the decision, she was not sure it was the right one. When Alison was ready to buy her next car, however, she was more confident. It didn't take her as

How much comparison shopping would you do to choose soap?

long to make a decision because she remembered what she had learned earlier, and she kept up with reports on different cars. After driving her car and knowing what her friends had, she knew the features she wanted and those she did not want. Knowledge and experience helped her to know what information was valuable, so she was able to streamline her process for comparing cars.

Sometimes, after comparison shopping a particular product a few times, consumers become brand-name buyers. They do little or no comparison shopping after their initial comparisons. This can save some time and effort when buying items that are purchased frequently or services that are used frequently. For example, when you are food shopping, having brand preferences makes it possible for you to shop in less time than it would take if you had to compare each product. Finding one brand of jeans that fits particularly well or wears out slowly cuts down on the time you spend shopping for clothes.

Brand-name buying for more expensive items may be satisfactory for some people if they are happy with the product and not concerned about paying less for a different brand. Other people, however, are not happy with a product unless they know they have done everything possible to get the most value for their money.

People who do all of their shopping in one or two stores are similar to brand-name buyers. They may have a particular salesperson whose judgment they trust (who, in effect, is doing their shopping for them), or

What knowledge and experience would be helpful to have when comparing fabrics?

they may like the services and policies of the store. It may cost them more not to shop around, but they may find the time they save makes it worthwhile. Confidence and trust in a store and its personnel are important to many people—sometimes more important than price.

When you are shopping for medical and dental care or banking and financial services or child care or repair services, you may comparison shop only once or twice and then stick with your initial decision. While in all these instances, it is important for you, as the consumer, to find the best service for your particular situation, it is impractical to comparison shop each time you need the service. In fact, better service may be given to loyal customers. Medical and dental care usually is better when there is an ongoing relationship between patient and doctor or doctors. Establishing a good relationship with whomever is providing the service may be more valuable than saving a few dollars. Of course, when needs change or dissatisfaction with the service, individual, or group offering the service occurs repeatedly, it may be time for more comparison shopping.

You can see that different situations require different decisions about comparison shopping. Each individual, group, or family must make these decisions based on their values, goals, and resources.

## Deciding Where to Shop

Stores may be large or small or any size in between. They may be fancy or plain, spacious or crowded. They may be owned by one or more individuals, one or more families, or by a large corporation. They may be independently owned, or they may be part of a chain of stores. No matter what their size, decor, or ownership, they all sell goods to consumers.

In a small community, there may be no stores at all, or only a few. Because there will

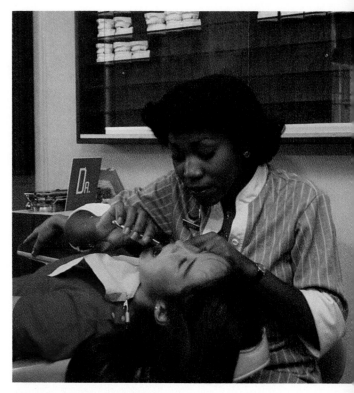

For quality health care, why is staying with one reliable, trusted source preferable to switching often?

be fewer shoppers in a small community, the stores are more likely to be small and may carry fewer goods than stores in larger communities. Stores in large cities or in malls that serve a large population or geographic area usually carry a wide variety of goods in many different styles, models, colors, and brands. Prices in these stores can vary considerably. As you visit the stores in your community or in a nearby community, you will become familiar with what they offer, and how they can meet your needs and wants when it is time to buy.

**Department Stores** Department stores sell a variety of goods, including clothes, small and large appliances, sporting goods, jewelry and other accessories, furniture, bedding, window coverings, floor coverings, gifts, books and records, and office supplies. Large department

If you are shopping for shoes, why might you be more satisfied with a specialty store than a department store?

**Specialty Stores** Specialty stores are stores that specialize in one particular product or a group of related products. A computer store may sell only computers, or it may sell software, furniture, and other accessories to be used with computers, as well as computers. Other examples of specialty stores include those that sell sporting goods, household appliances, home furnishings, auto parts, cameras, evening wear or formal clothes, maternity wear, uniforms for health-care workers, and gourmet foods. Specialty stores usually offer a wide selection of items in their particular areas of interest.

Employees at specialty stores often, but not always, are well informed about the product or products they are selling. If you need information about two or more products, they may be able to help you. For some products, such as microwave ovens, food processors, home computers, or sewing machines, some specialty stores may offer free classes to show you how to use the product properly to get the most benefit from it. Other services offered by specialty stores may include alterations, exchange and return privileges, pickup and delivery, phone orders, installation, and repair services. Most will take major credit cards, and many will accept personal checks.

**Supermarkets** Supermarkets are stores that sell a wide variety of food and food-related products. These can range from the basic fresh, frozen, canned, dried, and packaged foods to salad bars to deli and bakery items to gourmet foods to foods for special diets. Most supermarkets also carry laundry and cleaning products, housewares, paper goods, pet foods, magazines, and health and beauty items. Some large supermarkets sell toys, cards, books, records and tapes, small appliances, and plants and flowers. Some even have pharmacies.

Most supermarkets are self-service, although personnel are usually on hand to

stores may have different departments that offer similar goods in different price ranges. For example, there may be a department called "Better Sportswear" and another department called "Budget Sportswear." Some department stores have bargain basement sections as well, which are similar to discount department stores (see page 217).

Most department stores, particularly large ones, offer many services. They usually have a large number of salespeople available to help customers. They may offer a personal shopping service. Many of them accept personal checks as well as major credit cards. Many have their own credit cards. Alterations, telephone orders, exchange and return privileges, delivery and installation, parking facilities, and restroom facilities are other common services for department stores.

assist customers at the meat counter or in specialty sections, such as the deli or bakery. Sometimes employees bag the purchases and help customers take the groceries to their vehicles. Most supermarkets accept personal checks, and some will cash checks if the customer has the proper identification. Few, if any, supermarkets offer delivery service.

**Discount Stores** Discount stores sell products at lower prices than regular stores. The products may be the same brands or of similar quality as products sold in regular stores, or they may be of lower quality. Discount stores usually keep their costs down by having few displays or less elaborate displays, being located where buildings cost less to rent or buy, and by being largely self-service. Many discount stores will accept major credit cards and personal checks, although some operate on a cash only basis. Some do not provide bags for purchases or charge a small fee for each bag used. Usually discount stores have no repair or service departments and charge extra for delivery and installation, if they even offer the service. Customers may or may not be able to return or exchange purchases. Some stores issue a credit rather than a refund.

**Convenience Stores** Convenience stores are what their name implies—located conveniently, usually in a neighborhood, and open long hours or 24 hours a day. Usually, they are small and carry basic items such as bread and pastries, milk and other beverages, frozen and canned food, snack food, baby food, pet food, paper products, health and beauty aids, newspapers and magazines, and books. Selections are usually limited, and prices are often higher than at a supermarket.

Some convenience stores have small deli counters and fresh produce sections. Some sell sandwiches, soup, and hamburgers along with beverages and desserts.

**Factory Outlets or Outlet Stores** A factory outlet is a store that sells goods that come directly from the factory. These may be first quality items, or they may be *seconds,* goods that do not measure up to first quality. Usually the prices are lower than in other retail stores. Products are usually sold "as is," and there may be a policy of no returns or exchanges.

Most factory outlets deal in only one kind of product, shoes, sportswear, sweaters, woodenware, or furniture, for example. Services are usually extremely limited. There may be limited sales help, no delivery of large items, and no personal checks accepted.

While outlet stores are similar to factory outlets, they may be located away from a factory, for example, in a mall, and offer products from several factories rather than just one.

Some malls have several outlet stores offering a wide range of products.

# Tuned in to Shopping

You've probably heard the question "What's on TV?" thousands of times, but how often have you heard this reply: "Shopping!" Home shopping, as buying via television is called, is the newest rage in retailing. With a television, a telephone, and a credit card, you may be able to tune in to this technological marketplace. Here's how it works. Cable and UHF stations broadcast programs that offer products for sale. When you see what you want, you call in and charge your purchase on your credit card. A computer processes your order, and the item is mailed out to you.

The greatest advantage of home buying is its convenience. You can purchase anything from a blouse to a blender without leaving your living room. On the other hand, you cannot try on the blouse or test the blender before you buy it. In this way, home shopping is similar to buying from a catalog. And like many catalog companies, many TV retailers allow returns without explanation. Which method gives you a better idea of the style and quality of the merchandise? While you can see a product demonstrated on television, you only have a few minutes to evaluate it. On the other hand, you can reread a catalog entry as many times as you wish, and skip the items that don't interest you. Most of the early home-shopping programs were like general stores. They offered a long series of unrelated items to choose from. Now some newer shows are more like specialty shops. They may sell only electronics or home furnishings, so you don't have to sit through categories of merchandise you don't want. Nationally known retailers are also going into televised home-shopping, so you can judge their offerings by their reputations.

Part of the appeal of home buying is that it's new and it's fun! But remember, whether you are shopping at home or in a store, think about value, avoid impulse buying, and be an informed consumer.

***Sources of Used Merchandise*** Many products, including cars, appliances, household goods, clothes, and other items, can be bought already used from a variety of sources.

Secondhand stores sell used goods. Sometimes the merchandise is in excellent condition, having been worn or used only a little, and its price is much lower than its original price. Often, when the merchandise is not in good condition, the prices will be even lower.

Some secondhand stores take used merchandise on *consignment*. This means that the person who brings in the merchandise receives a portion of the selling price if it is sold. Sometimes the store sets the price; sometimes the person selling the item sets the price. Some secondhand stores prefer to sell items that have been donated.

Usually, secondhand stores dealing in used household goods, clothes, tools, and similar merchandise offer few services. They may demand cash, and there usually are no product guarantees or return privileges. If you are buying clothing, there may or may not be a dressing room for trying things on.

Places that sell used cars and used appliances often recondition them and offer them with some sort of warranty. If you buy one of these items secondhand, check the warranty carefully and ask questions about anything you do not understand. When there is a warranty, it usually is more limited than one on a new item.

Garage sales, yard sales, auctions, and newspaper advertisements are other sources of used merchandise. In most instances, the buyer of items from these places bears all the responsibility if the items do not perform or last as expected. Sometimes, however, there are bargains available if you know what to look for and can put in some time and effort to restore something.

## Investigating Other Shopping Sources

There are many other ways to shop besides going into stores. Mail order, telephone ordering, shopping clubs, direct buying in your home, and personal shopping services are other ways to shop. Each of these shopping methods has its own advantages and disadvantages. Whether you use any or all of these methods will depend upon your goals and the resources available to you.

***Mail and Telephone Ordering*** Shopping by mail or telephone can be convenient because you do not have to spend time traveling to and from stores and you can avoid transportation costs. Some catalogs offer items that you cannot get locally. At the same time, you cannot see what you are getting until it arrives; you

Catalog shopping is becoming increasingly popular. What are its advantages and disadvantages?

Magazine and newspaper advertisements are another way to shop by mail. The people or companies placing these advertisements may or may not be reputable. If the advertisement promises something for nothing, offers only a box number and not an address, and requires cash or check transactions, not credit cards, you should be especially cautious.

***Shopping Clubs*** Shopping clubs, such as record clubs and book clubs, are other ways to buy things without going to a store. Frequently, the consumer is offered a special deal to join—four books for $1.00 or several free tapes or records, for example. Most clubs require the purchase of a specific number of items within six months or a year. Some require the purchase of a certain number of items each year in order to maintain membership. Others have no requirements after the purchase of the first specified number of items. Some clubs offer discount prices to consumers. Others also have a program of bonus points. For each item purchased, the consumer receives so many bonus points. When enough bonus points are accumulated, the consumer can use the bonus points on an item and pay only shipping and handling costs.

While some clubs border on the fraudulent, many have few requirements and offer goods and/or services at prices similar to or lower than retail prices. You may be able to save money, or at least come out even after paying shipping and handling costs, if you restrict your buying to what you would normally buy if you were not a member. Keep in mind that members usually receive a catalog every few weeks, which may tempt you to buy more than you normally do. Even with lower prices, you may spend more than you would if you were not a member.

Before you join a buying club, be sure to read the membership requirements carefully. If it is not possible to save money, is the money

often have to pay shipping costs; and you have to wait a few days or even a few weeks to receive the merchandise.

Consumers receive catalogs that advertise all sorts of merchandise, even when they are not requested. Some catalogs or brochures are sent from local stores or stores where the consumer has a charge account. Some are from local companies. Some are from companies elsewhere in the country. Many well-known and reliable companies offer detailed descriptions and clear pictures of their products. These companies usually guarantee satisfaction and have a liberal return or exchange policy in effect.

you spend worth it in convenience? Does the club offer the type of selection you want? If you have to pay shipping and handling costs, you will want to add these to the purchase price. You may want to check with the Better Business Bureau or your state's attorney general's office to see if there are any complaints against the club you are considering. Many legitimate companies offer merchandise through the mail, but there are some that are out to defraud the consumer. As the consumer, you should investigate a club *before* spending your money.

**Direct Selling** Many products are sold by direct sale, or door-to-door sale, to the consumer at home. Vacuum cleaners, cookware, plastic storage containers, cosmetics, jewelry, cleaning supplies, clothing, encyclopedias, and craft kits are just a few examples. A salesperson may arrive at the door unannounced or may call ahead for an appointment. Sometimes, the consumer calls the local representative of a national company and arranges for a product party. The consumer then invites several other people to come to the party, and the company representative demonstrates the product or products being sold and takes orders from those who wish to buy.

Many of these salespeople represent their products honestly, give accurate information about costs, explain financing or methods of payment clearly, and then allow the consumer to decide whether or not to purchase the products. Because others are less honest and exert varying amounts of pressure on the consumer to buy, the consumer now has, by law, three days to change his or her mind about any order totaling $25 or more.

When you purchase an item being sold by means of direct sale, consider the product carefully. Is the company reputable? Is the product something you need? Can you get it elsewhere for less? If you can, is purchasing it as a direct sale item worth the extra cost to

you? If you need financing for the item, study any financing offers carefully. Find out what the financing costs are and compare them with the costs of borrowing from a bank or using a credit card.

**Personal Shopping Services** A new business—personal shopping service—has developed to meet the needs of people who dislike shopping or do not have time for it. Some stores as well as individual businesses offer this service.

Some personal shopping services shop for gifts and wrap them. Some help with wardrobe planning and the selection of clothes. Others shop for home furnishings. The costs

How does direct selling differ from buying products in a store? Are there advantages for the salesperson?

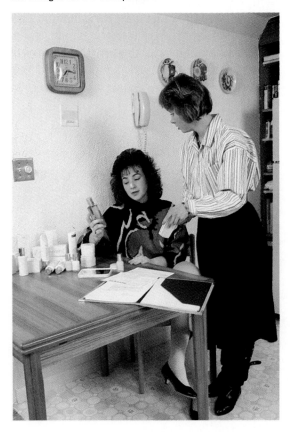

of these services vary and may seem expensive to some. To those who use them, however, they are worth the expense because of the time they save. Hiring someone who is considered an expert in selecting clothes or furnishings can make a person feel more confident that the selections are right for the situation or for the image or feeling that person wants to create.

## Evaluating Bargains and Sales

Many people enjoy bargain-hunting as much as they do the product they buy or the service they receive. The more money they can save, the happier they are. The appeal may range from feeling "I got the most for my money" to "I'm getting something for nothing or almost nothing."

Before you begin to bargain-hunt, you should consider the resources you may need in order to save money. Sometimes limitations on other resources can make it impossible to shop for the lowest price. Effective management

Some major department stores have bargain basements offering unsold items from the main store at discount prices.

involves balancing all your available resources, not just saving money.

### Deciding When to Look for the Best Price

Usually bargain-hunting for products and services can be considered a productive use of resources. If the purchases are made simply because they are bargains, however, they do not result in savings, especially when the money you use is needed for something else or when the product or service isn't something that will be used particularly by you.

Before you begin, you should consider the other resources you will use as you shop. For example, driving to three different supermarkets for different sale items may not result in any savings—the extra gas you use may make up for any money you save. The time and effort involved also must be considered in your plan.

People with limited money frequently have little or no choice in deciding to look for the best price. This may be the only way to have what is needed or wanted. People who have other limitations on their resources often are forced to make different decisions. For example, if transportation resources are limited, or there is only one store nearby, probably shopping is based on what is available nearby rather than the lowest price.

People with limited time need to be selective about the time they spend shopping for bargains. Visiting several stores to save a few dollars may not be the best use of time. If, however, you are looking for a loan for a new or used car, shopping around for the best interest rate can result in saving several hundred dollars over the life of the loan. This is usually time well spent, even if you are busy.

**Is It Really a Sale?** The term **sale** means selling something at an advantageous price. Most people think of a sale as selling products or services at prices lower than those normally charged. Knowing this, manufacturers and store owners or managers use the term SALE as a way to increase customers and encourage purchasing. The things on sale may or may not be at reduced prices.

When a sale involves selling goods and services at prices lower than those normally charged, you can save money if the product or service is something that is needed and part of an overall plan. Sometimes, if the price is reduced enough, it may make the difference between being able to buy that item and not being able to.

Unfortunately, unless you are familiar with regular prices, you may not be able to tell if a product or service is really on sale. You may know what you usually pay for items you buy frequently, such as food, clothing, and health and beauty aids. If you do, you will know whether or not the sale price will help you save money. Otherwise, you may have to guess.

Some stores have all their items marked with two prices—one labeled "regular price" (or something similar) and the other labeled "sale price"—all the time. Because these stores have never charged the "regular price," the sale price is not really a reduced price. It is, instead, what they normally charge. Unless you visit this type of store frequently, or you know others who do, you cannot tell whether the sale price is a reduced price or just made to appear that way.

Because the United States economy is based on competition, many stores often offer the same products. What is a sale price at one store may be the regular price at another. Unless you have the time and patience to do a great deal of comparison shopping, it can be difficult to get the lowest price possible on something. Sometimes it may be less tiring and time-consuming to buy something at what you feel is a fair price and not to worry about whether or not you could have found the object at a lower price. It all depends on your priorities, resources, and goals.

Before buying expensive products it is smart to find out if they really are on sale. How can comparison shopping help?

In the end, you have to depend on your own consumer knowledge and research. Advertisements or price tags in the store will not always tell you if the object is a bargain.

### What About Coupons and Special Offers?

Coupons, rebates, refunds, and other special offers are promotional devices designed to make consumers buy products or services. If you are planning to buy a product or service and can use one of these promotional devices, you may be able to save some money. Using them only for the sake of getting a "bargain" may not give you the desired results. You may end up spending money you would have used for some other purpose.

Probably the most well-known coupons are those for nationally advertised brand-name

What trade-offs are involved in using or not using coupons when you shop? How are time and money resources affected?

Sometimes local stores and businesses will put together a booklet of coupons for everyone living in the area. Many individual stores and businesses include coupons with their advertisements in newspapers. Often these coupons give a certain amount or percent off the prices of products or services. They may allow you to get two for the price of one or give you a free product with the purchase of another product or service. For example, you may find a coupon for 10 percent off a wash and wax job at a car wash or a coupon for two meals for the price of one or one small pizza free with the purchase of a large pizza. Sometimes these may be given to help the community celebrate a special event. Sometimes they are given to stimulate business. If you would normally buy the product or service, you can save money by using the coupon. If the coupon lowers the price of a product or service you usually cannot afford, you may be able to take advantage of the situation.

Although using coupons can save money, it does take time to clip and sort them. It takes some thought to remember to take them with you when you go shopping. For some people, the money saved is worth the time and effort. For others, the time involved is not worth the money saved.

**Refunds and Rebates**  Many businesses offer refunds or rebates when you buy a certain number or kind of products. For example, there may be a $3 rebate on a certain brand and style of hairdryer if you mail in the dated sales receipt and a certain portion of the packaging. You may be able to get $1 or $2 back when you buy three packages of light bulbs and send in the Universal Product Code (UPC) from each. There may even be a rebate of $200 or more on a certain style and model of car.

Before you take advantage of any rebate offers, however, you should ask yourself if you

foods. If the coupons are for brand-name products you would buy normally, you can save money. If your sole purpose in using coupons, however, is to save money, you may want to subtract the value of the coupon from the cost of the item and compare this price with that of a similar product. You may find that another brand or a generic brand is less expensive than the product even with the coupon.

would be making the purchase even without the rebate. Many rebate offers require considerable effort on the part of consumers. Sometimes you may have to soak labels off bottles, cut out weight or price stickers, peel off or cut out UPC codes, save sales receipts, and/or use special rebate forms. If you decide to take advantage of a rebate offer, you should read the instructions carefully and then decide if the time and effort are worth it to you.

## Deciding When to Buy

Once you have decided to buy a product or service, you may want to consider the timing of the purchase. Is it something you need right away, or can you wait until there is a sale, or you have saved more money for it? Perhaps the price is not likely to change, and you already have set aside the money. Deciding when to buy should be a part of your plan.

If you need a product immediately, waiting for a sale may not be possible or important. You should realize, however, that many items go on sale regularly at certain times of the year. Sheets and other bedding items, for example, often go on sale during White Sales in August and/or January. New cars frequently cost less at the end of the model year before the new models are introduced. There are also seasons for clothing. For example, when a merchant must make room for spring and summer clothes, prices on the remaining fall and winter clothes will be lower because the styles and colors of clothes may change and the merchant does not want last year's styles and colors left over. Whether or not you can profit from lower prices at the end of a season depends on your values. How important is the latest style to you? Is spending less money important enough to you that you can be happy without the latest style?

Some products go on sale almost every week. For example, supermarkets often have different specials each week. Many discount department stores have different health and beauty items, office supplies, small kitchen equipment, clothing, sporting goods, and other items on sale each week. Some drugstores have "2 for the price of 1" sales or "1¢" sales every so often. You may want to wait for these sales to stock up on things you normally need and use.

Many stores have "remodeling sales" or sales to celebrate holidays or in honor of special community events or activities. These sales may offer a certain percentage off the price of everything or certain items may be drastically reduced in price. Sometimes you can coordinate your needs and money with these sales.

Going-out-of-business sales are held when a store is closing permanently. Sometimes you can purchase goods at bargain prices at these sales. You should remember, however, that the store will not be there to take care of complaints or returns. Check anything you are thinking of buying carefully for defects before you purchase it.

Why would it be better not to purchase extremes of color or style at this sale? What would you buy?

# MONTHLY SALES CALENDAR

| JANUARY | FEBRUARY | MARCH | APRIL |
|---|---|---|---|
| • Dishes<br>• Furniture<br>• Household<br>  appliances<br>• Linens<br>• Rugs, carpets<br>• Sheets, towels<br>• Toys<br>• Winter clothes | • Air conditioners<br>• Bedding<br>• Drapes, curtains<br>• Home building<br>  supplies<br>• Household<br>  appliances | • Boots<br>• Garden tools<br>• Luggage<br>• Outdoor furniture<br>• Winter coats and<br>  clothing<br>• Winter sporting<br>  equipment | • Dresses<br>• Fabric<br>• Laundry<br>  appliances<br>• Men's suits<br>• Spring coats<br>• Wallpaper, paint |

| MAY | JUNE | JULY | AUGUST |
|---|---|---|---|
| • Blankets<br>• Camping<br>  equipment<br>• Housewares<br>• Lingerie<br>• Summer<br>  sportswear<br>• Televisions<br>• Tires | • Bedding<br>• Coats<br>• Fabrics<br>• Floor coverings<br>• Refrigerators<br>• Storm windows | • Air conditioners<br>• Coats<br>• Freezers<br>• Men's clothes<br>• Refrigerators<br>• Shoes<br>• Summer clothes<br>• Sports equipment | • Air conditioners<br>• Bedding, blankets<br>• Furniture<br>• New cars<br>• Tires<br>• Summer clothes |

| SEPTEMBER | OCTOBER | NOVEMBER | DECEMBER |
|---|---|---|---|
| • Bicycles<br>• Dishes<br>• Fabrics<br>• Fall clothing<br>• New cars | • Cars and car<br>  accessories<br>• Dishes, glassware<br>• Fishing equipment<br>• Lawn furniture | • Bathroom<br>  accessories<br>• Blankets<br>• Coats<br>• Men's suits<br>• Shoes<br>• Used cars | • Blankets<br>• Coats<br>• Dishwashers<br>• Holiday gifts<br>  and cards<br>  (after holidays)<br>• Men's suits<br>• Sweaters |

Because services seldom, if ever, go on sale, you need to use a different criteria when you try to time your purchase of them. In cold climates, for example, housing contractors are busy in spring, summer, and fall. Service stations are apt to be busier at the end of months when state automobile inspections must be made. Hair stylists often are busier at holiday times. Doctors, dentists, and veterinarians often are less busy at holiday times. If you can plan to purchase the service you need when things are less busy, you may receive faster service and better results.

## Looking for Quality

Many people associate quality with price. They assume that the most expensive product is the best quality and the least expensive is the poorest. This is not always true. While good quality does cost money, judging quality on the basis of price alone can be a mistaken use of your money resources.

You can learn to recognize differences in quality. The best product or service for you is not necessarily the best quality available. It may be the best quality for your purpose or for the money you have to spend.

Use the sources of consumer information that you learned about in Chapter 9 to help you decide about the quality of goods and services. If you can learn how things are made or how they work, it may be easier to decide if they will meet your needs and wants. For example, if you learn about fabrics, you will be better equipped to decide if a loose-knit sweater is what you want or whether you would be better off with a tighter knit. If you find out about belt-drive and direct-drive turntables or four, six, and eight cylinder cars, you will know which suits your purpose better or whether it makes any difference.

If you want good quality, look for goods that are safe, durable, convenient to use, and easy to maintain. In addition, be sure they perform well, that is, they do what they are supposed to do.

## Deciding How to Pay

Some businesses have a "cash only" policy. This may mean only coins or currency, or it may include personal checks and traveller's checks. Many offer some form of credit—layaways or charge accounts—or accept credit cards. How you decide to pay for your purchases will depend on your individual resources, your personal financial plan, and the policies of the business.

You learned about the advantages and disadvantages of using cash and credit in Chapter 7 and Chapter 8. As you shop, you will have to weigh these advantages and disadvantages carefully. If you put an item on layaway, will you have the time and the money available to make the regular installment payments you need to make to take possession of the item at the end of the time limit? If you pay for the item with cash or a check, can you still meet your other needs, including the basic ones? If you use a credit card or a charge account, are you going to have enough money to pay these bills when they come due? No matter how you pay for what you buy, try to keep track of what you spend. This can help you with your financial plan because you will know exactly where your money has gone.

Keep the sales slips for the products or services you buy. If you have a problem with something you buy, your sales slip is the record of its purchase. If the sales slip does not have a date on it, write the date on the slip when you get home from the store. Some warranties are not valid after a certain time limit, so having the sales slip can be helpful. If you have a problem with an item you have purchased, you usually need the sales slip to return the item or to exchange it for another.

## Solving Consumer Complaints

Sometimes even after carefully selecting goods or services, consumers are dissatisfied. What do you do if your hairdryer breaks down after you've used it only a few times? When you buy something, ask about the return policy of the store or how the service business deals with dissatisfied customers. This will help you to know what to expect if you are dissatisfied with the product or the service. Knowing how to return merchandise and register complaints can help you to get the results you want.

## Returning Merchandise

Complaining to your friends about your hairdryer will not solve the problem. Take it back to the place where you bought it and calmly explain to the customer service department or the sales clerk what has happened. If the item is too large to take back, call or visit the store to find out what should be done. If there is a warranty that has not expired and the product has not been abused, most stores will try to resolve the problem by repairing the product or exchanging it for another one that does work properly.

Obviously, services that have been performed, such as haircuts or yard work or building construction, cannot be returned, but depending on the nature of the service and the policy of the business, it may be possible to get some type of refund. Sometimes the business will refund your money. Sometimes the business will perform the service again so that it is satisfactory. Because most businesses want their customers to return and to recommend their services to others, they will try to make satisfactory adjustments when a customer is dissatisfied with the service.

## WRITING A LETTER OF COMPLAINT

When writing a letter of complaint, include:

1. business letter heading with the date and your address. Use the exact name, job title, and address of the person you are writing to.

2. a brief, clear statement of your complaint.

3. copies of receipts and/or warranties.

4. the name of the store or business where you purchased the goods or service and the date of purchase.

5. specific model numbers of goods or very specific description of the service.

# FEDERAL AGENCIES FOR CONSUMERS

| FEDERAL AGENCY | RESPONSIBILITIES |
|---|---|
| Consumer Product Safety Commission | Sets standards of safety for household products |
| Federal Trade Commission | Monitors advertising procedures and selling practices; regulates competition among businesses |
| Food and Drug Administration | Inspects food and drug production plants; regulates the quality of food, drugs, and cosmetics |
| Department of Agriculture | Inspects and grades food |
| Federal Communications Commission | Sets standards for radio and television broadcasting and advertising |
| Interstate Commerce Commission | Sets standards and regulates rates for train and bus travel |
| Postal Service | Prevents mail fraud; regulates mail practices |
| Office of Consumer Affairs | Provides consumer education |
| Securities and Exchange Commission | Regulates the sale of stocks and bonds |

## Sources of Consumer Assistance

Unfortunately, it is not always possible to prevent problems before they happen, and sometimes it is not possible to solve problems directly with the business where you bought the items or services. If this happens, there are public and private agencies and organizations that can help if you, as a responsible consumer, are willing to take the time and effort to follow up on your complaint.

**Consumer Hotlines to Manufacturers**
Some large businesses have national, toll-free numbers that a consumer can call if there are problems with the product or service that the consumer has not been able to resolve at the local level. This is the first step to take if you cannot resolve the problem with the people who sold or serviced the product. Automobile and appliance manufacturers are among those that sometimes offer toll-free numbers. You may find these numbers listed on the warranty or in the product's service manual.

If it is a nationwide chain of stores or a nationally distributed product that does not offer a hotline service, try the business headquarters. These names and addresses are usually on labels or in the instruction booklets that come with the product. Your librarian can also help you find the proper names and addresses of those to write. Keep a copy of the letter you sent so you have a record.

### Public and Private Agencies and Organizations for Consumers

It is the responsibility of a variety of government agencies to uphold the laws that protect consumers at local, state, and national levels. If you contact the manufacturer or the parent company, and there is still no satisfaction, your next step can be in any one of several directions.

Local, state, or federal government agencies may help in matters of safety and health. Many states have branches of these agencies. Most telephone books have listings that provide local telephone numbers and addresses in the white pages as well as in the front.

If the problem is product performance or dissatisfaction with authorized service on a product, an industry or trade organization or one of their consumer action panels may be able to help. For problems with products or services purchased from a nearby store or service business, the Better Business Bureau or the Chamber of Commerce may be able to help you. These may be local and/or state organizations. Sometimes your state's attorney general's office and/or consumer affairs office may be helpful.

### Legal Action

If public or private resources are not able to help, an individual consumer or a group of consumers can take legal action. Sometimes the consumer or the group of consumers can present the problem to a small claims court. A **small claims court** is a court where consumers and businesses present their own complaints and abide by a judge's decision. Proceedings are conducted in everyday language and technical legal terms are avoided. There is no lawyer's fee for the consumer because the consumer presents his or her own case. Small claims courts are designed to settle disputes that involve sums of money ranging up to $5,000.

Occasionally, the consumer may need a lawyer to take the matter to court. Individuals below a certain income level usually are entitled to help from a legal aid society, an organization that provides legal assistance to qualified low-income persons for little or no cost. The case may go to court or may be settled out of court.

If you follow up on consumer problems, you are helping anyone else who might buy those goods or services. Most complaints can be settled without taking legal action. They do require time and effort but being persistent conveys a message to the seller that you will not settle for unsatisfactory goods or services. When you express this fact, you are helping all consumers. At the same time, you may receive satisfaction for any unsatisfactory consumer purchases you may have made.

### For Review

1. If the store or business where you purchased unsatisfactory goods does not take care of your complaint, what step should you take next?

2. Name two organizations that may be able to assist you in solving any consumer complaints you may have.

3. How can a small claims court help a dissatisfied consumer?

# Management Application: Planning a Purchase

Imagine yourself in the situation described below. As you read, think about how the steps of the management process might apply to this situation. Then answer the questions that follow.

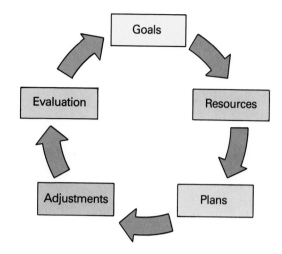

## Situation

April was in a hurry. She had a lot of shopping to do. School was starting next week, and she really wanted a great new wardrobe for the fall. She had earned more than she had expected to waitressing during the summer, so she had enough to buy a good, basic wardrobe. She had a list of specific clothing items she wanted and the estimated price for each item. She decided to look in the discount stores first, hoping to find the brand-name clothes she wanted. There were blouses and sweaters she wanted, but no jeans. The designer jeans she wanted were available in department stores, but they cost more there than three pairs of regular jeans. She made her other purchases and decided to think about the jeans. She knew she wanted them. They were really attractive, and she liked the style. They were also well made. The pair she had outgrown had lasted and looked great all year.

From her friends, she learned that there was an outlet store that carried the jeans she wanted, but it was a two-hour drive from her home. April decided it would be worth the time if her friends came along. She knew several girls who wanted the same kind of jeans. She talked to them and they decided it would be a good idea to go together. If they shared the price of the gas money, they would still save money. The problem was that none of them could make the trip before school started. She really did want to wear those jeans to school on the first day. Should she wait and pay less or go ahead and buy the jeans she wanted?

## Questions

1. What goal did April have?
2. Did she have enough resources to meet it? What about the resource of time?
3. What trade-offs will April make if she does decide to buy the jeans at full price?
4. What trade-offs will April make if she decides to wait?
5. Did April apply the steps of the management process to her shopping plan?
6. Which steps of the management process apply to this situation?

# 10 *Chapter Review*

## Summary

Having a clear understanding of your needs and wants helps you to make a shopping plan based on the resources you have. Being flexible allows you to adjust to changes and still remain on the path toward your goals. Learning how to comparison shop and deciding when and where to buy are important consumer procedures. Determining if products are really on sale and learning to recognize quality in products and services also are valuable shopping techniques. Finally, knowing how to return merchandise and register complaints can help you get the results you want when you are dissatisfied with a product or service.

## Vocabulary

Use the following vocabulary words to complete the paragraph below.

impulse buying

comparison shop

sale

small claims court

Jeff used to have a problem with __(1)__ ; he rarely thought about his budget and needs when he saw something he wanted. Then, last spring, he went into a shop that always advertises a __(2)__ , where he saw a VCR marked "Price Reduced For One Day Only." Of course the VCRs had been at the same price all month, but Jeff did not know that. To make matters worse, when Jeff got his VCR home, he discovered it was broken. The store blamed him and refused to replace it. Now Jeff is trying to get his money back through a __(3)__ , since he cannot afford a lawyer. He says he is going to start shopping wisely; from now on, Jeff insists, he will __(4)__ at several stores, before he buys anything.

## Questions

1. When may it not be worth the effort to do comparison shopping? Give examples.
2. What are some ways that discount stores keep their prices low?
3. What is the difference between a department store and a specialty store? What are some of the advantages and disadvantages of each?
4. What is a secondhand store? Explain selling merchandise on consignment.
5. Which two methods of shopping can be done by mail or phone? What are the advantages and risks of each?
6. What are the advantages and disadvantages of direct selling to the consumer?
7. Name three promotional devices. What factors should you consider before you take advantage of each?
8. What information should you include in a letter of complaint?

9. Which federal agency is responsible for each of the following:

   a. regulating train and bus travel

   b. regulating the quality of food

   c. setting standards of safety for household products

   d. providing consumer education

10. What is the purpose of a legal aid society? Whom do they help?

## Skill Activities

1. **Communication.** Practice writing a letter of complaint. Select a household item and pretend that it has broken or that it has not lived up to its advertising. Use the guidelines on page 228 to write your letter. Be sure to follow the form for a business letter.

2. **Critical Thinking.** Practice comparison shopping. Select an item such as a stereo, a radio, a major appliance, or a computer. You may want to refer to *Consumer Reports*. Follow the guidelines in this chapter for comparison shopping and decide which item is the best value. Keep notes on your findings, and share the results with your classmates.

   Now do your own medical or dental care comparison shopping. Choose either service and investigate the options available in your area. What additional factors are important in selecting these services that you do not have to consider when buying items? Discuss this as a class.

3. **Critical Thinking.** Stage a mock small claims court in your classroom. Choose either a service or a product (with a value of at least $500) that you will claim is faulty, damaged, or unsatisfactory. Have one student act as the displeased consumer and have another student represent the manufacturer or business owner. Learn about typical warranties for the situation before you begin. Ask the teacher to act as the judge.

   After each side has presented its case, the teacher will decide either in favor of the displeased consumer or the manufacturer or business owner. Then write a brief paragraph about your opinion of the judge's decision. Did you agree with it? Why or why not?

4. **Communication.** Do some research on any state or local agency that has been established to help consumers. What are its responsibilities? What actions can it take to help consumers with problems?

   Once you have looked into state and local agencies, learn more about the Office of Consumer Affairs of the federal government. Find out what consumer issues it has dealt with recently. Then write a letter to the Office of Consumer Affairs and request any consumer educational materials available.

# Unit 3

# Managing Time and Material Resources

# *11*

# *Making Nutrition Decisions*

## *As you read, think about:*

- [ ] how to identify foods from each of the five basic food groups.
- [ ] how to achieve a balance of nutrients in your diet.
- [ ] how to improve your eating habits for better health.
- [ ] how to plan meals that provide good nutrition and meet individual and/or family needs.
- [ ] how to apply the management process to personal decisions about nutrition.

## Vocabulary

nutrition
nutrients
calorie
saturated fats
cholesterol
Daily Food Guide
convenience food

How often have you heard the phrase "You are what you eat"? People are becoming more aware of the direct relationship between healthy eating and healthier, longer lives. Learning more about the nutrition in various foods and the best balance of foods for your diet can help you now and in the future. Acquiring good eating habits and learning to plan balanced meals will be important skills for you as you grow older.

## Learning About Nutrition

**Nutrition** is the science of food and its relation to health. With an understanding of nutrition you will be able to make other decisions about food. You will know which foods to include in your diet, or daily food intake. You will know which foods your body needs

for proper development and which foods you should eat less frequently. You will be able to make informed decisions when you are shopping or choosing foods in a cafeteria or in your favorite restaurant.

## Nutrients in Food

Food is important because it contains nutrients. **Nutrients** are the substances that your body needs for growth, energy, and good health. Nutrients also help to regulate body processes, such as digestion and circulation.

There are about 50 known nutrients needed by the body, and there may be others not yet discovered. Each nutrient has a special job and is needed in a certain amount to perform as it should. Many nutrients must work with other nutrients to be effective. No one food contains all the nutrients needed by your

Clean drinking water is vitally important for good health.

are three types of carbohydrates: starches (found in rice, pasta, and other grain products, such as bread), sugars, and cellulose. Cellulose is sometimes called fiber or roughage. It aids in the digestion process by helping to move food through your system.

**Proteins** Proteins are needed to build and repair body tissue. Animal products, such as fish, meat, milk, and eggs, are high in protein. Vegetables, fruits, and grains also contain varying amounts of protein.

**Fats** Fats help the body to store reserve energy and help to regulate body temperature. They also help in the storage and use of some vitamins. Fats are found in most foods other than fruits and vegetables. Butter, meat, salad dressings, cheese, and milk are among the food products that contain fats.

**Vitamins** These nutrients keep the body healthy and functioning. Because vitamins B and C are water-soluble, the body needs to have daily supplies of them. Vitamins A, D, E, and K are fat-soluble and therefore are stored in the body. The chart on page 239 shows how these vitamins help your body.

**Minerals** Minerals are a part of many body tissues. They are needed to maintain body processes, including circulation and breathing. Calcium, iron, sodium, iodide, phosphorus, potassium, and zinc are all minerals the body must have in order to develop and function in the proper way.

**Water** Water carries nutrients throughout the body. Sixty-five to seventy-five percent of your body weight is water. Since the body constantly loses water through elimination and perspiration, it is important to replace it. Many experts recommend drinking six to eight glasses of water every day.

body. That is why eating a variety of foods is important. It helps to insure that the body gets the nutrients it needs.

Based on their chemical composition, nutrients can be divided into six categories: carbohydrates, proteins, fats, vitamins, minerals, and water. Water is usually classified as a nutrient because it is necessary for the maintenance of life.

**Carbohydrates** Carbohydrates provide ready energy. They are found in many plant foods, especially grains, vegetables, and fruits. There

## SOME VITAMINS YOU NEED

| VITAMIN | WHY YOU NEED IT | WHERE IT IS FOUND |
|---|---|---|
| B Vitamins:<br>  $B_1$ (thiamine)<br>  $B_2$ (riboflavin)<br>  Niacin | Aid digestion<br>Help nerve and brain<br>  tissue function<br>Help body use other nutrients | Milk products, meats,<br>  cereals, breads |
| Vitamin C | Helps body build cells<br>Promotes healing<br>Helps form strong teeth,<br>  bones, and healthy gums | Citrus fruits |
| Vitamin A | Needed for good vision<br>Helps form healthy teeth and<br>  gums and strong bones | Yellow and leafy green vegetables |
| Vitamin D | Helps form bones and teeth<br>Helps body use minerals<br>  like calcium and phosphorus | In milk<br>Body can make vitamin D with<br>  sunlight |
| Vitamin E | Helps keep red blood cells healthy<br>Works with Vitamin A | Green leafy vegetables, peanut<br>  and corn oil, wheat germ, and eggs |
| Vitamin K | Helps blood to clot | Liver, leafy green vegetables |

## Calories

The body needs energy to carry on its internal functions, to digest and make use of food, and to be physically active. It gets this energy from the food you eat. The **calorie** is a measure of the energy produced by food when it is used by the body. Carbohydrates, proteins, and fats provide calories; vitamins, minerals, and water do not have any calories. When more calories are taken in than are used, the body converts the extra energy to fat. In other words, you gain weight. When fewer calories are taken in than are used, the body draws from its reserve of fat. In other words, you lose weight. When the calories taken in equal the number of calories needed and used, your weight stays the same.

## Nutrition and Health

What you eat or do not eat is related to your mental and physical health. Diet and eating habits can affect learning, concentration, and mood, as well as general health.

### Can Certain Diets Cause Health Problems?

A diet too high in fat can cause obesity, which may increase the risk of heart disease, may raise blood pressure, and may be a factor in adult diabetes. A high intake of **saturated fats** (fat from animal sources) can contribute to heart disease. A low-fiber, high-fat diet has been linked to certain types of cancer. Most experts now recommend watching cholesterol levels. **Cholesterol** (kuh-LESS-tuh-role) is a fatty substance. High cholesterol levels can lead to heart disease, high blood pressure, the blockage of arteries, and other problems. Saturated fats are solid at room temperature and include fats from animal sources and those from vegetable sources that have been hydrogenated. Polyunsaturated fats and mono-unsaturated fats may help to lower blood cholesterol. They are recommended in only small amounts because overconsumption can cause weight gain and may be linked to some types of cancer.

Too much sugar contributes to dental caries, or cavities. It also contributes to obesity and the problems related to it.

Too much salt often causes water retention and, in some people, contributes to high blood pressure and other problems.

Balanced nutrition can help you to be healthier at any age.

Too much protein in a diet can place a strain on the kidneys. It can interfere with the body's absorption of calcium, which is necessary for proper development.

Too much fiber can cause food to be processed by the body too quickly. When this happens, important nutrients are not absorbed by the body.

Too much caffeine, a substance found in coffee, colas, chocolate, and certain medications, can cause nervousness and insomnia. It also interferes with the absorption of calcium by the body.

**_What If You Don't Get Enough of Certain Nutrients?_** Deficiencies in certain nutrients also can cause health problems. For example, too little protein causes poor growth in infants and children. In adults, too little protein means the body is unable to repair and replace injured tissue.

Too little of the mineral calcium in children's diets can result in poor tooth and bone structure and interfere with normal growth. A lack of calcium in the adult diet may increase the risk of osteoporosis (OSS-tee-o-puh-RO-sis). Some research has suggested that too little calcium may contribute to high blood pressure and may increase a person's susceptibility to cancer of the colon.

Too little vitamin C contributes to gum problems and the slow healing of wounds. A lack of vitamin C interferes with the proper absorption of iron by the body.

Inadequate iron in the diet can cause iron-deficiency anemia. Infants, young children, teenage girls, women of child-bearing age, and the elderly are particularly at risk for this type of anemia.

Although fiber does not supply nutrients, it is important. According to some research, adequate fiber in a diet may help to prevent diverticulosis (DY-vur-tik-yuh-LO-siss), a condition of the intestine in which outpouchings form and then collect food residues. Diverticulitis (DY-vur-tik-yuh-LY-tiss) is the inflammation of these outpouchings.

Foods containing fiber can help in a weight-loss diet by contributing to a feeling of fullness. Additionally, some studies suggest that fiber can help to lower blood cholesterol levels and prevent cancer of the colon.

**Can Certain Foods and Diet Patterns Prevent Health Problems?** While research is inconclusive at this point, there are indications that certain foods and diet patterns can help to prevent some health problems. Planning your diet to include the nutrients you need in the right amounts will not guarantee good health, but it will help you to have the best health possible for you.

An adequate supply of calcium every day may help to avoid many health problems. Milk and milk products are obvious and important sources of calcium, but there are other sources. Canned salmon or sardines (both with bones) and cooked greens (kale, collards, and mustard greens, for example) also add significant amounts of calcium.

Some vegetables in the cabbage family (cabbage, brussel sprouts, broccoli, and cauliflower) are not only good sources of vitamin A but also may play a protective role in preventing cancer.

Whole grains, fresh fruits, and many other vegetables supply needed fibers and other valuable nutrients.

A low-fat/low-cholesterol diet emphasizes whole grain products, fruits and vegetables, low-fat dairy products, dried peas and beans, and small servings of fish, poultry, and lean meat. Since recent research has suggested that a special type of polyunsaturated fat found in fish helps to protect against heart disease, some experts recommend eating fish two or three times a week. You may also want to consider taking fish oil tablets, especially if you do not enjoy eating fish.

Yogurt, a thick semisolid milk product, is one source of needed calcium.

## Following the Daily Food Guide

To insure that people get the right amounts of the various nutrients you have been reading about, nutritionists have developed a guide called the **Daily Food Guide.** This guide divides food into five basic groups and outlines a daily recommended amount from each group. Following this guide can help people of all ages to eat a balanced diet. The food guide on page 242 shows the recommended minimum daily

# DAILY FOOD GUIDE

## VEGETABLE-FRUIT GROUP

Recommended minimum servings per day:
  all ages          4 servings

Examples of one serving:
  ½ c (125 mL) cooked vegetable or fruit
  ½ c (125 mL) fruit or vegetable juice
  1 c (250 mL) raw fruit or vegetable
  1 whole medium-sized fruit or vegetable

Major nutrient contributions:
  vitamin A and vitamin C
  variety of minerals
  carbohydrates (including fiber)

Note: Include 1 serving per day of a food high in vitamin C. Choose 1 serving 3 or 4 times a week of a food which provides vitamin A.

## BREAD-CEREAL GROUP

Recommended minimum servings per day:
  all ages          4 servings

Examples of one serving:
  1 oz (30 g) slice of bread
  1 oz (30 g) roll, muffin, or biscuit
  ½ bagel, hamburg or hotdog roll
  ½ c (125 mL) cooked cereal or rice
  ⅔ c (160 mL) cooked pasta
  1 oz (30 g) ready-to-eat cereal
  6 saltines
  1 pancake, 4″ (10 cm) in diameter

Major nutrient contributions:
  carbohydrates (including fiber)
  incomplete protein
  B-complex vitamins
  iron

## FATS-SWEETS GROUP

Recommended servings per day:
  No recommendations. A balanced diet
  includes some fats and sugars.
  Additional amounts are not necessary.

Major nutrient contributions: None

## MILK-CHEESE GROUP

Recommended minimum servings per day:
  children        3 servings
  adolescents     4 servings
  adults          2 servings

One serving = 1 c (250 mL) milk or its equivalent

Equivalents:
  1 c (250 mL)
  plain yogurt          = 1 c (250 mL) milk
  1 oz (30 g)
  hard cheese           = ¾ c (185 mL) milk
  1 oz (30 g)
  process cheese        = ½ c (125 mL) milk
  ½ c (125 mL)
  ice cream             = ⅓ c (80 mL) milk
  ½ c (125 mL)
  cottage cheese        = ¼ c (60 mL) milk

Major nutrient contributions:
  calcium and phosphorus
  complete protein
  riboflavin (a B-complex vitamin)
  vitamins A and D (if fortified)

## MEAT-FISH-POULTRY-BEANS GROUP

Recommended minimum servings per day:
  all ages          2 servings

Examples of one serving:
  2–3 oz (60–90 g) cooked meat, fish,
    poultry (without bone)
  3 oz (90 g) processed meats
  2 eggs
  4 Tbsp (60 mL) peanut butter
  1 c (250 mL) cooked dried beans or peas

Major nutrient contributions:
  complete protein and incomplete protein
  B-complex vitamins and other B vitamins
  iron and phosphorus

Note: Include milk, cheese, egg, or small amounts of meat, fish, or poultry with meals based on dried beans, peas, or nuts

servings from each of the five main food the groups. These consist of:

- the vegetable-fruit group
- the milk-cheese group
- the bread-cereal group
- the meat-fish-poultry-beans group
- the fats-sweets group

The final group includes foods that are high in calories but low in nutrients. Intake of these should be limited for good health. Usually, enough fat and sugar are found naturally in the foods you eat from the other four basic food groups.

## Sources of Nutrition Information

Publications from the U.S. government, the American Heart Association, American Dietetics Association, American Diabetes Association, American Medical Association, and American Home Economics Association usually are unbiased, reliable sources of nutrition information because they are based on extensive research and current knowledge in the field of nutrition. Scientific writers who base their writings on information from these sources are other good sources of information. Be careful about using information from specific organizations such as the Sugar Council. They sometimes advise the use of their products even if they are not nutritionally valid.

### For Review

1. Name six categories of nutrients and describe what each nutrient does for the human body.
2. Name three specific vitamins and tell why you need each one. What foods are they each found in?
3. Which foods and/or diet patterns do researchers recommend to prevent health problems?

Most nutritionists agree that eating fish has several health benefits.

After-school snacks such as
fruit and crackers and cheese
provide needed energy
without too much sugar.

## *Evaluating Eating Habits*

What you eat, when you eat, and how you eat play important parts in forming good eating habits. The U.S. Department of Agriculture and the Department of Health and Human Resources have published dietary guidelines for you to follow:

### DIETARY GUIDELINES

1. Eat a variety of foods.
2. Maintain an ideal weight.
3. Avoid eating too much fat, saturated fat, and cholesterol.
4. Eat foods with adequate starch and fiber.
5. Avoid too much sugar.
6. Avoid too much sodium.
7. If you drink alcohol, do so in moderation.

These guidelines will help you to form good eating habits and to stay healthy.

### *What You Eat*

Getting a balance of food in your daily diet from the basic food groups will provide the basis for a healthy nutrition program. As the guidelines suggest, avoid eating too much fat, saturated fat, cholesterol, sugar, and sodium. Foods to avoid include fried foods, candy, and chips. Substitute raw fruits and vegetables, whole grain breads, nuts, and seeds as healthier snacks. Eat more chicken and fish and less beef. If you eat sweets, try to do so with food from the other food groups. This will have less effect on your blood sugar level than eating sweets alone. For maximum energy, blood sugar levels should be kept fairly constant.

## When You Eat

When you eat is just as important as eating the right nutrients in the right amounts. Going without eating for a long period of time (skipping breakfast, for example) can cause a drop in concentration, interfere with learning, and cause a feeling of tiredness. This is because your body needs food on a regular basis to function properly and to keep you alert throughout the day.

Spreading out your food intake as much as possible during the day is a sensible approach. This helps your body to provide an even output of energy and avoids the overeating that may result from waiting too long between meals.

**Three Meals a Day**  Nutritionists recommend no less than three meals a day on a regular basis. In this country, three meals a day is a common pattern: breakfast in the morning, lunch or dinner in the middle of the day, and supper or dinner in the evening. This type of schedule is fine for those people whose work and other activities fall into this pattern. Many people, however, need to plan their meals around an irregular schedule or special individual needs. People who are up early and have long days or who don't eat a great quantity of food at any one time may be more comfortable with a four- or five-meals-a-day plan.

The morning meal is important because the body has not had food for several hours. To keep you alert and to give you enough energy, this meal should contain foods from the vegetable-fruit group, the bread-cereal group, and the milk-cheese group. It may also contain food from the meat-poultry-fish-beans group.

The midday meal should include food from each of the nutrient-rich food groups. A selection from the fat-sweets group can be added if you are not watching calories. A similar pattern is recommended for the evening meal.

## Practical Tip: Food Variety

■ To add variety to your meal plan, make a list of vegetables you have never tried. Look for these vegetables in your grocery store and include at least one item in your meal plan each week until you have finished the list. If you try this system for fruits and grains also, you can add still more variety to your diet.

**A Personal Eating Pattern**  If you are trying to control your weight or just don't need or want extra food, and your schedule is such that you wish to eat more often than three times a day, you can adjust your eating to meet your personal needs. For example, you might have a serving from the bread-cereal group and the milk-cheese group in the morning and save your serving from the vegetable-fruit group to have during your morning break. At lunch time, you might save your selection from one of the nutrient-rich groups to eat later. You could eat half your lunch at lunch time and the other half after school. You could even split up your food selections for your evening meal. You could avoid having anything from the fats-sweets group, or you could limit yourself to only a small serving from this group.

How you divide up your selections from the various food groups can be based on your schedule and how often you feel hungry. Most important is to try to get a balance of foods at each meal and throughout the day and to avoid extras from the fats-sweets group.

Think about the times of the day you usually eat. Do you eat in the morning? If not, how can you adjust your schedule to do so? If you do not think this is possible, what can you prepare the night before to eat on the way to school or when you get there? When do you eat at other times? When do you eat with other family members? With friends? Perhaps these times should be the basis for your own individual eating pattern. You can plan your food intake based on when you have some free time. If you seem to have no time to eat, perhaps you need to adjust your schedule to get the foods you need on a regular basis. What you eat or do not eat now will affect your health and well-being in the future.

## How You Eat

Many of us do not allow enough time for eating. We eat too quickly, which is not healthy. When you eat too quickly, you tend to overeat. Eating slowly helps your body's digestive process. It also helps you to know when you are full and gives you a chance to really taste and enjoy what you are eating.

Sometimes eating large amounts of food even when you are not hungry is a symptom of an unsolved emotional problem. If you are unhappy, frustrated, or angry, try exercising rather than eating. This will avoid establishing a bad eating habit, and the exercise may help your mental state.

## Losing Weight

There are many special diets for losing weight. Some are safe and do not endanger your health and well-being. Others range from inadequate to dangerous. Long-term success in losing weight is based on slow, gradual weight loss and the formation of good eating habits. Of course, when a safe plan for regular exercise is combined with a safe diet plan, weight loss is easier to achieve.

How is eating three meals a day similar or dissimilar to fueling a car?

A safe weight-loss plan includes the minimum number of servings of foods from the vegetable-fruit group, the milk-cheese group, the meat-poultry-fish-beans group, and the bread-cereal group. If the diet does not include foods from one or more of these groups or includes fewer than the recommended minimum servings, it is lacking in important nutrients and may be dangerous to your health.

A safe weight-loss plan does not have fewer than 1200 calories. Fewer than 1200 calories generally means that there is not enough food in the diet to provide an adequate amount of nutrients. Too few calories can upset body functions and cause you to lose muscle tissue rather than excess body fat. Health experts recommend that you do not lose more than 1 1/2 to 2 pounds per week. If you are planning to diet, your doctor can help you to figure out the exact number of calories you need daily based on your sex, age, present height and weight, and your activity level.

Research has indicated that a weight-loss plan is more effective when food intake is spread throughout the day with little or no intake after the evening meal. Apparently, the body makes better use of the food and burns calories more efficiently when your food intake is spread out. A morning meal is particularly important because it provides the energy needed for a good start on the day and helps to prevent feelings of hunger later on. Eating at midday is important for energy throughout the afternoon, but unless you are very active in the evening, a light supper and limited snacks are better for you at night. Subjects in research projects who ate all or most of their food late in the day lost less weight than those who spread their food evenly throughout the day.

Why is it important to eat breakfast, even if you are dieting?

## Gaining Weight

A plan for gaining weight also needs to be well-balanced. It should include increasing the intake of foods from the nutrient-rich food groups, not just from the fats-sweets group. Adding too many foods from the fats-sweets group can interfere with your appetite and make it difficult to get enough of the foods from the nutrient-rich food groups.

The timing of food intake also can help in a weight-gain plan. Instead of trying to eat large meals, four or more small meals spread out over the day may enable you to increase your total daily food intake. Unlike those who are trying to lose weight, eating during the evening may help you.

### For Review

1. Name the five basic food groups and tell which foods belong to each group.
2. Explain how good eating habits, including what, when, and how you eat, affect your health.
3. Describe a safe weight-loss plan and a safe plan for gaining weight.

## Planning Your Meals

Meal planning means planning ways to provide food while taking into consideration health, special nutritional needs, and schedules, as well as individual and family resources and goals. It may mean planning three meals a day for an entire family. On the other hand, it may mean planning meals or food for one person or for several people on different schedules. No matter what your circumstances are, you already know that meals should be planned using information from the Daily Food Guide. You also know that meals should be planned

Some meals require more time to prepare.

for food intake throughout the entire day. Keeping these facts in mind, you can now think about all of the other influences that affect meal planning.

## Influences on Meal Planning

There are many factors that influence your meal planning decisions. Special diets, family priorities, resources of time, energy, and money, and shopping and preparation skills are some of these factors. For example, if a special diet is required, it needs to be considered as you plan your meals. The time available to plan and prepare food for each meal also needs to be considered by you.

The resources you have available are other factors to think about when you are planning your daily food intake. Planning what you will eat and when you will eat it, based on the resources you have, helps to make it easier to carry out your plan. Knowing what your resources are also makes it easier to make last-minute adjustments in your plans.

**Special Diets** Some people have certain health conditions that require special diets prescribed by doctors or dietitians. Diabetes, heart disease, and high blood pressure are all health conditions that usually require special diets. Vegetarian diets and diets for losing or gaining weight are included in this category.

**Age** No matter how old you are, you still need the same basic six nutrients. There are periods in life, however, when certain nutrients are extremely important and may be required in extra amounts.

**Individual and Family Factors** Individual and family values, goals, and priorities affect meal plans. For example, if a high value is placed on nutrition, then a variety of foods probably will be available to all family members to choose from. If the family's goal is to eat three meals a week together, despite busy schedules, these goals and schedules need to be considered while you plan meals. Perhaps the only time everyone can get together is late at night. This may mean that family members who are up and out early need to divide their daily food intake into more meals because of the length of time between the first meal and the last.

Meal plans are easier to carry out if they are based on the schedules of those involved. If you and other family members eat most meals together, then meals can be planned for the times that are convenient. If you often eat by yourself because your schedule is different from the rest of your family, then your plan needs to accommodate this factor. If you have no plan, you may not get all the nutrients you need.

**Time and Energy** Once you understand daily nutritional needs and the other factors that affect what you eat and when, meal planning will become a simple task that does not take much time. If this is all you have to do, then the demands on your time are small. If you also have to shop and prepare food, then there are more demands on your time.

Skills in preparing food also take time to develop, but once developed, help speed up food preparation. For both experienced and inexperienced cooks, convenience foods are handy, because they require less preparation time than preparing everything "from scratch." **Convenience foods** are foods that have already been partially or completely prepared before you buy them.

Making meal plans helps you to make good use of your time. You can, if you wish, prepare some things ahead. You can also be sure that you have the foods you need for a meal. You won't be planning at the last minute and trying to do more than one thing at a time. When it is time for the meal, you will be more organized and the meal will go more smoothly. If you have used the Daily Food Guide to make your meal plans, you won't have to spend time thinking about nutrients as you prepare the food. That thinking will have been done ahead of time.

With planning, school lunches can be well-balanced and attractive meals.

On busy days, you may find that you have little time and energy for preparing food. When you know about these days, you can plan ahead for meals that use familiar foods and require a minimum of time and energy to prepare. Preparing food ahead of time, using convenience foods, or even eating out or bringing home food from some carry-out restaurant may become a part of your meal plan.

***Money and Shopping Skills*** Your meal plan should take into account the amount of money you have to spend. By making a shopping list from your plan, you can avoid last-minute decisions and impulse buying. You can take advantage of grocery store specials and sales when you plan ahead.

Skills in shopping for food can help you make the most of your money. You will know how to shop for good nutrition and how to compare prices. Chapter 12 has more information about saving money as you shop.

***The Need for Variety and Attractiveness*** The appearance of the meal you plan is almost as important as the nutrition it provides. A variety of colors, textures, flavors, and temperatures in the meal help to make it appealing and satisfying. A meal of meatloaf with tomato sauce or catsup, baked potato, harvard beets, and sliced tomatoes may be nutritionally sound, but the similar colors and the clash in flavors may make the meal dull and unappealing. Substituting a green vegetable for the beets and a fruit salad for the sliced tomatoes will provide more variety.

If you are planning a chicken sandwich for lunch, add a crisp green lettuce leaf and perhaps a tomato slice to the sandwich for some variation in color and texture. You might have some carrot sticks or an apple along with the sandwich. You might have a cup of soup, if you want to introduce something of a different temperature.

As a meal, fish sticks or strips of chicken, french fries, and carrot sticks repeat similar shapes and are in the same color range. Also, two foods are fried. Substituting a baked potato for the french fries and cooked peas for the carrot sticks will add more variety and make the meal more appealing to the eye.

**Preparation Skills**   When you plan meals that you will be preparing, take into account your skills in food preparation. The easiest meal is one for which all the menu items are purchased ready-to-eat. A meal that requires a recipe or has one item that has to be cooked while others are almost ready to eat requires more skill. A more complex meal may have several items that are more time-consuming to prepare.

If you are just learning how to cook and prepare food, you may want your meal plans to be simple. This allows you to practice what you know. To add to your skills, try to include a new dish or a new method of preparation when you have the time and desire to learn something new. As your skill increases, you will learn which menu items require a great deal of time, effort, and skill to prepare and which require less time and effort.

The first time you prepare something will take more time than the second. The more times you practice, the easier, smoother, and less time-consuming meal preparation will become. If you are interested in getting better at preparing food, you may decide that your leisure time is well spent in developing food

Learning to cook involves trying out new recipes. Cooking with a friend can add fun to the process.

# The Three Little Pigs and the Big, Bad Diet

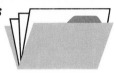

Once upon a time, there were three little pigs—at least that's what they called themselves. Molly, Polly, and Holly were really three average-looking freshmen at West High, and they were excited to be there. They were even more excited to be "rushed" by the best girls' club at West. The Cliques were known as the best looking and the best dressed group, all slim and stylish and sure of themselves.

"We'll never get in," the three sighed over after-school sundaes. "Look at the Cliques. There isn't one over size 8. And we look like Dumpy, Stumpy, and Lumpy. We have to lose weight—and fast!" They made a pact to go on the BBD Diet that all the Cliques were talking about. After all, if it was good enough for the Cliques, it was certainly good enough for them.

Molly stuck to the diet religiously, even though none of the prescribed meals sounded at all like the balanced diet she'd read about. Every time she drank the BBD Supplement, she felt ill, but she figured if it was good enough for the Cliques it was good enough for her. Polly tried the diet for a while, but she didn't like being too tired for volleyball practice, and she was worried about the strange-sounding ingredients on the BBD Supplement label. She took a long look in the mirror and checked a weight chart for her height and build. She decided her size 12 figure was right for her, and the Cliques would have to accept *all* of her or none. Holly decided to outdo the others; she stopped eating completely. She ignored the headaches and dizziness she felt in class and snapped at her friends when they asked what was wrong. She was determined to make her trim, athletic figure thinner no matter what.

Which of the girls do you think managed her "problem" best? Worst? Why? Who do you think will be happiest with herself in six months?

preparation skills. You will have to decide whether you want to use leisure time to practice or whether you prefer to get your experience as you go along preparing the food you are responsible for.

***Available Equipment*** As you plan your meals, you should consider the equipment, such as pans, bowls, small appliances, surface burners, and oven space, that is available to you. For example, if you plan a meal in which each item needs to be cooked in the oven, you need to be sure that your oven will hold everything. If you don't have an oven or yours does not work, then your oven-baked meal will not work.

A meal that has three items to be heated on stove burners when you have only two working burners may be a problem. You will have to decide if you want to juggle the pans on the

Convenience foods often are used when family time schedules are tight.

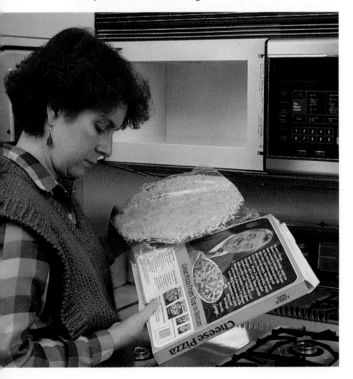

burners or change your plan. Maybe you can plan a raw vegetable instead of a cooked one, so you only need two burners. Decisions like these need to be part of the meal planning management process.

***Availability of Commercially Prepared Convenience Foods*** Dry mixes, canned and frozen foods, preformed meat patties, boned chicken, bottled and frozen juices, one-dish meals, completely baked products, and premeasured foods are just a few examples of convenience foods you can buy.

Some convenience foods are ready-to-serve foods, such as sliced bread, baked rolls, cheese slices, dry cereals, canned meats and fish, canned fruit, and bottled salad dressings. Some convenience foods are ready-to-use foods, such as instant coffee, tea, cocoa, and salad dressing mixes. Many convenience foods only need to be thawed, heated, or cooked. Some examples are frozen dinners, frozen desserts, canned and frozen vegetables, canned soups and stews, and ready-to-bake biscuits and rolls in a cardboard tube.

Although many commercially prepared convenience foods are expensive, the extra money for the savings in time and effort may make their use worthwhile. For other people, the savings from preparing food at home may be more important. Other considerations when planning your meals are the amount of enjoyment cooking gives, the level of cooking skill, and the taste preferences of the people eating the food. If you do use convenience foods, you should be aware of the extra sodium (salt) and additive content present in these foods. This may be important to you if you are on a special diet, for example.

## Eating Out

Eating out is very popular, and many individuals and families meet at least some of their

Some vending machines offer nutritious
food choices as well as chips or candy.

food needs by eating outside the home. While
eating out may meet some needs, it also requires some careful planning. Cafeterias at
school and work, restaurants for leisurely dining, and self-serve, drive-in, or take-out
restaurants all enter into decisions about meal
planning and food budgets.

***Advantages and Disadvantages*** Eating out
may solve some meal planning problems but not
others. It may be the answer to a lack of time
and energy for meal preparation or a lack of
skills and equipment. It may provide a chance
for all family members to eat together. However, if eating out is not part of the meal planning process, nutritional needs may not be met

and the family food budget may suffer as a
result of an unexpected expense.

***Know the Restaurant.*** Some restaurants specialize in just a few types of food. Others offer
a wide variety of selections. Although this variety makes it possible for more people to meet
their nutritional and caloric needs, many menu
selections are high in sodium, fat, and sugar
and low in fiber and certain important vitamins
and minerals. The nutritional value and calorie
content of foods eaten out are factors to be
considered when you are planning your meals,
particularly if you are on a restricted diet or
concerned about the prevention of certain
health problems.

Have a plan to accommodate one more guest.

**Use the Daily Food Guide.** If you eat in the school cafeteria or at snack bars or restaurants, you can plan your meals around the selections that are available. You can meet your nutritional needs by selecting foods from the nutrient-rich food groups and avoiding too many choices from the fats-sweets group. The foods you eat away from home contribute to your daily nutrient and caloric needs, so you may wish to round out your daily nutrition requirements with appropriate foods from the Daily Food Guide.

**Cost Factors** Since all of the mixing, preparation, cooking, and serving is done for you when you eat out, a meal out probably will cost more than the same meal prepared at home. Weighing the cost factor, the time and energy factors,

the nutritional value of the meal, and the circumstances at the time are a part of the meal planning process.

## Being Flexible and Prepared

Plans are helpful for getting organized and making good use of your time and resources. However, unexpected situations often occur and interfere with your plans. Having a written or mental "back-up" plan can be helpful in these situations. Suppose, for example, that you plan to make a sandwich for your lunch, only to discover that the bread is gone. If there are bulky rolls, you could use those instead of bread, or you could plan to make a salad or buy your lunch. Having canned or frozen spaghetti sauce on hand will help you to adjust your meal plan if you find you do not have enough time to make the sauce from a recipe.

When you make up your meal plans, think of alternatives you can use if you have a sudden change in resources, such as less time, no electricity, or unexpected company. Being able to adjust to the unexpected is a valuable management skill. Many of the things that affect meal plans are related to the resources you have. Try to have supplies on hand for at least one meal for unexpected company. This may mean just having a few extra boxes of pasta or macaroni and cheese stored away. Plan a meal you can stretch if you have to. Changes in resources can create the need for changes in your plans.

## For Review

1. List four of the factors you should consider when meal planning.
2. Explain how individual schedules and preparation skills affect meal planning.
3. List the advantages and disadvantages of eating out.

## Management Application: Making a Diet Plan

Imagine yourself in the situation described below. As you read, think about how the steps of the management process might apply to this situation. Then answer the questions that follow.

### Situation

Bob had been overweight for most of his life. Now, as he thought about entering high school next fall, he was really determined to lose the extra twenty pounds he was carrying. It was more than the twenty pounds that was bothering him. He was sick of pretending that fat jokes didn't hurt. He wanted to try out for the soccer team, too.

Bob went to his doctor and between them they worked out a 1200 calorie-a-day diet. It included the nutrients he needed each day and foods from each food group. It wasn't going to be easy. Hot fudge sundaes were *not* on the permitted snack list. He had tried diets before, but this time he set a realistic goal. He would lose two pounds a week. At that rate, he would have lost eighteen pounds by the first day of school. Bob tried to picture himself twenty pounds lighter. He was already looking forward to wearing more stylish clothes. More than that, he was looking forward to feeling better. Now he had trouble breathing when he tried to run. He also felt tired a lot, even when he hadn't done much. Gym class was a disaster because the extra weight made him so slow. Well, all of that was going to change. He was determined to succeed.

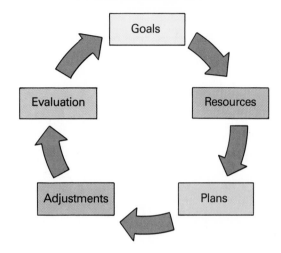

Bob's family was very supportive. His mother stocked up on fresh fruits and vegetables for snacks. His brother decided to diet with him, which helped. They biked to work every day instead of driving and kept each other on track with the diet. It was tough, but as the pounds came off, Bob felt better about himself. He was proud of his self-discipline. This time he was going to do it!

### Questions

1. What human resources did Bob need from himself and others?
2. What kind of professional resources did Bob use?
3. Was Bob's goal realistic? What might have happened if he expected to lose five pounds per week?
4. How will Bob evaluate the result of his plan in September? A year from now?
5. Which steps of the management process apply to this situation?

# 11 *Chapter Review*

## Summary

To make wise decisions about food, you should know which foods your body needs for proper development. Following the Daily Food Guide can help people of all ages to eat a balanced diet. When you eat and how you eat are as important as getting the right nutrients in the correct amounts. Many factors, including special diets, family values and goals, time, variety, and available equipment, influence meal planning decisions.

## Vocabulary

Complete each of the following sentences with one of the vocabulary words below.

nutrition                saturated fats

nutrients                cholesterol

calorie                  convenience foods

Daily Food Guide

1. Fats from animal sources are _____ .
2. A booklet that divides food into five basic groups and outlines a daily recommended amount from each group is the _____ .
3. The science of food and its relation to health is _____ .
4. _____ is a fatty substance; too much of this substance can lead to heart disease and other problems.

5. The substances that your body needs for growth, energy, and good health are called _____ .
6. A _____ is a measure of the energy produced by food when it is used by the body.
7. Foods that have been partially or completely prepared before purchase are known as _____ .

## Questions

1. In which food category would you find each of the following foods:

   butter      apples      carrots

   eggs        rice        chicken

   fish        bread

2. What vitamin(s) would you find in each of the following foods:

   oranges      eggs        cereal

   spinach      cheese      carrots

   peanut oil   hamburger

3. What can happen if you do not get enough protein? What does research indicate as the possible result of having too little calcium? Too little vitamin C?
4. What can happen if you consume too much salt or caffeine?
5. How many servings from the bread-cereal group should you eat each day? What are some of the foods you can choose from?

6. What are the seven dietary guidelines that are recommended by the Department of Agriculture and the Department of Health and Human Resources?

7. What is thought to be one advantage of eating fish regularly?

8. Explain why the appearance of a meal is almost as important as the nutritional value it provides to you.

9. What are the advantages and disadvantages of convenience foods? Explain your answer in terms of time and nutrition.

10. Explain how your family goals and schedules influence meal planning.

## Skill Activities

1. **Decision Making.** Keep a nutrition diary of the foods you eat during a week. Include all meals and snacks. At the end of the week evaluate your diet in terms of balance, vitamins, variety, and fats or sugars.

Write a short paragraph explaining what you have decided to do to improve the nutritional value of your diet.

2. **Resource Management.** Do you have a particularly nutritious and tasty family recipe? Write down the recipe, including ingredients and directions for preparation. Also make a list of the nutrients in the recipe.

Share your recipe with your classmates. As a class project, you may want to collect the recipes and create a recipe book. You may want to divide your book into sections such as "All-Time Favorites" and "International Cooking." Make copies for everyone.

3. **Science.** Divide the class into five groups. Each group will choose one of the sources of nutrition information listed on page 243. Write letters to these organizations requesting any current nutrition information they can supply. (If you cannot find addresses, your librarian should be able to assist you.)

To share the information you receive, have each member of the group give a short oral report to the class.

4. **Critical Thinking.** Start an investigation of the ingredients and nutrition information in cereals. On a sheet of paper, write your name. Beside your name, write the brand of cereal you want to investigate. Have each class member do the same. Try to use a different brand for each person. If you usually buy the cereal, cut out the ingredients label and take it into class. If not, copy down the ingredients in the store. Chart your results. How many cereals have sugar and/or salt included in their first three ingredients? Which are the top three cereals as far as nutrition per daily serving? Were you surprised by the results? Why or why not?

# 12 Managing Food Resources

## As you read, think about:

- how to improve your food shopping skills.
- how to control the cost of food and maintain quality.
- how to apply health and safety techniques to food preparation.
- how to follow a recipe and time a meal correctly.
- how to apply the management process to personal decisions about food preparation procedures.

food cooperative
shelf-life
menu plan
food additives
U.S. RDA
unit pricing
recipe

Managing food resources involves meal planning, shopping, cooking, and timing meals correctly. The skills needed in each of these processes are ones that you will use all your life. Learning to prepare nutritional meals safely and economically is what this chapter is all about.

## Making Food Shopping Decisions

Most people cannot grow all the fruits, grains, and vegetables they eat; even fewer can supply their own fish and meat all year long. Most of us need to purchase our food. Over the course of your life, you will spend many hours shopping for food. Learning where to shop, what to buy, and how to shop efficiently and economically are important life management skills for you.

## Where to Shop

There are many types of stores that sell food. You may have several supermarkets in your town, or there may be one small grocery store in your town and a large supermarket several miles away. If you can become familiar with the stores near you and the products they sell, it will help you to shop wisely. Before you decide where to shop, you might want to do some price comparisons to see if one store consistently has lower prices than another. Find out if coupons are accepted by the stores. Some stores even double the value of coupons.

Check the stores for cleanliness. Are the floors and displays clean, or is there dirt and dust and the remnants of broken packages in the aisles? Are the canned and packaged goods dusty? Does the produce look fresh? Is it kept cool? Are the frozen food cases free from a heavy buildup of frost or ice crystals? Are dairy products and meats properly cooled?

Some people shop for different items at different stores to get the best prices on each item. This may save money if you do not have to travel so far that you spend your savings on gas or bus fare. Many people, however, do not have the time to shop from store to store. They may try several stores, comparing prices, services, cleanliness, selection of food, and other factors, and then decide on one store as the place to do most or all of their shopping.

**Food Warehouses** Food warehouses are stores that offer limited services and lower prices. Because food warehouses are not paying for extras, you may have to bag your food at the check-out or supply your own bags or cartons. Usually these stores buy large quantities of certain brands of food, but they do not carry all the various brands that the average supermarket does. If these disadvantages do not bother you, you can usually save money by shopping at a food warehouse.

**Food Cooperatives: An Alternative** In many areas of the country, it is possible to join a food cooperative. A **food cooperative** is a group of individuals who have joined together to buy food in bulk from wholesalers or local growers or producers. The food they buy is sold to other members of the cooperative, usually at lower prices than you would pay in a supermarket or grocery store.

Members usually work for the cooperative a certain number of hours per week or

If you use food coupons, you may choose to shop where their value is greatest.

month. They may take orders, fill orders, unpack boxes, or work in the store itself, if there is a store. This can be a problem if a person is busy or if the cooperative is not nearby, but members do have a say in how the cooperative is run and in what foods are purchased. Because purchases usually are made in bulk, there are no individual packages, and members can often order as much or as little as they want. By providing their own containers for such items as dried beans and peas, flour, pastas, seasonings, and produce, they can conserve their resources. On the other hand, the cooperative may not offer as many food choices as a supermarket does.

## How Often to Shop

Some people shop every week because they are paid once a week. Others shop only once or twice a month because that is when they are paid. They may plan to buy only milk and fresh foods in between times. Still others may live so far from a store that they only plan one or two shopping trips a month. From these examples, you can see that many factors affect your decision about how often to shop.

The amount of storage space you have available also helps to determine how often you shop. If you have plenty of storage space in your cupboards, freezer, and refrigerator, then it is possible to make fewer trips but buy more each time. If your storage is limited, then more frequent shopping trips will be needed.

## When to Shop

The time a person has free for shopping is a major factor in deciding when to shop. Usually, school or work is scheduled for specific times, and shopping has to be planned around those times. Sometimes, shopping can be done on the way home so extra trips are unnecessary. Sometimes, schedules or other activities can be adjusted so that shopping can be done when it is most convenient for you.

If a large selection of food is important to you, you may want to find out when the store or stores you shop at have deliveries. Very large stores may have deliveries several times a week. Your selection of food is largest after a delivery. Knowing when stores have deliveries will help you to decide when to shop.

Buying marked-down products can save you money if you use them right away. Foods should be dated to show shelf-life. **Shelf-life** is the length of time that any food can be stored without spoiling. Food can be eaten safely during this time. Bread products have a short shelf-life and may be sold at a discount if they have not been sold by the date marked on the wrapper. Fresh food, such as ground beef or chicken, may be marked down on the last day it is to be sold. Fresh vegetables and fruits may

Wherever you shop, check items for shelf-life dating and ingredients.

be marked down after a few days. Sometimes markdowns take place just before a delivery date to help make room for the fresh products. If you buy marked-down fruits and vegetables, however, you should realize they lose nutritional value as they lose freshness. You should also check them carefully for spoilage.

Stores are more crowded at some times during the day than at others. For example, fewer people may shop early in the morning and in the evening than in the late morning or early afternoon. If you dislike crowded stores, you may want to visit your store at different times on different days to discover when most people shop. You may want to ask the store manager or a clerk when their busy times are. Perhaps you will be able to plan your shopping according to these times.

## Fresh, Frozen, Canned, or Dried?

Even with all the variety of items on shelves in supermarkets and grocery stores, most foods can be classified as fresh, frozen, canned, or dried. Each form of food has its advantages and disadvantages. These factors need to be considered when you are making your meal plans. Knowing which form of food best meets your needs also helps you to control food costs.

**Fresh Food** Fresh food is food that has not been processed by freezing, canning, or drying. Lettuce, carrots, oranges, and other produce from the garden, the local produce stand, or the fresh fruit and vegetable department of a store are examples. Ground meat, fish fillets, chicken, and other selections in the butcher shop, fish market, or meat department of a store, as well as meats and salads from the deli, are other fresh foods. Fresh rolls, bread, and other baked goods are also in this category.

Many people believe that fresh fruits and vegetables are more nutritious than canned or

Many food stores have bakeries that offer fresh rolls like these.

frozen ones. This is true only if these foods are really fresh when purchased, stored properly after purchase, and properly prepared and served soon after purchase. Improper storage, handling, and preparation cause nutrient loss. Improper home processing can also cause mild to severe nutrient loss. Commercial processing, such as canning fruit, is controlled carefully to preserve quality and nutrients. Frozen or canned fruits and vegetables may have a higher nutrient content than fresh ones that are out of season or have spent a long time in some type of storage.

Preparing fresh foods at home usually costs less than buying the same food partly or completely prepared, but it often takes more time and requires more knowledge and skill. For example, it takes time, some knowledge of recipe terminology, and some cooking skill to make lasagna or roast stuffed chicken or baked beans. It takes less time, knowledge, and skill to put a frozen lasagna or an already stuffed chicken in the oven or open a can of baked beans to heat them.

Fresh foods are popular with many people because of their flavor and texture, but many fresh foods must be stored in the refrigerator to maintain freshness and prevent spoilage. Many must be used within a few days or they will spoil.

**Frozen Food** Food to be frozen commercially is selected for quality and prepared quickly to maintain the quality. It is processed by subjecting it to very low temperatures that freeze it as quickly as possible. This protects the nutrients and prevents spoilage. The food is packaged to maintain its quality. Some examples of frozen foods are frozen vegetables and fruits, juices, main dishes, batters and doughs, dinners, and desserts. Frozen foods most closely resemble fresh foods in flavor and texture and, when stored properly, have the advantage of longer storage life than fresh foods presently have.

**Canned Food** Food to be canned commercially also is selected for quality and prepared quickly to maintain the quality. It is then sealed in cans or bottles and subjected to high temperatures to kill harmful bacteria and prevent spoilage. The high temperatures create an airtight seal. As long as the seal is not broken, the food will not quickly spoil.

Canned food often requires less preparation time than frozen foods because most of these foods are already cooked. Many are ready to use or eat from the can. Others only need to be heated. In contrast to frozen foods, canned foods are less like fresh foods in their flavor and texture.

**Dried Food** Dried foods are processed by doing a certain amount of preparation, then using special processes to remove moisture from the food. Examples of dried foods are dried beans and peas, nonfat dry milk, instant

Workers in a food processing plant check for quality before packaging begins.

coffee and tea, dry soup mixes, and dried fruits and vegetables.

When reconstituted by adding water, many dried foods are similar to fresh foods in flavor and texture. They are convenient because they can be stored at room temperature for long periods of time. For maximum shelf-life, they should be stored in a cool, dry place away from dampness.

## Knowing Your Resources

Even before you make a list, you should determine how much money you can spend on food. If you are shopping for your family, this amount may be determined by your parents. If you are shopping for yourself, you probably made this decision for yourself or at least helped in the process.

Knowing the amount you can spend helps you to make a plan. If the amount you have for shopping is limited, and your meal plans include several expensive food items, you will need to adjust your plans in order to buy enough food for all the meals. Setting a limit and sticking to it helps you to control what you spend for food.

Learn about less expensive sources of nutrients. You can lower your food costs, if you know some of the less expensive sources of important nutrients. Although meats, fish, and poultry are good sources of protein, they often take the largest bite out of your food budget. Dried beans and peas and peanut butter are less expensive sources of protein. They have high nutritional value when they are combined or eaten with milk, cheese, eggs, or small amounts of meat, fish, or poultry. Dry milk is less expensive than fluid milk and has the same nutrients. If you wish to save money, you can use reconstituted dry milk in place of all or part of the fluid milk you now use.

## Making a List

Shopping with a definite list of items you know you need is a smart technique. If you know what you need ahead of time, you are less likely to overbuy. Your list should be made after you have made meal plans and checked to see if you need any basic food staples or kitchen supplies.

***Menu Planning*** A **menu plan** is an outline or a listing of foods and beverages to be eaten at specific meals, and between meals, for a period of one or more days. The plan can be for

There are about nine grams of protein in two tablespoons of peanut butter.

one person or for several people. A menu plan is more specific than the more general meal plan discussed in Chapter 11.

Some people make menu plans for a week at a time. Others make their plans for shorter or longer periods, depending on the time they have for planning, how often they shop, the amount of money and time that is available to them, and the amount of storage space they have.

If you know what foods you will need and when you will need them, it will be easier to make your shopping list and easier to control costs by buying only the amount you will need and use. This will avoid waste and buying items you don't need. When necessary, you can adjust your menus to foods that have special prices or that are lower in cost.

***Taking Inventory*** After you have planned your meals, plus a "back-up" plan and "company" plan if appropriate, check to see if you have all the necessary food items on hand. Probably you already have some of the foods you need in the cupboard or in the freezer. You even may have fresh foods in the garden that are part of your menu plan. However, there are likely to be other foods you will need to put on your list.

***Checking for Staples and Nonfood Items*** Before you complete your list, check your supplies of staples, such as flour, sugar, seasonings, and other foods that you usually have on hand. If you are low on any of these, add them to your list. These foods do not have to be bought each time you shop, so you may not realize that your supplies are low unless you check them frequently.

As you add these supplies to your list, you may want to include all nonfood items you will need unless you purchase these at another store. Paper napkins, paper towels, and toilet paper are among these supplies as are soaps,

These coupon club members collect and share coupons to lower food costs.

detergents, and any other cleaning items that you feel you need.

***Looking for Specials and Coupons*** Many supermarkets and grocery stores have specials each week on certain foods. This means lower prices than usual. You may want to look over the newspaper ads and flyers to see if there is anything you or your family especially like. If you collect coupons, you may want to go over them before beginning your list. You may decide to change something in your menu plan because of a weekly special or a large coupon savings.

Clipping coupons and organizing them does take time and energy. Many people do not choose to use them for this reason. The resource of time saved is more valuable to them than the money resources saved by using coupons when they shop. This is an individual decision you will need to make when you are managing your food resources.

## For Review

1. Explain how being a member of a food cooperative differs from shopping for food at a store.
2. What are the advantages and disadvantages of buying fresh food? What are three other alternatives?
3. What should you include on the food shopping list you might write?

## Evaluating Food Costs and Quality

Now you have your shopping list in your hand and you are ready to head to the store of your choice. You have the coupons that you plan to use and have checked for specials and sale items. Once you are at the store, there are other things you can look for and do to make sure you are controlling food costs and getting the best quality food.

### Saving Money

There are certain steps you can take and things you can avoid while food shopping that will save you money. These are good consumer tips for you to learn. They will help you to keep your food budget under control.

**Buy the Correct Size or Amount for Your Situation.** If all the food you buy will not be used before it spoils, or if you cannot store it properly, it will be wasted. Buying small packages or containers, if this is all that you can store, or buying only the amount you will use will save you money.

Buying a lot of food on special only saves money if it is food that will be used and if there

Less expensive, generic brand foods may be as good as better known national brands. Have you tried any of them?

is room to store it properly. Stick to your shopping list unless the specials are items that will be used before they spoil.

**Avoid Impulse Buying.** As you know, impulse buying is buying without thinking about how an item fits into your plan or how it will affect your money resources. Depending on how much money you spend, impulse buying can upset your food plans a lot or a little. Also, avoid food shopping when you are hungry because you will probably buy more than you need.

**Avoid Excess Packaging.** Many foods need to be packaged to avoid contamination. Other foods, such as fresh fruits and vegetables, do not need to be packaged. Putting these foods on cardboard or foam-type trays and wrapping them in plastic uses more resources and costs you more money.

# Food Management

If you like managing family meals, and you are good at it, you may want a career in food management. Both chefs and dieticians plan and supervise meal preparation for large numbers of people.

**Chef** In a fine restaurant, the master chef runs the kitchen and is largely responsible for the style, quality, and reputation of the cuisine. This job requires skill, talent, and experience. Professional training at culinary institutes, junior colleges, and other facilities is becoming more important. Chefs also need "executive ability" to hire, train, and supervise a staff of *sous chefs* (assistant chefs) and specialists, such as pastry chefs or sauce chefs, as well as salad assemblers, dishwashers, and other kitchen personnel. The master chef coordinates the work of the staff, directs preparation of specialties, plans menus, decides serving size, and often purchases food supplies. When these activities are coordinated successfully, diners often say, "Our compliments to the chef!"

**Dietician** Dieticians are health professionals and food managers. They supervise meals in large food-service operations, such as cafeterias in schools and factories. They often hire, train, and direct cooks and other workers; budget and purchase food, equipment, and supplies; and enforce health regulations to ensure that meals are nutritionally balanced, as well as safely and economically prepared. Some dieticians work in health-related facilities, such as hospitals and nursing homes. Consulting with doctors and nurses, they determine patients' nutritional needs, develop their diets, instruct patients and their families, and evaluate patient progress. A bachelor's degree is required for this career. Registered dieticians (RD) must pass the American Dietetic Association examination and complete an internship program.

Still other foods have more packaging than is necessary for their protection. For example, some breads are wrapped in paper or put in a plastic bag for protection. Other breads, however, have both a paper or cellophane-type wrapping and a plastic bag. Individually wrapped cheese slices and individual packages of food inside larger packages use more resources and usually cost more than similar products with less packaging.

**Compare Brands.** There are several types of food brands to compare. National brands are the most widely advertised and generally the most expensive. There are also store, or house, brands and generic, or no-name, brands. The generic brands usually have the lowest price. If you are interested in the money savings, buy and compare a few of these brands for cost, taste, and quality. Some products may be just as good as the more expensive brands. Others may be such a disappointment in taste and quality that you will not purchase them again.

**Remember Your Coupons!** If you use them, have your coupons out and ready to turn in when you check out. In the process of unloading groceries from your cart, it is easy to forget to turn in coupons. Since they can mean sizable savings in your food budget, it is worth the effort to have them ready to use.

## Getting High Quality

High quality food is as fresh as possible, has good texture and flavor, and has the highest nutrient content possible for the type of food it is.

High quality fresh fruits and vegetables are ripe, firm, crisp, and free from bruises. Those that have started to spoil or look limp and pale are not good values, even if they are marked down. They are likely to have suffered nutrient losses.

**Grades** Meat and poultry are graded. The grades are an indication of their quality. In the

Although the food inside these dented cans may not be spoiled, it is wiser not to purchase them.

United States, top quality grades are Prime, Choice, and Good. Prime meats cost the most and are highest in quality, followed by Choice meats and Good meats, in that order. In addition, high quality fresh meats, fish, and poultry have a color that is characteristic of the product. There is no strong, offensive odor. If fish, for example, has a strong odor, it is not as fresh as it should be.

Eggs and dairy products also are marked with grades as an indication of quality. For judging freshness, check the dates that are marked on these products.

Many canned foods are marked with a grade as an indication of quality. Higher grades usually mean the pieces in the can or jar are whole or of uniform size. Lower grades can indicate broken pieces or variations in sizes. There is no difference in nutritional value. Lower grades generally cost less and may be useful when uniformity doesn't matter or when the food will be cut up anyway.

***Packaging and Containers*** You should check containers carefully when you buy canned food. The can should have no dents. There should be no rust. A bulging can may indicate food spoilage and perhaps the development of dangerous bacteria or other dangerous toxic substances.

Frozen food should be solidly frozen. If there are large ice crystals in the food, it has not been stored properly and the quality probably has suffered. If the packaging is clear, you can see the ice crystals. If packaging is opaque, you may want to feel the package for ice crystals.

Avoid frozen foods that are covered with ice crystals on the outside of the package or that are stored in frozen food cases that have a buildup of frost or ice crystals. These may indicate the food has been thawed at some point and the quality may have suffered. Frozen food that is not solidly frozen may have a lower nutritional value, and the flavor and texture of

MADE WITH 100% PURE VEGETABLE SHORTENING

INGREDIENTS: Whole wheat flour, enriched wheat flour (contains niacin, reduced iron, thiamine mononitrate [vitamin B1], riboflavin [vitamin B2]), vegetable shortening (partially hydrogenated soybean oil with hydrogenated cottonseed oil), sugar, salt, high fructose corn syrup, malted barley flour, turmeric oleoresin, annatto extract (vegetable colors).

How does food labeling help people who are on restricted diets?

it will have been affected by the thawing. Spoilage may have begun.

Packages of dried foods, mixes, and other packaged foods should not have broken or torn wrappings. These conditions expose the food to possible contamination and may make them unsafe to eat.

## Reading Labels

Most processed food is required by law to have certain information on labels. Reading this information can help you to decide what products are best suited to your needs. Labels have information about contents and nutrition. They usually also have unit pricing and shelf-life information for your use.

***Basic Content Information*** All food labels must have the *name of the food* on the label, "enriched rolls," "fish sticks," or "mayonnaise," for example. The *net volume,* for example, "16 fl oz (1 pt—473 mL)," or *net weight,* "13 oz (369 grams)," also must be on the label. When the contents contain solids and a liquid, the actual weight of the food without the liquid may be given, but this is not information required by law.

Other required information includes the *name and place of business* of the manufacturer, packer, or distributor of the food.

Most food products are required to provide a *listing of ingredients.* The ingredients are listed in order of descending weight. This means that the first ingredient listed makes up the greatest amount of the product by weight. The last ingredient listed makes up the least amount of the product by weight. You cannot tell from an ingredient listing exactly how much of a particular ingredient is in a product. However, you can find out what the ingredients are and how the amount of one ingredient compares to the amount of other ingredients. If you are looking at a can of mixed nuts, for example, you can tell which kinds of nuts are in the can, and you can tell if there are more peanuts than cashews in the mix.

Ingredient listing is helpful when you are comparing two or more products. For example, you may want more beef than potatoes in canned beef stew. By comparing the labels on various products, you can choose the one that has beef highest on its list.

Reading the list of ingredients is important for people who must follow special diets or have allergies to certain foods or substances in foods. If the ingredients are not listed, you can write to the manufacturer to find out what they are. Once you know the ingredients, you can avoid products that contain substances you want to avoid.

**Food additives** are substances that are added to foods to prevent spoilage, improve flavor and texture, enhance color, or improve nutritional value. By law, these must be printed on the ingredient list. Salt and sugar are commonly used as additives as are such substances as bisulfites (by-SUL-fites) and diglycerides (dy-GLISS-uh-rides).

Highly processed foods, such as mixes and ready-prepared foods and dinners, usually contain the largest amounts of additives. Foods that are less processed, such as flour or some cereals, usually contain fewer additives.

Although there are laws about the use of food additives and the Food and Drug Administration (FDA) enforces these laws, some people believe many food additives are not safe. Some consumers avoid foods with any additives. Others have cut back on the use of foods with additives. Still others try to eat a wide variety of foods in order to avoid consuming large amounts of any one additive.

***Nutrition Information*** Many food labels provide nutrition information. When this type of information is provided, the following information must be given:

- size of serving
- number of servings in the container
- calories per serving
- grams of protein, carbohydrate, and fat per serving
- percentage of **U.S. RDA** (United States Recommended Dietary Allowances) of protein, vitamin A, vitamin C, thiamine, riboflavin, niacin, calcium, and iron.

The U.S. RDA was developed by the Food and Drug Administration specifically for use in nutrition labeling. The figures for the amounts of each nutrient in the U.S. RDA are based on the recommended dietary allowances for adult males, established by the National Research Council of the Food and Nutrition Board of the National Academy of Sciences. The RDA figures are based on extensive research and include the intake of calories and specific nutrients recommended on a daily basis for males and females of different ages.

Additional nutrition information may include the cholesterol content, sodium content, sugar content, and fiber content.

**Use Unit Pricing Information.** Many states require the unit pricing of various foods. **Unit pricing** shows the price per unit of measure of the food, such as so much per pound or so much per quart.

Unit pricing information can be helpful when you are comparing the prices of two different sizes or brands of cans or packages. While often the largest size has the lowest price per unit, this is not always the case. Checking the unit price can tell you which size is the least expensive per unit.

Most unit pricing information can be found on a label on the shelf right below or above the product you want.

**Use Dating Information.** Most packaged food has a date on the label or package. The date may be preceded by the words "use by" or "sell by." This information tells you how long the food will stay fresh and retain its quality. The "sell by" date allows for a few days of storage at home. The exact length of storage depends on the type of food.

Sometimes the only information on the package is a date. This makes it hard to tell whether you should use the product by that date or if you can store it for a few days before you use it. Many consumers consider it to be a "use by" date just to be safe. If you are at all uncertain, ask the store manager exactly what the date means.

Sometimes food is marked down just before the date on the label expires. If you can use the food immediately or freeze it for use quite soon, you may want to buy it. You should check the product over carefully before deciding to buy it.

Grades and seals on meat indicate quality and safety. Check dating too.

## For Review:

1. Name at least five ways that you can control the cost of food shopping.
2. What things should you check for in packaging and in containers of canned, frozen, and dried foods?
3. Explain why the ingredient listing on food products is so important.

## Preparing a Meal

Food preparation involves many skills. Keeping the kitchen or cooking area clean and safe is one part of the food preparation process. Learning proper storage methods for various foods is another. Efficient work methods, following recipe instructions carefully, and timing meals properly are all part of preparing a meal. The more you know about the basic principles of cooking and how to use the equipment you need when preparing a meal, the easier your job will be.

## Sanitation, Cleanliness, and Safety

Commercial producers and processors of food must follow strict sanitation and cleanliness practices. These practices also are followed in restaurants, schools, hospitals, and other public places where food is served. This is necessary to provide consumers with uncontaminated food products. These same practices should be followed at home to avoid endangering the health and safety of all people who use the kitchen or eat the food prepared in the kitchen.

***Personal Habits*** Personal habits are important in maintaining clean, sanitary conditions. This means washing your hands with soap and hot water before handling food or beginning food preparation, after covering a sneeze or blowing your nose, and after using the bathroom. If possible, avoid touching your face or hair when you are working with food. Avoid working with food if you are sick. You should try not to work with food if you have an infected cut on your hand unless you wear rubber gloves.

Sometimes you need to taste something you are making to be sure it is seasoned properly. To do this, you may want to use the mixing spoon to transfer some of the food to a tasting spoon. You should try not to touch the tasting spoon with the spoon that is mixing the

Why do restaurants have such strict health procedures? Employees are trained to follow them as they cook and clean.

food. If what you are tasting is too thick to pour into a tasting spoon, use a clean spoon, not the mixing spoon, each time you take a taste.

When you put dishes away or set the table, you should try not to touch the rims of the glasses or the parts of the flatware that will go in the mouth or will be used to serve food.

Dishtowels are only for dishes. Do not wipe your hands on them or throw them over your shoulder as you do other tasks. A hand towel should be used only for wiping hands, not for drying dishes.

**Handling Food**  Fresh meat, fish, and poultry may have bacteria on their surfaces. If they are not handled properly, or if cleanup after preparing them is not properly done, food poisoning can occur.

When cutting meat, fish, or poultry, either fresh or cooked, you should use a cutting board that cannot be damaged by hot, soapy water. As soon as you have finished, wash the board and knife in hot, soapy water and rinse well with boiling water to kill bacteria. Wash your hands well and wash the counter with soap and water, then rinse well.

If you cut up fresh meat, fish, or poultry and plan to use the same cutting board for cutting the meat, fish, or poultry when it is cooked, you should wash it thoroughly in between and rinse it with boiling water. Bacteria from the fresh meat, fish, or poultry can contaminate the cooked food.

If it is possible, you may want to use a different cutting board for cutting up vegetables, fruit, bread, and making sandwiches than you do for cutting up meat, fish, and poultry. This board also should be washed thoroughly when you are finished, especially if you have made sandwiches with meat or other protein food.

**Keeping the Kitchen Clean**  A clean kitchen helps prevent food contamination. Cleaning as you go makes your task easier and helps to keep the kitchen clean.

Lay out food requiring refrigeration as close as possible to eating time.

Wash counters and work tables with hot, soapy water and then rinse them thoroughly. Wipe off the top of the oven or stove and the refrigerator door each time you clean up. Keep your cabinets and storage areas clean. If you put things away when you are done with them, you will find cleanup easier. Wipe up spills before they have a chance to spread or dry.

Rinse and dispose of cans and jars as you finish using them. Waste paper, vegetable peelings, and food scraps can attract flies, rodents, or other insects and animals. They also smell and, if left, may develop potentially harmful mold or bacteria.

Keep the sink clean. Clean out the drain or run the disposal frequently. Wipe around the sink area frequently.

Periodically, you will want to clean out your refrigerator. Dispose of food that has been stored too long, and defrost the freezer, if necessary. Wipe out the inside of the refrigerator with a solution of baking soda and water. If possible, wipe up spills inside the refrigerator as they occur.

Because they are good breeding grounds for bacteria, sponges should be washed out and allowed to dry after use and replaced frequently. When possible, use clean dishcloths and dishtowels for each meal.

Sweep or vacuum the kitchen floor frequently and wash it when needed. Wipe up spills immediately to prevent falls and to avoid attracting insects and rodents.

**Washing Dishes** To prevent the spread of illness and to destroy potentially harmful

Scrubbing cutting boards thoroughly between uses eliminates the spread of bacteria. Use hot, soapy water.

bacteria, you will want to wash dishes after every meal. The use of soap or detergent, water of the correct temperature, and thorough rinsing are all a part of dish washing.

If you are washing dishes by hand, scrape food scraps from the plates first. Rinse the plates, dishes, flatware, and pans. Put soap or detergent in the dishpan and add hot water. Wash the least soiled items first and work your way through the most soiled. Be sure to remove all traces of food and grease. Wash both sides of plates and the outside and inside of glasses, cups, and bowls. Rinse the dishes in scalding hot water and allow to air dry if possible. If you are using a dishwasher, scrape food scraps from the plates. Rinse any items with food residue if this practice is suggested by the manufacturer. Load the dishwasher according to manufacturer's instructions. Use detergent designed specifically for dishwashers. To insure thorough cleaning, the water temperature of the dishwasher should be at least 140° F (60° C).

## Storing Food Safely

When you store food, you want to maintain its nutritional value and to prevent its damage from environmental factors and unwanted bacterial growth and contamination. Clean, non-metal containers with lids are ideal for storing most foods safely.

**Protection from the Environment** Because various foods can be damaged by insects, rodents, heat, light, and moisture, proper storage is vital.

Sometimes *insects and rodents* can cause problems with staple foods stored at room temperature, such as cereal, flour, sugar, packaged mixes, and foods in paper or plastic bags. If you can store these foods in containers with snug-fitting lids, you can avoid these problems. Plastic containers with press-on lids are available in various sizes, shapes, and colors. In dry climates or storage areas, metal tins or cans can be used if their lids fit snugly. Although sealed plastic bags offer protection against insects, rodents can eat through them.

Sometimes *heat* can cause the deterioration of canned food and some packaged food and mixes. Storing these foods in a cabinet or on a shelf over the range or near another source of heat or in a sunny, warm corner exposes these foods to too much heat. When it is possible, you will want to store them in a cool, dark, dry place. Foods that contain moisture have a tendency to mold unless they are kept away from heat and moisture. Some whole grain products, such as whole wheat flour, full-fat soy flour, and wheat germ, become rancid in a few weeks when exposed to heat. Storing these foods in the refrigerator or freezer helps them to maintain their freshness.

Temperatures above 40° F (5° C) encourage the growth of bacteria in many moist, nonacidic, protein foods. Keeping these foods properly refrigerated will help to delay the process of spoiling.

Frozen foods must be kept at 0° F (-18° C) or lower to maintain their quality. Higher temperatures will shorten their storage life.

*Exposure to light* destroys certain nutrients in foods, such as riboflavin, an important B vitamin found in milk and many grain products. Milk in plastic containers or in clear glass containers that allow light to pass through should be stored away from light. Grain products, too, should be stored in opaque containers whenever possible to maintain nutritional quality.

*Air* also can destroy important nutrients. Vitamin C, for example, is destroyed by exposure to air. Cut fruits and vegetables should be tightly covered before storage to prevent this loss. Fruit juices should be stored in air-tight containers when possible.

*Too much moisture* in the air can cause crisp foods (cereals and crackers, for example) to become softer and stale tasting. Storing

Safely freezing portions of food in airtight bags helps to avoid waste.

these foods in a dry place that is slightly warm may help to keep them fresh and tasty. A cabinet over the range or stove may be a good spot for these foods.

**Preventing Bacterial Growth** Organisms that cause food poisoning grow most rapidly in temperatures between 40° F and 140° F (5° C to 60° C).

Highly perishable foods should be used within a short period of time. Fresh meat, poultry, and fish should not be kept at room temperature for longer than an hour. Cook them at the recommended temperature suggested by cookbooks and use a meat thermometer to insure proper doneness. Canned meat, poultry, and fish that has been opened should be refrigerated immediately after use.

When cooking or reheating foods containing protein, be sure the internal temperature is above 140° F (60° C) before you serve them. If your casserole bubbles in the middle as well as around the edges, it is hot enough. Foods that you need to keep warm after they have been cooked should be held at 140° F (60° C) or higher. These foods should not be left at room temperature for more than an hour after they have been taken from the burner or the oven. It takes as little as four hours for bacteria to multiply enough to cause food-poisoning. Leaving foods at room temperature until they are cool invites trouble. Whenever possible, put cooked protein foods into the refrigerator.

If you have a large amount of protein-containing food that has been cooked and must be stored, you may want to divide it into smaller portions before refrigerating it. Large pots of meat stew or soup or meat sauce or a large, deep casserole can be divided into individual servings for other times. You should, when possible, remove stuffing from turkey or chicken before you refrigerate it. If it is not divided or separated, the middle may not cool off soon enough to prevent the development of harmful bacteria.

## Following Recipes

A **recipe** is a written plan for a food that tells you what ingredients you need and what you are supposed to do with them. Recipes may include fresh ingredients, convenience foods, or packaged mixes as ingredients. The directions you find on packaged mixes are a type of recipe.

If you are a beginner cook, recipes with few ingredients and few steps usually are easiest to follow. When there are many ingredients and a lot of different procedures, more expertise is needed and more time and energy are involved in meal preparation.

Following directions when preparing food will help to prevent problems. Directions on packaged foods usually are written step by step. Recipes that list the ingredients in order of their mixing are the easiest to follow. It is

Once you become familiar with basic cooking techniques, you can advance to more complicated recipes.

## Practical Tip: Shopping Aid

■ Design your grocery list to save time and money when you shop. Group similar items, such as dairy products and fruits and vegetables, together. Arrange these groups in the order that you will first find them in your store to avoid retracing your steps as you select your groceries.

# MIXING TECHNIQUES

Ingredients can be mixed in many different ways. Recipes use special terms to describe the different ways of mixing. Using the proper mixing technique can help insure success when following a recipe. The information below explains various techniques for mixing ingredients.

**Alternate**

To take turns adding dry and liquid ingredients, mixing after each addition with a spoon or electric mixer

**Beat**

To mix ingredients rapidly using a spoon, rotary beater, electric mixer, or food processor

**Blend**

To thoroughly combine two or more ingredients using a spoon, blender, or food processor

**Cream**

To soften and blend ingredients (usually solid shortening and sugar) until smooth and light using a spoon, electric mixer, or food processor

**Cut in**

To chop solid fat into small pieces and mix into dry ingredients using two knives or a pastry blender

**Fold in**

To combine a light, whipped mixture with a more compact mixture by cutting down through both mixtures and lifting some of the mixture from the bottom up and over the mixture at the top using a spoon or rubber scraper with a slow, gentle motion so as to prevent loss of air from the whipped mixture

**Stir**

To mix ingredients with a circular motion using a spoon; slower action than beating

**Whip**

To beat one or more ingredients rapidly with a wire whisk or hand or electric mixer

also easier if the ingredients are grouped to show how they are to be combined. If a recipe you want to use has not been written in this way, you can rewrite it for yourself.

When you choose a recipe, read it through to be sure you understand the directions, have the time required to make it, and have the ingredients it needs. If there are terms you do not understand, find out what they mean before you start. The following abbreviations and symbols are often used in recipes:

| | | | |
|---|---|---|---|
| few grains | f.g. | hour | hr |
| teaspoon | tsp or t | minute | min |
| tablespoon | tbsp, Tbs, or T | inch | in |
| | | gram | g |
| cup | c | kilogram | kg |
| pint | pt | milligram | mg |
| quart | qt | liter | L |
| gallon | gal | milliliter | mL |
| ounce | oz | deciliter | dL |
| pound | lb | centimeter | cm |
| dozen | doz | millimeter | mm |
| square | sq | | |

If, when you are first learning to cook, you become familiar with basic cooking instructions and what they mean, you will enjoy the task more. If you can, buy a good cookbook for beginners that explains procedures clearly and simply. The chart on page 277 has definitions and illustrations for some of the most frequently used mixing techniques.

## Timing Meals

Have you ever prepared a meal and had part of it ready to serve, or worse, cold before another part is done? Have you ever had something take a longer or shorter cooking time than you or the recipe had estimated so that dinner was late or ready too soon? If you understand the factors that can cause differences in timing, you can make adjustments based on the situation. These factors include:

- the amount of food being cooked
- variations in the temperature of food to be cooked
- variations in pan size and/or size of food pieces
- variations in appliances
- variations in temperature (higher or lower than recipe calls for)
- the difficulty of the recipe
- the ability of the cook
- interruptions

**Prepare in Advance.** If you prepare food for breakfast or lunch the night before, you can have a meal even when you are short on time. Putting dinner in the slow cooker before you leave for school or work makes it possible to have dinner ready when you get home at the end of the day.

Setting aside some time to prepare food and package it for the freezer in meal-size packages is another way to prepare food in advance and save time. Sometimes you can make a double or triple batch of whatever you are fixing, such as meatloaf or a casserole or breads, and freeze what you do not eat. Planning and preparing ahead are helpful techniques when you have a busy schedule.

**Putting Tasks in Order** One good method for insuring that each part of your meal will be done at the same time is to put the cooking tasks in the order you will do them.

Some tasks can be done *ahead of time,* such as fixing raw vegetables or making a dessert or casserole that can be refrigerated and cooked later.

Other tasks should be done *more than two hours before the meal.* Taking meat out of the freezer and putting it into the refrigerator to thaw or making a stew or sauce that must cook for at least two hours should be done well ahead of time.

## TIMING A MEAL

### MENU

Oven Fried Chicken

Baked Potatoes

Frozen Peas

Coleslaw

Ice Cream
with Strawberries

Milk

Iced Tea

**SERVING TIME:** 6:00 PM

### SEQUENCE OF WORK

| Time | Task | Time | Task |
|------|------|------|------|
| 3:55 | Set table | 4:54 | Put potatoes and chicken in oven |
| 4:15 | Take out serving dishes | 4:55 | Prepare coleslaw and chill |
| 4:20 | Wash potatoes | 5:15 | Clean kitchen and utensils |
| 4:25 | Make iced tea | | |
| 4:30 | Put strawberries in bowl to thaw | 5:45 | Prepare and cook peas |
| 4:35 | Wash and prepare chicken | 5:55 | Serve food |
| | | 6:00 | Dinner |

Some tasks should be done *one or two hours before the meal*. Foods that take between one and two hours to cook, thaw, or chill need advance-planning.

A final category includes *last-minute preparations*. These preparations include such things as heating rolls or hot appetizers.

Before you begin your meal preparations, list the tasks in each of these groups in the order in which they must be done. Tasks that take the longest should be listed first. Now, working backward from your serving time, 6:00 p.m., for example, write down the time you must begin each task. This written plan will help to make sure that your timing is on target. The timing chart, given above, shows how this plan can be used to coordinate all the parts of a meal.

## Managing Meals for One

There may be times when you are making meals for yourself. If you have a part-time job or play sports, you may not be able to eat meals when the rest of your family does. If this is the case, there are certain meal preparation tips that can help you to prepare quick, nutritious meals for one.

One hint is to use small cans of vegetables and fruits that you will finish at one meal. If you do open a large can, you may store half of the contents in a glass or plastic container in the refrigerator to be used in the next day or two. Frozen vegetables come in bags that allow you to cook only the amount that you will eat.

Microwave cooking has become more popular. This method of cooking is fast and efficient, especially if you are cooking for one. Many packaged foods have both conventional and microwave directions on them so you do not need many cooking skills to prepare a fast, healthy meal.

There are several specific meals you can make for yourself with or without a micro-wave oven. Scrambled eggs and omelettes with toast or bread are fast, inexpensive, nutritious meals. You can add onion, green pepper or any other vegetable you like, cooked meat,

## CONSERVING ENERGY IN COOKING

These are energy-saving tips to remember as you cook:

1. For electric burners, use the right size pan for the burner.

2. If possible, cover food cooked on top of the range or stove.

3. Turn down the heat on the surface unit after the food starts cooking.

4. Preheat the oven only when necessary and close to the cooking time.

5. Use glass, ceramic, enamel, or stainless steel pans in the oven and set the temperature 25° F (10° C to 15° C) lower.

6. Use the full capacity of the oven.

7. Avoid opening the oven door frequently to check on food.

8. When cooking for a small number of people, use small appliances if they are available.

9. Cook foods only until done.

10. Turn the oven off for a few minutes before the food is completely cooked.

11. Open the refrigerator and freezer only when necessary.

12. Follow manufacturer's instructions for loading the freezer and refrigerator.

13. Use hot water only when necessary.

and cheese to omelettes. This will give you a well-balanced, tasty meal. Another specific suggestion is to toast English muffins or bread and add tomato sauce, cheese, vegetables, and cooked meat as desired. Put this under a broiler for a few minutes, watching until the surface bubbles and the cheese melts. This "homemade pizza" meal is fast, nutritious, and satisfying. Both of these meals for one include foods from four of the basic food groups. Using butter or margarine on bread would also include food from the fats-sweets group.

There are many other possibilities for meals for one, depending on your personal taste in food and your resources. A file of recipes you have developed will be a valuable source of meal ideas for any future occasions when you are eating alone.

## For Review

1. Describe the personal habits of cleanliness and proper handling of food that will help to prevent food contamination.

2. Explain how temperature, light, air, and moisture can contribute to food spoilage.

3. Plan a simple meal for one. Include foods from each of the five main food groups.

## Management Application: Handling a Food Budget

Imagine yourself in the situation described below. As you read, think about how the steps of the management process might apply to this situation. Then answer the questions that follow.

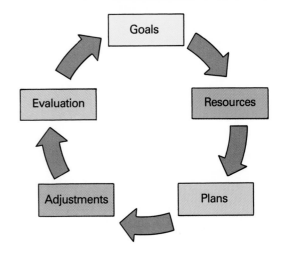

## Situation

Anna's mother had gone to stay with Grandpa while he was recuperating from his operation. She would be away for two weeks, and Anna was in charge of cooking supper while her mother was gone. She had the money for two weeks of food shopping for dinners according to her mother's usual budget.

The first two nights were easy. After a quick vote, she and her brothers decided to order pizza on Monday. Tuesday they went out for hamburgers and fries. However, as she checked the funds on Wednesday, Anna realized they couldn't afford to go out all week. There wouldn't be enough money for next week. Besides, two weeks of fast food would not be as nutritious as homecooked meals. She needed a menu plan. During study hall, she made a chart for each day's menu. She also divided the remaining food money by the days she had to cook to see approximately how much she could spend on each meal. She remembered that she needed quick meals for Thursdays because she had to get to work. Thursdays would be omelette nights. They were fast, inexpensive, and nutritious. She checked the newspaper that evening. Hamburger was on sale, and meatloaf was one thing she *could* make. She decided to make two and freeze one for next week. She bought enough extra hamburger to make patties. She froze them for next week also. Stew beef was also on sale. She convinced her brothers to help peel and cut up enough carrots and potatoes for two stew meals. Again, she froze one meal for next week. Anna calculated her remaining money. She realized she could afford a few nights using convenience foods. She bought frozen fish sticks and french fries and frozen pizza for two more meals. Only two more suppers to go. She had managed after all!

## Questions

1. What was Anna's goal?
2. What resources have to be used wisely?
3. How did she reevaluate her original plan?
4. How did menu planning help her to manage within her resources?
5. Were all of the steps of the management process applied?

# 12 *Chapter Review*

## Summary

Learning where to shop, what to buy, and how to shop efficiently and economically is an important life management skill. You can control the cost of food shopping by buying the right amount, comparing brands, checking unit prices, and using coupons. By reading labels, checking containers, and using date information, you can ensure quality. Food preparation involves many skills, such as cleanliness, safety, proper storage, and following recipes carefully. Learning to recognize how long it will take to prepare a meal and the tasks to be done in advance will further improve your management skills.

## Vocabulary

Complete each of the following sentences with one of the vocabulary words below.

food cooperative

shelf-life

menu plan

food additives

U.S. RDA

unit pricing

recipe

1. An outline of foods and beverages to be eaten at specific meals and snacks for a period of one or more days is a _____ .

2. _____ stands for the United States Recommended Dietary Allowance.

3. A group of individuals who have joined together to buy food in bulk from wholesalers or local growers or producers make up a _____ .

4. Substances that are added to foods to improve flavor or texture, enhance flavor, improve nutritional value, or prevent spoilage are _____ .

5. The length of time any food can be stored without spoiling is its _____ .

6. The price for a certain measure of a food, such as so much per pound, is known as the _____ .

7. A written plan for a food that tells you what ingredients you need and what you are supposed to do with them is known as a _____ .

## Questions

1. What are some of the factors that affect how often a person shops? How could these factors also influence where an individual shops?

2. What are the advantages and disadvantages of canned food?

3. How does shopping at different times of the day affect your buying pattern?

4. What steps should you take to prepare an adequate shopping list?

5. What steps can you take to control the cost of food shopping?

6. What steps can you take to check the quality of the foods you are buying?

7. What information do food labels contain? Why is it important to read this information when you shop?

8. Describe the proper methods for storing perishable food.

9. What is the meaning of each of the following abbreviations?

| | |
|---|---|
| pt | t or tsp |
| L | mg |
| qt | min |
| kg | c |
| doz | oz |
| T or Tbsp | mm |

10. What is the meaning of each of the following cooking terms?

| | |
|---|---|
| cream | fold in |
| blend | cut in |

## Skill Activities

**1. Science.** Working as a group, compare the different forms of a specific food available at a local grocery store—fresh, frozen, canned, and, if applicable, dried or smoked. You might, for example, choose tomatoes. Analyze each form of tomato for taste, price, food additives, and nutrition. Then share your findings with other members of the group. List the pros and cons of each form of the food, and compare the various forms. Then make a bulletin board that illustrates the group's findings.

**2. Resource Management.** Time the cooking of a meal for your family. Provide a family menu plan for one day of a weekend. Talk to all family members about their schedules. Ask those who will be at home for meals what they would like to eat, giving a few simple meals as choices. Help shop for the meal you have chosen, and keep track of your expenses. The meal should have food from each food group. Plan to have at least one fresh food and one frozen food.

Then prepare a brief timing chart like the one on page 279. When you actually prepare the meal, jot down the times for each step. Was everything ready at the right times? Could you improve your timing skills?

**3. Social Studies.** Go to your local grocery store, supermarket, or farm stand and ask what happens to extra, unsold food, such as bread and fresh produce. Interview store owners and managers to find out if foods that have a short shelf-life are given to local shelters or other organizations. Report your findings to the class. Are there other possible uses for these foods?

CHAPTER

# *13*

# *Making Clothing Decisions*

## *As you read, think about:*

☐ how to choose and wear clothes that create a good impression.

☐ how good grooming, correct posture, and appropriate clothing affect the way others view you.

☐ how to evaluate your present wardrobe and decide what you need.

☐ how to improve your wardrobe within the limits of your resources.

☐ how to choose colors and styles of clothing that best suit your features and your body type.

☐ how to apply the management process to personal decisions about clothing.

body language
fads
color value
color intensity
monochromatic
complementary
analogous
proportion

The clothes you wear and how you wear them affect your appearance. Whether this effect is positive or negative depends on many things, including the condition and cleanliness of your clothes and their suitability for the event you are attending.

Since clothing plays such a large part in the impression you make, certain skills are important to learn. Deciding what looks best on you, analyzing your clothing needs and wants, and learning to work within the limits of your resources will help you now and in the future.

## Communicating an Image

Everyone wants to make a good impression. Whether you are interviewing for a job, attending a formal dance, or going to a football game with friends, you want to look your best.

The clothing you wear and the way you present yourself have a lot to do with how others view you. The total impression you make depends upon a combination of factors that include your clothing, your personal grooming, your posture, and whether or not your clothing is appropriate for the occasion.

## Your Clothing

You may have heard the expression, "Clothes make the man." While this is an exaggeration, your clothing can influence others. Correctly or incorrectly, we all draw silent conclusions about people because of the way they dress. Imagine a man or woman impeccably dressed in a conservative, well-tailored suit. If you were meeting this person for the first time, you might use the adjectives "efficient" and "organized." These adjectives may or may

Good grooming begins with cleanliness.

The most beautiful dress in the world will not make a good impression if your hair is dirty or you haven't brushed your teeth. Before you think about what to wear, think about your own cleanliness. Bathing or showering regularly washes away the perspiration that causes body odor. Your hair should be washed as often as necessary to keep it clean. Your hands should be clean, and your fingernails should be trimmed. To avoid cavities and bad breath, brush your teeth after eating and see a dentist every six months.

There are hundreds of personal care products you may want to try. The soaps, creams, deodorants, shampoos, and toothpastes that work best for you are the ones you want to buy. They are not necessarily the most expensive ones. You may find it helpful to read ingredient labels and compare. Many generic brands contain the same ingredients and are just as effective as more expensive brands.

Besides basic personal care products, you may want to buy cosmetics. If you use cosmetics, keep them well sealed between uses to avoid the growth of harmful bacteria. Old cosmetics that you haven't used for a while should be thrown out. Eye cosmetics, such as mascara or eye liner, should be replaced regularly. Of course, you will not want to use products that contain unnecessary perfumes or dyes.

not be true, but the outfit being worn has influenced your impression, even before you have gotten to know the individual.

Your clothing reflects your taste, personality, interests, and even your mood. The style and the color of the clothing you choose add to the impression you make on others.

## Your Grooming

Grooming includes the way you take care of yourself and your clothing. If you want to make a good impression, there are certain rules of personal care and clothing care that you should follow.

**Personal Grooming** Good personal grooming means keeping yourself neat and clean.

**Grooming Your Clothing** After making sure that you are clean and neat, you must do the same for your clothes. This includes washing, drying, dry cleaning, and repairing your clothing when necessary. Chapter 14 provides more details about these procedures. For now, it is important to realize that the impression you want to make can be influenced by the way you groom, or do not groom, your clothing. Clothing that is dirty, wrinkled, and/or torn will not make a positive statement about you. You may find it helpful to schedule the time you need to keep your clothes clean, neat, and repaired.

These important procedures will help you to make a good impression when you are meeting people for the first time. They also will help to make the clothes you have last longer.

## Your Body Language

The way you carry yourself as you stand, walk, or sit also can influence others. The movements, gestures, and postures you use are commonly referred to as your **body language.**

You say something without words when you walk with your shoulders back and stand erect. You say that you are confident and self-assured. If you walk with stooped shoulders in a shuffling way you say that you are feeling defeated or you lack in self-confidence. These conclusions may or may not be true. The important thing is to realize that your body language adds to the impression you make with your clothing and grooming. Be aware of what your body language is saying to others. You may want to have a close friend describe the way you walk. Often we are not aware of our own poor posture, and another person can help us to improve it by pointing out habits we should try to change.

## Dressing for the Occasion

Appropriate clothing choices are important. You probably do not wear the same outfit for work as you do for a special occasion. Dressing for work, school, leisure, and special events will and should be different.

We all have favorite clothes. They are clothes that we wear frequently because they are comfortable and fit well. You may own a favorite pair of jeans and a favorite shirt, but even if you and your favorite clothes were perfectly groomed, you would not wear them when applying for an office job or going to a wedding. You would not because you know you would not make a good impression.

Although dress codes are not as common as they were in the past, they do exist. If your school or workplace has a written dress code, you need to choose your clothing accordingly. More often, there is an informal, unwritten dress code. By observing the accepted standards of clothing around you, you can decide on your own. This does not mean that you have to look exactly like anyone else. Your personal taste and style will show in your dress.

There are occasions when appropriate clothing calls for dressing up. The chart on page 288 defines some general categories of dress that you may find on an invitation. If you are not sure what type of clothing is called for, ask your host or hostess or other people who

Some occasions, such as school proms and dances, may call for formal or semi-formal clothing and corsages for the girls.

## DRESSING FOR AN OCCASION

You may be told what type of dress to wear for an occasion. These general categories are defined below.

| | |
|---|---|
| **CASUAL DRESS** | Men and women wear pants or shorts, shirt or leisure top |
| **INFORMAL DRESS** | Men: Tie and suit not required. Pants, sports coat or jacket, shirt and/or sweater<br>Women: A dress or skirt and blouse; pants with sweater and/or shirt, jacket if desired |
| **DRESS CLOTHES** | Men: Business suit, shirt, tie.<br>Women: Suit and blouse or a dress. |
| **FORMAL DRESS** | Men: Tuxedo<br>Women: Gown or long dress |

will be attending the event before you choose your clothing. This will avoid embarrassing situations.

## For Review

1. Why is grooming such an important factor in making a good impression? Explain grooming procedures for both you and your clothing.

2. How does your body language influence how other people think about you?

3. Explain what dressing for the occasion means and give an example.

## Evaluating Your Wardrobe

Closets often hold surprises. On looking over your wardrobe, you may find that you have enough clothes for your present needs. You may discover that you do not have the type of clothing you need for a special occasion. You may find out that you have not been wearing some clothing you like simply because you have not ironed it. You may also discover that you have more clothes than you thought you had. Taking an inventory of what you have is the first step toward a wardrobe plan.

## Taking an Inventory

To take an inventory of your clothing, you will need to go through all your clothes, group them in categories, list all of them, and write down certain information about each item. This information will become the basis of your plan.

Taking inventory takes time, so plan for a large enough block of time to start and finish the job. If you rush, you may miss some clothes or end up going through things more than once. Getting someone to help you can make the job go faster.

If you have enough space, you may find it helpful to remove all your clothes from the drawers, closets, shelves, and other places you have stored them. As you do this, group them into three groups or piles. One pile will be for all of the clothes you like to wear that do not need repair. Another pile can be for clothes that you are uncertain about or need repair. Clothes that you definitely don't like and don't intend to wear again should go into the third pile. This group will include any clothing you have outgrown or really dislike.

If you do not have the space to take everything out of storage, you can go through each drawer, your closet, and other places you have

clothes, listing the clothes for each of the three groups as you go.

As you make your list, don't forget to include the clothes you have on, those in the laundry, ironing, or mending basket, and any in another closet. You also will want to list the items you have let a friend borrow or the out-of-season clothes you may have stored.

**Decide What to Keep**  All of the clothes you put in your first group are clothes that fit, don't need repair, and you like. These should be counted and briefly described on your list, then put away again.

Now you are left with the other two groups to consider. The clothes in the third group are those you definitely don't want to keep. After you have made sure they are clean,

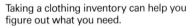

Taking a clothing inventory can help you figure out what you need.

you may want to put them in boxes or bags and use them as resources to swap, sell, or donate to charity. Any of these alternatives makes use of the clothes. Leaving them in your closet is a waste of resources because no one is using them.

The clothes in group two should be evaluated by asking yourself some basic questions about each item.

- Does it fit?
- Does it go with other clothes I have?
- Do I like it? If not, can I make changes in the garment so I do like it?
- What care does it require? Am I willing to give it the care it needs?
- Does it need repair? What kind? How can I get it done?
- If I keep it, will I wear it?

A hat is an example of an inexpensive fad item that is fun to wear.

Answering these questions will help you to decide which clothes to keep and which ones to add to group three. Before making a final decision, you may find it helpful to try on any of the clothes you haven't worn for a while. Perhaps some of them will go with the clothing you have decided to keep. If any of them need repairs, make plans to have them done. Many simple repairs can be done by you. The next chapter tells more about specific repairs. If you need to have someone else repair the clothing, get an estimate of the cost before deciding if it is worth fixing.

***Try New Combinations.*** Now that you can see exactly what you have and are keeping, you may want to try mixing and matching to create new outfits. Sometimes you can create a new look if you are willing to try different combinations of texture and color. You may have always worn your green sweater with your green pants. If you look carefully, you may notice other attractive combinations. That green sweater may match the green in your plaid skirt or go well with your navy blue pants, especially when you add a scarf to the outfit. Your shirt can be worn under a sweater or over a turtleneck jersey to look more like a jacket. Sometimes you can create a look by adding a belt or a tie, for example.

By experimenting with your clothes, you may be able to increase the variety in your wardrobe and extend the seasons you can use them. Once you have done some experimenting, you may discover that some of your clothes can be worn for more than one type of activity. By giving a new look to what you have, you may be able to decrease your need for more clothes.

## Deciding on a Basic Wardrobe

Your basic wardrobe should be useful, versatile, and made up of clothes you need for everyday activities. The basic wardrobe you need depends on your lifestyle. If you do not go to many formal events, your basic wardrobe does not have to include a tuxedo or a gown, for example. As you think about adding to your wardrobe, you may want to think in terms of quality and style. Simple, classic styles do not go out of fashion quickly. If you are interested in keeping your clothes for a long time, you may want to consider buying a blazer or jacket of this type rather than one with beads or a novelty design that will soon go out of style. This does not mean that all your clothes have to be practical. **Fads** are fashions that are popular for only a short time. Fad clothing is fun to have, and your basic wardrobe may contain some of these items. For the sake of your budget, you may want to balance less costly fad items with longer-lasting fashions. There are many ways to expand your wardrobe.

Thinking in terms of *outfits* helps when you are adding to your wardrobe. If you are buying a new sweater and skirt, try to coordinate them to make an outfit. Also, try to think of other items you already have that will go well with each other to create other outfits. This method will help you to build your basic wardrobe more quickly.

## Adding to Your Wardrobe

Now that you have inventoried, decided on the clothes you are keeping, and tried new combinations, you can begin to think about adding to your wardrobe. Some clothes may have to be replaced. If your favorite blue sweater that matched many of your clothes is too worn, you may want to get another. Sneakers or sport shoes that you have outgrown will need to be replaced. Other clothing additions will depend on your activities, the climate where you live, the standards of dress you follow, your personal preferences, and the resources you have.

Magazines can offer good fashion hints.

*Your Activities* The activities you participate in have an important effect on your clothing needs. If you participate in sports, such as swimming, running, or soccer, you may need special clothing. Special occasions, such as a school dance, a prom, a day of skiing, or a recital, may demand clothes other than the ones you usually wear to school. A member of an orchestra may need a dark suit or a long black skirt. If you have a job, you may need a uniform or protective clothing. Farmers and construction workers often need heavy, durable clothing.

You may find it helpful to start a list of the activities you participate in frequently and the clothes you need. Add activities that are less frequent but are coming up in the next few months. If you keep your list handy, you can add to it or revise it as you plan your wardrobe. Thinking ahead is a part of planning and can help you to be prepared for activities that are important to you.

# Retail Buyer

When you shop, you try to balance style, quality, and cost to get the most fashionable and useful wardrobe for your money. Mary Quinan, assistant sportswear buyer for a major department store, is responsible for purchasing clothes from garment manufacturers for her store. She is called a **retail fashion buyer.** This career requires fashion savvy and a keen business sense. Employers usually look for a bachelor's degree and previous retail experience. Most large stores also have their own training programs.

While being a fashion buyer sounds glamorous, it is hard work. Longer than average hours, travel, and pressure are typical in this competitive field. Since retail buying is done at least six months before merchandise appears in the stores, buyers have to predict future fashion and consumer trends. "It's important to stay on top of, even ahead of, trends," says Ms. Quinan. Word of mouth from others in the fashion industry, trade magazines, and European shows all help. So does keeping an eye on what's selling. "It's just as important to know when to get *out* of a trend," Ms. Quinan points out.

Buying decisions must suit the taste and pocketbook of the store's clientele. Successful buyers, however, often "educate" their customers in the newest styles by supervising how merchandise is presented and how it is advertised. Ms. Quinan adds that managing a budget is important. "You have to analyze your stock and sales as well as project future sales. That's how you determine how much you can spend. You also negotiate with the vendor (manufacturer) for the wholesale price and then set the retail price, allowing for profit, of course." Their study of sales records also reveals the buying patterns of their patrons.

Buyers travel to major cities around the world for fashion showings and buying trips. They weigh quality, style, price, their customers' tastes, and their employers' budgets to make the best purchases. Their decisions set the style for their stores.

***Climate*** The climate where you live will influence the types of clothes you need. Your clothes for school and other activities need to be appropriate for your climate. If it is warm to hot all year around, your clothing needs will be different than they would be if you lived in an area where the seasons changed dramatically from fall to winter to summer.

***Standard of Dress*** The standard of dress refers to the clothes that are appropriate for different occasions. While current fashions and national trends affect standards of dress, these standards also are based on community attitudes, customs, and cultural influences. In some places, for example, casual clothing is acceptable for such events as church, going out to eat, or attending sports events. In other communities, however, people may wear dressier clothes for similar occasions.

In addition to overall community and school standards, smaller groups in the community or school have their own standards of dress. Sometimes families or groups of families will have their own standards. Sometimes organizations have special standards of dress. You and your friends may have ideas about styles of clothes you will or will not wear or about what is appropriate or not appropriate for certain activities.

***Personal Preferences*** What your friends wear may have a lot to do with your personal preferences in clothes. Your own values and standards also influence your personal preferences in clothes. Both these influences will affect what you feel you need for clothes and what you want for clothes. It takes a lot of thought to sort out the influences that are important to you and then to decide what your needs and wants are. Spending the time to make these decisions will help you make a plan for a wardrobe that will meet your needs and make the most of your resources.

## Clothing Resources

Once you have developed your plan for adding to your wardrobe, it is time to figure out how you are going to get the clothes that you need and want. This requires analyzing your resources and deciding how you will use them to reach your goal.

There are many alternatives for getting clothes. Each requires different resources or different amounts of resources. Buying new clothes, for example, costs money. Buying used clothes costs money too, but usually not as much as new clothes. Repairing and altering clothes may not cost any money but they do require sewing skills, time to make the repairs

Although individual taste in clothing is still expressed, graduations call for a certain standard of dress.

or alterations, and probably a sewing machine. Learning new ways to mix and match the clothes you have takes time but does not cost money or require equipment. Knowing the alternatives you have and making the best use of the resources you have will help you to control clothing costs.

**Buying New Clothes** Depending on where you live, there may be many places where you can buy new clothes, or there may be few places to buy clothes. You may buy clothes through a mail order catalog, or you may try them on in a store. In either case, buying new clothes costs money. The amount depends on where you buy, the brand you buy, and the quality you buy. For example, prices at some stores are higher than at others. Certain brands cost more simply because of the brand name. Good quality and fit may cost more. Often, you pay more for the latest fashions. With all these variables, you can spend a lot for clothes or you can spend less. To a degree, you can control costs. Chapter 14 deals with shopping techniques in more detail.

For most people, money is a limited resource. When there is no money to spend on clothes or when money is extremely limited, buying one or more new garments may not be possible. Another alternative may be the answer.

**Buying Used Clothes** Buying used clothing is another possibility for getting clothes. You may have to look harder and make more inquiries to find places where you can buy used clothing, but if you know where to look, often you can find good, stylish clothes. The cost of used clothing is usually less than for new clothing.

You may find it possible to buy clothes from friends or relatives who have clothes they no longer wear. Thrift shops and consignment stores are other places to check. Sometimes you may see advertisements in the newspaper for used clothing, or you may find clothing at yard sales or garage sales. When you know what to look for in terms of quality and fit, you can get a lot of value for your money.

**Renting** You may want to consider renting expensive clothes that you are going to wear only once or twice, such as a tuxedo or gown, a costume, ski boots, or a wet suit. If you want to rent some types of clothing, check the telephone directory for rental clothing or check with some of the clothing stores in your area.

Although you were measured, try on your rented tux when you return to pick it up.

**Sewing** Sewing skills make it possible for you to repair and alter the clothes that you already have and any used clothing that you may buy. Maybe you have developed some sewing skills or have the time, interest, and equipment to learn to sew or to increase your skills. If you enjoy sewing, you may want to make some of the clothes you need or want.

Skirts, dresses, and pants can be lengthened or shortened, as you want and the material permits. A long-sleeved shirt or blouse can be made short-sleeved by cutting off the sleeves and finishing the edges. Collars or cuffs can be changed, removed, or added. New buttons can change a garment's appearance. Adding decorative stitching or trim to a garment can give it new life or at least extend its life until you are able to purchase something else.

Making your clothes is another alternative to buying. Sometimes it costs less to make clothes than to buy them new, but this is not always true. You need to compare the costs for making a garment against what it would cost to buy it.

To alter, repair, or make clothes, you need more than sewing skills. You need a sewing machine, either your own or one that you can use. You also need to have the desire to sew and an interest in using this skill. Most of all, you need to have the time to use your skill. If any of these resources is not available, then sewing is not an alternative.

**Barter** Barter involves trading one thing for another thing of equal value. It does not involve the transfer of money. You may find you can trade one or more of the garments you no longer wear for one or more of the garments a friend or someone in your family no longer wears. You each end up with the clothes you need or want, and you have not spent any money to obtain them.

You may be able to trade a service for a garment or for someone's skill in making

If you have a sewing machine and the time and desire to sew, you can make many of your own clothes.

clothes. For example, you might agree to type a friend's paper or do some chores for a friend in exchange for a garment no longer worn. You might agree to do some work at home or for a relative in exchange for a family member buying or making you something you need. Again, no money is needed, just the resources of time, energy, and the knowledge of how to do what you have agreed to do in exchange for the clothes.

**Sharing and Borrowing** Sometimes sisters or brothers or best friends share or borrow certain clothes, such as sweaters, blouses, or shirts. Coats, suits, and special occasion dresses are other possibilities for sharing or borrowing. Sports and outdoor activity clothes also can be borrowed or shared. Perhaps you have a friend you can borrow clothes from. In return, you can lend clothes to your friend. This makes it possible for each of you to have more clothes to wear without spending more money, although all your clothes will not be in one place for you to choose from.

Lending, borrowing, or sharing must be done carefully. You want to be sure that the person you lend to or share with will take good care of the garment. If the garment is damaged through careless use or improper care, it is

Sharing clothes can save money resources.

no longer a resource for either person. When you borrow something, taking good care of it helps to keep it wearable and makes it a valuable resource for both you and your friend or relative.

***Plan Timing of Purchases*** Probably you do not need all of the clothing items you want to add to your wardrobe immediately. Dividing your clothing needs into a time schedule will help you to see how your plan is going to take form. Clothes that you need tomorrow or for a special event in two days obviously need more attention than clothes for an event next month or next fall. If summer is drawing near and you need a bathing suit, you can wait for a winter jacket. Priorities are important. As you become a more experienced shopper, you may find it helpful to buy many clothes out of season when they are cheaper.

***Maintain Flexibility*** As you make your wardrobe plan, keep in mind that, like most plans, it needs to be flexible. You may have a change in resources that makes it impossible to get some of the clothes you planned. You may get a job that requires you to wear certain types of clothes. At this point, other things you have planned may become less important or not needed at all.

As you carry out your wardrobe plan, you will need to make changes and adjustments. Each time you add something to your wardrobe, you create a change in your resources. Each time you outgrow a garment or wear it out, you create a change in your resources. These changes require adjustments in your plan. A wardrobe plan, then, is something that constantly evolves. Once made, it does not stay the same. It must change to meet your changing wants, needs, and resources.

## For Review

1. Why is taking an inventory of your wardrobe important? What are the three categories that your clothing can be grouped into to help you?

2. Explain briefly how your activities, the climate in your area, the standard of dress, and your personal preferences affect your wardrobe choices.

3. What are three ways to add to your wardrobe other than buying new clothing?

## Analyzing Your Clothing Style

Before you add to your wardrobe, you may want to analyze how each item in your wardrobe looks on you. Your height, weight, and hair and skin coloring can affect the way you look in specific clothing. You may want to choose clothing that compliments your best features and disguises others. Line, color, proportion, texture, and print can work together to help you achieve the look that is best for you.

## *Line and Clothing*

The line of a garment refers to the angles that are created when it is sewn or put together, as well as to any lines or stripes of color on the clothing itself.

Different lines create different visual effects. Horizontal lines (lines going across) give an impression of increased width. Vertical lines (lines going up and down) give an impression of increased length. If you apply this information to your clothing, you will realize that clothing with horizontal lines or stripes of color may make a person look wider and heavier. Because horizontal lines or stripes take the eye back and forth rather than up and down, they tend to make a person look shorter than he or she is. In contrast, vertical lines or stripes take the eye up and down and tend to make a person look taller and thinner than he or she is.

Depending on your height, weight, and what you want to emphasize, you will choose clothing with either horizontal or vertical lines. The clothing you select should use a line that is becoming to you.

## *Color and Clothing*

Your skin tone, eye color, and hair color help to determine what colors look best on you. The total effect of your specific eye, hair,

The color wheel shows the primary colors (red, blue, and yellow), the secondary colors (green, orange, and violet), and the six intermediate colors. What are the intermediate colors?

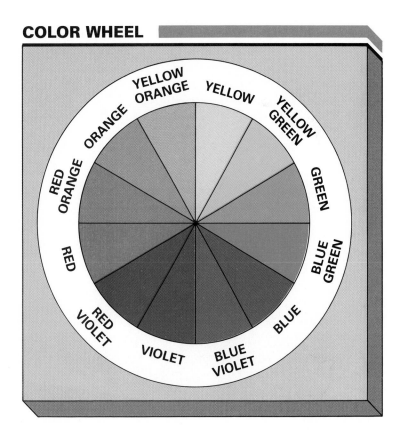

**COLOR WHEEL**

and skin coloring can be labeled as warm or cool. A person who has *cool* coloring usually has a blue undertone in his or her skin. A person with warm coloring usually has skin with a more yellow undertone. While there are exceptions, if you have cool coloring you usually look better in "cooler" colors, blues, violets, and greens. If you have warm coloring, the "warmer" colors of orange, yellow, and red probably will look better on you. Most people, however, can wear at least one shade or tint of almost every color.

***Color Analysis.*** To find out what colors are most becoming to you, you can consult a professional color analyst or you can do your own color analysis. To do your own analysis, use pieces of fabric or clothing that you already have and look into a mirror as you hold each item up to your face. You may want to have a friend help you. Try to make sure that you have items of different color value. **Color value** refers to the color's lightness or darkness. If possible, use items of different color intensity. **Color intensity** refers to the dullness or brightness of a color. You should do your analysis in the daytime, using natural lighting.

As you look into the mirror you will discover that certain colors compliment your own coloring better than others. Using this knowledge, you can choose clothing in colors that best suit you. Suppose, for example, you have decided to buy a basic jacket or blazer, which you want to last over several seasons. If your color analysis has shown you that you look better in cool colors, you probably will choose a

Choose new clothing for color as well as fit. Which color looks best on you?

navy blue blazer rather than a brown one. If your color analysis has shown that warmer colors compliment you, you probably will choose a brown jacket or blazer. These choices make sense because each will go well with the other cool or warm colors in your wardrobe.

*Color Schemes* There are three common kinds of color schemes that can be applied to your clothing choices to create combinations that are complimentary to you.

A color scheme that is **monochromatic** uses variations of the same color. A dark brown shirt worn with pale brown pants would be an example of this.

A **complementary** color scheme combines colors that are directly opposite. Refer to the color wheel on page 297. An orange sweater worn with a blue skirt would be an example of a complementary color scheme.

A color scheme that is **analogous** combines different colors that are closely related. A blue sweater worn with green slacks would be an example of this.

Finally, you may want to remember that dark-colored clothing has a more slimming effect than lighter-colored clothing.

## *Proportion and Clothing*

**Proportion** is the balance of one part in relationship to another. When you are trying to achieve a pleasing proportion in your clothing, you first have to look at your own body proportions. We all come in different sizes and shapes. Some of you may have long legs in proportion to the rest of your body. If you wear a long jacket that comes down as far as your hips, it will make your upper body look longer, make your legs appear shorter, and give better overall proportion to your look.

Use proportion changes in clothing to get the best results for you and your figure. If you want to look shorter or taller, for example, use proportion in your clothing to help you do this. Combining proportion with what you have learned about line can help you create the effect you want.

Tailors are trained to help you choose the size and styles that are in best proportion to your body type.

Experiment by combining various prints and textures to find new ways to use your present wardrobe.

## Print and Clothing

The size of the plaids, dots, stripes, or other patterns that cover the material of your clothing creates specific effects. Usually a tall person looks better in clothing with a large print. A short person tends to look overwhelmed in a large print and should wear smaller prints.

Prints add versatility to your wardrobe. They often contain several colors and allow you to mix and match with more than one solid color item of clothing. This makes your wardrobe more flexible.

Be aware of the effect that various prints have on you specifically and choose those that look best on you.

## Texture and Clothing

The texture of clothing is determined by the weave of the fabric used and the way it feels.

Tightly woven, fine fabrics, such as silks and polyesters, feel smooth and are actually thinner than the more loosely woven, bulky fabrics like wool. Be aware that bulkier fabrics tend to make you look heavier and smoother fabrics tend to make you look slimmer. Textures are often selected to suit the occasion. Tweeds, denims, corduroys, and wools are usually worn to more casual events. Silks, satins, chiffons, and other more delicate fabrics are usually worn to dressier, more formal events.

## For Review

1. Explain how the element of line can affect the way you look in clothing.

2. How can you determine the colors of clothing that will look best on you?

3. How do the elements of proportion, print, and texture affect the way clothes look on you?

## Management Application: Making Wardrobe Adjustments

Imagine yourself in the situation described below. As you read, think about how the steps of the management process might apply to this situation. Then answer the questions that follow.

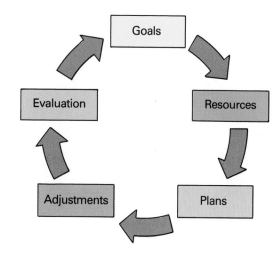

### Situation

Rachel had to smile as she surveyed her reflection in her full-length mirror. She had been in shorts and bathing suits all summer and hadn't worn these jeans since last May. She wouldn't be wearing them again the way it looked. There was now a full two-inch gap between the hem of her jeans and her ankles. Well, she'd always wanted to be taller . . . but, her clothes! She hadn't planned on buying many new clothes since she'd bought a lot of new things last spring. There were even a few pairs of slacks she hadn't worn yet! Now what? She had very little money and only a few weeks before school started. If only she could sew as well as her cousin Grace. Grace! Grace had real sewing talent. She had also taken sewing lessons and had her own sewing machine.

Rachel called Grace and described the disaster. Grace came over, and they took an inventory of the clothing that could be altered. Rachel offered to pay Grace for fixing her skirt and dress hems. However, they realized that Grace could wear many of the clothes that Rachel had outgrown. Grace said she would do the sewing in exchange for the clothes she

liked. She also told Rachel about a used clothing store that would try to sell Rachel's clothing on consignment and give her part of the profit if they did. Rachel gathered up all of her extra clothing after Grace left. Many items, including old prom gowns, were in excellent condition, and she knew she wouldn't wear them again. If they sold, she could buy plenty of pants and new jeans. She might even make a little extra money instead of letting all these clothes go to waste.

### Questions

1. What was Rachel's goal?
2. Which nonhuman resources was Rachel lacking for her goal?
3. Which human resources (talent) did she need? How did she get help?
4. When the time comes, how will Rachel evaluate the results of her plan?
5. Which steps of the management process apply to this situation?

# 13 *Chapter Review*

## Summary

The impression you make depends on your clothing, your grooming, your body language, and the appropriateness of your clothing for the occasion. Taking an inventory of your clothes to decide what to keep is the first step in making a wardrobe plan. Knowing about alternatives to buying new clothes and making the best use of your resources, helps to control clothing costs. Understanding the elements of proportion, texture, color, line, and print can help you to select the clothes that look best on you.

## Vocabulary

Match each of the vocabulary words below with one of the definitions below.

body language      monochromatic

fads      complementary

color value      analogous

color intensity      proportion

1. A color's lightness or darkness is known as its _____ .
2. A color scheme that combines colors that are directly opposite is _____ .
3. The movements, gestures, and postures a person uses are known as _____ .
4. A color scheme that combines different colors that are closely related is _____ .
5. A color scheme that uses variations of the same color is _____ .
6. Fashions that are popular for only a short time are _____ .
7. The dullness or brightness of a color is called its _____ .
8. The balance of one part of clothing in relation to another is _____ .

## Questions

1. What positive and negative messages can you send about yourself with the body language you use?
2. If you were asked to dress informally, what would be proper attire for a woman? For a man? What would not be considered proper attire?
3. Why is it important to vary your attire according to the situation?
4. What steps are involved when you take an inventory of your clothing?
5. Why is it a good idea to buy classic styles as well as fad clothing?
6. How does buying an *outfit* help you to build your wardrobe?
7. What is *bartering?* What are some other alternatives to buying new clothes?
8. How can a knowledge of line in clothing be useful for a person who is short and wants to look taller?

9. How can you use your knowledge of color to help you select the clothing that is most becoming to you?

10. How can you use your knowledge of color schemes to help control the cost of the clothing you buy?

## Skill Activities

 1. **Critical Thinking.** Analyze your clothes in terms of these general categories: casual dress, informal dress, dress clothes, formal dress. Do most of your clothes fit into one group? Are these the clothes you wear most of the time?

Do you get regular use out of all your clothes? Why or why not? Have you made good purchasing decisions in terms of the use you get of all your clothes?

 2. **Resource Management.** What did you discover when you started your inventory of your wardrobe? Any surprises? Write down your impressions, discoveries, surprises, and disappointments. Then write down your plans for your wardrobe, including items you need in order of their importance to you.

Choose one of the clothing items you need most. Find out if you can acquire this item at a used clothing store or by bartering with a relative or friend rather than buying new clothing. Can you make the garment yourself? Write down the resources you would need for each of these alternatives.

 3. **Critical Thinking.** Look through a fashion magazine and select an outfit that you think would suit your body type and would be attractive on you. Cut out the picture and write a short description of the outfit. Explain what gives the outfit its appeal and how it would complement you. Refer to the design elements on pages 296-300 of this chapter. Then, ask a good friend to look at your fashion selection and to offer his or her opinion about whether or not the outfit will suit your figure and skin, hair, and eye color. Have your friend select or describe an outfit he or she would like to have. Offer your honest opinion of that outfit. Support your opinion with facts about design found in this chapter.

 4. **Human Relations.** Do an investigation to determine if clothing manufacturers have special clothing items for the elderly, the handicapped, and small children. Special features for these items would include buttons, zippers, and velcro closings that are easy to manage and appear on the front of the garment. Are there garments in the stores that you could wear if you had a physical handicap, or would you have to alter your clothing? Draw your own design for a garment that would meet the special needs of either the elderly, the handicapped, or small children.

# 14

# Managing Clothing Resources

## As you read, think about:

- [ ] how to comparison shop to get the best clothing buys.
- [ ] how to check clothing for quality and fit.
- [ ] how to care for your clothing.
- [ ] how to do simple clothing repairs.
- [ ] how to store your clothing.
- [ ] how to apply the management process to make personal decisions about clothing resources.

# Vocabulary

pretreating
agitation
storage

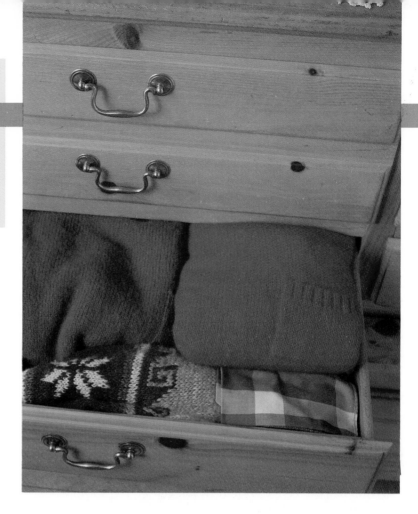

Buying new clothes can be fun; but once you own new clothes, it is important to learn how to care for them so that they will last and continue to look their best. Doing simple clothing repairs and learning about clothing storage are a part of the total clothing care process. The way you manage buying and taking care of your clothes will depend on your values, wants, and needs, as well as your resources.

## Shopping for Clothing

Since you will be shopping for clothing all your life, there are certain shopping skills you may want to develop.

In Chapter 13, you took a clothing inventory, so you know what items you need. Choose one of these items to shop for as the first step in your shopping plan. When you go

shopping, try to apply the skills you have learned in this chapter.

## Develop Shopping Skills

Shopping involves a variety of skills. Each one is important because it allows you to get the most from the money you have to spend. Knowing what you can spend, learning about the stores, and doing comparison shopping are some of the things that will make you a better shopper. As you are shopping for clothes, you will want to judge their quality and fit carefully to get the best buy you can for your resources.

### Know How Much Money You Have to Spend.
Before you go shopping, you probably will want to determine how much money you can spend on each item or the total amount that you can spend on what you need. The money you have

to spend may include money you have saved from your allowance or from your paycheck or have received as a gift. If you have a budget, you already know what you can afford to spend. Knowing the amount you have to spend helps you to make a realistic plan. Setting a limit and sticking to it will help you to control the amount you spend and allow you to have money for other things you need and want.

**Know the Stores.** There are many types of stores that carry clothing. Department stores, specialty stores, variety stores, and discount houses are only a few examples. Supermarkets, drug stores, and general stores may also carry certain clothing items.

Department stores usually have a wide variety of clothing in many sizes and styles for people of all ages. Each section or department will stock a selection of clothing in specific size ranges and different price ranges.

Some department stores have special departments for people with different needs.

Specialty shops usually offer a large selection of specific types of clothing.

You may find sections for preteens, teens, young adults, juniors, or for tall people.

Specialty stores stock clothes for specific purposes or specific groups of people. Menswear stores, sport shops, shoe stores, children's clothing stores, and dress shops are specialty stores. A store that sells only jeans or casual wear is another example of a specialty store you may use.

Variety stores, drug stores, and supermarkets often carry some items of clothing along with other types of merchandise. The selections may be limited to gloves, hats, and socks, for example, or may be much wider. Larger variety stores may have a selection that includes shirts, underclothes, sneakers, boots, jerseys, socks, and jackets.

Discount stores offer all kinds and qualities of clothing at less than original prices. The clothing may be first quality, or it may be damaged or imperfect. Garments with holes, stains, or imperfections in the fabric or construction are examples of damaged or imperfect merchandise. Sometimes, these imperfections will not affect the quality and appearance of the garment.

Ordering clothes from a mail-order house is one way to get things that are not available locally. Using a written description and perhaps a picture, you make your selection, then telephone or mail in your order. The merchandise is sent to you.

**Know What Makes Up the Price of Clothes.** Of course, the materials used and the cost of the labor to make the clothes affect the prices of them. Good quality materials, good design, and careful construction usually cost more. Original designs and certain brand names and designer labels also add to the cost and may or may not add to the quality.

When you buy clothes, you are paying for more than just materials and labor and perhaps a famous name. Overhead expenses,

Stores in high-rent locations often carry expensive merchandise.

or the costs of running a store, are added to the price of whatever the store sells. One major overhead expense is the cost of the building, either its rent or mortgage and taxes. Maintenance costs also are a part of the overhead and include the costs of heating, cooling, lighting, cleaning, and making any repairs or remodeling. Other overhead expenses include labor costs, the cost of benefits for employees, the cost of buying goods to stock the store, and the costs of storage for the items not on the floor. When a store advertises, the cost of the advertising is added to its overhead. Special services, such as credit plans, fashion advisors, restrooms, restaurants, elevators, escalators, alterations, ordering by mail or phone, and free parking, all add to overhead expenses.

Stores with high overhead expenses usually have higher overall prices. Stores with lower overhead and fewer services sometimes have lower prices. Some checking and comparing before you buy will help you learn about the stores in your area and the prices they charge.

***Do Some Preshopping and Comparison Shopping.*** To preshop is to look around but not buy anything. Sometimes you preshop to find out the prices of things you need. You comparison shop to compare stores and the prices they charge, the services they offer, and the kinds of clothes they carry. If you have just moved to a new city or town, or if you are not an experienced shopper, preshopping and comparison shopping can be especially helpful.

Impulse buying when you are comparison shopping could upset your clothing plan. If you want to compare prices once you know the quality you want, you may find it helpful to look at clothing catalogs either in your home or at a catalog store. Catalogs usually show a selection of various items in different sizes, colors, and qualities and a range of prices. Sometimes, using the telephone may be the easiest way to comparison shop. After a few calls, you can go to the store that has the lowest price.

Preshopping helps you to become an informed shopper, because you get to know the stores in your area and know where to find clothes you need or want. This knowledge will help you to decide where to shop for the best price and quality, where to shop when a particular service is important, and where to shop when you need a particular garment or style. Preshopping can help you to avoid wasting time when you are buying clothes. You already will have done some of the work and will know where to go to get what you need. Preshopping and comparison shopping can help you to make the best use of your resources.

***Learn to Judge Quality.*** Usually, a good quality garment is of good design, made of quality fabric, constructed carefully, and finished well. It is as durable as it needs to be for the type of garment it is. When used as intended and cared for properly, it continues to look new through several wearings and washings or cleanings.

A well-sewn lining and extra buttons indicate good quality.

**Check for Fit.** The fit of a garment is as important as its comfort and durability. Clothes look better on you when they fit right and are not too tight or too loose. They also are more comfortable when they fit right. Clothes that are too tight can wear out faster because of the extra strain on seams and fabric. Clothes that are too long will wear out around their hems because of constant dragging on the floor.

Buying clothes that do not fit well can be a waste of resources because you are not likely to wear something that is not comfortable. Your money works harder for you when you buy something that fits well.

**Consider Sale Items.** Buying clothes on sale can save you money if they fit into your plan in terms of what you need and when you need it. Buying something on sale just because it is on sale can be a waste of money if it doesn't fit into your plan.

If you are a wise shopper, you will watch for seasonal sales. Many stores run sales on specific items of clothing during off-seasons. Because stores must make room for spring merchandise, for example, they often hold sales on winter garments. You might find a winter coat for far less when winter is over. If you plan for these purchases, and if your clothing size does not change greatly from season to season, you can find some good bargains.

**Know the Purpose of Advertising.** You see advertisements for clothes in newspapers and magazines, in catalogs, on television, and in store windows. You hear ads on the radio. Obviously, stores and clothing manufacturers spend a lot of money for advertising, but advertisements do not always help you.

While some advertisements give you valuable information, such as style, price, color, and size range, you should remember that the major purpose of advertising is to sell. Clothes are shown to their best advantage and

The durability you need for your clothing will be different for each garment and will depend on its use. Clothes that are worn frequently or worn for rugged activities, such as sports or farming and construction work, need to be very durable. Clothes you wear infrequently, perhaps for a formal occasion such as a wedding or a formal dance, do not need to be as durable.

When you check the quality of the clothes you are interested in, there are certain things to look for. The fibers used to make the fabric, the way the fabric is made, the materials used in the construction, and the way the garment is constructed all affect the quality. The chart on page 309 gives you some specific information on things you should look for when you are checking quality.

# CHECKING CLOTHES FOR QUALITY

| FABRIC | • if fabric is woven, grainlines are at right angles to each other<br>• if fabric is knitted, rows are even and not stretched out of shape<br>• plaids and stripes match at the seams<br>• fiber content does not cause allergic reaction<br>• fabric construction is appropriate for garment use |
|---|---|
| SEAMS | • stitching is smooth and firm, no puckers or gaps<br>• stitches are short and close together<br>• seam edges are finished, if necessary, to prevent raveling<br>• seam allowances are at least ⅝ in (1.5 cm) wide<br>• thread matches fabric<br>• seam edges and corners lie flat |
| ZIPPERS | • stitching is neat and even<br>• thread matches fabric<br>• overlap is smooth and free from puckers<br>• overlap covers zipper<br>• zipper opens and closes easily and "locks" when tab is folded down |
| FASTENERS | • buttons, hooks, eyes, and/or snaps are firmly attached<br>• buttons slip easily through buttonholes<br>• buttons match or compliment the fabric and garment<br>• garment lies flat when buttons are buttoned<br>• buttonholes are evenly spaced, firmly stitched, and lie flat<br>• hooks, eyes, and snaps lie flat and invisible when hooked or snapped |
| HEMS | • depth of hem is even all the way around<br>• if fabric ravels, raw hem edge has hem tape attached or is overstitched<br>• hem lies flat and smooth against garment<br>• stitching does not show on right side of garment |
| GARMENT FEATURES | • collar is even, matches on both sides, and lies flat<br>• pockets are firmly attached or inserted and lie flat<br>• waistband lies flat<br>• garment details are neatly done<br>• the garment has a lining if it is close fitting and fabric stretches<br>• lining to prevent stretching is of tightly woven fabric, fits the garment<br>• lining for loose fitting garments is firm, but gives with movement |
| CARE | • care directions are attached to garment<br>• care directions are easy to understand<br>• all parts of the garment can be cleaned in the same way<br>• care is appropriate for use of garment |

words are used in ways to convince you to buy. Advertisers try to create a need for their product. If you can keep this in mind, it will help you to distinguish between information and appeals to your emotions.

**Read the Labels.** Most garments have care instructions on a label that is attached to the garment. This information tells you what care the garment requires. A "Dry Clean Only" label, for example, means that the garment has to go to the cleaners for several days or that you have to go to the coin-operated dry cleaners. Either way will cost time and money. A "Hand Wash/Line Dry" label means that the garment cannot be washed in the washing machine or dried in the dryer. This can be a problem for someone who has clothes that are easy to care for and does not have time for hand washing.

Consider the laundry facilities you use, your time, and how you want your clothes to look when evaluating a garment and the care it needs. You have to decide how much money, time, and effort you have and want to spend in

How can care instruction labels help you to make shopping decisions?

caring for your clothes. Reading the labels will help you to make a decision that matches the resources you have for care.

## Avoid Poor Shopping Habits

Poor shopping habits can destroy your wardrobe plans. Two poor shopping habits to avoid are buying too many fad or extreme fashions and impulse buying. Another habit to avoid is last-minute shopping.

***Fads and Extreme Fashions*** As you learned in Chapter 13, a clothing fad is a garment or accessory or a way of dressing that becomes popular but lasts for only a short period of time. Fashions, or popular styles, change with the times, but the change is more gradual and over a longer period of time.

Since fads and extreme fashions go out of style quickly, you can spend a lot of money if you try to keep up with all of them. This does not mean that you should never buy anything faddish or extreme. If you limit purchases to one or two items or accessories, however, you will have more money to spend on clothes that you can wear for a longer period of time before they go out of style.

Peer pressure and clever advertising may make you want to choose only certain designer labels. Think about these purchases carefully. What trade-offs are involved? Could you buy two pair of jeans for the price of one pair of designer jeans? Are the less expensive jeans of equal or better quality? Maybe it is worthwhile for you to choose the designer jeans anyway. If you do, check labels carefully to be sure you are getting a genuine designer garment and not a fraud or imitation label.

***Impulse Buying*** As you have learned, impulse buying means buying without thinking about how an item fits into your plan or how it will affect your budget. Depending on the amount of money you have to spend, impulse buying can upset your wardrobe plans a lot or only a little. You may find that the item bought on impulse doesn't go with the other clothes you have. You may find that you have to make major adjustments in your clothing plan because you have upset the balance of resources available to you.

Sometimes when you are preshopping, you find an item you have been wanting for quite a while. Sometimes you may find something you have been thinking about getting, but you haven't yet made it a part of your plan. If you buy the item, is it impulse buying? If you buy without thinking, it is. If you think about your plan, about the clothes you have and how the item will fit in, about the money and other resources you have to spend, and then make a carefully thought-out decision, it is not the same as impulse buying. Even though you were not shopping with the purpose of buying, thoughtful evaluation of the situation and recognition of the need to make adjustments in your plan make it a carefully considered decision rather than an impulsive act.

***Last-Minute Shopping*** Suppose you are going to a special occasion, such as a prom or formal dance. Before you realize it, the date has approached, and you have only a few days to get your clothing. You do not have time for much comparison shopping, and because there are several other proms in your area, the selection of formal clothing is poor. You may find that you have to settle on something you don't like very much or have to buy something very expensive because these are the only choices you have. Holiday shopping can be a similar experience. If you know that you have to make certain clothing purchases by a specific date, try to schedule some time for this in advance. This may help to save your shopping resources and leave you more satisfied with the quality of your purchases.

Before buying a garment, think about how it will go with your other clothes.

## Caring for Your Clothes

Caring for your clothes involves procedures that help your clothes retain their original appearance. This usually means getting clothes clean, dry, and wrinkle-free. The procedures that you follow depend on the fiber content of the fabric, its construction, and the construction of the garment.

The proper selection and use of detergents, bleaches, and fabric softeners are a part of the procedures you need to follow to keep your clothes looking new and undamaged.

## Follow Label Instructions

The Federal Trade Commission has required care instruction labels in clothing since 1972. The ruling was revised in 1984 to provide even more information to the consumer. Most instructions are on a label that is sewn into the garment, although the information may be stamped onto the garment or printed on a wrapper. Care instructions that are on a permanently attached label or printed on the garment itself are supposed to remain legible for the life of the garment.

The label will tell you if a garment is washable. If it can be damaged by hot water or by machine washing, the label must state that the garment should be washed in warm water or by hand. If any water temperature can be

Why are clothes that can be put in a dryer easier to care for?

used, and it can be either hand washed or machine washed, the label usually reads "Machine Washable."

Care instruction labeling can help you to handle your clothing care. If you have little time to spend on clothing care, you need to look for clothes with labels that specify simple procedures, such as "Machine Wash/Tumble Dry." You probably will want to avoid labels that say "Hand Wash Only" or "Dry Clean Only" or "Iron Wrong Side Only." If you have time to spend on special care procedures, and you are willing to use it for clothes care, you may have more alternatives to choose from.

When you have conflicting goals, your decisions are more difficult, and care information labels play an important part in them. For example, Jessica's favorite clothes are the ones that require special care, but she does not have time to spend on special care procedures. She has the conflicting goals of wearing her favorite clothes and spending as little time as possible on clothes care. She may decide that time saved is more important to her and wear her favorite clothes only on special occasions. Or, she may decide that wearing her favorite clothes is more important to her and take her chances with not following the care instructions. She may try to achieve both goals by enlisting the aid of her sister for some of her clothes care in exchange for money or for doing a task that her sister does not like to do.

If you take a few minutes to look at the labels in some of the clothes you wear often and not so often, you may discover a pattern in your own preferences. You may like your outfit that requires ironing, but if it is usually at the bottom of the ironing pile, it may not be doing you much good. You may wear clothes that are easy to care for most of the time. Knowing what you like and dislike in caring for clothes may help you to decide what to look for and what to avoid when you are looking for clothes in the future.

## Washing Your Clothes

There are several procedures you should follow before washing your clothing. If you follow them, you can reduce laundry problems and the amount of time you spend caring for your clothing.

**Check Pockets.** If possible, take a few minutes to make sure that all pockets are empty to prevent major problems. Ballpoint pens, colored pencils, and packs of gum are only a few of the objects that can turn a load of laundry into a major disaster.

**Sort Clothes.** Sorting clothes according to color, type of fabric, amount of soil, appropriate water temperature, and method of washing can help to prevent laundry problems. A useful guideline for you to follow is to wash similar colors and similar fabrics together.

Separating dark colors from light colors may help to prevent the transfer of color from dark items to light items. It is usually a good idea to wash white clothes by themselves as they tend to pick up colors and soil from other, darker fabrics.

When it is possible, sort according to the type of fabric. Heavy fabrics may cause the abrasion of lighter fabrics. Avoid combining heavy fabrics, such as denim jeans or a heavy cotton painter's cloth skirt or overalls, with lighter weight or delicate fabrics, such as shirts or blouses or underwear.

You may find it helpful to separate heavily soiled items from lightly soiled items or to prewash the heavily soiled items before combining them with other items that are similar in color and fabric to make a full load. Washing heavily soiled items separately or prewashing them prevents the transfer of soil from one item to another. Separate items that produce lint from ones that attract lint.

Consider the water temperature of the wash load. You do not want to combine clothes

Pens and markers left in pockets during a wash cycle can damage other garments in your wash load.

to be washed in hot water with those that should be washed in warm or cool water. Clothes that need warm or cool water may be damaged by hot water. Clothes that need hot water may not get clean in warm or cool water.

Don't forget to check the care label for the recommended method of washing before you begin your laundry. Obviously, clothes with "Hand Wash Only" labels should not be machine washed. Clothes with permanent-press finishes should be washed in the permanent-press cycle in the washing machine.

Sometimes you end up with partial loads when you sort your laundry. If you are using a washing machine that has water level adjustments for smaller loads, you can use a small-load setting. If you cannot adjust the water level, you may decide to combine some of these partial loads, or you may decide to wait until you have enough clothes to make a full load. Sometimes, loads can be combined successfully. Prewashing some heavily soiled items, for example, may make it possible to wash them with some less heavily soiled items.

Washing similar colors and fabrics together is a correct care procedure.

If you have to combine loads, you may find it helpful to use the water temperature and washing method recommended for the most delicate fabrics in the load.

**Pretreat Heavily Soiled Clothes.** Heavily soiled clothes may need some pretreatment before washing. **Pretreating** involves treating laundry to loosen or partially remove heavy soil and stains before beginning the regular wash cycle. Sometimes, it is as easy as brushing away loose dirt or mud. Sometimes, the clothes need to be put through a prewash cycle before being washed. A prewash cycle will help to remove some of the soil and will prevent soil from being deposited on other items in the wash load.

Presoaking for a recommended amount of time also helps to remove some of the soil

and will prevent soil from being deposited on other items. Presoaking with an enzyme-active product may help to remove stains as well as heavy soil.

**Pretreat Spots and Stains.** Spots and stains should be treated because the longer they stay in the fabric, the more difficult they are to get out. Many may become permanent after a short period of time. If you are unable to treat spots and stains immediately, you probably will want to take the time to do it before you begin your laundry. Most stains and spots do not come out during washing, and often washing will set the stain. Once stains are set, they are difficult or impossible to remove.

The first step in stain removal is to brush gently or scrape away any excess substance causing the stain. This makes it easier to treat the stain or soil in the fabric. The steps you follow after this depend on the type of stain and what caused it, as well as the fiber content and fabric construction of the garment.

When a stain is made up of a combination of substances, you may have to follow separate stain removal processes for each part of the stain. A cake batter containing flour, eggs, and oil, for example, would need to be scraped to remove as much as possible, sponged with cool water to remove the flour and egg, and then treated with a grease remover. Sometimes, one stain removal agent must be removed by another. For instance, if you use lard or oil to remove tar, you will need to remove the grease spot that the lard or oil leaves.

The temperature of the water is important for removal of many stains. Hot water is best for removing grease stains and sugar syrups, but it will set protein stains, such as milk, raw egg, or blood. Cool or lukewarm water should be used to remove protein stains. You may have to choose between hot water for stain removal and cool water, which is recommended for the fabric.

# All Washed Up

For as long as there has been clothing, there has been laundry—and people looking for easier ways to do it. The most primitive method, beating fabric against rocks in the river, was replaced in ancient Pompeii by slaves standing knee-deep in large pottery bowls and stamping on clothing with bare feet. Those snow-white togas of ancient Rome required frequent washing, and commercial cleaners, or *fullers,* did a booming business, also treading on the clothes in large vats.

For over a thousand years, there was little progress in laundry technology. As recently as the turn of the century, "doing the wash" meant carrying heavy buckets of water to the stove to heat, filling the tub, overturning the tub and refilling it, as well as scrubbing, wringing, carrying, and hanging heavy fabrics. No wonder even people of modest means sent laundry "out" or had help "in" to do it. Those who did their own could easily spend two full days per week in the hard labor of washing and ironing one load of family laundry.

The development of washing machines made laundry easier and less time consuming. Manually operated home washers appeared in the 1850s, but they often tangled or tore the clothes. In 1907, a motorized machine was developed, but filling and emptying the tub and running clothes through the wringer at the end of each cycle still had to be done by hand. The agitator was invented in 1922, but the fully automatic washer that could spin dry did not become common until the 1940s. Many women then began to use the time saved from the exhausting work of home laundering to take jobs outside the home. With today's machines, everything from water temperature to agitation speed can be preset, and clothes emerge clean and ready for the dryer. Now if they'd only invent something to fold the laundry and put it away!

## Using an Automatic Washing Machine

Clothes that do not require hand washing or dry cleaning can be cleaned in an automatic washing machine either at home or at a laundromat. Each machine has its own instructions, often found on the inside of the machine's cover or door. Using almost all automatic washing machines involves choosing laundry aids, selecting water temperatures and wash cycles, and properly loading the machine you are using.

**Water Temperature**  Although hot water usually cleans better than cold water, it is not always needed and may even damage a garment. If you use the correct laundry product, cold water can be effective. Cold water prevents shrinkage, rinses effectively, and is less expensive to use than warm or hot water.

**Wash Cycle**  **Agitation** is the force of the washing machine as it moves the water, detergent, and clothing during laundering. The strength of the agitation you need depends on how heavy the soil is and what fabric you are washing. Delicate fabrics usually require a *gentle* cycle, for example. Other common wash cycles are *normal* and *permanent press*. Checking care instructions and laundry product labels will help you to choose the correct wash cycle for each load of laundry.

**Laundry Aids**  Laundry aids are the products that you use to treat spots and stains, add to the wash water or rinse water, and/or use in drying and ironing clothes. The laundry products you choose and the ways in which you use them will affect the way your laundry looks after you have done it. There are different laundry products for different tasks and different water conditions.

*Cleaning agents* are added to the wash water to aid in soil removal. The most common

ones are known as soaps and detergents, although technically both are a type of detergent. Soaps are made from fat and lye. Detergents are nonsoap products, made from substances other than fat and lye. Soaps are actually better cleaning agents than some detergents, but they work best in hot water that is soft. Soft water contains few dissolved minerals. Since most of the water in this country contains varying amounts of minerals, and since many fabrics cannot tolerate hot water, detergents are used more frequently than soaps.

When soap is used in hard water, or water that contains large amounts of dissolved minerals, it combines with the minerals and forms floating, insoluble particles, called soap curds.

Why is it important to follow the directions on the machine and to select the correct temperature for the fabric?

The soap that has combined with the minerals is not good for cleaning, which wastes soap. In addition, soap curds form an insoluble, sticky film that clings to the fabric and holds dark soil and dirt. Since it does not dissolve in water, it will not wash out. The film builds up, washing after washing. When it is used with soft water, soap does not cause these undesirable effects. Although detergents do not form soap curds in hard water, they may not clean as well as desired in hard water.

There are many soaps and detergents available to choose from. They range from heavy-duty to light-duty to all-purpose. Some produce a lot of suds, and some are low suds-ing. Some contain other laundry aids, such as whiteners, bleach, or fabric softeners. To find the soap or detergent that is best for you, you may want to experiment with different ones. What works well for one person may not work for another because of the type of soil in the laundry or the types and amounts of minerals in the water. The directions on the container will tell you the right amount to use and when to add it for the best results.

*Water softening products* for the wash or rinse water help to prevent soap curds when you are using soap. They may help to prevent the redepositing of soil particles on your clothes when you are using detergent. Often you can reduce the amount of soap or deter-gent you normally use if you use a water softening product. For best results, follow directions on the package.

A water-softening system installed in your home near where the water supply enters the house is another solution to hard water. In addition to helping with laundry problems, this type of system prevents hard-water scale from building up in your plumbing systems.

*Bleaches* are used to whiten clothes that have become gray and stained. Bleaches whiten because they combine chemically with soil to form a colorless substance. Bleaching

Always read the directions on laundry aids carefully to get the best results.

does not remove soil; it simply makes some of it colorless.

There are several kinds of bleaches avail-able. Both liquid and dry chlorine bleaches can be identified by the chemical name sodium hypochlorite (SO-dee-um hy-puh-KLAWR-ite) on the label. These bleaches may be used on most white cotton or linen fabrics, but they will ruin silk or wool fabrics. Some white fabrics with special finishes turn yellow when they are bleached. Used in water that has a high iron content, chlorine bleach may cause brown spots and stains on clothes.

Liquid chlorine bleach should always be diluted before it is added to the clothes in the washing machine. If it is used full strength, or if it is just poured into the washing machine with the clothes, it can discolor fabrics and may even create holes in the clothes due to its strong chemical action. Too much chlorine bleach or soaking clothes in a bleach solution for too long a time can weaken or ruin a fabric.

Nonchlorine bleaches, or bleaches that do not contain sodium hypochlorite, usually are safe for all fabrics. Many require hot water to be most effective.

The information on the label of the bleach product will tell you on what type of fabric you can safely use the product. Follow the directions carefully for the amount to use and when to add it to the laundry.

*Fabric softeners* help to eliminate static electricity in clothes and to cut down on the stiff, harsh feeling that some clothes have after being washed in hard water and detergent. Many fabric softeners can be added to the rinse water. Others are added when clothes are put into the dryer. Follow the directions with the product to get the best results.

Fabric softeners that are added to rinse water work most effectively when the clothes have been thoroughly rinsed to remove other laundry aids. If all the detergent has not been removed before the fabric softener is added, the fabric softener will react with the detergent to form a sticky substance. This substance may cause spots or stains on your clothes or may cause fabrics to look a bit dull or grayed after several washings.

The regular use of a fabric softener can lead to a buildup on clothes and other items. The buildup can reduce the absorbency of fabrics and lead to problems in washing. Reduced absorbency means a fabric tends to be water repellent. Because water cannot get to the fibers as well, the fabric becomes more difficult to clean. Reduced absorbency is not a desired effect for towels or sport clothes.

Other laundry aids include spot and stain removers, enzyme presoaks, and starches. Each has special uses. Spot and stain removers

Why should you distribute laundry evenly around the machine's agitator?

help to remove specific types of spots and stains from certain fabrics. Enzyme presoaks are designed to remove heavy soil and protein-based stains. Starches add crispness, or stiffness, to fabrics. Read the labels on these products before choosing them and follow the directions on the labels.

You should use whatever laundry products you choose carefully. Using too much or using too little or not following directions can give you results you have not planned for and do not want. The more products you use, the greater the chance of a buildup on the laundry. Sometimes less is better. You may find you can get the results you want by using as few laundry products as possible.

***Loading the Washing Machine*** Proper loading includes following the directions on the machine itself. An overloaded machine cannot clean clothes efficiently and can be damaged by the load, because it has not been designed to hold so many clothes. To avoid problems, you may want to check that the clothes are moving freely. If they are not, you may want to remove several items. When loading a top-loading machine, try to distribute the clothes evenly around the agitator post to avoid having the machine off-balance during the spin cycle.

Usually, clothes are loaded first, then the machine is started, and finally the laundry aids are added. Check the instructions on each machine before loading the clothes.

## Drying Your Clothes

There are many ways to dry clothes. They may be tumbled in an automatic dryer with unheated or heated air, hung on a line to air dry, or laid on a flat surface to dry in the air. The care labels in your clothes will tell you what to do or not do with a garment.

***Drip Drying*** Drip drying means to hang a garment up without wringing or squeezing any water out of it. This should be done where the water can drip safely, such as in a shower, over a tub, or in the yard.

Clothes to be drip dried can be hung on a clothesline, draped over a clothes rack, or hung on a hanger that will not rust or discolor from dampness. You will want to use the method that creates the fewest wrinkles.

***Line Drying*** Line drying means to hang the clothes on a line to dry. They may be wrung or squeezed to get some of the water out, or they may be allowed to go through the spin cycle on the washing machine. Usually clotheslines for line drying are outdoors, but they may be on a porch or in a basement.

Of course, temperature and humidity affect line drying. On dry, hot days, clothes dry more rapidly than they do on cooler or humid days. A breeze can help to increase drying speed by increasing the evaporation rate. When the temperature is below freezing, clothes hung outside will take longer to dry because the water in clothes freezes. Eventually, the water will evaporate if the air is dry, but drying will be faster if the clothes are brought inside.

Line drying requires more time but saves money resources.

**Drying Flat** Some clothes must be dried flat. If they are machine washable, they usually can go through the spin cycle to remove some of the water in them. If a garment has been hand washed, rolling the garment between towels helps to remove some of the water without stretching the garment out of shape.

A screenlike flat rack, especially made for flat drying, can speed the drying process because it allows air to circulate around the garment. Drying on a solid surface, such as the top of the washer or dryer, takes longer because only the top surface of the garment is exposed to air.

If you are drying a garment on a flat surface, be sure that the surface you use cannot be damaged by moisture. You may want to be sure that there is nothing under the garment to cause a stain.

**Automatic Dryer** An automatic dryer uses a combination of heat and tumbling to dry clothes. The heat increases the rate of water evaporation; the tumbling action allows maximum air circulation in minimum space.

Overloading a dryer can cause the load to take longer to dry because there is little room for air circulation. It also can cause wrinkles because the clothes are too crowded to tumble properly. If it is extremely overloaded, the load may not dry at all, and the dryer may be damaged by overheating.

Dryer controls help you to control the heat used to dry clothes. The hotter the temperature, the faster the drying. A high setting is not always recommended, however. Many fabrics are damaged by temperatures that are too high. Some dryers have a no-heat setting that allows you to tumble dry items that may be damaged by heat.

If you have a load for the dryer that is a combination of fabrics requiring high and low temperatures, use the heat setting for the most delicate fabrics in the load. Although the fabrics that can be dried at high temperatures will not dry as quickly at lower temperatures, your delicate fabrics will not be damaged.

Removing clothing as soon as the dryer stops, especially if they have permanent press finishes, prevents wrinkles. If you can remove them and either hang them up or fold them right away, you may not need to iron or press them at all.

Be sure to locate the lint trap on the dryer you are using. As the dryer runs, lint is caught in this trap, which usually is a removable screen. Directions may vary, but most manufacturers recommend cleaning and emptying the lint trap after every dryer load. Too much lint in the trap can cause a fire, so you will want to follow dryer directions carefully.

Emptying the dryer lint trap after each load is an important safety procedure.

## Ironing Your Clothes

Some clothes need to be ironed even when you remove them promptly from the dryer. There are two basic types of irons you can use. A dry iron does not contain moisture. If the clothes you are ironing are severely wrinkled, you may want to dampen them before you use a dry iron. A steam iron has a container for water and holes on its surface to allow steam to escape as the iron heats. Steam irons are recommended for most washable fabrics, including permanent press. For some fabrics, an extra cloth should be used between the iron and the fabric to prevent damage. Read the instructions that come with your iron carefully and become familiar with the different heat settings for different fabrics. The care instruction labels on each piece of clothing will give further ironing directions.

A few good safety habits to develop when you iron include:

- Set up your ironing board where there isn't much household traffic.
- Stand the iron on end when you turn the garment and when you finish.
- Unplug the iron as soon as you have finished your ironing.
- Put the cooled iron away. Do not leave it on a high board where it can be knocked over.

There are many sizes, types, and models of irons available today. New features have made ironing easier and safer.

You may want to consider buying an iron that shuts off automatically when you are not using it. These models cost more but offer an important safety feature.

## Doing Simple Clothing Repairs

There are certain simple clothing repairs that need to be done quite frequently. These include sewing on a button, repairing a hem, sewing on a hook and eye fastener, repairing a seam, and applying a patch.

These common repairs can be done following basic procedures that do not require much sewing skill.

### Common Repairs

It is a good idea to do clothing repairs as soon as you notice them. A hem that has just started to unravel is easier to fix than one that has come down completely. Fixing a loose button when you notice it can save you from having to replace a lost one when you need your favorite outfit in a hurry.

How you do simple clothing repairs will depend on the resources you have. If you have a sewing machine and know how to use it, you can use it for most repairs. If you do not own a sewing machine and cannot borrow one, you can do simple repairs by hand. To repair a garment by hand, you will need a thimble, a sharp sewing needle, thread that matches your item of clothing or invisible thread, and scissors.

Thread your needle, pulling your thread through about five or six inches. Make a simple knot after you have cut off the length of thread you think you will need. Working with a single thread is fine for most simple repairs.

## Clothing Repair Alternatives

You may feel that you do not have the time or the skill needed to do even simple clothing repairs. If this is the case, you may want to barter with a relative or friend for help, or you may want to have your clothing repairs done by a professional tailor or seamstress. You must choose your clothing repair-plan on the basis of what is important to you and the resources available to you.

## Storing Your Clothes

Have you ever looked all over for a particular garment to wear to work or to school, then finally found it, only to discover it was unfit to wear? Developing and carrying out a plan for storage can help you to have your clothes ready to wear and easy to find when you want them.

**Storage** is a place to keep what you want to keep (in this case, your clothes) until you need it again. The particular type of storage each garment needs depends on the fiber content of the fabric, the fabric's construction, the garment's design and construction, and the length of time the garment is to be stored. Proper storage helps to extend the life of clothes by preventing damage and unneeded wear and tear.

This closet space clearly is organized to get the maximum storage possible while arranging garments neatly.

Convenience is another consideration in clothing storage. You want to be able to find a garment you have stored quickly and be able to get it out and put it away easily. Convenient storage encourages you to take proper care of your clothes. This applies to clothes that have just been laundered or dry cleaned and to those that you have worn and still are clean enough to wear again. It refers to clothes you are going to wear today, the ones you wore earlier this week, and those you are not going to wear until next season.

## Seasonal Storage

Protecting clothing during seasonal storage includes preventing damage from insects and other environmental factors, such as excess moisture, dryness, heat, cold, dust, dirt, sunlight, and odors. Damage from these conditions can be severe when clothes are stored for the season or for a long time. Holes, stains, and odors may appear during long storage and sometimes cannot be removed.

Knowing what your garment is made of can help you to protect it. Since most garments have labels that define their fiber content, you can check the labels to determine the best method of storage. Wool and fur garments, for example, should be stored with mothballs or flakes to prevent damage by moths.

You may find specially designed zipper bags for storing hanging and folded clothes convenient. You may prefer to store individual items, such as sweaters, in plastic bags like those used in the kitchen for food storage or garbage. Sealed plastic trash bags can hold your out-of-season clothes safely together until you need them again. If dampness is not a problem, cardboard cartons secured with tape are suitable storage containers.

Clean garments are the most important factor in preventing any damage during seasonal storage. Be sure your clothes are entirely clean before you put them away for the season. It is a good idea to polish any leather shoes or accessories a few days before storing them for the season to be sure the polish is dry.

## Daily Storage

A few guidelines for daily storage will help you to keep your clothes in good shape.

- Know which clothes should be hung up and which should be stored flat. This depends on the fabric. If hanging stretches a garment, it should be stored flat.

- Use the correct hangers for each garment. Heavier coats, jackets, and suits need wooden or heavy plastic hangers so they do not slip off.
- Use padded hangers to help retain the shape of a garment.
- Try to treat any spots and to do any repairs before daily storage.
- Close top buttons or other fasteners before hanging or folding garments.
- Hang skirts by the waistband; hang pants by the cuff or neatly folded over a wide hanger.
- Leave space between hanging garments.
- Keep closet doors open during the day to allow air to get at your clothes.
- Hang clothes in similar groups. For example, hang all your slacks together.
- Do not store anything that you cannot wear again as it is.

The hanger used depends on the garment.

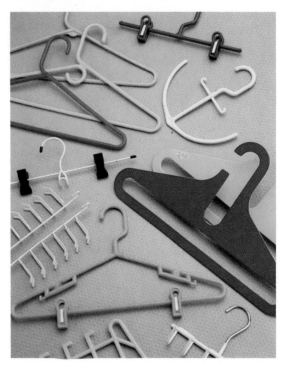

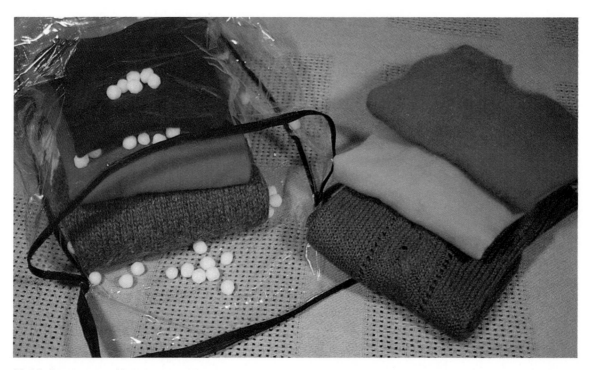
Mothballs protect wool between seasons.

## *Improving Storage*

Sometimes storage problems can be lessened by using special storage aids or devising special ways to make better use of the space available to you. Many department stores and hardware stores have storage aids that range from specialized hooks and hangers to special storage units that fit inside a closet. Most gift and housewares catalogs also have a variety of storage aids. Creativity and basic carpentry skills can help you to improve the use of your storage space with minimal expense. A few hooks added to a wall or to the back of a door do not require many resources. An extra rod added to your closet is another inexpensive way to double your hanging storage space.

## *For Review*

1. Name six environmental factors that can damage clothing. How do you store clothing for a season to prevent damage?
2. How do you decide which clothing to hang and which to store flat? Why do some garments need different hangers?
3. Name one way to improve storage.

# Management Application: Planning Clothes Care

Imagine yourself in the situation described below. As you read, think about how the steps of the management process might apply to this situation. Then, answer the questions that follow.

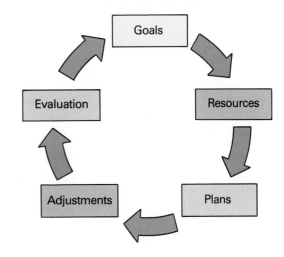

## Situation

Barbara knew she needed help. She had done two loads of laundry since she had been living in the college dormitory. The first load had resulted in pink socks and underwear because she had added her red sweatshirt at the last minute. The second attempt had turned her new cotton sweater into doll clothes. She knew how to do laundry. She had made those mistakes because she had been tired and in a hurry. Okay, so she would concentrate on her laundry but she didn't know how to repair clothing, and she had just ripped a pair of her new slacks. She had no desire to sew and no talent for it. The only hemline she had ever repaired had looked more like the Ohio River than a straight line. She wished there were some way to avoid clothes care altogether for the rest of her life.

That night, her roommate, Toby, was complaining about how much she hated housework and cleaning chores. She admitted that she wasn't very neat (as Barbara had already observed). A messy room drove Barbara crazy. At home Barbara always did the vacuuming and dusting; she really didn't mind doing housework at all. As the two girls talked, they had an idea. They decided to trade work. Bar-

bara would keep their room neat and clean. In exchange, Toby would do Barbara's laundry along with her own. Toby also knew a senior who did clothing repairs on his own portable sewing machine to earn extra money. If his prices were reasonable, it would definitely be worth it. There might be hope for her slacks after all!

## Questions

1. How are Barbara's priorities affecting the goals she has set?

2. What trade-offs will Barbara be making if she has her clothing repairs done?

3. Are both Toby and Barbara benefiting from their plan? Explain.

4. Think of one possible problem that might come up when Barbara and Toby put their plan into action. Could they make adjustments to solve it?

5. Which steps of the management process apply to this situation?

# 14 Chapter Review

## Summary

Knowing what you can spend, learning about the stores near you, understanding how to be a comparison shopper, and knowing how to judge quality will make you a better shopper. To keep your clothes looking fresh and undamaged, follow the care instructions on your garment labels and learn how to pretreat, wash, dry, and iron clothes properly. Doing simple clothing repairs as soon as they are needed will help to prevent major repairs. Following good storage procedures can help to extend the life of your clothes.

## Vocabulary

Use-the vocabulary words below to complete the paragraph below.

pretreating

agitation

storage

Sam is putting most of his winter clothes in __(1)__ for the summer. Unfortunately, he has to throw away two of his favorite garments, which were damaged because he failed to read his care label instructions. He tried __(2)__ a stain on his wool shirt with the wrong bleach. A pair of slacks that was supposed to be washed in the gentle cycle, was destroyed by the strong __(3)__ of the machine in a heavy-duty cycle.

## Questions

1. Compare the advantages of a specialty store with those of a department store and those of a discount house.

2. What should you look for when checking a seam for quality? When you are checking a hem?

3. What factors do you think influence the fads in your school as opposed to those in another school?

4. What does a label mean when it reads:

   hand wash          warm wash

   wash separately    tumble dry

   damp wipe only     line dry

5. Why is it important to sort clothes before washing? What procedure should you follow when you sort them?

6. What is the difference between the effect of a water softener and the effect of a fabric softener on your clothes?

7. What factors should you consider before selecting a bleach?

8. What is a lint trap? What procedure should you remember to follow after each dryer load? Why?

9. Why is it important to do simple repairs as soon as possible?

10. What are the advantages of using good storage procedures? List some of the procedures you should follow.

## Skill Activity

**1. _Communication._** Hold a brief class discussion about the influence of advertising and peer pressure on clothing decisions. Why do some clothing labels, those for jeans, for example, become popular? Include your personal experiences in the discussion. Have you found that these popular products are superior in quality or inferior? Ask volunteers to bring in designer or brand-name clothing items they own and the same clothing items that are not designer brands. Compare the stitching and workmanship and the quality of the fabric. Discuss the results and why you may choose clothing like that of your friends and whether or not you can do this and still have your own clothing style.

**2. _Decision Making._** Use the quality checklist on page 309 to help you rate the quality of three of your clothing items as good, fair, or poor. Then set up a chart to record your clothing expenses for three months. Put five columns on your chart. The first column will be for a description of the item you bought. The second column will record the brand name of the product and the name of the store where you purchased it. The third column will be for the date of purchase; the fourth will be for the price. Label the last column "Quality Rating." After a few months, fill in the last column. Use this information to help you make future buying decisions.

**3. _Human Relations._** Do some research and talk to people in your community about possible uses for clothing you have outgrown or will not wear again. Find out about agencies that may need good used clothing for either local or national purposes. Contact organizations such as the Red Cross to find out if they collect or receive donations of used clothing and what use they have for them. Perhaps your local churches or synagogues have clothing drives at certain times of the year. If you find an organization that needs used clothing, ask your teacher if you can hold a short used clothing drive within your class or school.

**4. _Critical Thinking._** Do an investigation into the subject of shoplifting, which is a major problem in our country. Think about two basic elements of the problem: why people shoplift when they can afford to pay for the goods and some of the consequences of being caught; and the effect of shoplifting on you as a consumer. If possible, talk to local retailers about the problem and what preventive measures they have taken to control it. How costly are these measures, such as installing hidden cameras? Is the cost passed on to you in the form of higher prices on goods? Discuss your investigation results as a class.

# *15*

# *Managing Housing Decisions*

## *As you read, think about:*

- ☐ how to choose the housing alternative that best suits your needs, wants, and resources.
- ☐ how to decide whether to buy or to rent housing.
- ☐ what choices you have in living arrangements.
- ☐ what you must know to make a final selection when acquiring housing.
- ☐ how to select appliances, equipment, and furnishings for your home.
- ☐ how to apply the management process to personal decisions about housing.

condominium
cooperative
lease (rental agreement)
security deposit
down payment
mortgage loan
fixed-rate mortgages
variable-rate mortgages
closing costs

We all like to think of our homes as places of comfort and safety. We need our own "living space" as families and as individuals within families. Of course, the size and type of living space vary for each of us, depending upon our family size and circumstances.

Perhaps you share your room with one or more brothers and sisters. Perhaps you have your own room. Perhaps you have plans to work on some attic space or other area to create your own room. The information in this chapter and the following chapter will help you think of ways to improve your living area.

The facts you learn in this chapter will help you in your future. Soon you will be faced with choosing your own housing. The more you learn now about housing resources, the better prepared you will be to make intelligent decisions about housing throughout your life.

## Housing Alternatives

At first glance, the many types of housing can be confusing. There are single-family dwellings, apartments, condominiums, cooperatives, and manufactured housing. Within each of these categories, there are many choices in size, construction, and style. The type of housing you choose will depend on your needs, wants, and what you can afford.

## Types of Housing

The single-family dwelling is a house that has been designed to be used by an individual or a family. It usually is described in terms of its style. It may be a ranch, a cape, a split-entry, a saltbox, or a Victorian, to name only a few styles.

An apartment is a room or set of rooms used as living space. It may be a part of an apartment building, or it may be a part of a house that has been converted. Types of apartments include high-rise, duplex, triplex, and fourplex. An efficiency apartment is one room that also has a kitchen area. Apartments almost always are rental units.

A **condominium** (kon-duh-MIN-ee-um) is living space that is bought, rather than rented, in a multi-unit building or group of buildings. The buyer owns his or her living space. All of the people who own condominium units then share in all the costs of keeping up jointly owned areas, such as the parking lots, elevators, and recreation areas.

A **cooperative** is living space that is under group ownership in a multi-unit building or group of buildings. An individual owns shares in the entire cooperative building, which entitles him or her to live in a unit. All the costs for repairs and maintenance are shared by the group.

Manufactured housing is housing that is partly or completely assembled at a factory and then moved to where it will be located. Mobile homes, precut housing, and prefabricated homes are three different, but common, types of manufactured housing.

# Deciding to Buy or to Rent

Your first major decision when you begin to look for housing will be whether to buy or to rent. The cost of both buying and renting housing is high. Most young people right out of high school or college have not had the chance or the time to save thousands of dollars. So, your first housing situation probably will involve renting. However, it is important to learn the advantages and disadvantages of both buying and renting before you decide.

## Renting Housing

When you rent living space, someone else owns the space, and you, as a renter, pay a certain amount each week or month for its use. Your rent includes taxes on the property. It may or may not include heating, lighting, telephone, and other utilities. Usually, repairs and routine maintenance are the responsibility of the landlord or owner of the living space.

Apartments are the most commonly rented living spaces. It is often possible, however, to rent single-family dwellings and mobile homes. Renting a condominium or cooperative is only possible if the owner or shareholder is willing to rent and the rules of the condominium or cooperative allow him or her to do so.

Because they are factory-built, prefabricated homes are usually less expensive.

***Rental Agreement*** Most rental housing involves signing a **lease,** or **rental agreement.** This is a document that sets forth the rental period, the rental fee and other fees, the due dates of payments, and the rules and regulations, or terms, the renter must follow. For example, pets may not be allowed. There may be restrictions on decorating the apartment. There may be restrictions on the number of people who can live in the apartment. If there are recreational facilities, there may be rules for their use.

Many times a renter must make a **security deposit,** or a payment that the manager of the apartment holds until the renter leaves. The deposit, which frequently is equal to one month's rent, is used to cover the costs of repairing any damage done to the apartment by the renter. It also protects the owner if the renter leaves without paying the final month's rent. Usually, the security deposit is returned to the renter when he or she leaves if rent payments are up to date and the premises have not been damaged.

At one time, it was less expensive to rent housing than it was to buy it. Renting for a few years while saving for a down payment on a house was common. However, housing costs have grown so much over the past several years that the cost per month for renting is often equal to one month's mortgage payment. For many people, so much of their income is spent for housing, utilities, and other necessities that there is little left over for saving.

When there is a lease for renting living space, the amount of rent is specified. The rent can increase when the lease expires. Increases each year or two are common due to increased taxes and the costs of maintenance and repairs, which the landlord must pay and then passes on to the tenants.

***Advantages of Renting*** Although rent payments have risen, the amount of money

It is important to read any rental agreement or lease carefully. Understand all the terms before signing it.

needed to start renting is usually less than the amount needed as a down payment for a house or a condominium. This may be an advantage if your income is low and you are trying to build up your savings. Renting may help you to save money because you do not have to worry about separate payments for property taxes, repairs, and maintenance. A renter does not have to pay for repairs. They are the owner's responsibility.

## Buying Housing

Buying housing usually refers to the purchase of a single-family home and the specified amount of land around it. There are other variations of home ownership, however. If you buy a mobile home, for example, the home itself is bought. The land it is located on often is rented, not owned.

***Financial Terms*** If you have decided to buy your housing, you may not have enough money to pay cash for it. Most lending institutions

When you own your own home, you must do any necessary repairs to keep up the value of your property.

will lend money for the purchase of living space. However, they will not lend prospective homeowners all the money they need. As a result, a certain amount of money is required for a down payment. A **down payment** is the amount of money the prospective buyer offers toward the purchase of an object. The minimum down payment may vary from 5 to 20 percent of the purchase price, depending on the lending institution, the type of loan, the type of housing, the credit rating of the buyer or buyers, and the present and potential income of the prospective buyer or buyers.

Once a prospective buyer has enough money for a down payment, most lending institutions will lend money for the rest of the

purchase price, provided that other conditions are met. A loan for housing other than a mobile home is called a **mortgage loan.** Interest rates on the money borrowed vary from lending institution to lending institution. The terms of the loan may vary from 15 to 30 or 40 years. Financing for a mobile home may be available through the dealer selling the mobile home or through a lending institution. The interest rate may be different from that for a mortgage. The maximum term of a loan for a mobile home usually is 15 years.

**Fixed-rate mortgages** have the same interest rate for as long as the mortgage lasts. **Variable-rate mortgages,** or adjustable-rate mortgages, may have a change in the interest rate over the life of the mortgage. A banker or financial adviser can explain the advantages and disadvantages of the different types of mortgages to you.

There are other costs associated with the purchase of housing. Many of these costs come under the heading of **closing costs.** These are the costs that must be paid in cash when the buyer takes possession of the living space, at the time of closing. Lawyer's fees for a title search, title insurance, mortgage processing fee, and points are just a few examples. A bank or other lending institution can provide specific information on all the costs of purchasing a house or other living space.

***Advantages of Buying*** Buying housing is usually a good investment. The value of housing usually increases over time—sometimes even over a short period of time. With each payment, the buyer owns more of the property and builds up equity. As you know, equity is the owner's interest in property over and above the claims against it.

Buying has tax advantages. Federal income tax laws presently allow the homeowner to deduct the amount of interest paid on the mortgage every year.

## Selecting Living Arrangements

Living arrangements concern the number of people in a living space and sometimes their relationship to each other. For example, a family usually occupies a single living space. With the higher costs of housing, however, there may be other arrangements. Young people may live at home after they finish school and have a job. Elderly parents may live with their children. A group of people may rent or buy living space together because that is the only way they can afford it.

## Living at Home

Because housing is so expensive, many young, single people and married couples choose to live at home. This may be a temporary measure until the young person or couple can afford a place of their own. It may be a permanent arrangement. Sometimes, parents do not charge for room and board, but in many instances, they ask for enough to cover the cost of heat, utilities, and food. Even then, the amount is usually less than it would be to rent another living space, furnish it, and live there.

Sometimes, young people live at home because their parents need the financial or emotional support they can provide. If the

What are some reasons for several generations of a family to live together?

young person or couple contributes to household expenses, respects parents' wishes and requests, shares in household responsibilities, and both parents and young people respect each other's needs for privacy and independence, this arrangement can work well. However, there is the potential for misunderstandings if there is poor communication. If parents were looking forward to having their children on their own, or if children remain dependent or refuse to follow "house rules" and share household tasks or accept responsibility themselves, relationships can become strained. If parents interfere with the young people's lives or do not encourage or allow independence, the young people do not benefit from the arrangement.

Sharing living space means sharing the work as well as the costs.

## Living Alone

Many young people look forward to their independence and to having a place of their own. Some advantages to living alone include being able to furnish the living space as you want and to set a schedule without worrying about others. At the same time, because you are responsible for the care and upkeep of the space, your living costs will be high and you may find that you are lonely.

## Sharing Living Space with Others

The traditional example of sharing living space is a married couple or a family with children living at home. In these examples, the sharing of living space is based on the social situation, that is, the blood relationships among the individuals sharing the space. When an extended family shares living space, it may be because of family ties. It may be because the relatives involved cannot afford a place of their own or because they are unable to care for themselves.

Sharing living space with others can help to lower housing costs for each individual and provide friendship and mutual support. Many young people rent their first apartments with friends. After working for a while, they may pool their resources with their friends to buy a house or condominium. When the costs are divided this way, it is more affordable. When the work is shared, it seems to go faster, or there may be less for each person to do.

Sometimes, people who do not know each other will share living space to keep their individual living costs as low as possible or to have benefits that they could not have living alone. These people may become friends or may continue to go their separate ways. While this arrangement reduces living costs, it may not provide the friendship that some people prefer.

The search for housing may begin by circling affordable locations in the paper.

When you share living space, others have to be considered. The same potential for problems that exists when you live at home exists in shared living space. Adjustments must be made to promote good relationships.

## For Review

1. Name the three major types of living arrangements available to most people.
2. What are the advantages and disadvantages of living alone?
3. Why do many young people continue to live at home? What part does communication play in this living arrangement?

# Choosing Your Housing

Many families move several times in the course of their lives. Whether you have moved ten times or are moving for the first time, moving takes time and effort and involves many different decisions.

There is certain information that you need before you even begin to look for housing. If you know how much you can spend for housing and related expenses before you begin, you will not waste time looking at housing that is too expensive. This type of information will allow you to compare housing costs and choose what is best for you. You may have other resources you can consider when looking for housing, such as time for and skills in remodeling or making repairs. These skills will allow you to look at places that others, without these resources, cannot consider. Once you know your resources and have determined what is available in the area where you want to live, you can begin to look at different possibilities. Knowing how to evaluate available housing will help you to make a wise final decision.

## Having a Housing Plan

Your plan for choosing housing must be logical and orderly. There are many important factors to be considered before you sign a lease or make a down payment on a house. You cannot afford any surprises in your monthly costs or in the housing itself once you have moved in. Finding a terrific, inexpensive apartment, renting it, then discovering that noisy trains pass by every hour will do you no good if you have signed a lease. The buyer or renter—YOU—should investigate the situation carefully before you sign a lease or make a down payment.

**Know What You Have to Spend.** Housing is expensive. It costs money to furnish a living

Make an estimate of all housing-related costs before the first bills arrive.

space and to have heat, electricity, and telephone service. You need to know how much you can spend to have a basis for your plan. A plan based on money that is not available to you is not realistic or helpful.

At one time, there were two general guidelines to help you determine how much to spend for housing. One guideline suggested that prospective homeowners should pay no more than 2 ½ times their annual income for their homes. Another guideline suggested that the annual costs of rent and renter's insurance or of principal, interest, taxes, and insurance, if you buy, should total no more than 25 percent of your income. These guidelines have worked fairly well and are still followed when it is possible. With housing costs increasing more rapidly than income, however, many people spend as much as 50 percent of their income for their homes.

Before you begin to look for housing, figure out what your income will be. You need to know your net pay, which is the money left after deductions for taxes, Social Security, and any other items have been taken out of your total, or gross, pay.

If you are just beginning to live on your own, talk to relatives and friends about approximate costs for each month. You will need to approximate food, entertainment, and transportation costs as well. Once you have estimated these, you can subtract them from your net pay to find what you can spend on housing.

If telephone, electricity, and fuel are not included in your rental price, you will want to estimate them. If you are buying, you will be paying all of these bills separately. Household insurance also must be estimated.

***Consider Needs and Wants.*** As you know, needs are conditions or things that are necessary; wants are conditions or things that are desirable but not necessary. Along with food and clothing, housing is a basic need for all human beings. Since all human beings are different, specific housing needs are different, too. Someone who is confined to a wheelchair, for example, needs a living space that allows easy access and moving about once inside. Someone without a car may need to be near public transportation or within walking distance of stores and work or school. An individual who enjoys people has different needs than one who prefers to be alone. A large family may have different housing needs than a small family has.

Sometimes the difference between needs and wants is not easily determined. After you have determined how much you have to spend on housing and housing-related expenses, and you have investigated the cost and availability of housing in the area you have chosen, you can begin to decide whether or not what you want is possible. You may have to make adjustments or give up some of your wants.

When you are looking for living space, making a list of needs and wants is helpful. If you will be sharing living space with one or more family members or friends, sit down together to make the list.

**Consider Nonmoney Resources.** Nonmoney resources include time, skills, knowledge, creativity, interest, enthusiasm, and patience. These resources can be used to repair or remodel a house, redecorate any living space, repair or refinish any needed furniture, make furnishings, and otherwise make a living space comfortable and appealing. When you have nonmoney resources and are willing to use them, you increase your options for housing.

**Find Out What Is Available in Your Area.** Reading real estate advertisements in the paper, talking to real estate agents, and talking to people you know are all ways to find out what type of housing is available in the area where you want to live. Visiting neighborhoods you are interested in may reveal more options. Many rentals are advertised only by a sign in a window.

The number of choices available to you depends on the supply of housing and the demand for it. In a town or city with one or more colleges, there may be little rental housing available because of high demand. In an area that is rapidly growing, there may be a housing shortage. In a small town, there may be houses for rent and rooms for rent but few apartments for rent.

As you read advertisements and talk to real estate agents, eliminate from consideration any housing that is too expensive or does not meet your needs. You may want to cut out advertisements from newspapers or ask real estate agents for copies of information about places that you feel are possibilities. You can number them in order of your preference, based on the information you have at this point. Some people like to see the location of each possibility before they look at any one place. This helps them to eliminate places that do not meet their criteria.

Once you have a few places you want to consider, you should make appointments to visit them. You may want to record the information you collect in a notebook to help you make your final decision.

It is possible to find housing advertised directly by the owner.

***Decide Whether to Buy or Rent.*** Because a substantial amount of money is needed to buy housing, you may have to weigh the advantages of buying or renting. If you are not sure you have saved enough money, an accountant or financial advisor can help you.

## Analyzing Possible Housing

Once you have decided what type of housing you want and have selected a few places to look at, there are still several factors to consider. Knowing what to look for will help you to select the housing that most closely meets your needs while making the best use of your resources. Some things to check include the condition of the roof, foundation, and building structure itself; the presence or absence of termites or other insects or pests; the presence, quality, and effectiveness of energy-saving measures; and the condition and quality of the heating, cooling, electrical, and plumbing systems.

***Structure and Condition*** Whether you buy or rent, you need to know more than how many rooms or closets your prospective living space has and how new its appliances are. If you know about the structure and general condition of the building, you will know about possible major problems, shortcomings, or things that need attention before you are committed to a lease or a purchase.

***Plumbing*** Whatever type of housing you look at, plumbing is important. Many years ago, lead pipe was used in construction. Unfortunately, lead is absorbed from the pipes into the water and can result in lead poisoning, which is dangerous to people of all ages and particularly dangerous to children.

Check for signs of leaking pipes, such as spots and stains on the wall or ceiling when there is a bathroom and/or kitchen on the floor

A professional inspection of a home's electrical system is a wise idea.

above. Look under the sinks for wetness. Some plumbing problems are simple to repair. Others are expensive projects.

You may want to turn on water faucets and flush toilets to check water pressure and to see how the fixtures work. If you do, turn on more than one faucet to see if this has any effect on water pressure.

Find out about the heating system for heating water. How is the water heated? Is it energy efficient? If there is a hot water tank, what is its capacity? How fast does it heat water? If you are thinking about renting, you will want to know if the cost of hot water is included in the rental fee.

***Electrical Service*** As you check the electrical system, look for any possible fire hazards. If you are considering housing in an older building, you may want to have an electrician evaluate the system.

Ask yourself if there are enough outlets. Is there wiring for new appliances? If not, you may need to know what would be involved in improving the wiring.

***Heating and Cooling Systems*** If you are buying your living space, the condition of these systems should be a major concern to you. Old, inefficient units are expensive to replace. If you do not know enough about these systems, a home inspector or energy specialist can help you to evaluate them. Even if you are renting and the cost of heating and cooling has been included in your rent, you will still want to know that these systems work well. Proper ventilation also falls under this category. Are there windows you can open for fresh air when you want it? The number of windows and their location will affect your heating and cooling systems. Many windows on the east and west side of your housing probably will reduce your heating costs in the winter, because the sun will help to warm your rooms.

If it is possible, you may want to test the heating and cooling systems by turning them on. Ask about the insulation. If it is very efficient, the heating and cooling systems will be more efficient.

Your comfort and the cost of it are important to you. Make sure you know as much as you can about both factors. Most cooling systems, for example, run on electricity. If air conditioning is not included in your rent, you may need to consider how much that will add to your electric bill.

***Living Space and Storage*** When you visit places you are considering, you need to decide if the number of rooms is adequate for your needs, and if their arrangement is practical. Do you have to walk through the bathroom to get to another room? Is there a hallway or another room between the living and sleeping area? Try to imagine yourself living there, and then ask yourself if the arrangement of rooms will work for you and those who will be living with you.

You are going to need adequate storage space wherever you live. As you visit places, you may want to check closets, basements, garages, and attics for their storage space. If you are renting, there may be a storage area that you can use. You should be sure you can lock or secure this area if it exists. Unexpected outside storage of any of your appliances or your belongings will increase your monthly expenses considerably.

How can cleaning procedures make your appliances more efficient?

# Welcome Home?

 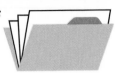

"Hi, Mom, I'm home!" Ellie's mother did not receive this news quite the way Ellie had imagined she would. Aren't your parents always supposed to be glad to see you? Even when you've just finished college, not yet landed a "good" job, and can't afford to live anywhere else?

More and more young adults are finding themselves in Ellie's position, and many parents are not sure how to welcome their grown-up children back to the nest. At first, Ellie's father was thrilled to "have his little girl back home," but Ellie had become quite independent at college. She wasn't used to being told when, how, and what to do. She didn't expect to go back to introducing her dates to her father before going out. Ellie's mother, too, had grown used to *her* independence: independence from doing her daughter's laundry, fixing her meals, and time-sharing the TV and car with Ellie and her friends. She had even turned Ellie's bedroom into a studio for her sculpting. How do you think this new/old living arrangement is going to work out?

It's human nature to want "the best of both worlds," but in real life there are always trade-offs.

"It's our house. We make the rules!" say Ellie's parents.

"I'm over twenty-one!" counters Ellie, right before asking, "What's for dinner?"

"Who's going to pay for the gasoline you use, for the snacks for your friends, and for your dry cleaning?" asks Ellie's father.

"You can't expect me to pay rent here!" protests Ellie.

In a trade-off, you give up something to gain something: some independence for some financial help; or some time and effort for some space; or some extra consideration for some companionship or for some privacy. How would you help Ellie and her parents manage realistic trade-offs that are fair to all?

**Location and Outdoor Space** Housing costs vary widely from one section of the country to another. Housing in suburbs close to a major city often is more expensive than housing in rural areas. Where you will be working and the amount of commuting you can afford to do (in terms of both time and cost) will limit your choice of location. Probably you will want to locate in the safest, most attractive, and most convenient housing you can afford. When you examine the condition of the outdoor space, be sure it is well maintained and that there is an area you can use for recreation and socializing. If you are looking at an apartment, you may want to find out if there is a specific parking space available. You may want to ask what your responsibilities, if any, are in the care of any outdoor space.

If you are buying a cooperative or renting, find out about use of outdoor space.

## For Review

1. How can you find out what housing is available in your area?
2. Explain how nonmoney resources apply to housing.
3. What should you know about heating and cooling systems in housing?

# Choosing Appliances, Home Electronics, and Safety Equipment

If you have chosen a furnished apartment, you may not need to buy any appliances. Let's assume, however, that your housing is unfurnished. Before you even begin to buy appliances, furnishings, and other equipment, you probably will want to consider carefully exactly what you need. Once again, you will want to decide how much you have to spend. You may find comparison shopping helpful. If you do not have time to go from store to store, you can use the telephone to compare prices at reputable stores. Sales may save you money, and guarantees will protect your purchases. Some stores offer free delivery and other services that you may want to take advantage of.

Once you know the appliances, furnishings, and other equipment you need right away, you may want to consider options other than purchasing. One option is *buying used merchandise*. This involves some risk, but if you are careful, you can save money and often get excellent values. Another option is *renting*. Sometimes, if you rent a major appliance, you can apply the rent you pay on it to its purchase price if you decide to buy it. Finally, you may want to consider *bartering*. Bartering involves

Do research before expensive purchases.

trading goods or services of equal value, rather than exchanging money for goods. For example, you might consider doing laundry for your roommate in exchange for the use of a washer and dryer. All of these options can help you keep expenses down and acquire the things you need and want sooner.

Before you shop, you will want to measure the spaces you have to fill. Whether you buy, rent, or barter, you will want your furnishings to fit those spaces.

## Appliances

Appliances usually are designed for specific uses and operated by gas or electricity. Household appliances often fall into two categories—large appliances and small appliances. Large appliances include ranges, refrigerators, and washing machines. Small appliances include fans, food processors, toasters, ovens, and slow cookers.

Often, the more features an appliance has, the more expensive it will be and the more things there are to need repair. You may need to decide whether the usefulness or convenience of extras outweighs the added cost.

Many consumer magazines give the performance records of various brand-name appliances. These models may be a little more expensive, but if they last longer and need fewer repairs, they may be worth the expense. Energy-saving features, when they are available, can save you quite a lot of money over the entire time you own the appliance.

**Refrigerators** Most experts recommend eight cubic feet of refrigerator space and two cubic feet of freezer space for two people. They suggest adding one more cubic foot of space for each additional person. You may find a freezer on top is more energy efficient than side-by-side models. You may want to ask the salesperson about self-defrosting models.

**Ranges** Ranges come in many styles and have varied features. They may be run by either gas or electricity. If gas is available where you live, you may want to consider a gas range. Many experts believe gas cooking is more efficient and economical. Ovens in ranges may be conventional, convection, or microwave. The microwave oven is the most energy efficient, especially when small quantities of food are cooked. You may want to check the range for ease of cleaning. Self-cleaning models can save you time and energy.

**Freezers** Freezers come in chest or upright models. If you shop in large quantities, have many people to feed, or preserve a lot of garden food, a freezer may be economical.

**Washing Machines** There are two basic styles of washing machines—top-loading and front-loading. Top-loading machines are usually larger than the front-loading ones and have an agitator in the center of the tub. If you are buying your machine for an apartment, you will want to be sure you have the plumbing hook-up before buying. Smaller, compact models may be better for apartments. Portable machines can be rolled up to the sink, and a hose hooked up during use. A machine with settings for different water levels will help you to conserve water.

**Automatic Dryers** Dryers may be run by gas or electricity. Gas dryers are usually more expensive, but they are more efficient to operate if you have gas available. Many sizes are available for apartments with limited space. A dryer that turns itself off automatically when the clothes are dry, rather than having a timed cycle, will be an energy saver.

**Room Air Conditioners** If you are putting yours into an existing window, you will want to measure carefully. You may want to check the EER (the Energy Efficiency Rating). An EER of 7.5 or higher is considered energy efficient. To avoid buying a more expensive model than you need, you should calculate the number of square feet you need to cool.

**Dishwashers** You probably will discover cleaning action is better with three washing arms than with two, and with many holes in the washing arms. Portable models are available. You may want to look for an energy saving option that allows you to air dry dishes. Solid food waste disposers are built into some machines, which can save you the water you would use in rinsing dishes before putting them in the dishwasher.

**Disposers** Garbage disposers may be continuous-feed (run by a wall switch) or batch-feed (a switch inside the cover). The batch-feed model is safer if there are children in the home. Most manufacturers do not recommend disposers if you have a small septic system.

Measure the space available for appliances before buying any.

**Small Appliances** You may want to consider buying several small household appliances, such as a toaster, toaster oven, coffee maker, electric fry pan, slow cooker, electric can opener, blender, or food processor.

Most of these appliances run on the ordinary household circuit, are convenient to use, and use less energy than the larger appliances. A toaster oven and electric fry pan can offer the cooking capabilities of a large, expensive range. As you should for all your purchases, do a lot of comparison shopping, check consumer publications, and ask sales persons to assist you before you make your final decision.

Some small appliances you may have purchased already include hairdryers and curling irons and brushes. When you shop for these items, ask for information from sales persons and compare features. If you want different temperature settings, for example, this feature will probably add to the total cost. You may also want to compare the warranties on these small appliances before you decide which one to buy.

When you are ready to buy luxury items such as televisions, do comparison shopping for price and quality.

## Home Electronics

Home electronic equipment includes such items as telephones, television sets, radios, video recorders, sound equipment, and home computers. Other than the telephone, these are usually considered luxury items. You do not need them, although you may want them. Because your money resources usually are limited, you may want to draw up a list of priorities. You may decide to postpone buying a television set, but you probably need to buy a refrigerator. It helps to plan your purchases in order of importance.

You may rent a phone from a phone company or buy one. Renting involves a monthly fee, but if you rent, the phone company takes care of needed repairs. If you buy, you will save the monthly fee, but you must take care of repairs. Before buying, you may find it helpful to find out if your service is tone or pulse, then you can look for the type of phone that matches your service.

## Home Safety Equipment

Some basic home safety equipment is vital for either renters or homeowners. New homes must have smoke detectors before they are sold, and landlords are required by law to provide these also. You should check to see if they have been installed and are in good working order in your housing. You may also want to buy a small fire extinguisher for your kitchen. If you do, read the instructions and know how to operate it before you need it for any emergency.

## Choosing Home Furnishings

Home furnishings include all the basic furniture, accessories, and lighting that you place in your living space. These items should be functional; they should fill your needs. At the same time, they should be things you enjoy. For the most part, your personal taste is reflected in your choice of home furnishings.

You may want to begin by making a list of the furnishings you think you want. As your plan takes shape, you may find you can eliminate some pieces of furniture you thought you needed. Some people think it is a good idea to get used to your housing before making any purchases. The amount of sunlight a room receives may make you decide to use a room as a den rather than a bedroom, for example. Your choice of furnishings may change according to the measurements of the room.

Another important factor to consider is the length of time you plan to stay in the housing. If it will be a short time, even a year, you probably will not want to spend a lot of money on furnishings.

Since color will figure into your furnishing choices, you may want to find out if you are allowed to paint the walls of rental housing and make other changes. For your own protection, you should check your rental agreement closely before changing anything or buying furnishings for your place.

You may want to consider used furnishings or renting or bartering for furnishings, as you did when you were acquiring appliances. Once again, nonmoney resources (creativity and talent) may allow you to make some of your own furnishings. Sometimes curtains, bedcovers, and wall hangings can be made, with little sewing skill, from sheets or large pieces of material. Woodworking can be a valuable resource, but it is not absolutely necessary. With some fabric and stuffing or polystyrene

Some inexpensive folding chairs can also be used as beds.

beads, you can make a large floor cushion that can double as a chair. You can make a lamp from a large bottle and a lamp-making kit. A desk can be made from a hollow core door and two filing cabinets or some cinder blocks stacked on top of each other. Fabric stretched on simple wooden frames that have been hinged together can become a room divider. Shelves can be created from cinder blocks and planks. "Do-it-yourself" books from your library may be helpful. If you have the time, are willing to make the effort, and have some imagination, you can use inexpensive things to meet your furnishing needs and wants.

You may find garage sales, thrift shops, and auctions are not only fun but also provide you with inexpensive furnishings. If you take the time to sort out quality merchandise, you can find some great bargains.

## Furniture

Furniture comes in many styles, sizes, and materials. Prices range from very expensive to moderately expensive to quite inexpensive. The quality also varies. The furniture you choose depends on your needs, the purpose you want the furniture to serve, and your resources. Basic furniture items include beds, tables, chairs, sofas or couches, bookcases, and desks.

Wood, metal, fabric, plastic, and various combinations of these materials are used to make furniture. An upholstered chair, for example, usually has a wood frame, metal springs, foam and other types of padding, and fabric covering. A plastic chair may have a fabric-covered seat. A kitchen or dining room table may be made of wood but still have a plastic-coated top. Chairs may have wooden legs or metal frames.

Furniture styles range from country to traditional to contemporary. Some styles are massive and heavy. Others are more delicate and ornate. Still others are quite simple. The style you choose will depend on your personal preference and how you wish to use the item.

Good quality new furniture is often expensive, so many people repair, refinish, or reupholster the furniture they have or buy used furniture to fix up. This is one way to create a new look or to have quality furniture without spending as much money.

**Checking the Quality** Even if you are buying inexpensive furniture, you will want the best quality you can get for your money. Two major factors determine the quality of furniture: the materials used to make it, and the way the furniture is made. Refer to the checklist given below for things you should look for when buying any type of furniture.

## FURNITURE SHOPPING CHECKLIST

Before buying, make sure:

1. there are no scratches, chips, or broken parts.
2. the joints, legs, and all connecting pieces are sturdy and solid.
3. all doors and drawers open and close smoothly.
4. the materials used (wood, metal, plastic or other) are strong enough to support weight necessary for use.
5. all edges are smooth, not sharp or rough.
6. surfaces are not warped or uneven.
7. fabrics can be cleaned. Check for protective coating; coverings that can be removed to wash or dry clean are better to buy.
8. that the furniture you will be sitting or lying on is comfortable. Try It!

Assembling simple shelving or bookcases does not require many carpentry skills.

**Types of Furniture** Preassembled furniture is furniture that has been put together in the store. Sometimes, new furniture is available in kits or "knock down" form for you to assemble with basic tools. If you are interested in this type of furniture, you may want to check the model in the store for quality before buying. Some of this furniture is inexpensive and functional. Unfinished furniture is available in kits or already assembled. If you paint or stain it yourself, you can save money. Multipurpose furniture is furniture that can be used for more than one function, for example, a sofa bed. If you are in a one-room apartment you might want this type of furniture. Some chairs can be converted to single mattresses by unfolding them. These types of furniture are practical purchases for small living spaces.

## Wall, Floor, Ceiling, and Window Coverings

A wide variety of materials can be used as wall, floor, ceiling, and window coverings. Each material has its own characteristics, advantages, and disadvantages. Paint, for example, may be oil-based or latex, washable or not. You should study each situation to see what you need. Before purchasing anything, you may find it helpful to visit a reputable store and talk to a salesperson, keeping in mind your needs and financial resources.

## Accessories

Accent lamps, pillows, magazine racks, pictures, and other wall decorations all fall into the category of accessories. They can be inexpensive ways to create a new or different look and to add interest to a room.

Some accessories are strictly decorative, such as pictures and wall hangings. Many accessories, however, are functional as well as decorative. Magazine racks, for example, serve a purpose and add a decorative touch. Pillows may be decorative, but they can serve a purpose as well.

Accessories vary widely in price. Many people find they can be creative and spend more time and effort than money in personalizing their living space with accessories. Magazines and books are available to help anyone who wants to make their own accessories. Craft and fabric stores, evening education classes, and classes offered by your local recreation department are sources of learning how to make accessories.

## Lighting

There are three types of lighting for a living space. Each serves a definite purpose. General lighting provides enough light to allow you to walk into a room or down a hallway without difficulty. It helps to prevent glare when you are watching television or using task lighting. Task lighting gives adequate light to the work or activity you are doing, such as reading, cooking, typing, or building something in a workshop. Accent lighting is for accenting special things in a living space, such as pictures, plants, or special architectural details.

**General Lighting**  General lighting does not have to be bright. A low-watt bulb is adequate and helps to save on electricity costs. Often a bulb in an overhead light fixture will provide enough general lighting.

**Task Lighting**  Task lighting needs to be brighter so that you can see what you are doing without straining your eyes. Some lighting manufacturers suggest that task lighting should be about three times brighter than softly lighted adjacent areas. This may mean a 200- or 250-watt incandescent bulb or a 40-watt fluorescent tube. Of course, different types of bulbs and lampshades may produce equivalent amounts of light without requiring such high wattage bulbs. You should be sure the lighting fixtures you have will accommodate a high-watt bulb before you put one in. Many lamps only will take a maximum of 60- or 100- or 150-watt bulbs.

**Accent Lighting**  Accent lighting does not need to be extremely bright. There are special picture lights for paintings or other framed artwork. Track lighting or other fixtures that can be directed down or up onto objects often work well for accent lighting.

## Household Textiles

Household textiles are items made from fibers, such as bedspreads, blankets, sheets and pillowcases, curtains or draperies, tablecloths, dishtowels and dishcloths, and towels and washcloths. There is a wide variety of prices and qualities available.

Usually a fabric that is tightly woven or knit is more durable than one that is loosely woven or knit. Tightly twisted strands of fibers (called yarns) also contribute to durability. On looped surfaces, such as terry cloth towels and washcloths, the closer the loops, the more durable the item.

Many household textiles have special finishes to make them easy to care for. Most sheets, for example, now have permanent-press finishes. Tablecloths or place mats may have soil- and stain-resistant finishes to prevent staining. Items with special finishes may cost more, but they may be worth it because of their ease of care.

## For Review

1. What are the two primary factors that determine the quality of furniture? Name five of the things you should check before buying furniture.

2. What are accessories? How can they be useful as well as decorative? Give one example of a useful accessory.

3. Which of the three types of lighting requires the brightest light? Why?

## Management Application: Making a Housing Choice

Imagine yourself in the situation described below. As you read, think about how the steps of the management process might apply to this situation. Then answer the questions that follow.

### Situation

Jeremy was ready to find a place of his own. After finishing college, he had lived in his parents' home for a year. Now, he had a good job as an accountant and was making enough money to live on his own. He wanted to buy a small house or condominium, but he knew it would be a few years before he could afford a down payment. Although he could save more by continuing to live at home, he valued his independence and privacy more. He figured out the maximum amount he could spend on rent and began to look for an apartment on weekends. Most of them made his parents' home look like a palace. Those that he could afford to live in alone were pretty shabby and cramped. He liked one place, but it was $100 per month more than he wanted to spend. If he lived there, he wouldn't be able to save toward buying housing. Having no extra money would limit his social life too. He wanted to be able to afford to go out with his friends a few times a week at least.

The other alternative was a great three-bedroom apartment with a swimming pool and tennis courts. Of course, the drawback was he would be sharing the place with two roommates. It was furnished and close to his job. In fact, it was the least expensive option. He remembered how he had disliked dorm life—the noise, no privacy. Well, maybe if the three of them set definite rules. . . . He asked the realtor to set up an interview but also told her he was still interested in the small single apartment he had seen. He probably should decide soon. Rental costs were getting higher all the time, and both of these places could be gone if he didn't decide quickly. How could he decide?

### Questions

1. How will Jeremy's values influence the decision that he makes?
2. What trade-offs will Jeremy make if he chooses to live with others?
3. What is Jeremy's long-term goal? How is this affecting his choice of housing now?
4. What should Jeremy find out before making a final decision?
5. Which steps of the management process apply to this situation?

# *15* *Chapter Review*

## *Summary*

Many types of housing are available with considerable variety in size, construction, and style. There are always advantages and disadvantages to buying or renting housing.

Living arrangements depend on a person's age, family situation, and finances. A housing plan and the ability to recognize building problems help you to evaluate housing. Good shopping procedures when choosing appliances and furnishing a home will allow you to get the most for your money.

## *Vocabulary*

Complete each of the following sentences with one of the vocabulary words below.

condominium

cooperative

lease or rental agreement

security deposit

down payment

mortgage loan

fixed-rate mortgages

variable-rate mortgages

closing costs

1. A _____ is a document that sets forth the rental period, rental fee, and terms the renter must follow.

2. _____ is money lent to a buyer to purchase housing other than a mobile home.

3. A _____ is a loan for housing that may undergo change in the interest rate over the life of the loan.

4. A _____ is a payment, which may be used to cover the costs of repairing any damage done to the apartment by the renter, that the manager of an apartment holds until the renter leaves.

5. A _____ is a living space that is bought, rather than rented, in a multi-unit building or group of buildings.

6. A _____ is a loan for housing that has the same interest rate for as long as the period of the mortgage.

7. A _____ is the amount of money the prospective buyer of a house offers toward the purchase of the house.

8. A _____ is a living space that is under group ownership in a multi-unit building or group of buildings.

9. _____ are the expenses that must be paid in cash when the buyer takes possession of the living space at the time of closing.

## *Questions*

1. Why would the manager of an apartment ask for a security deposit? Under what circumstances might you lose your deposit?

2. Explain the difference between a condominium and a cooperative.

3. What are some factors that affect a person's living arrangements?

4. Which two general guidelines should you use to help you determine how much to spend for housing?

5. What should you know about plumbing when you are buying or renting? What should you know about living space and storage? Why are these things important?

6. Name some alternatives to buying an expensive new appliance. What are the advantages and disadvantages of each?

7. What factors should you consider when you are deciding what furniture you need for your living space?

8. What should you check when you are shopping for furniture?

9. What kinds of wall coverings are available? What factors should you consider before making a choice?

## Skill Activities

1. **Decision Making.** What are the housing costs in your area for buying and renting? The first place to check is the newspaper, and the Sunday newspaper is best. Look over the real estate section. Jot down the costs of buying a single family home, a condominium, and a cooperative in your area. Try to choose housing with the same number of bedrooms. Include all important information.

Then review the cost of renting a unit of comparable size. Include all important information. Using the information you have gathered, decide which would be most practical for you if you had an annual salary of $19,000 and no dependents.

2. **Math.** Select one of the units that were for sale in Skill Activity 1. Investigate the cost of a mortgage. Check two banks. Try to find out what the closing costs would be. Calculate the down payment at 5%, 10%, 15%, and 20%.

After you have figured the down payment, calculate how much interest you would be paying over the entire period of the mortgage if your mortgage extended over 20 years.

3. **Decision Making.** Go to a furniture store and compare the cost and quality of two items of furniture, for example, two couches, two beds, two sleeper sofas, or two dining room tables. Make sure that one of the items of furniture is significantly more expensive than the other. Use the checklist on page 346 of this chapter. What is the difference in quality? What is the difference in style? Which would you choose? Why?

# *16 Organizing Your Living Space*

## *As you read, think about:*

- ☐ how to arrange rooms and furnishings to make your housing as functional and attractive as it can be.
- ☐ how to set up storage, work, and activity centers in your housing.
- ☐ how to develop the best methods for home cleaning, maintenance, and repairs.
- ☐ what you can do to conserve energy and control housing costs.
- ☐ how to apply the management process to personal decisions about organizing your living space.

# Vocabulary

floor plan
traffic pattern
center
weatherization
central heating system
direct, or space, heat
cost-effectiveness
payback period
insulation
energy audit

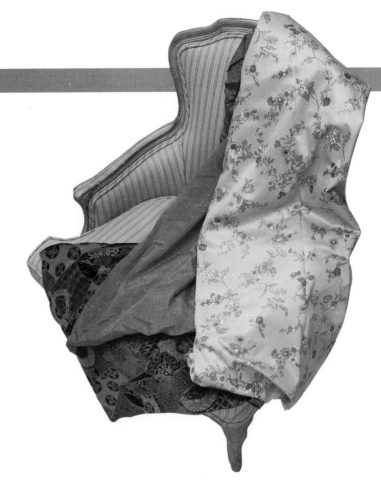

Have you ever rearranged all of the furniture in your room to give your living space a new look? Have you changed the color scheme? Perhaps you have put up inexpensive shelving or taken out a piece of furniture you do not really use to make your room more functional and less cluttered. Perhaps you have a plan for keeping your own room clean. Perhaps you have repaired broken possessions yourself. Probably you already know that you should shut off lights and other electrical devices before you leave your room.

All these things will help you to realize how much planning goes into arranging, decorating, and maintaining an entire home.

## Planning and Decorating

There are many things you should consider when you are deciding how to use your living space. These things include deciding which rooms will be shared by the entire family, how the furnishings will be arranged in each room, and how you can plan for your storage needs. Before you make any final decisions, you may find it helpful to work out a plan.

## Making a Floor Plan

Whatever your living space is, you should decide first how you will use each room. If you have an efficiency apartment, or one-room apartment, you will want to consider the best possible arrangement for your furniture. Once you have decided on the best possible use for your room or rooms, you can begin to draw up floor plans. A **floor plan** is a sketch of a room and its furniture drawn to scale. To make an accurate floor plan, you may find it helpful to use graph paper when you sketch the room that you want to arrange.

# MAKING A FLOOR PLAN

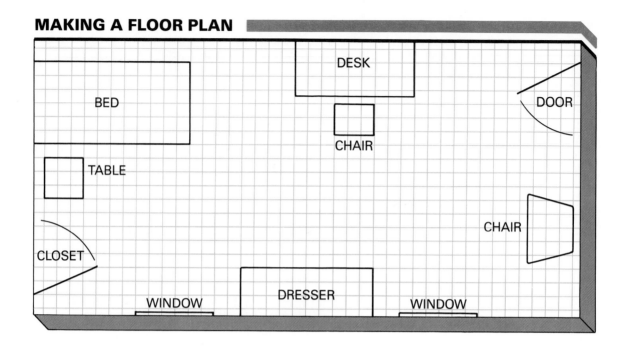

**Measure the Room.** As you begin your floor plan, measure the room and mark off these measurements on an equal scale on the graph paper. Suppose, for example, the room is 10 by 12 feet. You could mark the width on your paper as 10 inches and the length as 12 inches. You will want to decide how many squares on the graph paper will be equal to one foot.

**Indicate Room Features to Scale.** After you have marked off the room on your paper, show windows, doors, fireplaces, and anything in the room that would affect the placement of furniture. Although you can sketch your furniture to scale directly on the plan, you may prefer to draw furniture to scale on a separate piece of graph paper. You can then cut it out and move it around on your floor plan to experiment with the best placement.

**Consider All Activities and Traffic Patterns.** You will want your arrangement of furnishings to be realistic and based on all the activities that may take place in the room. For example, a family room may be used for watching television, studying, playing games, writing letters, working on hobbies, or just sitting and talking. If you can, list all the activities you would like to be able to do in a room; it will help you to arrange your furniture. A folding, multipurpose table, for example, may be better for some rooms than a table that takes up a lot of space and cannot be stored easily.

Traffic patterns in each room also should be considered as you plan your arrangements. **Traffic patterns** are the paths people usually take to get from one room to another. For example, one traffic pattern in your bedroom may be from your bedroom door to the closet. If you have built-in furniture or bookcases, another path may be from your bedroom door to these locations.

It is important to sketch traffic patterns lightly on your plan as you arrange or rearrange furniture. Keeping furniture out of traffic paths or arranging furniture to route traffic paths around work or activity areas can make a room or area more functional.

You may want to keep traffic paths from going through the middle of a special purpose area. To do this, you can position furniture to force a minor change in a traffic path. In an area used for watching television, you may want to arrange things so that people have to walk around the seating area and television set, rather than between the seating area and the television set.

It is easier to get into and out of rooms if you place large pieces of furniture away from doorways. As you arrange your furniture, remember to allow enough room to open doors and drawers and to move chairs away from desks or tables. Of course, you do not want your furniture to block your sources of heat or light. If you have planned or need to use electricity in certain areas (lighting for studying or reading, or power for stereos or hairdryers, for example), you will want to be sure you have electrical outlets near these areas. Try as many arrangements as you can think of and your space will allow, always keeping in mind the best possible way to use the space as you have planned.

## Arranging Furniture for Special Needs

There may be special family situations that affect your furniture arrangement. Maximum safety, comfort, and convenience are your goals.

**Children**  Babies or young children in a household mean special furniture arrangements. When children are just learning to walk, you will want to put away or avoid furnishings that tip over easily or have sharp edges. As you will discover, a commonsense approach to furniture placement is your best guide when young children are involved.

**Handicapped Family Members**  People with limited mobility, for example, may be using wheelchairs, crutches, walkers, or other equipment. You will want your furniture placement to allow them to move safely through the living space. There are many accommodations you can make when arranging furniture that will be helpful to any handicapped family member.

## Arranging Furniture for Appearance

Once all the functional reasons for arranging furniture have been considered, you probably will begin to think about the area's appearance. Which arrangement will be most attractive and inviting? The use of color, texture, patterns, space, shape, and line all figure into the total look of a room.

Using scale model furniture can help you to decide on the best floor plan.

**Colors** Colors related to the sun and fire—yellows, reds, and oranges—can give a room or area a feeling of warmth and create a feeling of liveliness and activity. Colors related to water and the earth—blues and greens—can give a room or area a feeling of coolness or create a feeling of calmness.

**Patterns** Stripes, plaids, checks, and geometric patterns or floral prints can add interest to a room. Careful combinations of a variety of patterns can result in an attractive room without creating a feeling of clutter or confusion.

**Textures** Smooth, shiny surfaces in certain colors can give a feeling of coolness. In other colors, these textures result in a feeling of drama or simplicity. Highly textured surfaces, like carpeting or burlap, can create a feeling of

How can furniture arrangement and use of color create a friendly atmosphere?

warmth and coziness. Open textures, such as loose-weave curtains or mesh chairs, can give a feeling of airiness or coolness. Combining textures and colors results in different feelings and appearances.

**Special Decorating Techniques** It is possible to make a room appear wider or narrower or longer just by the way the furniture is arranged. If you want to create a feeling of spaciousness, you can use reflective surfaces, such as mirrors. Clear glass or acrylic furnishings also add to a feeling of openness and help a room or area to appear less crowded.

**Balance** A room or area is more inviting and pleasing to the eye if there is a feeling of balance in the way furniture is arranged. There are different ways to achieve this.

One way is to scatter large pieces of furniture throughout a room or area. Putting all the large pieces in one part of a room can make it seem visually heavy in one area or another. Large pieces of furniture mixed with smaller pieces throughout a room create a more balanced feeling. Another way to create a feeling of balance is to keep large pieces of furniture away from doorways. This draws your attention into the room where the larger pieces have less visual weight.

**Accessories** Accessories can add to the attractiveness of a room or area when their arrangement is visually pleasing. A large hanging plant, a tall lamp, or a tall plant in the corner of a room can help to make the end of the room seem wider. Placed between the center of a wall and the corner, these accessories can make a wall appear shorter or narrower.

You may want to place small tables or other small pieces of furniture at angles to other pieces of furniture or on the diagonal in a corner to add interest to the furniture groupings or to the general appearance of the room.

Some planning before you hang pictures or other items on the wall can help these accessories add to the attractiveness of your room or area. If you are going to group several pictures or items together, you may find it helpful to experiment with their arrangement on a large flat surface before hanging them. Once again, you will want to create a feeling of balance among the items. Sometimes, scattering large pictures through a grouping rather than keeping them in one area will do this. You may want to balance dark colors with light colors or to create a rectangle or square or other shape with your grouping.

Interior design books can offer more information on using color, texture, and patterns in decorating. By using these and other elements of design creatively, you can add to the appearance of a room or area.

## Planning for Storage

People store several types of things. How frequently these items are used affects the kind of storage they will need. As you plan storage, you may want to think about how often you use different items or equipment.

**Daily or Frequent Use** Some things to be stored are used frequently. This may mean every few days, daily, or even several times a day. Grooming items, such as combs, brushes, and toothbrushes, kitchen cleanup items, such as dishpans, detergents, and dishcloths, and some clothing items, such as sleepwear, jackets, and shoes, fall into this category. In many families, certain foods and equipment are used every day. During the school year, reference books, study supplies, and a typewriter or home computer may be used frequently. A radio or stereo and records (or tape deck and tapes) may be used every day. Items that are used frequently need to be stored conveniently to make them easy to take out and put away.

---

### GUIDELINES FOR STORAGE

1. Store frequently used items at the place where you use them most often.

2. Store items that are used often in a place where you can see, reach, grasp, and replace them.

3. Store heavy items that are used often near the height of the elbow.

4. Use all three dimensions of storage space.

5. After using every item, store it back in its place right away.

---

**Infrequent Use** Some items to be stored may be used only a few times a month or a few times a year or perhaps even just once a year. Movie cameras, canning supplies and equipment, popcorn poppers and electric frypans may fall in this category. Certain hobby supplies and equipment also fall in this category.

Items that are used less frequently do not need to be as conveniently located as those that are used more frequently. If you store these items in less accessible spots, you will have the easy-to-get-at places available for frequently used items.

**Seasonal Storage** There are many things that are used in only one or two seasons. Seasonal decorations, such as those used during holidays or in the spring or fall, are good examples of these items. Canning equipment and gardening supplies are other examples. In parts of the country where the seasons change greatly, there are more seasonal items, such as winter clothes, summer clothes, ski equipment, patio furniture, and lawn mowers.

The storage area for things that are out of season can be in out-of-the-way places, such as an attic, a storage shed, a garage, a top shelf, or the back of a closet. When these items are in season, you probably will want to have a space for them that takes into account their frequency of use. Sometimes these items can trade places with items that need to be put away for a season or two.

## For Review

1. What is a floor plan? Why would you make one?
2. Explain how color can affect the feeling of a room. Give one example of how a room can achieve balance through furniture arrangement.
3. How does the frequency of use affect an item's storage?

Cooking is easier when a work center is organized. Here, spices are labeled and put on a convenient wall rack.

## Setting Up Work and Activity Centers

Space that is designed for a specific task or recreational activity is called a **center.** A center for tasks such as cooking, studying, paying bills, or doing laundry often is called a **work center.** Centers for hobbies or leisure activities often are called **activity centers.** Sometimes these two terms are used interchangeably because their components and functions are the same.

When you are setting up either a work or activity center in your living space, you want the design or plan to be functional. The space must be easy to work in, with a place for things to be conveniently arranged and stored. To plan a work or activity center successfully, you need to know the tasks or activities you will be doing there, the equipment and supplies you need for the activities, the amount of space you need, and the preferred height of the work surface you will be using. You may find it helpful to work your plan out on graph paper.

### The Study Center

A study center needs to include a work surface for writing, adequate lighting, any reference books you use frequently, and your supplies, for example, paper, pens, and rulers. If you use a typewriter for papers, the typewriter and supplies used with it need to be included in the study area. A home computer and related supplies and equipment also may be included.

If you have a specific desk or table for your center, you may want to put it where it is most convenient for you. If you want a quiet area, you may want to put the desk in your room or in a place away from family or group activities. Locate the books, equipment, and supplies you use within easy reach of your work surface.

The work surface height for writing should be a height that is comfortable for you—usually below elbow height. Most desks are about 26 1/2 to 28 inches (67.3 to 71.12 cm) high. Most tables are about 30 inches (76.2 cm) high. If the work surface is too low for you,

perhaps you can build a platform to put your writing on. If the work surface is too high, you may want an adjustable chair. Once you have found the chair's proper height in relation to the work surface, you can find or build something to rest your feet on.

Using your typewriter or computer keyboard on a surface as high as a table or desk for long periods of time can be tiring because your arms are not held comfortably. You may want to arrange for a slightly lower surface.

Think about where you study now. Is it the best place to do this? You do not have to spend a lot of money creating a study center. You do need to spend time planning how to organize it. If you do, you may find you are studying more efficiently than you did before.

Work surface height is important for safety and efficiency. Does this look like a well organized work center?

## The Workshop

A basement or garage workshop is common in many homes. It may have hand tools and power tools for woodworking, for building, or for making repairs. It may have the repair equipment needed for working on automobiles, trucks, motorcycles, or small engines like those found in lawn mowers, chain saws, snow blowers, and other small equipment.

If work is going to be done on a workbench, the work surface needs to be at a comfortable height. Usually, you will be most comfortable if the top of the item you are working on is about elbow height or a little lower. If you work on items of various sizes or heights, you can build several workbenches to meet your needs, or you can adjust the height of the workbench you have with different platforms to put your work on or to stand on.

When you work on car engines or do other repairs, you often have to bend at the waist, which can cause muscle strain and fatigue.

This is a music and recreation center.

Sometimes, work under a car requires lying on your back and working with your hands above your body. A *creeper,* a board with wheels underneath, may help. Lying in a creeper reduces the distance of your reach and increases the ease of moving around under the car.

You will want to store the equipment and supplies you use in your workshop in the area where you work. This way they are available and you can avoid extra walking back and forth to get what you need.

Adequate lighting is important. If the work area is large and many activities take place there, you may want general overhead lighting as well as task lighting.

## The Recreation or Entertainment Center

In many homes, there are family rooms or recreation areas set aside for entertainment or recreation. In other homes, the living room may serve this purpose. The recreation or entertainment center may have one or more of the following things: a stereo and/or tape deck; piano and/or other musical instruments; television; video games; video equipment; seating space; bookcases; pool table; table-tennis table; exercise equipment; weight-lifting equipment; space for dancing, exercising, or weight lifting; or a card table or game table with cards and other games. Of course, many homes have only a few of these items. They may be located in one area or in several different rooms. Depending on how the equipment is used and where it can be located, there may be one recreation or entertainment center or several.

Electronic equipment, such as a stereo or tape deck, needs to be located where it is easy to use, yet out of the way of other activities. If there is going to be dancing or some other form of activity in the area, the equipment needs to be set up so that it will not be jarred or affected by the activity. A storage area for records or tapes and accessories will be convenient for everyone.

Television sets and related video equipment also need to be located where they are not easily bumped or jarred. The recommended distance for viewing depends on the size of the screen. Larger screens require more distance between the viewers and the television. Unless the screen is small, you will want to have viewers seated at least six feet away to prevent eyestrain.

Musical instruments need two kinds of space: space for storage and space for using the instruments. Storage space for music and accessories should be a part of these centers.

A center for cards and board games usually includes the playing surface (usually a table), chairs, cards and games, paper, and pencils. If the playing surface and chairs can be folded up and put away, the cards or games can be stored with them. If the table is permanently set up, cards and games can be stored conveniently nearby.

For any activity, and particularly for reading, you need adequate lighting. Ideally, the light should be arranged to light up the focus of the activity, as well as some of the surrounding area. Visibility is better when people and objects do not cast shadows on the activity.

### Safety Tip: Flammable Fluids and Fumes

■ Keep storage areas free of oily rags. Store any flammable fluids, such as gasoline, in fire-safe containers. Never light a match or turn on a light if you smell gas fumes. Open the windows and leave the house. Use a neighbor's phone to contact the fire department.

***Look Around.*** There are many other work and activity centers in homes. The study, workshop, and recreation centers are just a few examples to show you the types of things you must plan for in a center.

See if the centers you have in your own home are used efficiently. By observing the activities and spaces in your home, you may see that some spaces are being wasted. Sometimes you can improve the way a center functions or give it better lighting just by moving your furnishings.

### For Review

1. What facts must you know before setting up a work or activity center?
2. Draw up a list of the important parts of a study center.
3. Draw a floor plan for an entertainment or recreation center that includes a television, a stereo, and a game table. Sketch traffic patterns and plan your center and furnishings accordingly.

## Managing Cleaning, Maintenance, and Repairs

Routine cleaning, maintenance, and repairs are an important part of making the most of your housing resources. If you make frequent, routine checks of your home and repair and clean things as soon as possible, you may be able to avoid major problems. Some repairs can be done with a few basic tools and "do-it-yourself" information. Major repairs, such as fixing an oil burner or rewiring your living space, usually require expert help. If you are able to do some simple repairs and maintenance yourself, and you have time to do these tasks, you can cut down on your costs.

Many no-wax floors require specific cleaning products.

## Common Cleaning Tasks

There are some steps you can take to lessen the time you spend cleaning. Doormats and sweeping the porch or entry sidewalk areas frequently will help to keep dirt out of the house in the first place. Cleaning mud and spills as soon as possible will make weekly cleaning jobs easier. Easy-to-clean fabrics and furnishings will save you some time and effort, which you may want to use for other things.

When you do begin your housecleaning, your first task should be to identify the material you are cleaning. If you read the labels of all cleaning products and read all the steps for using them, you may find that you can finish your work more quickly.

**Hard-Surface Floors** Vacuuming hard-surface floors will remove dirt. If the dirt is gritty,

however, a soft, dry mop may prevent scratching. Washing should be done with a wet mop and whatever product is recommended for the specific surface. Most products require rinsing, but some do not.

Depending on your type of floor, waxing is an added protectant. There are different types of waxes for different types of floors, so you will need to follow the product directions on the container carefully.

**Carpets and Rugs** Frequent vacuuming helps to prevent embedded dirt, which can shorten the life of your rug or carpet. You should try to remove all stains as soon as possible with the correct product for the fiber or material. If you shampoo your own rugs once or twice a year, you will want to avoid leaving shampoo residue in the rug and allow plenty of time for drying.

**Walls** A sponge, dampened with a neutral cleaning solution, will wipe off fingerprints and soil from washable paint or wallpaper. Try squeezing the dirty sponge into an empty container to keep your cleaning solution clean.

**Windows** You can conserve your resources by making your own cleaning solution out of ammonia and water or dish detergent and water (about a capful of either to a gallon of warm water), or you can buy a window cleaner. You may want to use a squeegee and sponge. Squeegees allow you to apply the solution with the sponge, let it stay on for a few moments, and then remove the solution and the dirt. If you start across the top of the window and work your way down, you can avoid streaking.

**Furniture** Upholstered furniture needs to be vacuumed often. If you turn cushions regularly, you can prevent too much wear on one side. Sometimes, covers can be taken off and washed or dry cleaned. Although you will want to dust any wood surfaces, you may want to avoid overusing polishes containing wax or oils.

# Nothing's New Under the Sun

The earliest heat source enjoyed by people was, of course, the sun. Learning to burn wood for heat was a big step toward civilization. Today, some of the latest advances in home-heating technology and conservation of fossil fuels once again involve heat from the sun and from wood fires. These two new/old heating methods were given a boost by the oil shortages of the 1970s. They continue to be popular with consumers, and technologists are studying ways to improve their efficiency, economy, and availability.

**Solar Heat**  Solar energy was not a practical home-heating source until it could be collected, concentrated, and stored. Now, solar collectors, placed on rooftops, trap sunlight. A flat, black, metal plate is heated by sunlight. Glass covers and fiberglass insulation prevent heat loss. As liquid passes through tubes inside the plate, it absorbs the heat. The liquid then flows to a storage tank and exchanger where the heat is transferred to the home's central heating system. The cooled liquid is returned to the collectors by a pump, and the cycle starts over again. An auxiliary electric system provides backup heat in cloudy weather.

**Wood Stoves**  Much less complicated than solar heating is the use of a wood stove as a space heater. It warms a room directly by radiation and convection, but wood fires need tending and produce "dirt." Some modern iron stoves need to be fueled only once a day and have doors to control the draft. Connecting stoves to a chimney can improve their efficiency as can catalytic converters. In fact, catalytic converters create extra heat by burning the gases produced by the burning fuel that would otherwise create air pollution. Convertors also decrease the formation of creosote, a substance that can cause chimney fires.

**Bathroom**  It is usually a good idea to wear rubber gloves during bathroom cleaning. A toilet brush and a disinfectant cleaner will clean and sanitize the inside and outside of the toilet. To prevent scratching, use a clean cloth or sponge to do the sink and bathtub. You will want to use a product recommended for the type of surface you have.

## Weatherization

As a part of your yearly maintenance routine, you probably will want to check your home for protection against the weather. **Weatherization** is any work that helps to prevent the loss of heat from your living space. Routine weatherization tasks include putting

Adding fiberglass insulation to attic spaces decreases heat loss.

up storm doors and windows and checking insulation, weatherstripping, and caulking before the heating season starts.

Storm doors and windows (exterior and/or interior) are those doors and windows put up in addition to the doors and windows installed as a part of the building or living space. Storm doors and windows help to cut down on heat loss during cold weather. This saves heating costs and helps to cut down on drafts, thus making the living space more comfortable.

Weatherstripping and caulking are simple procedures that can be done by most homeowners. They are inexpensive to do, cut down on heat loss, and help to prevent drafts.

## Heating Systems

While there are many kinds of heating systems, they usually can be categorized as either central heating systems or direct (space) heating systems. A **central heating system** is one that provides heat to all parts of a living space. Most of these systems are oil-fired or gas-fired by a furnace or a boiler that generates the heat. **Direct,** or **space, heat** provides heat directly to a room or an area through a heating device located in the room or area. Electric baseboard heat, woodburning or coal-burning stoves, and various types of space heaters are examples of direct, or space, heat.

The maintenance and repair needs of different kinds of heating systems vary widely. Since your comfort, heating costs, and sometimes your health and safety are affected by your heating system, you will want to learn as much as you can about how yours works. If you heat with coal or wood, you may want to check for any cracks or warped surfaces. If you have a woodburning stove, you can learn how to clean the chimney to avoid the buildup of a flammable substance called *creosote*. If you have a central heating system, you will want to know where the master switch is so you can

Installing space heat safely is vital.

Because central air conditioning systems are quite complex, you may want to have major repairs done by an expert. If you read the owner's manual, you may be able to do some routine maintenance. Lubrication, checking fans and belts for wear, and cleaning blades and filters are some of the routine tasks that need to be done. Room air-conditioning units frequently need to have their bearings oiled, and their air filters cleaned and replaced. Fans also can be lubricated and cleaned quite easily.

## Plumbing

Clogged drains and leaky faucets are common plumbing problems for homeowners and renters. Other problems may include leaking or burst pipes, frozen water lines, and improperly working toilets.

The location of the main water supply for your living space and how to shut it off are probably the most important things to know about your plumbing system. Knowing this can prevent problems caused by leaking or burst pipes. Knowing where the shut-off valve is for each fixture or appliance, such as the sink or tub or dishwasher, also is important.

Drains can become clogged with food scraps, coffee grounds, hair, grease, and a variety of other substances. If you can prevent these things from going down the drain, you can avoid some problems. Sometimes you will need to use a special product for dissolving whatever is clogging the drain. Because these products often are strong chemicals, you should use them with great care. They should not be used when there is a garbage disposer. If do-it-yourself measures do not work, call in a plumber.

Frozen pipes can occur when the pipes are located in an area that is below freezing. If the problem is not taken care of immediately, the pipe can burst because water expands as it freezes. To care for the problem, you should

shut it off in case of emergency. Lack of heat, too much heat, or too little heat may be caused by a variety of factors. Usually, calling an expert is your wisest plan. Many oil and gas companies offer maintenance and repair contracts. For a yearly fee, they will check your system over and do any repairs required, depending on the terms of the contract.

## Cooling Systems

Central air conditioning, individual air-conditioning units, whole-house fans, attic fans, and window or freestanding fans are all types of cooling systems.

The maintenance and repair required depend on the type of cooling system you have.

turn off water to the frozen supply line and open all the faucets on the line. You are going to want to melt the ice in the pipes slowly, working from the part closest to the faucet back toward the water supply. Use rags wrung out in hot water and wrap them around the pipe. You may need to repeat the process frequently. Sometimes you can use a hairdryer to heat the pipes. Propane torches, butane lighters, and other open flames are extremely dangerous. They can cause a fire easily. You may want to consider insulating the pipes to help prevent similar problems in the future.

If the pipes burst, or there is a major leak, call a plumber. Sometimes small leaks can be repaired temporarily with a rubber-lined clamp or a special epoxy seal, but you will need a

You may be able to fix many plumbing problems if you have reliable information and the tools needed.

plumber as soon as possible to repair any major problems permanently.

Leaky faucets often waste water and can be annoying to listen to. Often a new washer will take care of the problem. Single-control, lever-style faucets often require special washers and tools for repair. Washers in standard faucets are easier to fix. A reference book or a knowledgeable hardware store or plumbing supply salesperson can tell you what you need and how to make the repair.

## Electrical Systems

Electrical repairs can range from resetting a circuit breaker to replacing a fuse, outlet, or light switch to rewiring your entire living space. With appropriate precautions, some of these tasks can be done by the homeowner or renter. Most electrical tasks, however, should be left to a professional.

You should know how to turn off the main source of electricity for your living space. The location of the switch and the type of service will vary, so you may need to have someone show you where the switch is and how and when to turn it off.

Never do any electrical work with wet hands or while standing in water. Water is a conductor of electricity, and you may get a severe or even fatal shock.

Defective wiring or electrical problems that you cannot find causes for need to be handled by a professional. Putting off repairs may result in an electrical fire.

## Exterior Maintenance

A yearly check of the exterior of your living space can help you to discover things that need cleaning or repair before they become major problems. A loose shingle can be repaired quickly. Leaving it for several years may

Spotting outside home problems early can avoid costly repairs.

cause others to come loose, can cause leaks, and may create the need for a new roof or major repairs inside and out.

Here are some important things to check for on the outside of your housing:

- cracks in the foundation
- peeling paint
- rotten wood and signs of carpenter ants or termites
- clogged gutters and downspouts
- loose or damaged roofing material
- broken windows and torn screens

## For Review

1. Who should handle most major repairs of home heating and cooling systems? Why?

2. Describe the procedure to follow if you have a frozen pipe.

3. List the important things to check on the exterior of housing. Which problems would require expert help?

# Conserving Energy Resources

Conserving energy is one way to save money as well as to conserve natural resources. Some energy conservation practices make your living space more comfortable by cutting down on drafts.

There are many ways to practice energy conservation. Some cost no money; they only require a change in everyday habits or ways of living. Other measures require the purchase of materials and/or equipment that can range in price from relatively inexpensive to quite expensive. Installing and/or making use of these materials or equipment may be simple do-it-yourself tasks or may require a skilled technician. The chart on page 368 lists the steps you can take to conserve electricity, hot water, and fuel.

## Money Matters

Two terms, often used in relation to energy conservation measures, are **cost-effectiveness** and **payback period.** Both these terms refer to how much money is saved by taking certain steps.

**Cost-Effectiveness** Cost-effectiveness refers to the amount of money you save compared to the amount you spend. For example, if you spend $25 for some interior storm windows for your apartment and save $75 on your heating bill for the year, the windows are a cost-effective measure. If you could not reuse the windows and saved only $25 on your heating bill, they would not be cost-effective.

**Payback Period** The payback period refers to how quickly you can recover any money you spend. In the example above, the payback period was relatively short—the money you

## CONSERVING ENERGY

| To Save  ELECTRICITY | To Save  HOT WATER | To Save  FUEL |
|---|---|---|
| 1. Reduce use.<br>2. Investigate off-peak rates.<br>3. Buy energy-efficient appliances.<br>4. Make use more efficient. For example, bake several things at once.<br>5. Shut off all lights and electrical equipment when they aren't needed. | 1. Install reduced-flow shower heads.<br>2. Take short showers, not baths.<br>3. Make sure dishwashers and washing machines are full before use.<br>4. Use cold or warm water in washing clothes.<br>5. Lower temperature setting on the hot water heater if it is set too high for your needs.<br>6. Insulate the water heater. | 1. Maintain heating system properly.<br>2. Set thermostat at 65°F to 68°F at night.<br>3. Buy an automatic setback thermostat.<br>4. Close off unused rooms.<br>5. Replace old, inefficient heating systems.<br>6. Weatherproof with caulking or weatherstripping.<br>7. Install storm windows and/or doors if you don't have them.<br>8. Use window coverings.<br>9. Cover unused doors.<br>10. Insulate or add to present insulation.<br>11. Have an energy audit done on your housing. |

saved on heat paid for the windows. For expensive measures, such as installing a solar water heater or a new air conditioning system, the payback period usually extends over a period of years. Consulting an energy expert can help you to determine the payback periods for each different situation.

## Insulation

**Insulation** slows down the flow of heat from a warm area to a cooler area. Installing insulation is particularly beneficial in cold climates where it can help to keep heat in the living space. In hot climates, insulation can help to keep heat out of the living space, but adding insulation may not be the most cost-effective way to reduce cooling costs.

*Where to Insulate* In a house with no insulation, most experts recommend adding insulation to the attic first. Because heat rises, more heat is lost through the roof than through the walls. Walls are the next most important place to insulate, then the basement or crawl space. When a living space already has some insulation, adding more may help to reduce heat loss further, but it is possible to reach a point where adding more insulation does nothing.

*Types of Insulation* The three most frequently used types of insulation are batts or blankets, loose fill, and rigid board. The type to use depends on where it is to be put. Batts or blankets are easy to put up in new construction or unfinished areas. They are made in widths to fit between floor joists and wall studs. Loose fill is blown into finished walls or floor cavities or poured between floor joists, as in an unfinished attic, for example. Rigid board insulation often is put up around the outside of newly constructed buildings before the clapboard, stucco, or other exterior finish is added. Board insulation can be used under wallboard in new construction.

**R-value** The R-value of insulation is based on its resistance to heat flow. Each type of insulation has an R-value rating. An energy specialist can tell you what R-value would be good for the areas you want to insulate.

**Vapor Barrier** No matter what type of insulation you use, it is important to have a vapor barrier between the heated living space and the insulation. Damp insulation is not effective. A vapor barrier prevents moisture from condensing in the insulation.

## The Energy Audit

An **energy audit** is an evaluation of the energy used in a particular living space. It may be done by a computer analysis of answers on a form that the homeowner or renter has filled out, or it may be done by a person trained to do home energy audits. The person may be an employee of a utility company or may be employed by a company that sells energy-conservation supplies or does energy-conserving home improvements.

An energy audit conducted by someone who is properly trained may be more beneficial than filling out a form for computer analysis. At the same time, a utility company representative may be more objective in his or her analysis than someone from a company that sells energy-conservation equipment, supplies, and services. The audit by a trained individual may cost nothing, or a small fee may be charged.

A well-done energy audit includes a detailed evaluation of your present situation,

### NONENERGY WAYS TO HELP COOL YOUR HOME

The following are ways to help cool your housing without air conditioning or fans.

1. Install awnings or exterior window shades, especially on the east and west sides of the house.
2. Paint your house a light color to reflect the sun's rays. Light-colored roofing also helps.
3. Plant trees and shrubbery to provide shade.
4. Use heat-producing appliances early in the morning or late at night.
5. Add insulation if you don't have any and if it will be cost-efficient.

including windows, doors, building exterior, basement and foundation, heating system, water heater, walls and ceilings, attic, and roof. It also includes specific recommendations for improvements as well as potential cost savings. An energy audit can help renters and homeowners learn about more specific ways to conserve energy, based on the structure and location of their particular living space.

## For Review

1. Define the terms cost-effectiveness and payback period. How do they figure into your decisions to invest or not invest in energy conservation?

2. How does insulation work? What are the three main types of insulation?

3. What is an energy audit? Given the cost, would it be beneficial? Why or why not?

other ways for them to control housing costs. Your goal is to get the most from the money you spend, while having the kind of living space you want and enjoy. There are techniques to help you exert control over what you have for a living space and what you spend for it.

## Keep Track of Housing Expenses

Keeping a record of what you spend for your rent or mortgage and property taxes, insurance, heat, electricity, telephone service, maintenance and repairs, and improvements is a matter of writing down any money you spend, when you spend it, and what you spend it for. This record can help you to see where your money goes, what you spend on housing-related expenses, and any areas where it is possible to cut back on expenses.

## Take Care of What You Have

By putting things away regularly, cleaning periodically, and taking care of maintenance promptly, you can help to keep a living space comfortable and liveable. These actions will help to prevent accidents and fires, stop small problems from becoming major repair jobs, and conserve resources. These procedures also slow down the deterioration that naturally occurs in your living space. Taking care of what you have will mean you have lower repair costs and lower replacement costs.

Taking care of what you have involves following a workable storage plan, developing a cleaning plan to meet your needs, and doing routine maintenance and repairs when needed. Cost-effective improvements also fall into this category. Energy conservation, safety, and security measures help to protect and add to the value of your housing.

Closing up spaces around windows by weatherstripping can reduce heating and air conditioning costs.

## Managing Total Housing Costs

While individuals and families cannot fix the rent they pay or the interest rate on a mortgage or the tax rate on property, there are

## Allow for the Unexpected

No matter how well you plan for maintenance and repairs, the unexpected is likely to happen—the liner in the water heater will crack or your two-year-old niece will try to flush a toy down the toilet or the furnace won't run on the coldest night of the year! Knowing what to do or who to call can prevent the situation from becoming worse. Having money set aside in a household maintenance and repair account helps to prevent a budget disaster.

## Learn What You Can Do Yourself

Do-it-yourself skills can save the money that you would otherwise pay someone else.

Many books contain good, basic information for doing simple maintenance and repair tasks. Others deal with more involved tasks, such as building or remodeling. There are even classes that deal with basic maintenance and repairs as well as carpentry and woodworking skills. With time, patience, and a willingness to learn, these skills can be mastered and become valuable resources to homeowners and renters.

## Hire Others Carefully

You may not want to do some work yourself. Perhaps you don't like the work, or the job is too complicated for you to handle. Service persons and/or contractors are expensive to hire. If you have an extensive project to be done, such as putting in a new driveway or

Many do-it-yourself books at your library and bookstore are valuable resources.

How can personal recommendations of neighbors help you to hire help wisely?

several companies or individuals for estimates on the same job. Get your estimates in writing with a breakdown of individual costs. Make sure that the total job is included in the estimate you are given.

Ask the businesses you consult for the names of other people they have serviced. If possible, see the work they have done. Ask former customers if they would recommend using the services of the individual or company you are thinking of using.

**Make Your Choice.**  Once you have done all of the preliminary steps, you can make a wise decision. You are ready to hire.

**Ask for a Written Contract.**  If you are having a major job done, it is a good idea to get a written contract and perhaps have a lawyer look it over before signing it.

**Check the Work.**  As the job is done, check on the quality of the work. Ask questions if you have any and clear up any problems that arise early in the process.

**Evaluate the Completed Work.**  Ask yourself if you are satisfied with the completed work. Was the work schedule on time or late? You may want to provide positive or negative feedback to the individual or business you hired.

adding a room, there are important procedures to follow before you hire someone. Following these procedures can help you to get quality work at a fair price.

**Be an Investigator.**  Check newspaper ads and the yellow pages and talk to people you know who have hired others. You may want to call the Better Business Bureau or the Chamber of Commerce in your area to see if any complaints have been lodged against a business or service person you are considering. Sometimes a state or local consumer agency can give you this information.

**Get Estimates and References.**  Check to make sure that the estimates are free, then ask

## For Review

1. List and explain five ways to control housing costs.
2. How can the Better Business Bureau help if you need to hire a business to do work on your home?
3. List the steps you should follow in the hiring procedure.

# Management Application: Arranging Living Space

Imagine yourself in the situation described below. As you read, think about the steps of the management process in relation to the situation. Then answer the questions that follow.

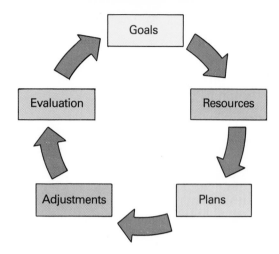

## Situation

Joelle wanted her own room. Now that she was in high school, her schedule was not the same as her ten-year-old sister's. She studied late at night and liked to play her radio. Sometimes she wanted to have a friend come over to talk. After talking her problem over with her parents, Joelle decided the attic was a possibility. It was used for storage now, but there was plenty of space. With effort and imagination, it could work. Furniture was the big drawback. Her parents didn't want her to move things from her present room, so she would have to come up with a new bed and bureau. Joelle made notes as she looked through the do-it-yourself books and magazines at the library. She couldn't afford to buy furniture. Her aunt had an old double mattress and box spring that was in good shape. She told Joelle that she could have them if she could get them from one house to the other. Her cousin brought them over in his pick-up truck, and they took them upstairs. Joelle went to the lumber company and got three boards, four cinder blocks, and some paint. She painted and then stacked the blocks and boards to make a bookcase. Then she painted an old crate to use for a table. She got cartons at the grocery store where she

worked. After decorating them with old posters, she filled her new bureau with sweaters, socks, and underwear, and jeans. She also decorated the large carton their new refrigerator had come in. She cut one side open and hung an old broom handle inside. Now she had a small closet! She bought three colorful sheets — two for her bed and one to string up to create a "wall" between her and the storage side of the attic. It wasn't finished, but her new room was taking shape!

## Questions

1. What was Joelle's goal?
2. Would you say that Joelle needed more human resources or more nonhuman resources to reach her goal? Explain.
3. Would you say that Joelle's new room was a need or a want? What values motivated her to achieve her goal?
4. Which of the steps of the management process apply to this situation?

# 16 Chapter Review

## Summary

To make the best use of your living space, create a floor plan that accommodates all your activities and needs in an arrangement that is also attractive and inviting. A work or activity center requires a functional design. Doing routine cleaning, maintenance, and repair jobs as soon as possible can help you to avoid major problems. You can manage your total housing costs by keeping track of your expenses, taking care of your things, learning to do certain things yourself, and hiring others carefully.

## Vocabulary

Match each of the following vocabulary words below with one of the definitions.

floor plan

traffic pattern

center

payback period

insulation

energy audit

weatherization

cost-effectiveness

direct, or space, heat

central heating system

1. A method of warming housing that provides heat to all parts of a living space is a _____ .

2. The amount of money you save on an energy conservation measure compared to the amount you spend on it is _____ .

3. An evaluation of the energy used in a particular living space is an _____ .

4. A sketch of a room and its furniture drawn to scale is a _____ .

5. Any work that helps to prevent the loss of heat from a living space is _____ .

6. A method of warming housing that provides heat directly to a room or an area through a heating device located in the room or area is _____ .

7. The paths people take to get from one room to another form a _____ .

8. Material that slows the flow of heat from a warm area to a cool area is _____ .

9. A space that is designed for a specific task or recreational activity is a _____ .

10. The time it takes to recover money you spend on an energy conservation measure is the _____ .

## Questions

1. Why should you consider traffic patterns when designing a floor plan?

2. How can textures be used to enhance the appearance of a room? How can balance? Give an example of each.

3. What factors should you consider when planning for storage?

4. If you were planning a kitchen center and had a small child, what safety features would you want?

5. How can routine cleaning, maintenance, and repairs save money?

6. How should you maintain furniture, walls, and rugs?

7. What are some simple weatherization procedures that can be done by most home-owners?

8. What information can you get from an energy audit?

9. Before you hire someone to do a repair, maintenance, or building project for your home, what procedures should you follow?

## Skill Activities

**1. *Social Studies.*** Draw up a floor plan of one room in your home. Follow the guidelines on page 354 in this chapter. Be sure that your floor plan is to scale. Use arrows to indicate the traffic flow in this room.

Is the space arranged well? Can you offer any simple suggestions that might improve traffic flow?

**2. *Critical Thinking.*** Design a fantasy bedroom for yourself. Make a floor plan of your fantasy bedroom. It should be 10 feet by 12 feet. Be sure to include a bed, a dresser, a window, and a closet. (Optional furniture: a desk, a bookshelf, a chair.) Explain how you would make your space functional to meet your personal needs.

Using ideas from decorating magazines as well as other popular magazines, explain how you would use accessories, colors, textures, patterns, balance, and any other elements of design to decorate your room.

**3. *Resource Management.*** Find two rooms in your home, including the room where you spend the most time, to manage. What common cleaning tasks should be done on each room? Refer to pages 362–364 "Common Cleaning Tasks." Draw up a schedule to show what tasks should be done and when you would do them.

**4. *Science.*** Study ways to regulate the temperature in your home. Begin by charting the temperature of each room at different times of day. Chart when each room is used and for what activity. Then list ways to get the greatest comfort for the least cost. For example, you might close shades or curtains to insulate windows and keep a room warm at night, and open them so that the sun could heat up the room during the day.

If you live in a warm climate, design a plan to best utilize ventilation, fans, or air conditioners.

# 17

# *Making Transportation Decisions*

## *As you read, think about:*

- how to evaluate your transportation needs.
- how to decide which form of transportation best fits the needs, wants, and resources you have.
- how to make the best consumer decisions when buying a bicycle, car, moped, or motorcycle.
- how to estimate the total expenses involved in buying and owning a car.
- how to apply the management process to personal decisions about the type of transportation you use.

public transportation
carpooling
disclosure statement
title
sticker price
options
book value

Can you imagine what your life would be like without cars, bikes, airplanes, buses, and all the other forms of manufactured transportation you have?

We have many types of transportation available to us, depending on where we live. The type of transportation you use will depend on your needs and resources. Learning how to make wise transportation choices will help you now and throughout your life.

## *Choosing Your Transportation*

Take a moment to estimate how much time you spend going from one place to another on an average day. Just how long is the walk, the drive, or the train or bus ride to and from school and/or work? Once you have given it some thought, you can easily see that a large part of your life is spent just going from one place to another.

Cost is an important factor in the method of transportation you choose to use. If you use public transportation and pay a daily fare, the cost is not too difficult to calculate. If you own your means of transportation (bicycle, motorcycle, car, or other vehicle), there are many different kinds of costs to estimate.

The type of transportation you choose depends upon your individual needs. Location, activities, financial resources, safety, and convenience all contribute to the type of transportation you choose to use.

### *Your Location and Activities*

Where you live, in a rural area, a suburb, or a city, and where your daily activities take you will help to determine the type of transportation you use. If there is public transportation nearby, you may choose to use it. **Public transportation** is transportation that is operated for the benefit of the general public. A fare is paid to use it. Buses, subways, trains, and ferries are all forms of public transportation that you may use.

Your need for transportation is determined primarily by your personal circumstances. Right now, transportation to and from school may be most important to you, but you may also need to get to and from a job. Dates and social activities with friends require transportation. Like most young adults, you probably are looking forward to having your own source of transportation. You may be thinking about a bicycle or a moped now and planning to buy a car in a few years. These purchases require a clear understanding of your financial resources.

## Financial Resources

For many people, transportation is a major expense. The first step in figuring out what you

Many commuters pay tolls each day as they go to and from work.

can spend on transportation is to determine what your income is. The next step is to figure your expenses. If you are already earning an income and have transportation expenses as well as other expenses (food, clothing, and insurance, for example), you have some idea of what it costs you to live. You may know where you can cut back on expenses and where you cannot. You probably know whether you can spend more on transportation or whether you should spend less. If you are getting your first job or a new job or are moving into your own place for the first time, you will need to do some careful calculating.

If you already have a vehicle, you probably know what it costs you. If you do not, you may find it helpful to talk with people who own different types of vehicles to get some idea of the expenses involved in owning them. If you are planning on using public transportation, you need to know what the fares are and how often you will be using it.

No matter what form of transportation you are considering, you should determine ahead of time all of the expenses before making a decision. This is true whether you want to buy a bike or car or any vehicle. If you buy a car and then realize you can't afford insurance or repairs, you still will be without transportation. By adding all of your monthly budget expenses and subtracting the total from your monthly take-home, or net, pay, you can estimate what you can afford to spend on transportation.

## Safety

Obviously, your own safety and the safety of all who travel with you are your primary concerns. Safety factors vary from one form of transportation and the circumstances to another. While cost may dictate your means of transportation, there are certain safety precautions you can and should be aware of as you go to and from school, work, or play.

Why is the ability to fix your own bicycle so important on a long trip?

**Use Safety Equipment.** On public transportation, use seatbelts, hand straps, or whatever other equipment is advised. In your own car, use seatbelts and other safety equipment, such as snow tires, when needed. If you are riding a bicycle, moped, or motorcycle, wear a helmet and any protective clothing necessary.

**Check Weather and Road Conditions.** Depending upon the weather, some forms of transportation will be unsafe. Bicycles, mopeds, and even some motorcycles do not perform safely on icy roads. When road conditions are really hazardous, public transportation may be safer. Leaving your car at home to take a train to work on a snowy day is one example of a responsible safety decision.

**Maintain Your Vehicle.** If you regularly use public transportation, you may want to find out how often it is maintained and repaired. If you operate your own vehicle, you will want to keep it in good shape for your own safety, as well as the safety of others.

**Control Your Emotional and Physical State.** Drivers of any vehicle who act out their frustrations or anger as they drive are dangerous. If you are ill, overtired, or under the influence of alcohol or drugs, you cannot drive safely. Call a friend or family member or a taxi if you need transportation. Do *not* try to drive.

## Convenience

Although not as important as safety, convenience is a factor when you choose a form of transportation. You want the most convenient form of transportation that you can afford. If you have to walk two miles to a bus stop and wait in the rain or snow because the bus is rarely on time, you probably will want to look for another way to get to school or work.

If you have a long drive into the city every day, have to struggle through traffic jams, and then have to hunt for a parking space, you may find a train more convenient.

Some people who live in large cities believe that public transportation for local travel is more convenient and less of a worry than owning and operating a car. Other people use public transportation for commuting to and from work and have a car for other activities. Still other people find it inconvenient to adjust their schedules to the schedules of buses, trains, and subways. They prefer to drive their own cars or to take taxis. In areas that are not served by public transportation, people must have their own vehicles or depend on others to take them where they wish to go.

Taxis are more expensive than some means of public transportation, but often they are more convenient because they operate "on demand," rather than according to a set schedule. Unlike buses and trains, which stop only in certain places, taxis will deliver you to your door.

If you live in an area where most people drive, you may want to try a carpool to cut down on your expenses. **Carpooling** is an arrangement in which people share driving and driving expenses. One person may drive all the time, or everyone may take turns. Often, the riders

Car ownership involves making repairs.

are picked up at their own homes and dropped off where they work or go to school. Carpooling conserves energy and eliminates the air pollution that would be created if each person drove a car.

## For Review

1. How can you determine what you can afford to spend on transportation?
2. List at least three ways that you can make your form of transportation safer.
3. How important is convenience in choosing transportation? Describe carpooling.

## Buying a Bicycle

Although bicycles often are thought of as recreational vehicles, many people use them for getting to and from their work or school. Mopeds and motorcycles are motorized, two-wheel vehicles that can be used for recreational purposes and as means of transportation.

Bicycles probably are the least expensive of the two-wheel vehicles. Because they require human energy and strength for power, rather than fuel, they are not expensive to run. Since they do not have gasoline engines, they usually are less expensive to maintain and to repair than mopeds, motorcycles, and four-wheel vehicles.

### Types of Bicycles

Bicycles vary in their styles and basic purposes. The most popular type of bicycle is the *10-speed touring bicycle,* which has thin tires, racing-style handlebars, and a derailleur gear system. *All-terrain bicycles* and *city bicycles* have heavier frames, balloon-type tires, and straight handlebars. They may have as many as

18 speeds to make it easier to maneuver the heavier weight over rough roads and terrain.

Touring bicycles are lightweight and designed for speed on smooth-surface roads, comfort for long-distance riding, and ease of operation over hills and on flat terrain. The thin tires, lightweight frame, and racing-style handlebars, which force the rider to bend over while riding, help to cut down on wind resistance, thus allowing for greater speed. The 10- or 12-speed gear system is designed to make it easy to ride up and down hills, as well as on flat surfaces, while maintaining a fairly constant pedaling rate.

All-terrain bicycles and city bicycles are heavier than touring bicycles because they are subjected to more stress from riding on rough terrain or on bumpy city streets. The fatter tires help to absorb the shocks from riding over bumpy surfaces. The pronounced tread on the tires helps with traction on muddy, wet, or grassy surfaces. City bicycles may have slightly narrower tires with less tread than the tires of all-terrain bicycles.

All-terrain bicycles need low gears for ease of riding on steep trails and mountains, but because there is little opportunity for high-speed riding, they do not need many high gears. City bicycles need fewer low gears because there are usually few steep hills to climb. They may have gears in the higher ranges for flat-surface riding. Some all-terrain bicycles have as many as 18 speeds, which allows them to have the low gears needed for off-the-road use and the higher gears needed for roads with smoother surfaces.

The straight handlebars on all-terrain bicycles and city bicycles force the rider to sit up straight, which allows him or her to pay close attention to any obstacles in the path. The increased wind resistance, caused by the rider sitting up straight, reduces the need for the high gears that are necessary for high-speed riding on smooth surfaces.

This man is following road safety rules and wearing appropriate clothing as he bikes to work.

## Safety Factors

Knowing how to ride the bicycle you have, how to use the gears and brakes, and how to ride on different road surfaces and in different kinds of weather will help you to be a safe bicycle rider. If you are unfamiliar with the type of bicycle you have, or if you are a new rider, you may want to practice riding in areas where there are few people and vehicles until you feel comfortable with your bicycle.

In most places, for the safety of those who are walking, bicycles are not permitted on sidewalks. When bicycling is allowed on sidewalks or other areas where people are walking, you should be extremely careful. Pay

## BICYCLE SAFETY RULES

- Ride with the traffic.
- Use the bicycle lane for riding when there is one. Do not ride on the sidewalk.
- Stop at stop lights and stop signs.
- Use hand signals when turning.
- Cross at corners and crosswalks. Walk your bike across the street.
- Keep both hands on handlebars unless signaling.
- Wear a protective helmet when you are riding in city traffic or long distances.
- If you ride at night, wear light-colored clothing marked with reflective tape.
- Equip your bike with reflective lights and a headlight.
- Follow the same rules of the road that drivers are expected to follow.

attention to what you are doing and to what others are doing. You should be able to stop quickly if someone walks or runs in front of you. Racing is dangerous to you and the pedestrians on the walk.

When you are riding on the road, you should ride with the traffic. You are expected to know and obey the same rules of traffic that drivers obey. Try to ride on the side of the road or in an area where you cause the least disruption of traffic, and pay attention to stop signs and traffic lights. Of course, you will want to use hand signals when turning.

Since head injuries can occur if you are in an accident, safety helmets are recommended, particularly in city traffic, on long-distance rides, or when riding off the road. Long pants

and a long-sleeved shirt can help to minimize scratches and scrapes if you are riding off the road or fall. You may want to use pant clips to keep pant legs from becoming tangled in the bicycle chain.

Be sure your bicycle has reflectors on the front and back as well as on the spokes and pedals. If you ride at night, you will need a working headlight. For night riding, you need to be as visible as possible to avoid being hit. A shirt or jacket with reflective tape can help to make you more visible. A riding flag or pennant may make you more visible both day and night.

## Shopping for a Bicycle

There are certain steps you should take and things you should consider before you buy a bicycle. These procedures are similar to the ones you follow when you make other important purchases.

*Gather Consumer Information.* You may find it helpful to read consumer magazines and publications for information about types and brand names of bicycles that have proven their performance. Your library is a good source for this information.

*Comparison Shop.* Once you have decided on the type and brand of bicycle you want, check several stores and bicycle shops to compare prices. Ask about sales that may be coming soon. If you read newspaper ads, you may discover more sales. Try to find out about warranties and where and how you could have major repairs done if they were necessary.

*Ask About a Test Ride.* If you can try out a bicycle before you buy it, you can check for certain things. As you try out a model, see if it pedals easily, responds properly when you are turning the wheel, shifts easily and smoothly, and makes quick and easily controlled stops.

You probably will want your bicycle to have a fairly comfortable seat, a sturdy, rigid frame, and sturdy pedals with serrated metal treads. If you are looking at a touring bicycle, the frame should be lightweight. An all-terrain bicycle or city bicycle can have a slightly heavier frame. Check to see that you have enough gears in the proper ranges to pedal easily on the terrain where you will be riding.

***Consider Buying a Used Bicycle.*** If you want to save money or cannot afford a new model, you may want to think about buying a used bicycle. Perhaps one of your friends is selling a bicycle, or perhaps you can find one at a yard or garage sale. Of course, you will want to test ride it before you buy it. Gear repairs are expensive, so you will want to make certain that the gears function correctly and that all parts are in good working order. Sometimes you are able to get a signed warranty from the seller, but usually you must take the bicycle "as is" and deal with any repairs yourself, so choose carefully. You may be able to bargain about the asking price if something needs to be fixed, but be sure the problem can be repaired before buying.

***Figure Out the Total Cost.*** In some areas of the country, bicyclists must pay registration and license fees. Other expenses may include a helmet, a bicycle lock, and a headlight and/or reflective clothing for safety. All of these factors add to the total cost of your transportation.

## Mopeds and Motorcycles

Two other popular, but more expensive, two-wheeled vehicles are mopeds and motorcycles. Mopeds are motorized bicycles that can be pedaled. Their engines are small and their top speed is not high, so they are appropriate for traveling for short distances. A motorcycle is heavier in weight and larger in size than a

Before buying a bike, check out all its features and ask about a test ride.

moped. It cannot be pedaled. Both mopeds and motorcycles get better gas mileage than a car.

There are many different models of motorcycles available. In general, the larger and heavier the motorcycle, the larger the engine size (designated in cubic centimeters) and the more powerful the vehicle.

Usually, smaller motorcycles are recommended for beginning riders because they are lighter in weight and easier to handle than larger ones. This type of motorcycle is adequate for local transportation since speed and long-term comfort are not important factors.

Experienced riders may prefer larger motorcycles with more power. These are more comfortable for long rides and may perform

What are the age restrictions in your state for a driver's license?

protective outer clothing are necessary. Like bicycles, mopeds and most motorcycles should not be driven in certain weather conditions.

Before you buy a motorcycle or moped, you may want to gather information from dealers and anyone you know who owns one. If possible, you should try driving the vehicle you are considering to see if it feels right for you before you buy it.

## For Review

1. Describe safe bicycle behavior when you are riding on the sidewalk and the road.
2. What are the five steps you should go through before purchasing a bicycle?
3. Why can mopeds and motorcycles be considered more dangerous to drive than a car?

better than some of the smaller, lighter weight models. A reliable salesperson can help you choose the appropriate size and style for your level of experience and the intended use.

Some motorcycles are designed for use on the road only. Others are designed for off-the-road use. If you plan to use a motorcycle for transportation rather than recreation, you should choose an appropriate model and style.

Obviously, safety is an important consideration when you choose a moped or a motorcycle as your form of transportation. Both types of vehicles offer you little protection. Being bumped by a car when you are on a moped or motorcycle may mean a serious injury rather than the dented fender you might have if you were in a car. Helmets and tough,

## Buying A Car

If you have analyzed your transportation needs and have decided you need a car, you have many options to consider and a lot to learn before making your choice. You need to obtain a license to drive. You need to gather all the information you can about various models before you make your decision. Finally, you need to consider *all* your car-related expenses to be sure you have the financial resources you need to own, operate, and maintain a car.

### Getting a License

In most states, there are age restrictions on driving motorized vehicles, and drivers must be licensed. The age restrictions vary from state to state. Usually a permit is required for a certain period of time before a license is issued. To get your permit, you must pass a

# Managing Mobility for the Handicapped

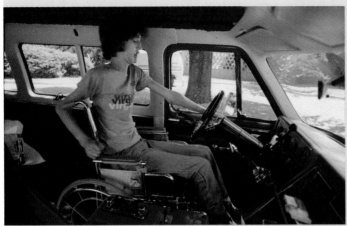

How do you *go* to school? *Go* to work? *Go* to the movies or a sports event? *Go* shopping or on vacation? Did you ever wonder how you would get there if you were handicapped? According to a government report, there are over seven million "transportation handicapped" people in American cities. Transportation barriers—things that block the way of those who require aid in walking, for example—can deny handicapped people "rights" that most of us take for granted: the right to education, to working for a living, to going where and when we wish. Study skills, job skills, and a desire for independence don't help if your wheelchair doesn't fit through a doorway, if you can't make the first big step onto a commuter bus, or if you can't get through a subway turnstile. Many organizations, some government sponsored, see it as their responsibility to remove these barriers to handicapped people.

While airlines will accommodate wheelchairs and some train stations are wheelchair accessible, driving a car modified for their condition gives the handicapped the best opportunity to manage their own transportation. The Veterans Administration tests and certifies driver aids such as *hand controls* that allow braking and accelerating by hand rather than foot; *low-effort steering devices; wheelchair lifts* and *tie-downs* for vans; and *emergency brake adapters* that allow paraplegics to use the emergency brake.

Choosing the right model and options is important. Two-door cars have larger door openings, allowing easier wheelchair access. Bench seats that "sit low" or have power adjusters also make wheelchair access easier. Power steering and power brakes are essential; power windows, door locks, and outside mirrors are worthwhile options as are air conditioning and cruise control. Finally, a CB radio or cellular telephone is an all-important backup for getting help if it is needed.

written test. To get your license, you must pass a road test as well as a written test. Most states insist that you renew your license after a certain period of time. Many states insist that you take an eye test and/or a road test before you renew your license. Whether you are getting your license for the first time or renewing it, there is a fee involved. Your state motor vehicle department can tell you what the age restrictions and licensing requirements are for your state.

Driver education courses teach you driving rules and give you on-the-road experience before you take the road test for your license. There is a fee involved, but if you complete the course, there is usually a reduction in your car insurance cost, since you are considered to be a safer, more educated driver. Sometimes these courses are available through your high school.

## Types of Cars

Frequently, cars are described in terms of their size. Commonly used terms include subcompact, compact, intermediate, and full-size, or standard. *Subcompact cars* are the smallest cars. Usually, they are the least expensive size to buy, run, maintain, repair, and insure. They are easy to maneuver in crowded city streets and into and out of parking spaces, but they have the least room for passengers and luggage. For the most part, they do not have powerful engines, tend to be less comfortable on long trips, and are more likely to be severely damaged in an accident.

*Compact cars* are larger than subcompact cars. While they are economical, they still cost more than subcompacts to buy, run, maintain, repair, and insure. They offer more room for passengers and luggage but are small enough for good maneuverability. Their comfort and performance on a long trip may be less than that of a larger car. Although they are less vulnerable than subcompacts, the risk of severe damage is still higher than in a larger car.

*Intermediate-size cars* are the next largest size cars after compact cars. They are less economical than smaller cars and usually offer more space and comfort. For the most part, their highway performance is better than that of smaller cars because of the option of larger, more powerful engines and other features not found on smaller cars.

*Full-size* or *standard cars* are the largest cars. Usually, they are the most expensive to own and operate. Full-size cars lack the maneuverability of smaller cars but offer great power, comfort, and passenger and luggage space. They also provide greater protection than a small car in the event of an accident.

Most cars come in a variety of body styles. Two similar styles are the sedan and the hardtop with either two doors or four doors. The main difference is in the presence or absence of a side pillar, which is most noticeable in four-door models. Sedans have the pillar; hardtops do not. While many people prefer the appearance of the hardtop, the presence of the pillar in the sedan can provide greater stability in case of an accident.

Of course, four-door cars allow easier access to the back seat than two-door cars, but two-door cars have larger openings for the

### Safety Tip: Nighttime Driving

- As a road alert, apply fluorescent tape in a large "x" shape to the underside of your trunk lid. When you raise the lid for a nighttime emergency or tire change, this glowing symbol can be seen easily by other drivers. It is also a good idea to keep a working flashlight and flares in your car at all times.

driver and passenger doors than four-door cars. The larger openings are necessary for the use of the back seat.

Station wagons are designed for utility. For the most part, they are heavier and more expensive to operate than sedans or hardtops of comparable size, but they hold more passengers and have much greater cargo space. The back seat in a station wagon usually goes down, which allows you to transport large and/or long items.

Some compact and subcompact cars are available in hatchback models. The entire back is hinged to open upward, giving easier access to the cargo area and providing more storage space than a model with only a trunk. Usually a hatchback model has a rear seat that folds flat, which gives it carrying capacities similar to those of a station wagon.

A convertible is a hardtop model with a heavy fabric roof that folds back or a roof that can be removed. Although passengers can ride in the open air, there is greater chance of injury in case of accident. A fabric roof has less insulation value than a roof made of the same material as the car. Frequently, it is difficult to control the temperature in a convertible in very hot or very cold weather.

Most sports cars have seating space for only two people and limited space for luggage or other cargo. They usually have a special design and more power than comparably sized cars in other models.

## Gathering Information About Cars

Perhaps you have always been interested in cars and already know a great deal about the different types and how well they perform. Even if you know most of these things, you will want to learn more. Buying a car is a big investment, and you will want to make the best-informed decision you can. Consumer

Who might need the space advantages of a van or station wagon?

publications, personal recommendations, advertisements, and individual car dealerships are all excellent sources of information. Once you have gathered all the information you can, you will have to sort through conflicting information and advertising claims to make the most responsible decision you can.

**Consumer Publications** *Consumer Reports* is an excellent source of information. You can purchase it at a bookstore, or you may be able to find it at your local library. There are many other automobile magazines that rate models and makes of cars in terms of safety, comfort, reliability of performance, and repair record. Many of these magazines also rate cars in terms of their resale value.

You may discover after some research that the car you were thinking of buying performed poorly in a crash test. It is usually better "to do your homework" before buying, especially if it can save your life.

**Personal Recommendations**  You may want to ask relatives and friends whether or not they are satisfied with the cars they own. They can tell you advantages and disadvantages because of their experiences. Sometimes car repair shops will tell you the makes and models they repair most often.

**Advertisements**  Although there are laws to protect the consumer against false advertising, you still need to be able to sort through the glamour and glitter of car advertisements to get the facts. A car that looks nice but guzzles

A used car may not have a warranty.

gas is not a good buy. A small compact car may go 40 miles on a gallon of gas but weigh so little that it crumbles in an accident. You will want to look for all the negatives that the advertisement does not tell you.

**Dealerships**  Once you have narrowed your choices down to a few makes and models, you may want to visit the dealerships near you. Most dealerships have brochures and pamphlets available on the various models. You can ask to test drive the car you are interested in and have the salesperson answer any specific questions you have.

## Making a Final Selection

Once you have gathered all your information and decided which make and model you want, you can move on to the actual purchase. Deciding between a new or used car, whether to buy or lease, and settling on a fair purchase price, including the options you need and want, are part of the process.

**New or Used?**  If you do not have enough money for a new model or if you want to save money, you may consider buying a used car. Some used cars include options that you couldn't afford on a new car. However, a used car often has a limited warranty or no warranty at all.

If you buy a used car from a dealer, read the window sticker carefully. This sticker is the buyer's guide and is required by the Federal Trade Commission (FTC). It should tell you if the vehicle has a warranty and what the terms of it are. It will also suggest that you have your own mechanic check the vehicle before you buy it and that you get in writing any promises made by the dealer.

Usually, low-mileage vehicles have fewer problems than high-mileage vehicles. Although some dealers and individuals once turned back odometers to register fewer miles than the vehicles actually had, this practice is now illegal. If you buy a used car, you should receive a **disclosure statement** at the time of purchase, which will certify that the mileage is accurate. This statement should contain the vehicle make, model, and year, as well as the vehicle identification number and the signature, name, and address of the seller. If you buy a vehicle without a disclosure statement, you may get a vehicle that is more used than you realized.

Before you buy a used car, you should have a mechanic test drive it and check it over for any major problems. While you can check for obvious signs of wear, such as rust or torn upholstery, only a mechanic may be able to tell if the car has been in an accident. Once you have bought the car, be sure the seller gives you the **title**, a document that proves legal ownership.

A certificate of title is required as proof of ownership for all vehicles newer than 1972. If the vehicle is used, the seller has to sign over the present title to you. When you register the car, the state motor vehicle department will take the title and issue a new one. If you finance your purchase, the lender will hold the title until the vehicle is paid for. If you pay cash, you should receive the title at the time of purchase. Once you have the title, keep it in a safe place. It does not belong in the vehicle.

***Leasing*** One possible alternative to buying a car is leasing one. For some people, especially those who must do a lot of traveling, there are advantages to this plan. Some leasing plans include basic repair costs and insurance; others do not. Some include the option to buy the car when the term of the lease ends; others do not. Carefully investigate all of these points and costs to see if leasing is a good idea for you before signing any agreements.

***Purchase Price Including Options*** The **sticker price** of a new car is the suggested

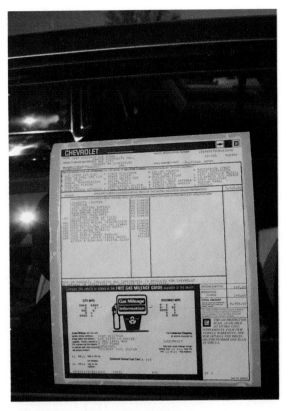

This window sticker on a new car lists options and prices and gives estimated gas mileage for city and highway.

retail price. Usually it is found taped on a window of the car. It will list the costs of the individual options included in the car. **Options** are nonessential, additional features, such as air conditioning or a tape deck.

If you special order a car, you have to order the options you want. If you buy a car the dealer has, it probably will have at least a few options. Knowing what the options are and their benefits and drawbacks can help you to decide whether you need or want them. Each option you buy adds to the price of the car, although sometimes "packages" are available that offer certain options for a price that is less than the total of the individual options. You may want to keep in mind that the more options you have and the more complex the

Keeping up with routine care helps you get more for your car at trade-in time.

*Used Car Guide* lists the book values of most cars. If you cannot get approximately the book value of your car from a dealer, you may want to sell your car privately. Usually this method will get a better price. It may take longer than you had planned, however, since you must advertise and wait for prospective buyers to come to you.

**Sales Contract**  If you buy a new car, be sure to get a purchase agreement from the dealer. The purchase agreement is a legal contract that states the rights and responsibilities of both buyer and seller. You must be of legal age to sign a contract. If you are not, someone who is will have to sign for you or cosign the contract. The person who signs the contract is legally responsible for it.

A purchase agreement should include the total price of the vehicle, the costs of any individual items, the amount of the deposit you are making to hold the car until purchase, the date of delivery, and any other matters related to the sale of the vehicle. Be sure you read the contract and understand all the terms before you sign it. Sometimes purchase agreements are not legal if the dealer does not sign them, so you will want to be sure that the dealer, as well as the salesperson you are working with, signs your agreement. If you do not like some of the terms of the contract, you may be able to convince the dealer to make adjustments. Once again, you will want to be sure that both you and the dealer initial any changes.

**The Warranty**  A warranty on a new car usually covers parts and workmanship for a specified period of time or number of miles for no cost or for a low cost. Of course, any problems have to be the result of normal use, not the result of an accident.

Warranties on new vehicles are honored if the owner makes sure the car is properly maintained according to the schedule specified by the manufacturer. Usually, maintenance

options are, the more things there are to repair and the more expensive the repairs can be.

If you do comparison shopping and get price quotes from several dealers, you may be able to negotiate with a dealer. Sometimes this means that you can pay less than the original asking price or the sticker price.

Some people decide on the maximum amount they will spend, then make an offer lower than that amount. If the seller accepts the offer, they come out ahead. If the seller does not accept the offer, there is still some room for bargaining. Be firm in your final offer and be prepared to leave if you and the seller cannot come to an agreement. This is better than paying more than you can afford.

**Trade-ins**  If you have a vehicle to trade in, do not discuss it until you have settled on the price of the vehicle you want. You can get an idea of what your vehicle is worth by finding out its book value. The **book value** is the standard price of a specific used car, depending on its make, model, and year. Options are also figured in. The *National Automobile Dealers Association*

involves changing the oil, the filters, and the spark plugs, and checking certain things. Sometimes the warranty specifies that the work must be done by an authorized dealer. Be sure you read and understand the warranty that comes with any vehicle you are considering.

## Other Four-Wheel Vehicles

The car is only one of the many four-wheel vehicles available to a consumer. There are a variety of pickup trucks, vans, and all-purpose utility vehicles. Each of these vehicles is available in many different sizes, styles, colors, and price ranges.

If you are interested in buying any one of these vehicles, the process of gathering information and making a final selection is similar to the process you followed in buying a car.

Before signing a purchase agreement, be sure you understand its terms.

## For Review

1. Explain how subcompact, compact, intermediate, and full-size cars compare in size, price, and safety.
2. Which four sources of car information usually are the most helpful?
3. If you choose to buy a used car, what things should you do to protect yourself before buying?

## Paying All Car Expenses

Now that you and the dealer (or individual) have agreed upon a price, you should figure out all of your costs, including the costs of financing a loan. Other costs will include the cost of your license, taxes, the cost of registration, insurance, maintenance and repairs, and weekly expenses, such as gas and parking fees.

## Loan Payments

The least costly way to pay for a vehicle is to pay cash. There are no interest charges, and you do not tie up future income by taking out a loan. Even if you take the money from your savings account, you probably will lose less in interest than you would pay in financing the vehicle through a dealer or a bank.

Frequently, however, it is not possible to pay cash. If your credit is good, and the amount you want to borrow is not out of line with your present income and expenditures, you may want to look into financing. Sometimes dealers offer financing at a lower rate than banks, but they may offset the costs of low rates by refusing to negotiate on the price of the vehicle. You will want to do some comparison shopping before you decide where to borrow money.

Your monthly installment payment on a car loan will be based on the amount that you are borrowing. The larger your down payment, the less you will have to borrow, and the smaller your monthly payments will be.

If you work full time, your place of work may offer a credit union. Credit unions frequently have the lowest interest rates of all financial institutions. If you are not working full time and do not have a credit union, you will be comparing the interest rates of other financial institutions.

Suppose, for example, that you want to buy a used car for $6,000 and that you can afford $2,000 as a down payment. You will need to borrow $4,000. You compare percentage rates at the banks, with the dealer, and at work. Your best deal is through a bank at nine percent yearly for two years. Nine percent of $4,000 is $360. As you make payments, the amount to be paid off on your loan decreases. Because of this, $360 is estimated as the total interest for two years, so the total cost will be $4,360. The total cost of your car, $4,360, divided by 24 months (the number of months of the loan), will give you monthly payments of $181.25.

## Sales Tax

The sales tax depends upon the tax rate in individual states. Even so, the higher the purchase price, the higher the amount of the sales tax will be. You will need to calculate this amount so that you will be prepared to pay it.

## Insurance Costs

Many states require insurance on any motorized vehicle, and many factors contribute to the cost of this insurance. For example, newer, larger, and more powerful vehicles cost more to insure than older, smaller, and less powerful ones. Younger drivers have higher insurance rates than older drivers. Rates usually are higher in more highly populated areas where there is more traffic and, therefore, increased chances of accidents. Your state department of transportation can tell you if there is mandatory insurance in your state and what the minimum coverage requirements are.

Because there are many types of insurance coverage, you will want to talk at length with a reputable insurance agent who can help you to decide how much coverage you need. Compare the costs and services offered by several insurance agencies before selecting one. If you are ever involved in an accident, you will want to receive prompt, fair service from your insurance company.

## Registration

All motor vehicles must be registered with the state motor vehicle department. Usually, the registration has to be renewed each year, and there is a fee involved. In order to register your car, you must provide certain information about the vehicle, such as the sales contract. In many states, you must prove that your car is insured. To be sure you have all the information you need, you may want to check with the motor vehicle department in your state.

Sometimes the dealer you buy your car from takes care of getting the title, registering the vehicle, and getting the license plates if you do not have them. When you receive your registration, you will want to keep it in your vehicle.

## Inspection

Many states require the regular safety inspection of motor vehicles. This usually involves checking the brakes, lights, steering mechanism, wheels and tires, and any other aspect of the car related to safety. It also may involve checking exhaust emissions to be sure the vehicle is not creating excess air pollution.

Usually, only licensed inspection stations can inspect vehicles and give stickers that indicate the vehicle has passed inspection. The fee for inspection varies from state to state. If your vehicle needs repairs or adjustments in order to comply with inspection requirements, it is another cost to keep in mind.

## License Fee

The cost of obtaining an automobile license varies from state to state. Remember to figure the fee for your license into your total automobile cost and to be prepared to pay this fee the day you take your driving test. If you lose your license, there is an additional fee to replace it, which may or may not be equal to the original fee. Check with a motor vehicle department near you for information about these fees.

## Maintenance and Repairs

All vehicles require maintenance on a regular basis to keep them running properly and safely. Engine tune-ups, oil changes, keeping the proper air pressure in the tires, and checking the brakes are a part of regular maintenance. Sometimes, maintenance involves replacing batteries or brake pads.

If you put your car on a regular maintenance schedule, it will add to the life of the car and protect your investment. You may want to consider learning how to do some basic car maintenance tasks yourself. There are many courses you can take, but they will require an investment of money, time, and effort.

The owner's manual for your vehicle offers a number of suggestions for its maintenance. In addition to these, simply keeping your vehicle clean can help to prolong its life. Washing it regularly will remove dust, dirt, bird droppings, and other things that can harm the finish. If you live in an area where the roads are salted or treated chemically to melt ice (or live near the ocean), more frequent washings can help to minimize the damaging effects of these chemicals. Pay special attention to the under parts of the vehicle, and touch up paint chips as soon as possible. Waxing your vehicle when it is needed will protect the finish.

Feeding parking meters adds to car costs.

## Daily Operating Expenses

The *cost of fuel* to run your vehicle should be figured into your total transportation budget. Depending on how far you travel to and from work or school each day, this may be a substantial amount of money. Your driving habits will affect your gas mileage, or the number of miles you can drive on a tank of gas. Driving at high rates of speed can cut down on gas mileage. Leaving a vehicle idling for more than a minute uses more gas than turning off the ignition and starting it up again. Conservation methods not only help you to avoid wasting fuel but also help you to cut down on the amount of fuel you use and thus save money.

*Parking and/or garage fees* also can be costly, regular vehicle expenses if you have to face them on a daily basis. You should figure these into your budget. You may want to do comparison shopping to find the least expensive situation, or you may be able to save if you pay on a monthly basis rather than daily. If parking is too difficult to find or pay for, perhaps you should consider taking your car part of the way to work or school and then taking some form of public transportation. Frequently, if you take the train, for example, there is free parking at the railroad station.

*Tolls* for highway and/or bridge use are a final cost factor to take into account as you calculate your transportation budget.

## Auto Clubs

An optional cost related to car ownership is membership in any of several auto clubs. Depending on your needs and circumstances, this may be a wise yearly investment. Membership in an auto club usually entitles you to service, wherever you are, in the event of a breakdown. Changing flat tires and battery restarting are examples of this on-the-spot service.

If you are considering an auto club membership, you will want to compare services. Some clubs offer discounted hotel or motel rates as well as other benefits.

## Planning Transportation for the Disabled

Most of us take for granted walking as a means of getting from one place to another. For some disabled persons, however, walking is impossible or possible only with some type of help.

Some people with disabilities that involve legs and/or feet may use crutches or one or two canes or a walker for extra support. Others may require a wheelchair. Some wheelchairs must be propelled by physical strength from the arms and hands; others are motorized. While these objects may improve mobility, there are still many obstacles to face.

Many towns and cities have sidewalks without curbs at their corners so that people using wheelchairs can cross streets easily. Some newer buildings are wheelchair accessible or able to accommodate those with handicaps. Although some older buildings have been adapted to be more accessible to those with disabilities, many still have only steps, not ramps. Frequently, these buildings have no elevators or elevators that do not accommodate wheelchairs. These factors limit the ability of the disabled to operate as independently as they wish.

People with vision problems may use seeing-eye dogs, or guide dogs, in order to walk without endangering themselves or others. Others may use a special cane to guide them in their walking.

Some people with physical disabilities, such as paralysis of the legs (paraplegia) or the loss of an arm or leg, are able to drive with the aid of specially equipped vehicles. While these vehicles can be quite expensive, having one enables the disabled person to function with greater independence.

Public transportation is not always easy or possible to manage for people who have mobility problems. Buses, trains, and airplanes may not be equipped to handle persons with certain mobility handicaps or to handle the equipment these individuals need. A Supreme Court ruling in 1986 stated that airlines had the right to refuse to board passengers they did not feel equipped to handle. For those with any type of handicap or disability, checking with the specific train, airline, or bus line under consideration before planning a trip can help to prevent any serious problems or unpleasant, last minute surprises.

## For Review

1. Besides loan payments, what other car expenses are there?

2. What type of information must you provide in order to obtain a registration for your car?

3. List the most common daily operating expenses of a car.

## Management Application: Deciding on Transportation

Imagine yourself in the situation described below. As you read, think about how the steps of the management process might apply to this situation. Then answer the questions that follow.

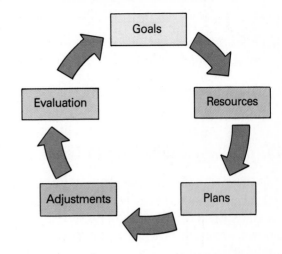

### Situation

Adam's goal was to buy the new racing bike he had been reading about. He visited the bicycle shop in town and saw just the one he wanted. He needed a bike to get to and from home and his after-school job because the one he had was ready to fall apart. He had owned his bike for five years and had used it every day. He had also had it repaired several times in the past. The only problem with the new bike was its price tag. This bike cost $375.00, and Adam had only $100.00 to spend. He thought hard to come up with some plan to buy the new bike. If he washed the car and did extra chores, his parents might pay him. The only problem with that plan was that between school and homework, his job, and fun with his friends, there wasn't much time to do extra chores. His job paid $50.00 a week, but he had to budget some of each check for lunch money, entertainment, and any extra clothes he wanted. Even if he saved half of every check, it would take him eleven weeks to earn the $275.00 he needed to buy the bike. That would be about 3 months from now. It might just work. Adam decided to try it. A week later as he was coming home from work, the gears on his old bike gave out. Repairing the bike was foolish. It was too old,

and the tires were in bad shape, too. Besides, he needed transportation right away. He had to be able to get to work. He now had $125.00 saved. He had seen a used racing bike for sale at the bike shop. His friend Tony also was selling his bike. He would test ride them both tomorrow. If they were in good shape, he would compare their features and prices and probably buy one of them. For now, it looked as though the new racing bike was completely out of the question.

### Questions

1. What was Adam's goal?
2. What forced him to revise his goal?
3. Explain how limited time and money resources affected Adam's decision to set a new goal.
4. Do you think Adam made a wise decision? Why or why not?
5. Which steps of the management process apply to this situation?

# 17 *Chapter Review*

## Summary

Convenience, location, cost, circumstances, and safety factors affect your choice of transportation. Bicycles are less expensive to run, maintain, and repair than other two- and four-wheel vehicles. The type of bicycle that you purchase depends upon where and why you are riding it.

Cars come in several sizes and many styles. If you are buying a car, make a well-informed decision, based on several sources of information and a consideration of new and used cars. Besides the price of the car, other costs include license, taxes, registration, insurance, maintenance, repairs, and weekly expenses, such as fuel and parking.

Public transportation is not always possible for those with mobility problems. There are, however, specially equipped vehicles that allow some handicapped individuals to function with greater independence.

## Vocabulary

Complete each of the following sentences with one of the vocabulary words below.

- public transportation
- sticker price
- carpooling
- options
- disclosure statement
- book value
- title

1. Nonessential, additional features, such as air conditioning, that come with a car are called _____ .

2. A used car certificate that indicates that the mileage showing in the car is accurate and contains a vehicle identification number, and the vehicle make, model, and year, is a _____ .

3. The standard price of a specific used car, depending on its make, model, and year, is the _____ .

4. Transportation that is operated for the benefit of everyone is _____ .

5. A document that proves legal ownership of a car is a _____ .

6. The suggested retail price of a car is known as its _____ .

7. An arrangement in which people share driving and driving expenses is referred to as _____ .

## Questions

1. If you drive a car, what steps can you take to be more sure of your safety? What safety procedures should a bicycle rider follow at all times?

2. Of the three types of bicycles mentioned in this chapter, which one would you choose? Give several reasons for the choice you have made.

3. What are the advantages of owning a car over a motorcycle?

4. What are the advantages of a compact car? What are the disadvantages?

5. What are the two most objective sources of information about cars? Why are these sources more objective than advertisements or manufacturers' brochures?

6. What is the difference between a purchase agreement and a warranty?

7. Why is it important to know all of your car expenses when you are buying a car?

8. What steps should you take before you purchase car insurance?

9. What should you do to maintain your car? Why is regular maintenance important?

10. Do you think your town or city has provided adequately for the mobility needs of the physically handicapped?

## Skill Activities

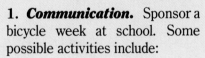

1. **Communication.** Sponsor a bicycle week at school. Some possible activities include:

• Ride a bicycle to school every day and write a short paper on "The Pleasures of Bike Riding."

• Write a paper on the benefits of bicycle riding for good health and how riding a bicycle reduces transportation costs.

• Write a poem called "Joys of Biking" or "No More Smog."

• Have a bicycle repair person discuss bicycle maintenance and repairs and the cost of these procedures with your class.

2. **Critical Thinking.** Rate one car model that you would like to own. Use the sources of information described in this chapter and as many personal sources as you can find, including friends and relatives who may own the same model car.

Using the information you have gathered, how would you rate the car? One star (poor)? Two stars (still not up to par)? Three stars (good)? Four stars (very good)? Explain your reasons. Have you changed your mind about wanting to own this particular car? Why or why not?

3. **Math.** Do a cost comparison for transportation. Choose a city or town at least 20 miles from your home. Imagine that you were commuting there daily to go to your job. Find out the cost of taking public transportation (if it is available) for one week. Calculate what you would be spending for gasoline if you drove to work for one week. (Estimate your car's gas mileage at 25 miles per gallon.) Add parking costs for one week. Finally, calculate what it would cost to take a taxi to work and back each day for a week. (Make a phone call to a local cab company to find out the cost.) Record your final results. Which method of transportation is the least expensive?

# *18*

# *Managing Your Leisure Time*

## *As you read, think about:*

- how to analyze the way you use your leisure time.
- how to choose both short-term and long-term recreation activities.
- how to fit recreation into your resources of time and money.
- how to achieve a realistic balance between recreation and other areas of your life.
- how to apply the management process to personal decisions about recreation and leisure time.

leisure time
hobbies
vacation
short-term recreation
long-term recreation

Everyone makes management decisions about recreation. You decide what you want to do with your leisure time. You plan daily and yearly recreation activities that range from a bicycle ride to a family vacation. Once you have learned how to set recreation priorities according to the time and money resources that you have and how to fit recreation into your life pattern, you will have acquired skills you can use both now and in the future.

## *Planning for Leisure and Recreation*

Just hearing the word *recreation* may make you smile. You may think about the last baseball game you played or attended. You may remember swimming at the lake during the summer or collecting shells on the beach. No matter what you think about when you hear the word, it probably will be pleasant. Recreation time is important. It is a time to renew your energy and spirits, to develop new skills, and to have fun.

The time we use for recreation purposes is **leisure time.** You may associate leisure with such words as freedom, spare time, relaxation, recess, and holiday. Depending on your own needs, wants, and resources, the way you choose to use your leisure time is completely up to you.

## *Leisure Now and in the Future*

You have more leisure time than people who lived only a few generations ago and far more than the early pioneers. Without mass transportation systems and modern, time-saving machinery, the early settlers needed

Developing an interest in animals can be
a lifelong leisure activity.

almost their entire day to manage food, clothing, and shelter. Of course, they had some
recreation, but the hours of leisure were few.

As more and more advances in science
and technology are made, the more likely it
becomes that you will have more time for
leisure during the working years of your life.
As more strides are made in modern medicine,
people have longer life expectancies. With
people living longer after retirement than ever
before, how they use their leisure time
becomes more and more important.

***Your Leisure Time Now*** Think about the
number of hours you spend in leisure now. On
an average day, you probably spend about six
hours in school and a few more doing homework. To this, add the time you spend eating,
since mealtime is not considered pure leisure

time. The time you have before you go to
bed can be defined as leisure time. Perhaps,
because of needs and wants, you have a part-
time job during the time that normally would
be for leisure. If you do, these hours should be
deducted from your daily leisure time. You can
figure out the number of real leisure hours you
have in an average week by adding up your daily
totals as you go through the week. You might
want to keep a brief diary of what you do during these hours to give yourself a realistic picture of how you spend your leisure time. Do
you use your leisure time well? Do you plan
ahead to do something you really enjoy? Do
you spend most of your daily or even weekly
leisure time watching television? The answers
to these questions will help you to set a pattern
now for an enjoyable and productive use of your
leisure time in the future.

***Your Leisure Time in the Future*** At present and throughout your school years, depending on your wants and needs, you may be working during summer and school vacations. Individual situations may vary, but usually as you move toward middle age and then old age, your leisure time increases. What will you do with that time? Even though retirement seems far away at present, the way you choose to manage your leisure time now will have a lot to do with the way in which you manage it then. Unfortunately, many retired people are unprepared for the long hours that used to be filled by a job. Instead of being excited by the new freedom they have, many feel a sense of loss and uselessness. It seems likely that retirees who feel this way never used their earlier leisure time to develop interests, hobbies, or skills outside their work.

## Assessing Your Special Interests

Everyone has some area of special interest. These interests have developed and grown as you have had more life experiences.

This chapter could never discuss all of your possible interests. There are simply too many. But we can consider a few categories of special interests. As you think about each of these, you should realize that areas of special interest and special ability often go hand-in-hand. It is likely that you will choose a job or career that is tied closely to your special interests. Even if you do not, all the learning experiences you have in your area of special interest will make you a better educated, more well-rounded individual. Special interests help you to use your leisure time pleasantly.

**Hobbies** are leisure activities that develop over time as you pursue your special interests. They vary widely, but all provide satisfaction, pleasure, and even some financial rewards, depending on how much time and

Using leisure time to stay physically active and socially involved can contribute to a happier retirement.

effort you put into them. As you think about each area of special interest, you may want to think about hobbies that might grow out of each one.

***Music*** Perhaps you have developed an interest in music by attending concerts, listening to different types of music, collecting records, reading about famous composers, or learning to play an instrument. Maybe you have done all of these things. Using music as just one example, it is easy to see how many leisure time activities and hobbies there are for every area of special interest.

Sculpting is only one of a variety of artistic hobbies you may enjoy.

**Sports** Perhaps a sport is your greatest area of interest. If so, you probably spend a lot of time practicing and playing it. Perhaps you enjoy many sports. Basketball, baseball, hockey, tennis, soccer, and softball are just a few of the sports interests you may have. You may choose to use your leisure time coaching a team in the sport you like best. Playing, practicing, and competing in sports are healthy, productive uses of leisure time that allow you to meet new people, develop new skills and self-confidence, learn more self-discipline, and get needed, regular exercise.

**Mechanics** Perhaps your special interest lies in mechanics. You like to fix things and figure out how they work. If so, you may use leisure time to fix an old car engine or a lawnmower or a clock. You may be using your leisure time to take a course to learn more about your interest. If you develop your interest in mechanics, you will be able to fix many things yourself, rather than paying others for these services. You may find that you enjoy learning and saving money resources at the same time.

**Art** Perhaps you enjoy drawing or painting or both. Perhaps you are interested in watercolors, acrylics, or oils as painting media. You may like to draw portraits or landscapes, or you may enjoy sculpting. If you are interested in art, you may be interested in the principles of design. Do you enjoy choosing decorating schemes for rooms? Do you like to draw designs for clothes? Have you considered entering an art contest or competition? Have you helped to design backgrounds for play productions or shows at school or in your community? All of these are exciting leisure activities if art is your special interest.

The world is full of fascinating things to do and learn. Deciding on one or several of these things should be fun and stimulating, not a chore. If you pursue one or more interests, you may find many rewards beyond getting a job or more money. You will find that you have the pleasure of learning more about something you like. You will never be bored, and you will be preparing to enjoy your future leisure time.

## Developing Basic Skills

Another direct benefit of leisure time is the development and improvement of basic skills that last throughout your life. Biking and swimming are just two examples of these skills that you usually learn during leisure hours. Other skills, such as reading, can be improved during leisure time. Learning more about any subject by reading and researching is a valuable use of leisure time. You not only improve your basic study skills, you also become an "expert" in your chosen subject area.

## Planning Vacations

Official vacation periods call for planning leisure time according to your individual values, interests, time, and money resources. A **vacation** is a period of time away from the usual duties involved in work or school. The weekend is not a vacation unless you usually go to work or to school on weekends. If you do, then a free weekend is a two-day vacation for you. Although a vacation can range from one day to a month or more, one to two weeks of vacation is common for many working people.

How do you decide what to do on your vacation? What factors should you consider in the decision-making process? Many people look forward to their vacations all year, but without proper planning, they are often disappointed or let down when their vacations do not meet their expectations. This will not happen to you if you take into account individual values and interests, the realistic use of time, and the realistic use of money resources.

***Individual Values and Interests*** You may want to poll each member of your family or everyone who will be vacationing with you to be sure the location and activities satisfy everyone. If they do not, make some compromises before making your final decision. If you are on a school vacation yourself and no one else is on vacation with you, plan ahead of time to please your own values and interests.

Why does planning allow everyone to enjoy family vacations more?

**Realistic Use of Time** Try not to overschedule your vacation by planning to do too many things. A vacation is for relaxation as well as activities you enjoy. Frequently, the first day or two of a vacation is an unwinding period for everyone. It may take them this long to relax mind and body and to forget the hectic pace they usually maintain.

**Realistic Use of Money Resources** Your vacation plans will be determined in part by the amount of money in your personal budget. After you have figured out what you can spend, think of all the choices this will allow. You do not have to go to Hawaii to be happy and relaxed during vacation. If your resources are limited, you may want to plan ahead to attend free concerts or lectures, go biking with friends, or play tennis. Use your creativity to come up with inexpensive ideas if you do not have a lot of money for your vacation. Planning ahead will avoid many money frustrations. If you would like to go out to eat with friends but can't afford to, you may want to plan a potluck dinner with everyone bringing one dish. This type of activity allows you to socialize with friends over a meal and not stretch your money resources too far. If you overextend your finances during a vacation, it will cause added stress when you return to work or school and find you cannot afford some basic needs.

## For Review

1. Explain why most people have increased leisure time as they get older.

2. Why is an area of special interest so important? Name two of these special interest areas and list as many related leisure activities as you can for each.

3. What three basic factors should be considered when planning a vacation?

## Practical Tip: Packing Efficiently

■ One space-saving way to pack for a trip or vacation makes use of a technique that involves rolling clothing. Lay out several layers of shirts or sweaters or pants. Roll the layers of similar clothing tightly into one bundle. You will fit more clothing into your suitcase or duffle bag and keep wrinkles to a minimum.

# Setting Recreation Priorities

The decisions you make about the types of recreation you choose are based on priorities. The time and money resources you can afford to invest in recreation will help you to set your priorities.

## Time Priorities

The time you put into recreation and leisure activities should be in proportion to the time you can spare from other life responsibilities. In terms of time, recreation can be divided into two main categories: short-term recreation and long-term recreation.

**Short-Term Recreation** Short-term recreation is made up of the separate, isolated leisure activities that you fit into your daily or weekly schedule. These activities may include going to a movie or taking time out to watch a favorite television show. In terms of time, you plan and set priorities each time you enjoy this type of recreation. While you might like to watch television all evening, you know that tomorrow's test in Spanish is your major priority for the evening. You learn to balance the time you can afford to spend in recreation against the other things you have to do. Each day's schedule will vary, depending on the time demands of work or school. Therefore, as you make decisions about how to manage your short-term recreation, your plans will have to be flexible.

It is important to try to plan some short-term recreation time every day, even if it lasts only for a few minutes. Your mental and physical states, for example, can be improved by taking a fifteen-minute break after several hours of concentrated studying. Stretching, getting some fresh air, or enjoying a few minutes of exercise are all examples of important, even if very short-term, recreation. Every plan for short-term recreation will be a very individual one.

***Long-Term Recreation*** Long-term recreation is made up of the leisure activities that you enjoy throughout your life. Hobbies and any other activities of special interest that you continually build on and improve are included in this category. As with short-term recreation, you must set time priorities to fit these activities into your life. It is important to devote time to long-term recreation because the skills and interests that develop out of it will enable you to be happier in your later years when your time is no longer taken up with work or school.

Hobbies such as carpentry, crafts, sewing, and collecting are examples of long-term recreation. Skiing, swimming, and biking are other examples. Volunteering in any of hundreds of areas can be considered a form of long-term recreation.

## *Money Priorities*

Although some types of recreation are free, most involve some expense. Deciding what types of recreation you can afford will depend on your personal finances and the money priorities you must set. Few of us, for example, can afford to go downhill skiing or play indoor tennis at a club every day, even if we have the time to do it. The money you spend on recreation usually is what is left over in your budget after deducting such essential living costs as housing, food, clothing, and transportation. For this reason, you will make your recreation choices based on the expense category each falls into.

Scouting activities combine long-term recreation and community service.

# Managing Time to Volunteer

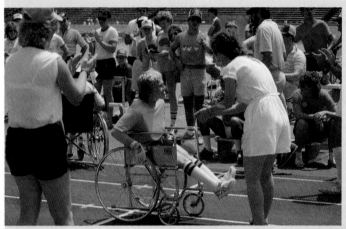

"What do you want to do?"

"I dunno. What about you?"

Leisure time! Everyone looks forward to it, but most of us waste a large part of it. Although hanging out on the corner or dozing in front of the TV may be a break from routine, they do not bring the sense of satisfaction and accomplishment you can get from volunteering. While you may have a choice of reading, swimming, or going to the zoo on a nice summer day, there are handicapped and elderly people who are unable to do these things on their own. Helping them with leisure activities can give you as much pleasure as it brings them.

What leisure-aid activities are open to you? There are as many answers to this question as there are activities that people enjoy. Your local United Way or a similar "umbrella organization" can tell you what volunteer programs are available in your community. Here are some suggestions from United Way: singing for nursing home residents, serving as a guide for blind athletes, teaching handicapped children to swim, reading to the blind, and working with the Special Olympics. You can probably think of many other programs like these and contact them on your own. If you are looking for other suggestions, check with your school guidance office, local church or synagogue, Y, or Scouts.

There are several advantages to volunteering in an organized program. No matter how well-meaning people are, leisure time often slips away. Before you know it, another month has gone by without your participation. Scheduling some of your volunteer activities ensures that you will do them and gives both you and the people you are aiding a special time to look forward to. When you meet your schedule you receive the added satisfaction of knowing you are a person who can be counted on to do something—in this case something especially worthwhile.

***Free Recreation*** Taking a walk is free recreation. We tend to think of swimming and jogging as free recreation, too, but although these are relatively inexpensive types of recreation, you do have to spend money to do them. You need a swimsuit, good jogging shoes, and comfortable clothing to jog in, for example. In many areas of the country, the weather will not permit year-long enjoyment of this type of recreation. You might have to join a community center or a private club to swim or jog all year. All of these costs have to be analyzed before you can determine what you can afford to spend for recreation.

***Special Equipment for Recreation*** Most sport-related recreation involves buying special equipment. Football and hockey gear is very expensive. Skiing equipment is also costly. If these are your recreation choices, you may have to make other trade-offs to afford them. You may have to consider used equipment when you first start, or you may need a part-time job to earn money. Musical instruments and art and craft supplies are other examples of activities that can be expensive. To fit them into your budget, you need to plan for these expenses. Much of this special equipment will last for a long time if it is properly cared for. While your money investment will be high at the start, you will get a great deal of use and enjoyment in return. If you are considering an activity such as skiing, you may want to borrow or rent equipment for the first few times to see if you really enjoy the activity enough to buy what you need.

***Continuous Recreation Expenses*** Some types of recreation cost money each time you take part in them. Once you have bought a bicycle, a helmet, and appropriate clothing, you do not have to spend money each time you go for a bike ride. On the other hand, if you decide that you want to learn to play the guitar,

Good jogging shoes may cost more, but they provide needed support.

you will have a continuous recreation expense for as long as you decide to take lessons. The daily fees involved in downhill skiing are another example of a continuous expense. If you can afford to go downhill skiing only two or three times a year, it may not be worth buying the equipment. Renting until you can use the equipment more often may be smarter, especially if you are still growing and will not be able to use the same equipment for several seasons in a row.

Although the price of joining a club may be a set fee for a year, there are often other continuous expenses. Sometimes, even as a member, you must pay hourly fees for the use of tennis, squash, or other courts.

None of this information should discourage you from pursuing some type of recreation. Becoming informed, deciding what you can afford, setting priorities, and having a plan can help you to choose recreation that fits into your personal budget.

## For Review

1. Why is it important to fit short-term and long-term recreation into your life?
2. How can you determine the amount of money you have for recreation?
3. Describe two kinds of continuous recreation expenses you might have.

# Working Recreation Into Your Total Life Budget

Your recreation needs and wants will need to be worked into the total scheme of your life. In Chapter 7, you learned how to create a budget to fit your income and expenses. Although you may not face food and housing expenses right now, you probably are responsible for paying for your recreation. If you want to go to a movie or to a sports event, you probably have to contribute toward their cost in some way.

Your individual recreation budget right now depends on the other things you have to buy. If you buy most of your own clothing, for example, the amount of money you have to spend on recreation will be smaller in proportion to your clothing budget.

## Managing Your Recreation Budget Now

You may want to ask yourself some questions about how you are handling your recreation budget. Do you spend more than you can afford? Do you borrow money from friends or family members for recreation purposes? Do

you find that you have no money for anything else because you have spent too much on recreation? In terms of the time spent on recreation, you may want to ask yourself a few more questions. Do you spend more time than you should for recreation? Are you at a movie the night before a big test when you should be studying? If the answers to these questions are "Yes," you may want to try to balance your recreation budget better. Learning to use self-discipline now will help you to establish better control over your total budget in the future.

## Managing Your Future Recreation Budget

As we discussed earlier in this chapter, your resources of time and money for recreation probably will increase as you grow older. Even when they do, however, you will have to put recreation into balance with your other budget expenses. Housing, food, transportation, and health costs should take priority over recreation because they are more important needs. You may have to learn to postpone recreation wants or find less expensive forms of recreation. You may need to moderate your recreation budget to put it into proportion with the other parts of your total life budget. If all the parts are in balance, you will be managing your resources successfully.

## For Review

1. What types of needs should take priority over recreation needs in terms of your money resources?
2. Explain why recreation priorities must be set in terms of both time and money.
3. What factors should be considered when deciding on a realistic recreation budget for the future?

## Management Application: Planning Vacation Time

Imagine yourself in the situation described below. As you read, think about how the steps of the management process might apply to this situation. Then answer the questions that follow.

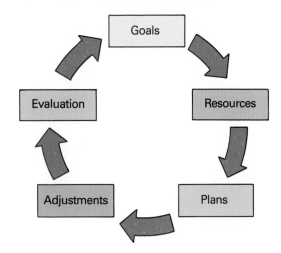

### Situation

Hank finished his algebra homework and looked at his watch. Ten more minutes of study hall were left. He looked out at the late winter grayness and began to daydream about summer vacation. He remembered how bored he had been last year and how sorry he was that he hadn't found a job before summer. Making last-minute plans to do things with his friends hadn't worked out well either. He had learned his lesson. This year he was already making vacation plans. His older brother had invited him to his beach house for two weeks. His parents had agreed he could go if he earned his own train fare. He had saved half of it already. Hank could almost hear the surf and feel the motion of his surfboard beneath his feet. He really relaxed at the beach. It was great to have that leisure time to look forward to. He would go there two weeks before school opened again because that would allow him to work through the rest of the summer. He wanted to work outdoors and had already talked to the owner of a local landscape company. Hank had to call him back next month to confirm that he wanted the job. This daytime job would also allow him to have fun with his friends in the evenings. Hank and his best friend Tim had

even figured out what to do on rainy days when they couldn't mow lawns. Tim's dad had an old car that he told Tim he could have if he could get it going. He and Tim had decided to use spare time to work on it. He wanted to learn more about cars so he could fix his own when he got one. This would be a good time to begin learning.

The bell rang, and Hank smiled as he gathered his books. He knew he would have a great summer vacation this year, and he couldn't wait for it to begin.

### Questions

1. What is Hank's goal?
2. What is his plan for summer vacation?
3. What human and nonhuman resources will he need to carry out his plan?
4. Would you say that Hank will be managing his vacation time well? Why or why not?
5. Which steps of the management process apply to this situation?

# 18 *Chapter Review*

## Summary

Leisure time is a time to renew your energy and spirits, to develop new skills, and to have a good time. Learn to use your leisure time well by developing interests, hobbies, or skills outside of work. This will lead to productive and enjoyable use of leisure time in the future. Establish recreation priorities based on the time and money you can afford to invest.

## Vocabulary

Match each of the following vocabulary words with one of the definitions below.

leisure time        short-term recreation
hobbies             long-term recreation
vacation

1. Separate, isolated leisure activities that are part of your daily or weekly schedule are called _____ .
2. The part of our lives we use for recreation purposes is _____ .
3. Leisure activities that you develop and enjoy throughout your life, including hobbies and other special interests, are known as _____ .
4. Leisure activities that develop into strong interests over time are _____ .
5. A period of time away from work or school is known as a _____ .

## Questions

1. How are your present patterns of leisure time important to your future?
2. How do you calculate leisure time?
3. What are the benefits of developing special interests into hobbies?
4. What steps can you take to make sure your vacation meets your expectations?
5. Give one example of a creative, inexpensive vacation activity.
6. What is the difference between short-term and long-term recreation?
7. Give one example of short-term recreation that you can do daily.
8. Select two specific types of recreation you enjoy and describe the expenses of each.
9. What questions should you ask yourself when you try to determine whether you are handling your recreation budget well?
10. Which needs take priority over recreation needs in terms of time resources?

## Skills Activities

**1. Communication.** Select an area of interest or a hobby such as music, art, mechanics, or sports to investigate.

Find out what sorts of activities, clubs, meetings, programs, shows, or speakers are

available in your area during the next month. Keep track of the cost of each.

You may want to start a bulletin board in your classroom of local events that other students may be interested in pursuing with you.

**2. *Critical Thinking.*** How do you spend your leisure time? Refer to the section on "Your Leisure Time Now," in your book on page 400 to calculate how much leisure time you have. Keep track of your leisure time during a one-week period.

Are you satisfied with how you spent the time? Would you like to make changes? How? Write a short paragraph answering these questions. If you are not fully satisfied, what changes would you make?

**3. *Math.*** Choose a location in the United States that you have always wanted to visit. Plan a one-week vacation to that location. Do a comparison of travel costs for airplane, train, car, bus, and boat transportation, if applicable. Remember to calculate your return trip costs also. Decide on the form of transportation you would use. Then talk to a travel agent or write to the Chamber of Commerce in that city or town to get information about possible accommodations, including hotels, inns, and camping facilities, if they are available. Calculate how much you would be spending to stay where you have decided to

stay for one week. Now add the estimated costs for meals, depending on whether or not you will have cooking facilities where you are staying. Add transportation costs during your vacation, including car rental if needed. Finally, estimate how much spending money you will need for entertainment and other expenses. How much will your dream vacation cost?

**4. *Social Studies.*** Choose a historical site or monument in our country that you would like to visit. If you do not have a map of the United States in your classroom that shows these locations, look for one in your school or local library. Why is this historical site or monument significant? What person or historical event does it stand for? Gather as much detailed information as you can about this place from history books and other sources, such as encyclopedias.

Use a highway map to track your route from your home to the historical site or monument. Figure out approximately how many miles you would be traveling on highways and roads to reach your destination.

Write to the Chamber of Commerce or the tourist bureau in the area to ask when they would advise planning a visit. Usually, they can supply information about the times of the year when the number of tourists is heaviest. With this information, you could avoid crowds if you were to travel.

# Glossary

A

**abstinence** Refraining from; not having sexual relations.

**abuse** Wrong, bad, or excessive use; ill-treatment of a person. Abuse may be verbal, physical, or both.

**aerobic exercise** Dynamic exercise, involving rhythmic, repetitive motion, that forces a continuous flow of oxygen-carrying blood through the heart and large skeletal muscles.

**agitation** A stirring or shaking motion; the action of a washing machine as it moves water, detergent, and clothing during the laundering process.

**AIDS** Acquired Immune Deficiency Syndrome, a fatal, sexually transmitted disease that has no known cure at this time.

**alcoholism** A disease characterized by addiction to alcohol. An alcoholic drinks uncontrollably once he or she starts to drink.

**analogous** Similar or comparable in certain respects; referring to a color scheme that uses colors closely related, or next to each other, on the color wheel.

**annual percentage rate (APR)** The ratio of the dollar finance charge to the average amount of credit in use for the length of the contract. APR is always expressed as a yearly percentage.

**annual percentage yield (APY)** The rate at which the money in a savings plan will earn interest in one year.

**anorexia nervosa** An eating disorder characterized by overdieting, sometimes to the point of starvation. Anorexics have a distorted image of their bodies; they feel they are too fat even when they are dangerously thin.

**apprenticeship** A method by which an inexperienced worker can learn a specific trade or skill from one or more experienced workers.

**attitude** The idea or opinion a person has of himself or herself, others, and various events and situations; a general mind set.

**autonomy** Independence or self-governing. The state of being free from the care of parents, relatives, or guardians; functioning on your own.

## B

**bankruptcy** A formal, legal procedure in which a person is declared unable to meet his or her debts, and the court seizes and sells the individual's possessions in order to pay some part of those debts.

**blended family** A family unit made up of stepparents and stepchildren as the result of remarriage.

**body language** The movements, gestures, and postures that communicate a person's feelings, attitudes, and personality.

**book value** The standard price of a specific used car, based on its make, model, and year. Book value does not take into consideration the condition of a particular car.

**budget** An estimate of income and expense for a fixed period of time.

**bulimia** An eating disorder characterized by alternate binging (overeating) and purging (self-induced vomiting and/or overuse of laxatives). Bulimics want to lose weight and want to eat; they carry both to extremes.

## C

**calorie** A measure of the energy produced by food when it is used by the body.

**carpooling** An arrangement in which people share driving and driving expenses.

**center** A place where an activity or several related activities are carried on; a space designed for a specific task or recreational activity.

**central heating system** Any method of providing heat to all parts of a living space.

**cholesterol** A fatty substance found naturally in the body and in some foods. A high level of cholesterol in the blood has been linked to high blood pressure, heart disease, and other circulatory problems.

**closing costs** Fees that must be paid in cash when a buyer takes possession of property. They often include lawyer's fees for a title search, title insurance, and mortgage processing fees.

**collateral** Property or goods pledged for repayment of a loan if the borrower cannot repay.

**color intensity** The dullness or brightness of a color.

**color value** The lightness or darkness of a color.

**communication** A process by which information is exchanged between individuals through a common system of symbols, signs, or behavior.

**communication inhibitors** Combinations of attitudes with verbal and nonverbal communication techniques that interfere with communication.

**comparison shop** To carefully compare the goods or services of several sellers as to quality and price.

**complementary** Together, adding up to a whole or making up what is lacking; referring to a color scheme that uses colors directly opposite on the color wheel. Complementary colors of the spectrum produce white light when combined.

**condominium** A living space that is bought rather than rented in a multiunit building or complex. It also involves joint ownership of common areas.

**consumer** A person who selects and buys goods and services for his or her own needs and not for resale.

**contract** An agreement that is legally binding between two or more persons or parties. A contract does not have to be in writing to be binding.

**convenience foods** Foods that have been partially or completely prepared at the time of purchase.

**cooperative** Done or owned jointly for mutual benefit; living space in a multiunit building or group of buildings that is owned jointly by all tenants.

**cost-effectiveness** The evaluation of a particular measure in terms of the money saved by its use compared to the money spent on it.

**CPR** Cardiopulmonary resuscitation, a first-aid technique applied when breathing has stopped. It involves alternate breathing and heart-pumping procedures.

**credit** The privilege of taking possession of money, goods, or services in exchange for a promise to pay for them at a future date.

**credit rating** A rating or evaluation given to an individual to indicate how good a credit risk he or she is. A credit rating is based on past uses of credit and financial status.

**custody** Guardianship or care; the legal responsibility of an adult for a child.

## D

**Daily Food Guide** A division of foods into five basic groups, and recommendations for the daily amount needed from each group to create a balanced diet.

**diet** What a person usually eats and drinks; daily food intake.

**direct, or space, heating** A method of providing heat directly to a small area, such as a room, through a heating device located in the room.

**disclosure statement** A document stating the vehicle make, model, year, identification, number, and mileage as well as the signature, name, and address of the seller of a used car.

**down payment** The amount of money offered in cash by the prospective purchaser of an item. The remainder of the selling price is financed on credit.

## E

**emotions** Specific, strong feelings, often combined with physiological, or bodily, responses. Emotions include love, hate, fear, and happiness.

**empty nest syndrome** The sense of loss and lack of purpose that may occur in parents, especially mothers, when their children have left home.

**energy audit** An evaluation of how effectively energy is used in a particular space.

**environment** The total of the conditions, circumstances, and influences surrounding and affecting an individual.

**equity** The value of a piece of property to the owner above and beyond any claims against it.

**express warranty** Specific assurances by the seller about a product. Express warranties are usually, but not always, in written form.

**extended family**    A family unit consisting of several generations, such as parents, grandparents, and any children, living together and functioning as one family.

## F

**fads**    Styles or fashions that are popular for only a short time.

**fats**    Energy-rich nutrients made up of fatty acids. Fats are oily or greasy substances.

**finance charge**    The total of all the fees for obtaining credit.

**fixed expenses**    Payments that must be made on a regular schedule and that usually do not vary in amount, such as mortgage or rent payments.

**fixed-rate mortgages**    Property loans that have the same interest rate for as long as the loan lasts.

**flexible expenses**    Payments that vary over time in type and amount, such as those for clothing and recreation.

**floor plan**    A sketch of a room and its furniture drawn to scale.

**food additives**    Substances that are added to foods to prevent spoilage, improve flavor, enhance color, or improve nutritional value.

**food cooperative**    An organization of individuals or families who jointly buy food in bulk from wholesalers or producers and then sell or distribute the food among members at lower than usual prices.

**full warranty**    A promise by the seller to fix or replace an item, or part of an item, free of charge for a certain length of time.

## G

**goal**    An objective or end that a person strives to attain; an aim.

**gross pay**    The total amount paid to an employee by an employer; salary.

## H

**Heimlich Maneuver**    A simple, effective technique for dislodging an object that is causing someone to choke. It involves quick, sudden pressure under the diaphragm; the resulting air pressure forces the object back up into the victim's mouth.

**heredity**    The total of all characteristics passed on to an individual by parents and ancestors.

**hobbies**    Activities or subjects that a person likes to do or study during leisure time.

## I

**implied warranty**    An unwritten, but understood, assurance by the seller that a product will perform properly for a reasonable length of time and be suitable for the use indicated by the seller. The length of time of this consumer protection varies from state to state.

**impulse buying**    Making a purchase on the spur of the moment, without thinking about budget and needs.

**income**    The gain, usually measured in money, that comes from a variety of sources.

**income tax**    A tax based upon the income of earnings of an individual or business.

**infatuation** A foolish or all-absorbing passion; an attraction often focused on only one characteristic of a person rather than on the whole person. It is usually intense but not long-lasting.

**inflation** An increase in the general level of prices due to an increased volume of money and credit.

**insulation** Material that does not conduct heat (sound, electricity, or other similar substances or qualities) and is used to prevent their passage or leakage to nearby areas.

**interest** Money paid for the use of money, as in a loan; income a depositor (or saver) receives from a bank for the use of the depositor's money by the bank (usually for loans to others).

**investment** The placing of funds into businesses, real estate, stocks, bank accounts, or other enterprises in order to obtain income or profit.

# L

**lease (rental agreement)** A contract by which the owner of property gives temporary use and/or possession of the property to someone else; the document that sets forth the terms of this agreement (such as rental period, fee, and restrictions).

**leisure time** Free, unoccupied time, often used for recreation.

**life cycle** The course of development from the beginning of the life of an organism until its end; the stages of human development from infancy, through childhood, adolescence, adulthood, and old age.

**limited warranty** A promise made by the seller to take certain actions to repair or replace a defective product if the consumer meets certain conditions. These conditions may include part of the cost of the repair.

**long-term recreation** The leisure activities enjoyed all through life, such as hobbies or sports.

# M

**management** The act of using, handling, and directing resources to reach particular goals.

**menu plan** An outline or listing of foods and beverages to be consumed at specific meals and between meals for a period of one or more days.

**modified extended family** A family unit in which members of several generations live nearby and often interact with one another.

**monochromatic** Referring to a color scheme that uses variations of the same color, such as different shades of blue.

**mortgage loan** A loan for the remainder of the purchase price of property after the down payment has been made.

# N

**needs** Things or conditions that are required or necessary.

**net pay** The amount of money actually received as payment, after necessary deductions have been made from gross pay. Net pay is sometimes called "take-home pay."

**nonverbal communication** The exchange of information or feelings without using words.

**nuclear family** A family unit made up of parents and their dependent children living in the same household.

**nutrients** The substances that the body needs for growth, energy, and good health.

**nutrition** The science of food and its relation to health; the way food is used by the body to promote growth, to replace worn or injured tissues, and to carry on the body processes.

## O

**options** Choices; nonessential, additional features that can but do not have to be ordered on a car. There is an extra charge for options.

## P

**payback period** The time it takes to recover or save the funds spent on a money-saving item or procedure.

**personal financial plan** A plan for spending, saving, and investing tailored to a particular individual's income, needs, and wants.

**plan** A scheme or program decided ahead of time for the accomplishment of a goal.

**pretreating** Procedures to loosen or partially remove heavy soil and stains before beginning the regular wash cycle.

**process** A series of actions, thoughts, operations, or changes that lead to a particular result, condition, or end.

**products** Material items produced by nature or made by human industry or art; goods.

**proportion** The balance or comparative relation among parts of a whole.

**public transportation** A system of transport operated for the use and benefit of the general public.

## R

**recipe** A written plan for a dish that lists the ingredients and gives directions for its preparation.

**resources** All the things available for use; the things, knowledge, skills, abilities, services, and people available to help in the attainment of a goal.

**resume** A written summary of a person's work history, education, experience, interests, and other information pertinent to a job application.

## S

**sales** The special offerings of goods at lower than usual prices.

**saturated fats** Those fats that are solid at room temperature; containing as much hydrogen as possible in their chemical makeup.

**security deposit** A payment made by a renter to a landlord at the beginning of a lease. It is usually equal to one month's rent. It can be used to cover repairs or missed payments; otherwise it is returned at the end of the lease.

**self-concept** The beliefs and feelings a person has about himself or herself, including abilities, worth, and faults.

**services** Actions or labor that have value. Services may not result in the production of a specific item.

**shelf-life** The length of time that a food can be stored without spoiling.

**short-term recreation** The separate, isolated leisure activities that are part of a person's daily or weekly schedule.

**small claims court** A court where individuals or businesses present complaints or disputes that involve sums of money up to $5,000. The complainant does not need to be represented by a lawyer; proceedings are conducted in everyday language, and the decision is made by a judge.

**standard** Something established as a rule or basis of comparison for measurement. Standards are guidelines for measuring values and goals.

**STDs** Sexually Transmitted Diseases. Diseases that may be passed on through sexual intercourse.

**stereotype** A generalized attitude or opinion about a group of people, allowing for no individuality or critical judgment.

**sticker price** The suggested retail price of an item.

**storage** A place to put things aside until they are needed.

**stress** Any factor that causes bodily or mental tension; strain.

# T _____

**tax** A charge or fee (usually a percentage) imposed on persons or property for the support of a government.

**title** Right to ownership; a document that proves legal ownership.

**trade-offs** Exchanges, particularly the giving up of one benefit or advantage to gain a more desirable one.

**traffic patterns** The paths people usually take to get from one room to another or from one part of a room to another.

# U _____

**unit pricing** Expressing the price of an item per standard unit of measurement (such as gram, liter, or pound) rather than by container unit (such as box, bottle, or can).

**U.S. RDA** United States Recommended Dietary Allowance. The recommended dietary amounts of protein, vitamin A, vitamin C, thiamine, riboflavin, niacin, calcium, and iron for adult males. The amounts have been established by the National Research Council of the Food and Nutrition Board of the National Academy of Sciences.

# V _____

**vacation** A period of time away from the usual duties involved in work or school.

**values** Ideas or beliefs about what is important; the social principles or standards accepted by an individual or group.

**variable-rate mortgages** Sometimes called adjustable-rate mortgages; these are property loans in which the interest rate varies according to specific conditions.

**verbal communication** The exchange of information by written or spoken words.

**violence**  Rough force in action. Domestic violence (violence within the family) may involve the use or threat of force.

## W

**W-4 form**  A document that authorizes an employer to deduct a specific amount of federal income tax from an employee's paycheck for each pay period. The employee claims the appropriate number of tax exemptions and signs the W-4 form.

**wants**  Things or conditions that are desirable but not necessary.

**warranty**  A guarantee or assurance by the seller of an item that it will perform satisfactorily for a certain length of time. It also includes conditions under which the seller will repair or replace it or refund the buyer's money.

**weatherization**  Any work done to a living space that helps to make that space more energy efficient.

**work policies**  Rules set by a business or employer that are related to work safety, efficiency, and standards.

# *Index*

*c indicates a chart or table*

manufactured, 330
needs and wants and, 336
renting, 330–331, 334
sharing, 56, 334–335
single-family dwellings,
329, 330

# I

Identity crisis, 52
Illness
    colds and flu, 114
    fever, 113–114
    headache, 114
    nausea and vomiting, 113
    in old age, 58
    *see also* Health
Implied warranty, 203, 205
Impression
    clothing and, 285
    creating a good, 40
    in an interview, 130
    on the job, 133, 135
Impulse buying, 211, 249,
266, 307, 310–311
Income, 143
    and financial planning,
143, 145
    fixed, 176
    gross and net, 148
Income tax, 158, 159
Individual Retirement
    Accounts (IRAs), 186
Industrial banks, 171
Infancy, 49–50
Infatuation, 57
Infection, 110, 113, 114
Inflation, 170
Inheritance tax, 160
Insulation, 368–369
Insurance, car, 392

Interest, 151
    on checking accounts,
151–152
    on loans, 169–170
    on savings accounts, 151,
180, 182
Interest inventories, 132
Internal Revenue Service
    (IRS), 158–159
Interview, job, 130–131
Investments, 180, 183
    counseling on, 168
    factors to consider in,
184–186
    information on, 184
    savings accounts,
180–181, 184
Iron (mineral), 240
Ironing, 321

# J

Job(s)
    advancement, 136
    applications, 129–130
    benefits, 137
    changing, 138
    employee expectations,
131, 135–137
    employer's expectations,
131, 133–135
    finding, 128–130
    interview for, 130–131
    paychecks, 136–137
    personal characteristics
for, 134–135, 139
    resumés, 129–130
    succeeding on the,
131–138
    working conditions, 136
    *see also* Career; Work

Job skills, 124–128
    apprenticeship, 128
    basic, 126–127
    on-the-job training, 134
    specialized, 127–128,
133–134

# K

Kennedy, John F., 191
Keogh Plans, 186
Kitchens, cleanliness in,
273–274

# L

Labels, 201–202
    on clothing, 310, 312,
313, 323
    on foods, 296–271
Language, communication
    and, 36
Laundry, 313–319, 325
Laundry products, 316–318
Leadership skills, 42–44, 45
Lease (rental agreement), 331
Legal action, 230
Leisure time, 4, 399–401
    art, 402
    hobbies, 401, 405
    improving basic skills,
402–403
    mechanics, 402
    money resources and,
404, 405–408
    music, 401

Unit pricing, 271
Unwed mothers, 65–66,
105–106
U.S. government publications,
243
U.S. RDA (United States
Recommended Dietary
Allowances), 270

## V

Vacations, planning, 403–404,
409
Values, 5–6
and decision making, 18
and financial planning,
144
and goals, 8
and peer pressure, 43
Verbal communication, 36, 44
Violence, 102. *See also* Abuse
Vitamins, 238, 240
Voice, tone of, in
communication, 37
Volunteer activities, 406
Vomiting
induced, for poison, 107
treatment of, 113

## W

Walls
cleaning, 362
decorating, 347

Wants, 8
financial planning and, 144
housing and, 336
working to meet, 121–122
Wardrobe
adding to, 291–296
basic, 290–291, 298
evaluating your, 288–296,
301
flexibility in, 296
taking inventory, 288–290
trying new combinations,
290
what to keep, 289–290
*see also* Clothing
Warranty, 202, 227
car, 390–391
express, 204–205
full, 204
implied, 203, 205
limited, 204
for services, 205
on used or reconditioned
items, 219
Washing machines
buying, 343
using, 314–319
Water, in the diet, 238
Weatherization, 364
Weight control, 76
Weight-lifting, 76
Weight loss. *See* Dieting
Wellness, 71. *See also* Health

W-4 form, 137, 158
Wheelchairs, 336, 394
Windows
cleaning, 362
energy conservation and,
364
Women
abuse of, 102
career, 122
heads of households,
64–65
pressures to marry, 56,
65
Wood stoves, 363, 364
Work
for income needs and
wants, 121–122
and leisure, balance of, 78
permanent, 123–124
to satisfy personal
interests, 122, 126
for self-support, 122–123
temporary, 123, 126, 137
volunteer, 126
*see also* Careers; Jobs; Job
skills
Work center, 358
Work habits, 133
Working conditions, 136
Work policies, 134
Workshop, 360
Writing skills, 39, 126
W-2 form, 159

# Acknowledgements

**i:** John Curtis. **ii–iii:** John Curtis. **v–x:** John Curtis. **xii–1:** John Curtis. **2:** John Curtis. **3:** John Curtis. **4:** Lou Jones/Uniphoto. **5:** Sue Klemen/Uniphoto. **6:** Nancy Sheehan. **8:** Dave Repp/DPI. **10:** David Witbeck/The Picture Cube. **11:** Paul Conklin. **12:** Susan Van Etten. **13:** Nick Pavloff/The Image Bank. **14:** Susan Van Etten. **15:** Dave Schaefer. **17:** Paul Conklin. **18:** Jim Levitt/Uniphoto. **19:** Paul Conklin. **24:** John Curtis. **25:** Nancy Sheehan. **26:** Paul E. Johnson. **27:** Ronda Bishop/DPI. **28:** Susan Johns/Photo Researchers. **29:** Larry Kolvoord/Texastock. **30:** Cary Wolinsky/Stock Boston. **31:** Mary Houtchens-Kitchen/The Picture Cube. **32:** Bruce Roberts/Photo Researchers. **33:** Susan Van Etten. **34:** Paul Conklin. **35:** A. Boccaccio/The Image Bank. **36:** Freda Leinwand/Monkmeyer Press Photo Service. **37:** Chris Cross/Uniphoto. **39:** Christopher S. Johnson/Stock Boston. **40:** Bob Daemmerich/Stock Boston. **41:** Michal Heron/Woodfin Camp and Associates. **43:** Richard Hutchings/Photo Researchers. **48:** John Curtis. **49:** John Curtis. **50:** DEK/Texastock. **51:** Dave Schaefer. **52:** B. Christensen/Stock Boston. **53:** Paul Conklin. **54:** Bob Daemmerich/Stock Boston. **56:** Susan Van Etten. **57:** Paul J. Vinci, Jr. **58:** Rick Brady/Uniphoto. **59:** Dave Schaefer. **61:** Dick Luria/FPG. **62:** Paul Conklin. **64:** Philip Jon Bailey/The Picture Cube. **66:** John Lei/Stock Boston. **70:** John Curtis. **71:** John Curtis. **72:** Hilary Wallace. **73:** Richard Hutchings/Photo Researchers. **74:** Susan Van Etten. **75:** John Curtis. **76:** Kelly Langley/DPI. **79:** Olivier Rebbot/Stock Boston. **81:** Paul Conklin. **82:** Paul Conklin. **85:** Susan Van Etten. **91:** David Lissy/The Picture Cube. **92:** Dave Schaefer. **98:** John Curtis. **99:** John Curtis. **100:** Susan Van Etten. **101:** Larry Kolvoord/Texastock. **102:** Bob Daemmerich/Uniphoto. **105:** Bob Daemmerich/Uniphoto. **106:** Dave Schaefer. **107:** Kennedy/Texastock. **109:** Dave Schaefer. **110:** Ellis Herwig/Stock Boston. **111:** Susan Van Etten. **112:** Ralph Barrera/Texastock. **118–119:** John Curtis. **120:** John Curtis. **121:** John Curtis. **122:** Paul Conklin. **123:** Smiley/Texastock. **124:** Billy E. Barnes/F.P.G. **125:** Dave Schaefer. **126:** Stephen Hopkins/F.P.G. **127:** Carolyn A. McKeone/F.P.G. **128:** Paul Conklin. **129.** Susan Van Etten. **130:** Michael Grecco/Stock Boston. **131:** Paul E. Johnson. **132:** Hilary Wallace. **133:** Dave Schaefer. **134:** Michal Heron/Woodfin Camp and Associates. **135:** Ellis Herwig/The Picture Cube. **136:** Susan Van Etten. **137:** Paul Conklin. **138:** Stacy Pick/Stock Boston. **142:** John Curtis. **144:** Paul Conklin. **146:** Steve Miedorf/The Image Bank. **149:** Janeart, Ltd./The Image Bank. **150:** Frank Siteman/The Picture Cube. **151:** Peter Chapman. **153:** Dave Schaefer. **154:** Susan Van Etten. **155:** Andrew Brilliant/The Picture Cube. **156:** Mike Mazzaschi/Stock Boston. **157:** Susan Van Etten. **159:** Andrew Brilliant/The Picture Cube. **160:** Susan Van Etten. **164:** John Curtis. **165:** John Curtis. **166:** Carol Palmer/The Picture Cube. **168:** George Ferriar. **170:** Andrew Brilliant/The Picture Cube. **172:** Paul E. Johnson. **173:** Susan Van Etten. **175:** Susan Van Etten. **178:** R. Phillips/The Image Bank. **179:** Susan Van Etten. **180:** Brett Froomer/The Image Bank. **181:** Andrew Brilliant/The Picture Cube. **182:** Susan Van Etten. **183:** Peter Chapman. **184:** Susan Van Etten. **185:** Dave Schaefer. **186:** Susan Van Etten. **190:** John Curtis. **191:** John Curtis. **192:** Teresa Zabala/Uniphoto. **193:** Dave Schaefer. **195:** Paul Conklin. **196:** Hilary Wallace. **198:** Jeffry Meiers/Uniphoto. **199:** Hilary Wallace. **200:** Paul E. Johnson. **201:** Paul Conklin. **202:** Susan Van Etten. **204:** Dave Schaefer. **206:** Susan Van Etten. **210:** John Curtis. **211:** Hilary Wallace. **212:** Dave Schaefer. **213:** Bobbie Kingsley/Photo Researchers. **214:** Alvis Upitis/The Image Bank. **215:** Paul Conklin. **216:** John Coletti/The Picture Cube. **217:** Susan Van Etten. **218:** Hilary Wallace. **220:** Sally Weigand/The Picture Cube. **221:** Paul E. Johnson. **222:** Nancy Bates/